D0897841

✧ FROM SHE-WOLF TO MARTYR

FROM SHE-WOLF TO MARTYR

THE REIGN AND DISPUTED REPUTATION OF JOHANNA I OF NAPLES

ELIZABETH CASTEEN

CORNELL UNIVERSITY PRESS
Ithaca and London

First published 2015 by Cornell University Press

Printed in the United States of America

Library of Congress Cataloging-in-Publication Data

Casteen, Elizabeth, 1979– author.
    From she-wolf to martyr : the reign and disputed reputation of Johanna I of Naples / Elizabeth Casteen.
        pages cm
    Includes bibliographical references and index.
    ISBN 978-0-8014-5386-1 (cloth : alk. paper)
    1. Johanna I, Queen of Naples, 1343–1382. 2. Queens—Italy—Naples (Kingdom)—Biography. 3. Naples (Kingdom)—History—Johanna I, 1343–1382. I. Title.
    DG847.5.C37 2015
    945.7'05092—dc23
    [B]   2015014131

Cornell University Press strives to use environmentally responsible suppliers and materials to the fullest extent possible in the publishing of its books. Such materials include vegetable-based, low-VOC inks and acid-free papers that are recycled, totally chlorine-free, or partly composed of nonwood fibers. For further information, visit our website at www.cornellpress.cornell.edu.

Cloth printing   10 9 8 7 6 5 4 3 2 1

For Frank

✿ CONTENTS

❧ ACKNOWLEDGMENTS

The number of debts—intellectual, personal, professional—I have incurred in the writing of this book is staggering. My first and greatest thanks are owed to Robert E. Lerner. His support, patience, advice, humor, and friendship have been invaluable, and this book would not exist without his unfailing generosity in sharing his knowledge and the fruits of his research. I was blessed to benefit from his mentorship, as from that of Richard Kieckhefer, Barbara Newman, Edward Muir, and Dyan Elliott, each of whom has been unstintingly generous and gracious with his or her time, expertise, and editorial wisdom.

William Monter shared his thoughts on the challenges of queenship with me at an early stage in this book's inception, and his perspective—like his insistence on the importance of numismatics—helped me think through many of the conceptual difficulties Johanna faced. Daniel Lord Smail kindly offered guidance on navigating Marseille's archives. Anna Qureshi generously allowed me to read her master's thesis about misogynistic judgments of Johanna (written under Dr. Smail's direction), helping to fill gaps in my reading.

Theresa Earenfight and an anonymous reader offered valuable expert criticism and insight on the manuscript that have made the book stronger.

My colleagues in the History Department and in the Center for Medieval and Early Renaissance Studies at Binghamton University have been wonderful supporters, editors, and critics. Marilynn Desmond, Richard Mackenney, and Tina Chronopoulos have read most or all of the manuscript at various stages, and I thank them for their advice and generosity. Leigh Ann Wheeler has been a superb sounding board and crisis counselor. Thanks are due as well to Nancy Appelbaum, Ken Kurtz, Howard Brown, Steve Ortiz, Diane Sommerville, Jean Quataert, Kent Schull, Olivia Holmes, Dana Stewart, Heather DeHaan, Julia Walker, Kevin Hatch, Heather Welland, Sean Dunwoody, Jerry Kutcher, and Barbara Abou-El-Haj for their friendship and moral support.

Much of the research that went into this book was supported by the Fulbright Association, which allowed me ten months of intensive research in French libraries and archives. Much of the writing was supported by the American Association of University Women and by the Harpur College Dean's office, which also funded additional research in Naples.

I have presented portions of this book to a number of groups. I presented an early version of chapter 1 at the Sewanee Medieval Colloquium in 2006. At that time, Charles Briggs offered perspective that helped direct my research going forward. I shared portions of chapter 4 with the participants in the California Medieval History Seminar (February 2009) and the Newberry Intellectual History Seminar (November 2010); both groups offered feedback and commentary that helped me better articulate my argument. I also benefited from the insight of my fellow panelists and the audience at a panel on "Rumor and Infamy in Political Culture" at the 2013 meeting of the Medieval Academy of America. Finally, my thinking about Boccaccio's treatment of Johanna gained sharpness and clarity thanks to conversations with participants at a conference in Binghamton in honor of Boccaccio's 700th birthday.

My family and friends are owed the most profound gratitude. My father, John T. Casteen III, and my mother, Lotta Löfgren, have always been my intellectual models and heroes. They have been my best editors, and they have gone well above and beyond the bounds of parental duty in their willingness to read drafts, talk through ideas, and offer moral support. I thank them, Betsy Casteen, Andy Hord, and Michael and Katherine Chang for their encouragement. My brother, John Casteen, is a tireless, compassionate listener and a beloved friend who has been quick to offer needed morale boosts. I thank Lars Casteen and Sonny von Gutfeld for their hospitality and generosity, as for their support and friendship. Jenny Miller, too, offered hospitality, fellowship, and a place to stay during a vital stage in my research. Thanks are due as well to Elizabeth Carpenter Song, Meghann Pytka, Dana Polanichka, Courtney Kneupper, Suzanne LaVere, Alex Wolff, Noah Peffer, Joel Westendorf, Candice Lin, Jon Mingle, Laurie Casteen, Lily Casteen, Luke Casteen, Alex Barker, and Lily Robinson.

Above all else, I am grateful to and for Frank Chang, whose love and friendship mean everything.

❦ ABBREVIATIONS

ADBR   Archives départementales des Bouches-du-Rhône
AMM   Archives municipales de Marseille
ASPN   *Archivio storico per le province napoletane*
RIS   *Rerum Italicarum Scriptores*

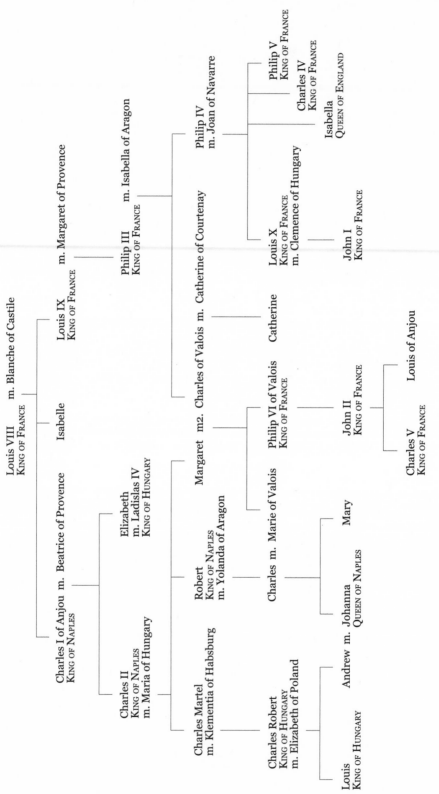

Figure 1. The Capetian, Angevin, and Valois dynasties

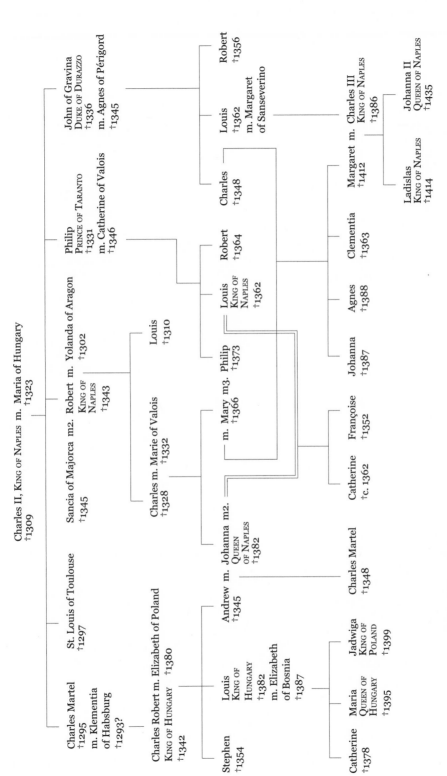

FIGURE 2. The Angevins of Naples and Hungary

Angevin lands in the mid-fourteenth century.

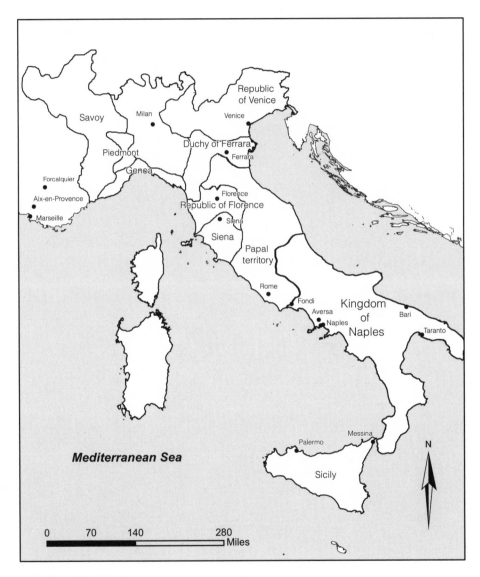

Italy in the mid-fourteenth century.

Introduction

> I saw the Queen of Naples in great estate, I swear to
> you, in my Lady Fortune's court. No single woman
> in the world was more honored—and, apparently, as
> loved—by my Lady! . . . For a long time Fortune
> maintained her, and kept her in state, but afterward,
> very suddenly, she turned her back most cruelly.
>
> Christine de Pizan, *The Book of Fortune's Transformation*
> (1403)

During the latter half of the fourteenth cen-
tury, both Provence and the Kingdom of Naples were ruled by a woman. In
both cases, the woman became vital to regional memory. Provence's Countess Jeanne is remembered as pious, beautiful, courtly, wise, and committed
to her subjects' well-being. In the words of an eighteenth-century historian,
she was "a woman endowed with all the agreeable traits possible in her sex."[1]
Naples's Queen Giovanna is another story entirely. A century after her death,
according to a fifteenth-century Neapolitan historian, people still whispered
about how she strangled her first husband as retribution for his sexual inadequacies.[2] Hopelessly debauched and voraciously lustful, she squandered
her kingdom's resources until she met a fitting end, murdered by her heir to
avenge decades of misrule.

These two historical portraits appear dichotomous, but they actually
describe the same woman. Variously known (depending on who was or
is describing her) as Jeanne, Jehanne, Joan, Giovanna, Zuana, or Joanna,
in life she was most often called—at least in writing—by her Latin name,

---

1. Pierre de Bourdeille, *Oeuvres du Seigneur de Brantôme*, vol. 2: *Contenant des dames illustres Françoises et étrangeres* (London: Aux dépens du Libraire, 1779), 426.

2. Pandolfo Collenuccio, *Compendio delle historie del Regno di Napoli, composto da messer Pandolfo
Collenutio iurisconsulto in Pesaro* (Vinegia: Michele Tramezino, 1548), 143.

Johanna. Johanna of Naples, queen of Sicily and Jerusalem and countess of Provence and Forcalquier (r. 1343–82), was a controversial, complex figure in life and after her death. Her posthumous reputations serve as a reminder of the mutability of historical memory and how contingent and culturally determined reputation is: One person's Jeanne is another's Giovanna. This book is about Johanna's various, contradictory reputations; through this lens, it examines the cultural mentality of late medieval Europe, particularly diverse, multifaceted reactions to regnant queenship, female sovereignty, and Johanna herself.

Johanna's Life and Reign

The fourteenth century has famously been characterized as "calamitous" and as "an age of adversity."[3] To study Johanna is to study the upheavals of her century. Her life and reign coincided with the Black Death, the marauding of the Great Companies, the so-called Babylonian Captivity of the Church, and the Western Schism. Johanna did far more than experience these calamities: they shaped her life, but she was also, to varying degrees, implicated in them. She figured in contemporaries' efforts to make sense of catastrophe and occupied a major role in their cultural imaginary. Indeed, Johanna appears in the work of her century's most celebrated writers, from the visionary Birgitta of Sweden to Giovanni Boccaccio and Francesco Petrarch—two of the Three Crowns of Italian literature—who commented and passed judgment on her, helping to shape her reputation and enshrining her as a pivotal figure in fourteenth-century history.

Johanna's date of birth is unknown, but she was likely born in 1326 or 1327, the daughter of Marie of Valois (1309–32) and Charles of Calabria (1298–1328), the son and heir of King Robert of Anjou (r. 1309–43). Charles's death made Johanna and her sister, Mary (b. 1329), Robert's only direct lineal heirs; Robert designated Johanna his successor in 1330.[4] The complex questions of legitimacy and sovereignty that her succession raised assured that Johanna remained an object of scrutiny throughout her reign. She became the heiress of the self-consciously French Angevin dynasty shortly after her maternal uncle, Philip VI (r. 1328–50), became the first Valois king of France on the strength of the so-called Salic Law

---

3. Barbara Tuchman, *A Distant Mirror: The Calamitous Fourteenth Century* (New York: Random House, 1978); Robert E. Lerner, *The Age of Adversity: The Fourteenth Century* (Ithaca: Cornell University Press, 1976).

4. Robert's testament is preserved in ADBR, B 269, fols. 325r–327v.

principle that thrones could not pass to or through women.[5] Valois apologists helped to elaborate political theories that defined sovereignty as incompatible with femininity, building on Scholastic discussions of gender and politics to argue that, in the words of François de Meyronnes (1288–1328), a polemicist for both the Valois and Angevin dynasties, "a woman, even when the only child, cannot inherit" a kingdom.[6] Their arguments took shape as Johanna came of age; her reputation became caught up in a larger cultural conversation about female nature and capacity, as about how to define sovereignty itself.

Johanna grew up in a court noted by contemporaries for its scholarly culture—although she apparently received no formal education.[7] Instead, she came under the tutelage of her step-grandmother, Sancia of Majorca (ca. 1285–1345), after her mother died in 1332. Sancia was famous for her piety, her devotion to the Franciscan order, and her active religious patronage, and she provided an important model for Johanna.[8] She lived austerely even before widowhood, when she retired to a Clarissan convent, and she had more interest in contemplation and prayer than in the more worldly aspects of queenship, but she wielded great power at court and took a forceful role in the dispute about evangelical poverty.[9] The Angevin court was not entirely given over to piety, however. The Angevins had long patronized arts and letters, and Robert was famous for his

---

5. Ralph E. Giesey has recently argued that the initial impetus behind the exclusion of women from the French throne was politics rather than principle. See Ralph E. Giesey, *Le rôle méconnu de la Loi Salique: La succession royale, XIVᵉ–XVIᵉ siècles*, trans. Franz Regnot (Paris: Les Belles Lettres, 2007), esp. 40–47. Nonetheless, by the time of Johanna's succession, the argument that women did not succeed to the French throne was taken as a statement of principle.

6. On Valois apologetics, see Giesey, *Le rôle méconnu de la Loi Salique*, 69–89. On François de Meyronnes's role as an Angevin polemicist, see Samantha Kelly, *The New Solomon: Robert of Naples (1309–1343) and Fourteenth-Century Kingship* (Leiden: Brill, 2003), esp. 30–38, 278–80.

7. On Johanna's education, see Émile G. Léonard, *Histoire de Jeanne Iʳᵉ, reine de Naples, comtesse de Provence (1343–1382)* (Monaco: Imp. de Monaco, 1932–36), 1:169–74. In 1346, Johanna wrote to Pope Clement VI that, as a woman, she lacked Latin learning ("mulier sim et litteras non noverim nisi paucas"). The letter is ADBR, B 176, fol. 183. Léonard provides an edition in *Histoire de Jeanne Iʳᵉ*, 2:437–39.

8. On Sancia's piety, see Caroline Bruzelius, "Queen Sancia of Mallorca and the Church of Sta. Chiara in Naples," *Memoirs of the American Academy in Rome* 40 (1995): 69–100; Ronald G. Musto, "Queen Sancia of Naples (1286–1345) and the Spiritual Franciscans," in *Women of the Medieval World: Essays in Honor of John H. Mundy*, ed. Julius Kirshner and Suzanne Wemple (Oxford: Blackwell, 1985), 179–214; and Kelly, *The New Solomon*, 83–86.

9. Sancia was famous for her asceticism and desire to become a nun. She remained chaste (although Robert had a mistress and illegitimate children). Sancia petitioned unsuccessfully to have her marriage annulled in 1317 and 1337 so that she could enter a convent. Cf. Musto, "Queen Sancia of Naples," and Kelly, *The New Solomon*, 85.

learning.[10] His court attracted and fostered the leading lights of fourteenth-century culture, including Giotto, Petrarch, and Boccaccio. It was frequented as well by Robert's younger brothers, Philip, prince of Taranto (1278–1331), and John of Gravina, duke of Durazzo (1294–1336), and their wives and children, including six sons whose rivalry dominated court gossip and helped shape the first two decades of Johanna's reign. Johanna was thus the product of a court marked, on the one hand, by religious fervor and a fledgling humanist culture and, on the other, by intrigue and simmering factionalism.

In 1343, Johanna succeeded Robert ahead of nine male cousins who could (and did) stake claims to her throne. She would struggle with their resentment, as with their plays for power. From the outset, she faced criticism for the perceived iniquity of her succession, along with uncertainty about what it actually meant for her to inherit Robert's throne. Would she truly govern? Would she incorporate her husband into her reign, or would he become the kingdom's ruler? The conceptual and political importance of the Kingdom of Naples made such questions particularly pressing. It was the most significant European polity yet to be ruled by a woman in her own right. From their capital in Naples, the Angevins ruled the southern half of peninsular Italy, the counties of Provence and Forcalquier, and portions of the Piedmont, Albania (the duchy of Durazzo), and Greece (the Morea). Under Johanna's forebears, the Angevin realm had approached empire; its kings exercised de facto rule over much of northern Italy while aggressively spreading their territory to the East. Until 1282, it also included the island of Sicily; even after its loss to Aragon in the Sicilian Vespers, Angevin kings fought to reclaim the island and referred to their realm as the Kingdom of Sicily—although historians refer to the kingdom as it existed after 1282 as the Kingdom of Naples, or simply as the Regno. In addition, the Regno's kings had claimed the symbolically potent (but territorially empty) title king

---

10. On Angevin patronage, see Jean Dunbabin, *The French in the Kingdom of Sicily, 1266–1305* (Cambridge: Cambridge University Press, 2011), 189–279, and Dunbabin, *Charles I of Anjou: Power, Kingship and State-Making in Thirteenth-Century Europe* (London: Longman, 1998); Kelly, *The New Solomon*, esp. 22–72; Caroline Bruzelius, *The Stones of Naples: Church Building in Angevin Italy, 1266–1343* (New Haven: Yale University Press, 2004); Janis Elliott and Cordelia Warr, eds., *The Church of Santa Maria Donna Regina: Art, Iconography and Patronage in Fourteenth Century Naples* (Farnham: Ashgate, 2004); Cordelia Warr and Janis Elliott, eds., *Art and Architecture in Naples, 1266–1713: New Approaches* (Oxford: Wiley-Blackwell, 2010); Andreas Bräm, *Neapolitanische Bilderbibeln des Trecento: Anjou-Buchmalerei von Robert dem Weisen bis zu Johanna I*, 2 vols. (Wiesbaden: Reichert, 2007); Ferdinando Bologna, *I pittori alla corte angioina di Napoli, 1266–1414, e un riesame dell'arte nell'età fridericiana*, ed. Giuliano Briganti, Saggi e studi di storia dell'arte 2 (Rome: Ugo Bozzi, 1969); and Cathleen A. Fleck, *The Clement Bible at the Medieval Courts of Naples and Avignon: A Story of Papal Power, Royal Prestige, and Patronage* (Farnham: Ashgate, 2010).

of Jerusalem since 1277, when the first Angevin king, Charles I (1227–85), bought the title from Marie of Antioch.[11] By the time of Johanna's succession, the Regno's rulers were as prominent as the king of France or England or the emperor himself.

The competing claims of the senior branch of the Angevin family, which ruled Hungary, rendered Johanna's succession particularly controversial. According to the rule of primogeniture—widely accepted by the fourteenth century—Robert, the third son of Charles II (1254–1309), should not have become king. Rather, the son of his eldest brother, Charles Martel (1271–95), should have done so. However, when Charles Martel died, his young son, Charles Robert, or Carobert (1288–1342), was removed from the line of succession to protect the Regno from instability. Charles II's second son, the future St. Louis of Toulouse (1274–97), had become a Franciscan friar and bishop and renounced his hereditary rights, so Robert succeeded Charles in Naples, while Carobert inherited the Hungarian crown.[12] Carobert insisted that he and his sons were the Regno's rightful rulers—a charge that his son, Louis "the Great" of Hungary (1326–82), took up in his turn. That Robert should bequeath his kingdom to a female child when Carobert's youth had barred him from the succession added insult to injury and was to have profound ramifications for Neapolitan history.

The thorny question of the Hungarian Angevins' rights to Naples formed the backdrop to the early years of Johanna's reign. As a child, she was betrothed and then married to Andrew of Hungary (1328–45), the second of Carobert's three sons, in an effort to secure peace and stability.[13] The Hungarians saw their union as reparation for Robert's unjust succession. Yet Johanna refused to accept Andrew as a coruler, and he was murdered after a protracted power struggle in 1345. The ensuing scandal, which included accusations that Johanna had first cuckolded and then murdered Andrew, would haunt her throughout her reign. It also nearly cost her kingdom: Louis of Hungary twice invaded Naples (1348–50) to avenge his brother and claim what he insisted was his birthright—an argument with which many contemporaries agreed.

---

11. Kelly, *The New Solomon*, 5.

12. Charles Martel's mother was Maria of Hungary (1257–1323). Through her, he became titular king of Hungary, although he died before he could make good on that claim. His son Carobert ruled Hungary from 1312 to 1342.

13. On Robert's negotiations with Carobert regarding the marriage, see Kelly, *The New Solomon*, 281–82.

Marriage, and the balance of power within marriage, posed a consistent challenge to Johanna. It had important implications for her reputation, as contemporary expectations of marriage and femininity shaped how contemporaries responded to Johanna. After Andrew's death, she married Louis of Taranto (1320–62), another cousin with designs on her throne. Louis was the only one of Johanna's four husbands to rule in his own name, effectively co-opting her power from 1350 to 1362 and inspiring sympathy for Johanna. Her subsequent two marriages proved less problematic for her exercise of sovereignty. Her third husband, James IV of Majorca (1336–75), was reportedly insane, and Johanna was able to enforce his secondary status and govern independently without incurring contemporaries' ire. Her fourth husband, Duke Otto of Brunswick-Grubenhagen (1320–98), acted as the Regno's military leader without seeking the throne and supported Johanna loyally until her death.

The latter half of Johanna's reign differed starkly from its beginning, which was wrought with scandal, violence, and strife. Johanna emerged, over the course of the 1360s and 1370s, as a respected figure on the European political stage. She became a noted papal ally and a leader in the league that defended papal prerogatives in northern Italy. She helped to return the papacy from Avignon to Rome, and she formed friendships with the most celebrated female religious of her day, Birgitta of Sweden, Catherine of Siena, and Katherine of Vadstena. She emulated her grandparents in patronizing religious orders and foundations, and she helped to foster a vibrant artistic culture in Naples. In the process, Johanna became known and acted as a legitimate, sovereign monarch.

Ironically, her leading role in religious politics proved Johanna's downfall after the Great Schism of the Western Church began in 1378. She was the first monarch to recognize Clement VII as pope. Her abjuration of Clement's rival, Urban VI, led many of Johanna's former allies to turn against her. It also resulted in her deposition and, ultimately, in her death, after Urban crowned her cousin, Charles of Durazzo—backed by her old enemy, Louis of Hungary—king in her place. Johanna died in prison, reportedly at Charles's hand, in 1382. Childless, she had adopted the French prince Louis of Anjou as her heir; Louis and Charles waged a long war that permanently divided Johanna's realm, plunging Angevin lands into disorder. Johanna's reign ended even more bloodily than it had begun, leading many—particularly in Urbanist lands—to see violence and suffering as her legacy to her people.

Angevin Sovereignty and Female Succession

The legacy of Angevin sovereignty rendered Johanna's inheritance of the Regno particularly problematic. The kingdom's origins lay in the early twelfth-century Norman conquest of southern Italy and Sicily. It was a rich (thanks to bustling ports and fertile fields), culturally diverse region coveted by rulers throughout the Mediterranean world. Under Frederick II (1194–1250), it had become part of the Hohenstaufen Empire. Frederick—a Sicilian born and bred—favored the cosmopolitan Regno, a center of thriving trade, as of culture and scholarship. It was the jewel of his empire, boasting Europe's first secular university (in Naples), its first medical school (at Salerno), and one of the greatest libraries of the thirteenth century.[14]

The Regno was a rich prize, one Johanna's ancestors came to possess as a result of the papal crusade against the Hohenstaufen. The papacy claimed suzerainty over the Regno when it deposed Frederick in 1245, and a series of popes sought a champion to wrest the kingdom from his illegitimate son, Manfred (1232–66).[15] Charles I of Anjou—the youngest son of Louis VIII of France and brother of the crusader king and future saint Louis IX—ultimately assumed the mantle of papal champion. After Manfred's death, the capture and execution of Frederick's grandson, Conradin (1252–68), and the imprisonment of Manfred's sons, Charles became the Regno's king, ruling with papal sanction and blessing and founding an Angevin kingdom that remained at the forefront of European politics until it was conquered by Aragon in 1442.

Naples's Angevin rulers were, paradoxically, both powerful, independent monarchs and papal vassals. Charles and his successors dominated Italian politics and claimed leadership of the Guelf party. They portrayed themselves as crusaders, even incorporating the crusaders' cross into their coat of arms, and as kings whose kingship had spiritual dimensions—a claim bolstered by currents in eschatological thought that identified Frederick II with Antichrist and predicted that a French prince would champion the Church

---

14. On the pre-Angevin Regno, see Hubert Houben, *Roger II of Sicily: A Ruler between East and West*, trans. G. A. Loud and D. Milburn (Cambridge: Cambridge University Press, 2002); John Julius Norwich, *The Normans in the South, 1016–1130* (London: Longmans, 1967); David Abulafia, *Frederick II: A Medieval Emperor* (Oxford: Oxford University Press, 1988); and Abulafia, *The Two Italies: Economic Relations between the Norman Kingdom of Sicily and the Northern Communes* (Cambridge: Cambridge University Press, 1977).

15. Sicily's Norman rulers asserted autonomy from imperial rule by insisting on their status as apostolic legates. Constance of Sicily (1154–98) amplified the kingdom's ties to the papacy during Frederick II's minority by placing him under papal tutelage. The special status claimed by Norman rulers set important precedents on which Angevin rulers would later draw. On papal claims to lordship over the Regno and the Angevin crusade against the Hohenstaufen, see Salvatore Fodale, *Comes et Legatus Siciliae: Sul privilegio di Urbano II e la pretesa Apostolica Legazia dei Normanni di Sicilia* (Palermo: U. Manfredi, 1970); Norman Housley, *The Italian Crusades: The Papal-Angevin Alliance and the Crusades against Christian Lay Power, 1254–1343* (Oxford: Oxford University Press, 1982); Steven Runciman, *The Sicilian Vespers: A History of the Mediterranean World in the Later Thirteenth Century* (Cambridge: Cambridge University Press, 1992); and Dunbabin, *The French in the Kingdom of Sicily.*

in the Last Days. The Angevins represented their vassalage to the papacy as a sign of their "special sacrality," linked to an inborn holiness that was the product of a "sacred lineage or *beata stirps*" that imbued their bloodline with sacred power.[16] Charles I forged a dynastic union with the Hungarian Árpád dynasty—with serious repercussions for Johanna—by marrying his son, the future Charles II, to Maria of Hungary (1257–1323). The marriage united two bloodlines with saintly members, and it allowed later Angevins to publicize their kinship not only with Louis IX (canonized 1297), but also with a line of Hungarian royal saints, including, most recently, Elizabeth of Hungary (d. 1231).[17] Angevin kings insisted on the holiness of their blood, their quasi-sacral status as protectors of the papacy, and their sacred rights as kings of Jerusalem. Angevin publicists argued that their rule was divinely ordained and that Angevin kings trod a unique path between worldly rulership and ecclesiastical power, making them monarchs both secular and sacred.[18]

Johanna was the Regno's fourth Angevin monarch. Under her predecessors, the Regno had risen to international preeminence, growing in size, prestige, and influence. It reached its cultural zenith under Robert, who became known as a "second Solomon" for his learning and penchant for preaching erudite sermons. Robert is significant both for resisting the efforts of the emperor Henry VII (1275–1313) to force his submission to the imperial principle of universal rulership and for creating a new kingly type—that of the scholar-king. Robert's reign thus began a new period in European political history, signaling the final end of imperial hegemony and redefining medieval kingship. His contemporaries understood that "the Neapolitan king was emperor in his own domain," exercising sacral, even quasi-sacerdotal

---

16. Kelly, *The New Solomon*, 74. The Angevin bloodline included numerous saints of both sexes, the most recent of whom was Johanna's great-uncle, St. Louis of Toulouse. For a detailed discussion of the Angevin *beata stirps*, see André Vauchez, "'*Beata Stirps*': Sainteté et lignage en Occident aux XIIIᵉ et XIVᵉ siècles," in *Saints, Prophètes et Visionnaires: Le pouvoir surnaturel au Moyen Âge* (Paris: Albin Michel, 1999), 67–78.

17. On the importance of saintly kin to the Capetian, Angevin, and Árpád dynasties, see Vauchez, "'*Beata Stirps*'"; Gábor Klaniczay, *The Uses of Supernatural Power: The Transformation of Popular Religion in Medieval and Early Renaissance Europe* (Princeton: Princeton University Press, 1990); Klaniczay, *Holy Rulers and Blessed Princesses: Dynastic Cults in Medieval Central Europe*, trans. Éva Pálmai (Cambridge: Cambridge University Press, 2002); Klaniczay, "La noblesse et le culte des saints dynastiques sous les rois angevins," in *La noblesse dans les terroires angevins à la fin du moyen âge*, ed. N. Coulet and J.-M. Matz (Rome: École française de Rome, 2000), 511–26; Jean-Paul Boyer, "La 'Foi Monarchique': Royaume de Sicile et Provence (MI-XIIIᵉ–MI-XIVᵉ siècle)," in *Le forme della propaganda politica nel due e nel trecento*, ed. Paolo Cammarosano (Rome: École Française de Rome, 1994), 85–110; and Dunbabin, *The French in the Kingdom of Sicily*, 189–98.

18. Kelly, *The New Solomon*, 116–17.

kingship.[19] His reign paved the way for future kings who, like Charles V of France (1338–80) and Charles IV of Bohemia (1316–78), emulated his model of wise kingship.[20]

Johanna's position as Robert's heir—while perfectly in keeping with Neapolitan law, which allowed daughters to inherit in the absence of sons—was complicated by the legacy he bequeathed to her of a monarchy whose king was treated as a "quasi-religious figure."[21] The succession of a queen to a European throne was not without precedent: Urraca of León and Castile ruled the realm she inherited from 1109 to 1126, setting an example for her descendant, Berenguela (r. 1217), while Navarre had two regnant queens just before Johanna's succession, and the Latin kingdom of Jerusalem (over which Johanna claimed sovereignty) had no fewer than five.[22] Nonetheless, female succession was unusual, particularly as monarchs were becoming more powerful and political theory—especially in France and the Empire—insisted that sovereignty was a solely male prerogative. While emphasis on divine election and sacral kingship had served earlier Neapolitan monarchs well, this tradition placed Johanna at a disadvantage. Naples's queens were often influential and took an active role in the Regno's governance, but they also, as Johanna could not, adhered to traditional expectations of queenship, acting as consorts or, in some cases, as regents who wielded authority without claiming sovereignty, which remained vested in their husbands or sons.[23] The difficulties inherent in regnant queenship were compounded, in Johanna's case, by the distinctive qualities with which her forebears imbued their kingship: Women could not preach, nor could they be crusaders, raising questions about what it meant for a woman to be Naples's sovereign.

Both Robert and Johanna conceived of Johanna as heir not merely to Robert's throne but also to his sovereignty. Despite having a large pool of eligible potential male successors, Robert was determined that his direct line should rule Naples. While he sought to sooth the ire of the Hungarian Angevins by

---

19. Walter Ullmann, "The Development of the Medieval Idea of Sovereignty," *English Historical Review* 64 (January 1949): 1, 19.

20. Kelly, *The New Solomon*, 19–20.

21. Boyer, "La 'Foi Monarchique,'" 86, 110

22. On regnant queens in medieval Europe, see Armin Wolf, "Reigning Queens in Medieval Europe: When, Where, and Why," in *Medieval Queenship*, ed. John Carmi Parsons (New York: Palgrave Macmillan, 1998), 169–88.

23. On Angevin queens, see Mario Gaglione, *Donne e potere a Napoli: Le sovrane angioine; Consorti, vicarie e regnanti (1266–1442)* (Catanzaro: Rubbettino Editore, 2009). Gaglione argues that some queens—most notably Maria of Hungary, Violante of Aragon, and Sancia of Majorca—wielded great influence, particularly in the traditional queenly role of mediator or intercessor (34). Sancia provided an important model for Johanna, but her power differed markedly in its source and conceptualization from that which Johanna claimed.

marrying Johanna to Andrew, Robert had no intention of allowing them to control Naples or of allowing Andrew to rule in Johanna's place or in her name (as many contemporaries expected). As far as Robert was concerned, Johanna's blood legitimated her queenship, and her sex should present no obstacle.

Robert's ambitions for Johanna are on display in the *Anjou Bible*, commissioned in the mid to late 1330s as a gift for Johanna and Andrew.[24] Its visual program, executed by the Neapolitan Cristoforo Orimina, asserts the justice of Johanna's succession and her claim to sovereignty. The second of the manuscript's two frontispieces (see figure 3) presents a pictorial Angevin genealogy, showing the three generations of Angevin kings and queens and drawing on them to legitimate the impending fourth generation.[25] In the top register, Charles I sits enthroned with his queen, Beatrice of Provence (1231–67), and blesses a crowned, kneeling Charles II. In the second tier, Charles II sits alongside Maria of Hungary and looks to his left, where his three most illustrious sons—Charles Martel, Robert, and Louis of Toulouse—stand. Robert and Charles Martel are both crowned, a visual argument for the justice of Robert's succession and the division of the family into two ruling dynasties. A haloed Louis of Toulouse stands behind them, looking toward Robert, who consistently evoked his brother's intercession and blessing as legitimating features of his kingship.[26] Robert's two sons, Charles and Louis, kneel at his feet. In the bottom tier, Robert and Sancia sit enthroned, surrounded by Robert's descendants. Charles and Louis—both dead when Orimina painted the frontispiece—stand to Robert's left. To his right, Marie of Valois presents Johanna and Mary, whose clothing and posture mirror those of their father and uncle in the tier above, to Sancia—who extends her hand to the girls, taking charge of them—and Robert. A young man, who may be Andrew of Hungary, kneels to kiss Robert's feet, a gesture of obeisance that sets him apart from the other figures in the tableau and differentiates him from Johanna. The entire

---

24. Leuven, Maurits Sabbe Bibliotheek, MS 1. An excellent study of the bible, including reproductions of the miniatures, was published in 2010. See Lieve Watteeuw and Jan Van der Stock, eds., *The Anjou Bible, Naples 1340: A Royal Manuscript Revealed* (Paris: Peeters, 2010). On the dating of the manuscript and its relationship to Johanna's succession, see Michelle M. Duran, "The Politics of Art: Imaging Sovereignty in the Anjou Bible," in Watteeuw and Van der Stock, *The Anjou Bible*, esp. 74.

25. Leuven, Maurits Sabbe Bibliotheek, MS 1, fol. 4r.

26. Robert pressed for Louis's 1317 canonization and drew heavily on his image in his artistic commissions. The most famous instance is Simone Martini's altarpiece (ca. 1317) depicting Louis crowning Robert, now in Naples's Museo Nazionale di Capodimonte. On Robert's iconographic use of Louis, see Kelly, *The New Solomon*, esp. chap. 3.

Figure 3. Angevin pictorial genealogy from the *Anjou Bible*. Leuven, Maurits Sabbe Bibliotheek, MS 1, fol. 4r. © Bruno Vandermeulen, KU Leuven, Maurits Sabbe Library. Maurits Sabbe Library, FTRW, KU Leuven.

frontispiece is, thus, an artful statement about Angevin succession, portraying both Robert and Johanna as the legitimate inheritors of the Regno's throne.

Johanna was to rule Naples alone, just as Robert had before her, and the *Anjou Bible* portrays Andrew not as a king but as Johanna's consort. Many of the manuscript's miniatures reinforce his secondary status. Folio 249r shows a seated couple, commonly believed to be Johanna and Andrew (see figure 4). The man caresses the cheek of the woman who, unlike him, is crowned and who sits, facing regally outward, while the man looks and moves toward her, focusing all of his attention on her. The same couple appears again on folio 278r; the man's head is again bare as he embraces his crowned wife. Andrew is portrayed bareheaded and in profile as well on folio 309r, where he kneels to receive the finished bible from Robert. Johanna, by contrast, often appears alone, crowned and facing forward, as on the bottom of folio 308v, where she sits enthroned, holding an orb and scepter.[27]

Robert's conception of Johanna's sovereignty proved difficult for many contemporaries to accept, and Johanna would battle public opinion that favored other heirs throughout her reign. Indeed, Johanna was as controversial as she became because she insisted on her sovereignty. She defined her role as a regnant queen as active and powerful, one that entailed divinely sanctioned rulership without the interference or participation of her consort. As Michelle Duran has pointed out, Johanna's own artistic commissions represent her alone, despite the fact that she spent almost all of her life as a wife.[28] The best expression of her artistic self-presentation can be found in the *Book of Hours of Johanna I*, completed between 1362 and 1375.[29] On folio 234v (see figure 7, chapter 3), Johanna kneels before a lilied background—a reminder of her Capetian descent—with a book. The heavenly host and Trinity gaze benignly down at her, and the Father hands her a scepter, signaling divine approbation of her sole sovereignty. Thus, Johanna and Robert both insisted

---

27. See Watteeuw and Van der Stock, *The Anjou Bible*, 269, 274, 295, 296, as well as Duran, "The Politics of Art," 74–75, 85–86. For a different interpretation of the bible's imagery, see Bräm, *Neapolitanische Bilderbibeln des Trecento*, 1:15, 180; 2:404–5. Ronald Musto has suggested that the miniatures depicting Johanna and Andrew "counter the early slanders of their mutual disdain and then open hostility." See Ronald G. Musto, "Review: Lieve Watteeuw and Jan Van der Stock, eds., *The Anjou Bible: A Royal Manuscript Revealed* and Cathleen A. Fleck, *The Clement Bible at the Medieval Courts of Naples and Avignon: A Story of Papal Power, Royal Prestige, and Patronage*," *Renaissance Quarterly* 64 (Summer 2011): 588. This is a problematic argument; the bible's visual program is a statement of Angevin ideology and not a transparent reflection of relationships at court. The portrayal of Andrew as an honored but secondary figure is perfectly in keeping with court rhetoric.

28. Duran, "The Politics of Art," 88.

29. Vienna, Österreichische Nationalbibliothek, MS Cod. 1921.

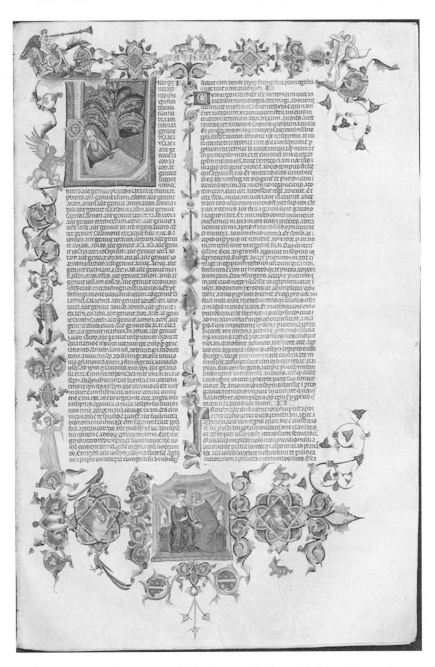

Figure 4. At bottom royal couple, probably Johanna of Naples and Andrew of Hungary. Leuven, Maurits Sabbe Bibliotheek, MS 1, fol. 249r. © Bruno Vandermeulen, KU Leuven, Maurits Sabbe Library. Maurits Sabbe Library, FTRW, KU Leuven.

that Johanna was the continuation of a line of pious, divinely appointed monarchs whose blood enabled and justified their succession.

Reputation and Queenship in Medieval Europe

Throughout her long reign, Johanna occupied an important place in Europe's cultural imaginary. Her reputation evolved as it did because she mattered—deeply—to her contemporaries, whether they admired or hated her. Her public image became caught up in a larger cultural conversation about women that would come to be called the *querelle des femmes*, or "woman question." She was always, even for her apologists, most noteworthy as a woman and representative of the virtues, potential, weakness, or threats associated with femininity. After Andrew of Hungary's murder, she became typed as a she-wolf—a sexualized, bloodthirsty predator—while as a papal ally she became the loving, obedient daughter of the Church. During the schism, Clementists described her as saintly and self-sacrificing, even as Urbanists denounced her as the embodiment of female irrationality and vice. On both sides of the ecclesiastical divide, Johanna was incontrovertibly significant, a potent figure whose motivations and character were crucial to understanding the crisis facing the Church and European society.

Modern scholarship has paid substantially less attention to Johanna and accorded her less importance than did her contemporaries. Scholars of Angevin Naples—a vibrant, flourishing field—conventionally treat Johanna's reign as a decisive break, a rupture that represents the end of Angevin greatness.[30] The definitive study of Johanna was published between 1932 and 1936 by the French scholar Émile Léonard.[31] No English-language study of her reign has appeared in more than a century, and most surveys of the period anachronistically dismiss her as an ineffective ruler with little impact on history.[32]

---

30. Samantha Kelly's *New Solomon*, for instance, frequently offers the disasters of Johanna's reign as evidence of the relative stability of Robert's. Jean Dunbabin's *French in the Kingdom of Sicily* ends in 1305, while works on a number of facets of Angevin culture, such as Caroline Bruzelius's *Stones of Naples*, end with Robert's death. Similarly, a conference on Neapolitan Angevin history held at Cambridge in 2013 did not consider Johanna's reign or the period after it.

31. Léonard, *Histoire de Jeanne Ire*. Léonard's *Les Angevins de Naples* (Paris: Presses Universitaires de France, 1954) also provides a summary of Johanna's reign.

32. See Welbore St. Clair Baddeley, *Queen Joanna I of Naples, Sicily, and Jerusalem, Countess of Provence, Forcalquier and Piedmont: An Essay on Her Times* (London: W. Heinemann, 1893), and Baddeley, *Robert the Wise and His Heirs, 1278–1352* (London: W. Heinemann, 1897). A recent English-language biography by Nancy Goldstone relies heavily on Léonard and published primary texts to provide an overview of Johanna's "notorious reign." See Nancy Goldstone, *The Lady Queen: The Notorious Reign of Joanna I, Queen of Naples, Jerusalem, and Sicily* (London: Walker and Company, 2009). There have been numerous biographies in French and Italian; they focus on the sensational aspects of chronicle accounts, particularly regarding Johanna's rumored promiscuity. See Italo de

Scholarly neglect of Johanna serves as a reminder of the power of historical memory and the lingering potency of reputation: One eminent historian of southern Italy characterizes Johanna's reign as "a constant record of court intrigues," while a recent survey of medieval queenship speaks only fleetingly—in one sentence—of Johanna's reign immediately after noting, "many queens-regnant ruled for short periods of time and often in moments of crisis."[33] Johanna's reign was long by any standard, and for much of it, her contemporaries described her as a wise, able ruler. Yet because of her posthumous reputation, modern accounts focus on scandal and crisis, as on her supposed sexual licentiousness—perhaps explaining why, until quite recently, political history has ignored her reign. Fortunately, the tide is turning. William Monter describes Johanna as Europe's first successful "female king" in a recent study of female sovereignty, while Mario Gaglione provides a balanced overview of her reign and a brief, somewhat reductive survey of her reputation in a collective biography of Angevin queens.[34] Art historians as well have begun the important task of examining Johanna's patronage and self-presentation.[35] This book, by taking Johanna's reputation as its focus, examines *how* and *why* she came to be remembered as she has been, analyzing the complex interplay between historical events, gossip, rumor, and propaganda that shapes both reputation and historical memory to reconstruct Johanna's place in her century's cultural imaginary. Close examination of her reputation reveals that Johanna was intimately associated in contemporaries' minds with many of the most important political and religious issues of her day. Their attitudes toward her, as toward gender, sovereignty, and femininity, were remarkably fluid. Many contemporaries perceived her as a successful monarch, and her sovereignty, under the right conditions, was accepted and even celebrated.

Feo, *Giovanna d'Angiò, regina di Napoli* (Naples: F. Fiorentino, 1968); Felice Froio, *Giovanna I d'Angiò* (Milan: Mursia, 1992); Vittorio Gleijeses and Lidia Gleijeses, *La Regina Giovanna d'Angiò* (Naples: T. Marotta, 1990); Louise Michel, *La reine Jeanne de Naples et de Provence: Histoire et légendes* (Grasse: TAC Motifs, 1995); and Dominique Paladilhe, *La Reine Jeanne, Comtesse de Provence* (Paris: Perrin, 1997).

33. David Abulafia, "The Italian South," in *The New Cambridge Medieval History*, ed. Rosamond McKitterick et al. (Cambridge: Cambridge University Press, 1995), 6:511–12; Theresa Earenfight, *Queenship in Medieval Europe* (London: Palgrave Macmillan, 2013), 190.

34. William E. Monter, *The Rise of Female Kings in Europe, 1300–1800* (New Haven: Yale University Press, 2012), esp. 61–67; Gaglione, *Donne e potere a Napoli*, 50. Gaglione does acknowledge the divergence between Neapolitan and Provençal treatments of Johanna.

35. In particular, see Bräm, *Neapolitanische Bilderbibeln des Trecento*; Duran, "The Politics of Art"; and Paola Vitolo, *La Chiesa della Regina: L'Incoronata di Napoli, Giovanna I d'Angiò, e Roberto d'Oderisio* (Rome: Viella, 2008).

Johanna's position as the sole regnant queen on the European stage during most of her reign, the scandals of her court, and her relationship with the papacy kept her in the public eye. Her reputation gained international dimensions, spreading via oral rumor that is largely irretrievable, but also in chronicles, prophecies, letters, poetry, and art, much of which echoes and refracts rumor. Such texts reveal not only how Johanna was perceived by her contemporaries but also how those contemporaries sought to define her and how they understood the complex of problems—queenship, femininity, royal succession—at whose nexus she stood.

The commentators who helped to shape Johanna's reputation likely did so consciously. Reputation was of paramount—and growing—importance in medieval Europe. A person's reputation, or *fama*, had crucial implications for her or his ability to take part in public life and determined her or his place in society and in what Daniel Lord Smail has called the medieval "economy of honor."[36] *Fama* was accepted as a form of proof in canon law at the turn of the twelfth century.[37] By the thirteenth century, the great canonist Hostiensis accepted as a matter of course that criminal trials began with an inquiry into the reputation of both defendant and accuser, because public estimation was integral to identity and spoke to reliability and character.[38] *Fama* had probative value and could serve as legal evidence, while *infamia* (infamy) was a legal status incurred by those who had committed (or were thought to have committed) a crime of which "certain public knowledge" was "so widespread

36. See F. R. P. Akehurst, "Good Name, Reputation, and Notoriety in French Customary Law," in *Fama: The Politics of Talk and Reputation in Medieval Europe*, ed. Thelma Fenster and Daniel Lord Smail (Ithaca: Cornell University Press, 2003), 75–94, and Jeffrey Bowman, "Infamy and Proof in Medieval Spain," in Fenster and Smail, *Fama*, 96; Daniel Lord Smail, "Hatred as a Social Institution in Late-Medieval Society," *Speculum* 76 (January 2001): 90–126.

37. On the legal evolution of *fama*, see Francesco Migliorino, *Fama e Infamia: Problemi della società medievale nel pensiero giuridico nei secoli XII e XIII* (Catania: Editrice Giannotta, 1985); Richard M. Fraher, "Conviction According to Conscience: The Medieval Jurists' Debate Concerning Judicial Discretion and the Law of Proof," *Law and History Review* 7 (Spring 1989): 23–88; Julien Théry, "*Fama*: L'opinion publique comme preuve judiciare. Aperçu sur la révolution médiévale de l'inquisitoire (XII*ᵉ*–XIV*ᵉ* siècle)," in *La preuve en justice de l'Antiquité à nos jours*, ed. Bruno Lemesle (Rennes: Presses Universitaires de Rennes, 2003), 119–47; Massimo Vallerani, "Modelli di Verità: Le prove nei processi inquisitori," in *L'Enquête au Moyen Âge*, ed. Claude Gauvard (Rome: L'École française de Rome, 2008), 123–42; Vallerani, *Medieval Public Justice*, trans. Sarah Rubin Blanshei (Washington DC: Catholic University of America Press, 2012), 106–13; and Laura Ikins Stern, "Public Fame in the Fifteenth Century," *American Journal of Legal History* 44 (April 2000): 198–222.

38. Edward Peters, "Wounded Names: The Medieval Doctrine of Infamy," in *Law in Medieval Life and Thought*, ed. Edward B. King and Susan J. Ridyard (Sewanee, TN: University of the South Press, 1990), 85.

as to constitute in effect the testimony of an eyewitness."[39] In cases when no one came forward to lodge a formal accusation, *infamia* could be personified as the accuser, not only testifying against the defendant but also initiating an inquest.[40] This was particularly common in later medieval Italian communes, which provided the social and cultural context for much of the textual consideration of Johanna's reputation.[41] It was understood that *fama* and *infamia* reflected communal knowledge, and even what we would now call hearsay had legal standing.[42] In many parts of Europe, "common knowledge" was sufficient to convict a person of a crime—or at the very least to justify the use of torture to elicit a confession.[43]

The consequences of infamy were dire. Thirteenth-century French judges were empowered to imprison the defamed, who represented a danger to their communities.[44] In both Roman and common law, infamy carried with it a range of "legal disabilities" designed to shame the infamous and bar them, and even their children, from full participation in society.[45] As Edward Peters argues, later medieval Europe was "a world in which status, capacity, reputation, and honor were not merely widely known and closely linked, but culturally reinforced by rigid exclusionary practices" that led to the marginalization and isolation of the infamous.[46] For women, whose political and social activities were more proscribed than those of men, *fama* was of even greater significance: A woman's reputation could condemn her if she were accused of a crime—particularly adultery or prostitution—and it had direct bearing on her social standing, her ability to marry, and the status of her children.

---

39. Akehurst, "Good Name, Reputation, and Notoriety," 84. Cf. Peters, "Wounded Names," 69. Canon law—setting precedent for civil law—accepted *fama* and notoriety as evidence in adultery cases. See James A. Brundage, *Law, Sex, and Christian Society in Medieval Europe* (Chicago: University of Chicago Press, 1987), 411–12.

40. Vallerani, "Modelli di Verità," 126.

41. Fraher, "Conviction According to Conscience," 28.

42. Stern, "Public Fame in the Fifteenth Century," 198.

43. This was the position of the thirteenth-century Italian jurist Albertus Gandinus, who argued that the infamous, even if they were not guilty of the crimes of which they were accused, deserved punishment via torture for the things that had created their bad reputations in the first place. See Vallerani, "Modelli di Verità," 131–32.

44. Théry, "*Fama*," 137.

45. Peters, "Wounded Names," 79; cf. Bowman, "Infamy and Proof in Medieval Spain," 97–99, 104; Akehurst, "Good Name, Reputation, and Notoriety," 79; and Chris Wickham, "Gossip and Resistance among the Medieval Peasantry," *Past and Present* 160 (August 1998): esp. 4–6.

46. Peters, "Wounded Names," 85; cf. Migliorino, *Fama e Infamia*, 139, 172.

Fama, in both the legal and cultural senses, was powerful, but it was also—late medieval commentators recognized—unstable and easily manipulated. Albert Russell Ascoli argues that Dante Alighieri (himself the victim of defamation) mistrusted *fama*, because "the biased report of either friend or enemy gives rise to a series of exaggerations which gain force as they recede in time and space from the person whose name is repeated."[47] *Fama* reflects the biases of those whose accounts give it life, as Dante recognized, rather than an objective reflection of reality. Indeed, as Dante notes in the *Convivio* (1.3.11), "the image generated by fame alone is always greater . . . than the thing imagined in its true state."[48] *Fama*, as Dante demonstrated in the *Commedia*—which Justin Steinberg has aptly called "an infamy-making machine"—could also be a potent tool, one that literally rewrites history and remakes character.[49] Gossip and rumor—among the building blocks of *fama*—could easily be employed to construct infamy, regardless of their factual basis. Indeed, penitential manuals routinely warned against gossip's unreliability and destructive potential.[50] Medieval commentators recognized that *fama* was unreliable, and that it was inescapable: as Geoffrey Chaucer points out, "every speche or noise or soun, / Thurgh his multiplicacioun, / Though it were piped of a mouse, / Mot nede come to Fames House."[51] Chaucer goes on to argue that Fame is difficult to cultivate, and that one often winds up with "the contraire" of what one seeks.[52] Jurists shared Dante's and Chaucer's suspicion of *fama*, giving voice to uncertainties deeply rooted in medieval thought. Isidore of Seville notes in his *Etymologies* (V.27) that "*fama* . . . creeps like a serpent through tongues and ears."[53] Like a serpent, it is insidious and potentially deceitful, acting as an index of communal knowledge, an expression of subjective public opinion, and an illusion that obscures the person it purports to represent.

---

47. Albert Russell Ascoli, *Dante and the Making of a Modern Author* (Cambridge: Cambridge University Press, 2008), 92. Cf. Justin Steinberg, "Dante and the Laws of Infamy," *PMLA* 126 (October 2011): 1118–26.

48. Steinberg, "Dante and the Laws of Infamy," 1122.

49. Ibid., 1120.

50. On the power and use of gossip in the later Middle Ages, see Susan E. Phillips, *Transforming Talk: The Problem with Gossip in Late Medieval England* (University Park: Pennsylvania State University Press, 2007).

51. Geoffrey Chaucer, *The House of Fame*, II.783–86, in Geoffrey Chaucer, *Dream Visions and Other Poems*, ed. Kathryn L. Lynch (New York: W. W. Norton, 2007), 62.

52. Ibid., III.1540, p. 79.

53. Cited and translated in Peters, "Wounded Names," 45.

Given the cultural and legal importance of *fama*, studying reputation reveals a great deal about the people who constructed *fama* and the values and beliefs they held. Max Gluckman argued in a seminal 1963 article that "gossip and scandal" are "among the most important societal and cultural phenomena" for anthropological analysis.[54] He points out that they maintain group unity and morality and help control competing factions within a community.[55] Chris Wickham, building on Gluckman, argues that gossip is an especially important object of historical study because of what it reveals about communal values and identity.[56] This is particularly true when it comes to discerning the cultural significance of a woman like Johanna. She lived at the center of a constantly accruing mass of gossip, which makes her reputation a particularly instructive window on later medieval culture. *Fama*, as Thelma Fenster and Daniel Smail argue, is always under negotiation and shaped by multiple and competing pressures. Gossip, or "talk," to use Fenster and Smail's preferred term, is the medium by which "we monitor and record reputations," and which "in medieval societies . . . did many of those things that in modern society are handled, officially, by bankers, credit bureaus, lawyers, state archives, and so on."[57] As the conduit for communal bias, morality, and self-policing and self-definition, *fama* is one of the most important indices of medieval mentalities that remains to us. As such, talk or gossip tells us a great deal about the people who feed, report, and shape it—more even than about the people who are its subject.

Medieval commentators were well aware of the power of *fama*, as of its usefulness and slipperiness. Chroniclers, polemicists, and writers of conduct literature touted the importance of royal reputation. The reputations of queens, in particular, were contested and subject to almost prurient attention. Queens faced "propaganda and character assassination" by political opponents, "because the question of fitness to rule and legitimacy" centered on their sexual morality, and because royal courts were places where "the politics of the personal produce a hotbed of gossip, intrigue, and suspicion."[58] Indeed, chronicles reveal "preoccupation with queenly sexuality" that often

---

54. Max Gluckman, "Papers in Honor of Melville J. Herskovits: Gossip and Scandal," *Current Anthropology* 4 (June 1963): 307.

55. Ibid., 308.

56. Wickham, "Gossip and Resistance among the Medieval Peasantry," 12.

57. Thelma Fenster and Daniel Lord Smail, "Introduction," in Fenster and Smail, *Fama*, 9.

58. Pauline Stafford, "The Portrayal of Royal Women in England, Mid-Tenth to Mid-Twelfth Centuries," in Parsons, *Medieval Queenship*, 146.

led to accusations of adultery and "other royal misbehavior to blame queens for past conflicts" or to discredit or delegitimize their husbands and heirs.[59]

Fascination with the character and reputation of queens reflects the political significance and the ambiguity of queenship. For much of European history—and, indeed, for most modern historians—a queen was defined as "the king's wife."[60] Most recent studies of medieval queenship, driven by feminist concerns, have striven to demonstrate queens' agency, analyzing the power and influence many queens wielded as the wives and mothers of kings. Such studies demonstrate that queens consort and regent were able administrators, and that their cultural activities often won them great respect and admiration—even as their proximity to power and central position in the court gossip mill rendered them vulnerable to slander. Throughout Europe, the queen was "an integral part of the institution of monarchy"—something scholars have stressed in analyzing queens' roles as intercessors, mothers, wives, and patrons, often within a well-defined familial context.[61] Perhaps most valuably, Theresa Earenfight has convincingly argued for the "corporate character of monarchy," demonstrating that queens were as vital as kings to the functioning of monarchy.[62]

---

59. John Carmi Parsons, "Introduction: Family, Sex, and Power: The Rhythms of Medieval Queenship," in Parsons, *Medieval Queenship*, 7.

60. Ibid., 3.

61. Lois L. Huneycutt, *Matilda of Scotland: A Study in Medieval Queenship* (Rochester, NY: Boydell Press, 2003), 93. Theresa Earenfight has been the most prolific recent contributor to the field of queenship studies. See Theresa Earenfight, *The King's Other Body: Maria of Castile and the Crown of Aragon* (Philadelphia: University of Pennsylvania Press, 2009) and Earenfight, *Queenship in Medieval Europe*, as well as an edited collection, *Queenship and Political Power in Medieval and Early Modern Spain* (Aldershot: Ashgate, 2005). Other recent studies of queenship include Elena Woodacre, *The Queens Regnant of Navarre: Succession, Politics, and Partnership, 1274–1512* (New York: Palgrave Macmillan, 2013); Janna Bianchini, *The Queen's Hand: Power and Authority in the Reign of Berenguela of Castile* (Philadelphia: University of Pennsylvania Press, 2012); Nuria Silleras-Fernandez, *Power, Piety, and Patronage in Late-Medieval Queenship: Maria de Luna* (New York: Palgrave MacMillan, 2008); Helen Guadette, *The Piety, Power, and Patronage of the Latin Kingdom of Jerusalem's Queen Melisende* (New York: City University of New York Press, 2005); Miriam Shadis, *Berenguela of Castile (1180–1246) and Her Family: Political Women in the High Middle Ages* (New York: Palgrave MacMillan, 2009); Therese Martin, *Queen as King: Politics and Architectural Propaganda in Twelfth-Century Spain* (Leiden: Brill, 2006); Elena Woodacre, ed., *Queenship in the Mediterranean: Negotiating the Role of the Queen in the Medieval and Early-Modern Eras* (New York: Palgrave MacMillan, 2013); Lisa Benz St. John, *Three Medieval Queens: Queenship and the Crown in Fourteenth-Century England* (New York: Palgrave Macmillan, 2012); William Layher, *Queenship and Voice in Medieval Northern Europe* (New York: Palgrave Macmillan, 2010); J. L. Laynesmith, *The Last Medieval Queens: English Queenship, 1445–1503* (Oxford: Oxford University Press, 2005); Kathleen Nolan, ed., *Capetian Women* (New York: Palgrave Macmillan, 2003); Anne J. Duggan, ed., *Queens and Queenship in Medieval Europe* (Bury St. Edmunds: Boydell Press, 1997); and Helen E. Maurer, *Margaret of Anjou: Queenship and Power in Late Medieval England* (Woodbridge: Boydell Press, 2003).

62. Earenfight, *The King's Other Body*, 13.

Johanna's career deviates substantially from that of most medieval queens in that she ruled in her own right rather than via a husband or son. Indeed, monarchy as she practiced it could not be corporate, because Johanna could not brook competition from her consort. She stood on the cusp of a period in which women did frequently inherit thrones: She was the only regnant queen during most of her life, but the generation after her saw a woman crowned king of Poland and regnant queens in Hungary, Sicily, the united Scandinavian kingdoms, and Portugal, while her great niece, Johanna II, held the Neapolitan throne from 1414 to 1435.[63] She was in some sense a test case, a prominent queen whose reign witnessed the articulation of ideas about the feasibility and pitfalls of regnant queenship and paved the way for future sovereign queens like Elizabeth Tudor and Isabella of Castile.[64]

Queens were always under scrutiny, even when they played more traditional roles. Louise O. Fradenburg has argued that, in medieval literature and political thought, "the queen is a paradoxical figure because she links sovereignty to the feminine."[65] The power—direct and indirect, symbolic and concrete—that queens wielded made them both fascinating and troubling. They represented a disquieting incongruity, a fracture in "the structure of thought."[66] Johanna's unusual position and eventful reign made her particularly fascinating, even beyond the borders of her realm. As scholars of queenship have recognized, queens regnant "presented conceptual and legal difficulties."[67] They represented the tension in political thought between concerns of gender and concerns of lineage. Queens regnant challenged and were challenged by prevailing gender norms, which taught that women were intellectually, physiologically, and morally inferior to men. The prevailing understanding was that "a woman who inherited supreme authority would marry and produce a son to replace her implied submission to a husband as prescribed by Christian teaching."[68] Female monarchs were conceived of as placeholders upholding hereditary principle, their blood allowing them to

---

63. See Wolf, "Reigning Queens in Medieval Europe," and Monter, *The Rise of Female Kings in Europe.*

64. This is how William Monter sees her: see *The Rise of Female Kings in Europe*, 61–67.

65. Louise O. Fradenburg, "The Love of Thy Neighbor," in *Constructing Medieval Sexuality*, ed. Karma Lochrie, Peggy McCracken, and James A. Schultz (Minneapolis: University of Minnesota Press, 1997), 141.

66. Ian Maclean, *The Renaissance Notion of Woman: A Study in the Fortunes of Scholasticism and Medieval Science in European Intellectual Life* (Cambridge: Cambridge University Press, 1980), 66.

67. Anne J. Duggan, "Introduction," in Duggan, *Queens and Queenship in Medieval Europe*, xx.

68. Parsons, "Introduction," 8.

occupy the throne only "to transmit that power to their sons."[69] They were "representatives of their families, agents for their fathers, husbands, and sons," and contemporary commentators often described them in a familial context rather than portraying them as rulers in their own right.[70] At the same time, queens regnant, because of dynastic concerns, needed to marry and were placed at risk by marriage. As Anne J. Duggan has pointed out, "the rights of the king-by-marriage were ill-defined."[71] The usual expectation was that kings consort actively ruled, either in place of or alongside their wives, often generating controversy about the introduction of a foreign prince to the throne or the equally problematic elevation of "a non-dynastic male" from within the kingdom.[72] Johanna's many marriages were the subject of rampant gossip, both because of her refusal to allow her consorts to rule and because of the potential threat each posed to her autonomy and the interests of Naples's ruling class. Johanna's assertion of personal sovereignty clashed with expectations of women and wives, and it lay at the center of discussions about her, which always pondered her femininity.

Medieval antifeminism, building on classical precedent, posited that women should be subject to male authority, and that any subversion of the gender hierarchy—including within marriage—was unnatural and even dangerous.[73] Learned opinion throughout the high and late Middle Ages barred women from positions of authority and defined them as, at best, in need of care and guidance and, at worst, an active danger to men. For Johanna's reputation, as for descriptions of powerful women more generally, one of the key differences between men and women was that women were thought to be more lustful.[74] In the seventh century, Isidore of Seville—whose *Etymologies* remained influential throughout the Middle Ages—reported that the Latin *femina* derived from the Greek for "fiery," a reflection of women's greater

---

69. Lois L. Huneycutt, "Female Succession and the Language of Power in the Writings of Twelfth-Century Churchmen," in Parsons, *Medieval Queenship*, 195.

70. Ibid., 196.

71. Duggan, "Introduction," xxi.

72. Ibid., xx.

73. To discuss medieval "antifeminism" may seem anachronistic, as there was no such thing as medieval feminism. However, I prefer "antifeminism" to "misogyny" as a way to describe anti-woman tropes that are common throughout medieval texts. Much antifeminist language draws on stock ideas and images to contribute to a widespread conversation about women. Such language does not necessarily have the emotional valence that the word "misogyny" implies—medieval writers could take part in antifeminist discourse without hating women.

74. For an overview of medieval medical understandings of sex difference, see Joan Cadden, *Meanings of Sex Difference in the Middle Ages: Medicine, Science, and Culture* (Cambridge: Cambridge University Press, 1995).

lust.[75] Theorists posited that "women's capacity for sexual pleasure" far out-strips that of other animals (with the exception of mares) and "deviates from the ideal course of nature."[76] It was "an expression of irrationality and lack of control"—a form of weakness that meant women required strict oversight and that Johanna's critics cited in their arguments against her.[77]

The arguments of medical theorists and natural philosophers dovetailed—although they never fully agreed—with theological wisdom that saw women as easily led astray and prone to temptation. Similar arguments shaped both legal and literary culture. Medieval literature of all kinds portrays women as lustful and weak. Women's natural defects were a legal commonplace; canon law, for instance, identified women as less credible witnesses than men.[78] In many parts of Europe, women were denied the right to inherit immovable property, and they were excluded from most positions of political power—hence prevailing suspicion of queens. There were, however, important regional differences in inheritance patterns and aristocratic power structures. In some places, women of high birth attained positions of great wealth and power, particularly in southern France and Provence, where aristocratic women often acted as territorial lords. Elsewhere, women had less access to dynastic power. Such differences led to divergent attitudes toward female rule that helped to shape Johanna's reputation—her rule was never as contested in Provence as it was in Naples, where women could not generally inherit immovable property and enjoyed less legal autonomy.

All of these factors contributed to widespread ambivalence to regnant queenship and to Johanna herself. They form the cultural matrix or discursive field within which her reputation took shape, and they set the terms of talk or gossip about her throughout her life. The sovereignty she asserted was provocative; the reputation she strove to create for herself, like those her contemporaries created for her, reveals the contradictions and tensions inherent in the very idea of regnant queenship, the instability of the concept of sovereignty, and the power and malleability of reputation.

Methods and Sources

This book examines the talk that built around Johanna and assessed her as a queen, as a woman, and as a reigning monarch, listening for what such

---

75. Isidore of Seville, *Etymologiarum sive originum libri XX*, ed. W. M. Lindsay (Oxford: Oxford University Press, 1911), 11.2.24; cf. Cadden, *Meanings of Sex Difference in the Middle Ages*, 48.

76. Cadden, *Meanings of Sex Difference in the Middle Ages*, 148–49.

77. Ibid., 151; Ruth Mazo Karras, *Sexuality in Medieval Europe: Doing unto Others* (New York: Routledge, 2005), 39.

78. Brundage, *Law, Sex, and Christian Society*, 411.

talk reveals about contemporary attitudes toward those subjects. Talk about Johanna survives in the texts that both helped to shape and recorded her reputation: contemporary chronicles—carefully constructed works of social commentary that artfully transmitted (or fabricated) hearsay using the language of gossip, such as "as it is said" (*ut dicitur*) or "as it is told" (*ut fertur*)— poetry, letters, religious and prophetic texts, municipal records, and papal legislation. Such texts, regardless of their genre, were part of an ongoing conversation about Johanna. They were almost all intended to reach a large audience, even as they reflected the terms of the conversation to which they contributed. This is true even of letters. The medieval letter was a rhetorical form, rather than a private communication; often, its contents were intended for an audience wider than its putative recipient. Thus, few of the texts that considered Johanna did so in private, and most were constructed as part of a larger debate about Johanna and her cultural significance.

This book draws on a range of sources to reconstruct Johanna's reputation, incorporating diverse voices and opinions. Many of my sources are literary, and many of the voices—such as those of Giovanni Villani, Boccaccio, Petrarch, Catherine of Siena, or Birgitta of Sweden—are well known, even if they are not often treated together. Other sources are archival, although I read them as constructed texts. Scholars of Angevin Naples have long been handicapped by the 1943 destruction of the Grand'Archivio di Stato as German troops left the city.[79] Fragments of the archives survive, and a reconstruction project, largely based on pre–World War II inventories, is underway, although it is doubtful that it will yield much to help scholars interested in Johanna.[80] The loss of the Neapolitan archives might make Johanna an interesting but inaccessible historical oddity, and it makes sources like Léonard's biography of Johanna—produced in the 1930s—invaluable. However, the departmental archives for the Bouches-du-Rhône (which preserve Provence's comital archives) and the Archives municipales de Marseille are rich sources of documentation for Johanna's reign. They preserve records of municipal deliberations, copies of papal bulls and legislation, and letters by and about Johanna. Such documents provide a precious window on Johanna's style of rule, on how she portrayed herself to her subjects,

---

79. Jole Mazzoleni, "Les archives des Angevins de Naples," in *Marseille et ses Rois de Naples: La diagonale angevine, 1265–1382*, ed. Isabelle Bonnot (Marseille: Edisud, 1988), 27.

80. Ibid. Even before 1943, the records for Johanna's reign—due to riots, war, and natural disaster—were incomplete and badly damaged. See ibid., 26.

and on how they and her successors described her.[81] I have supplemented this
Provençal material with archival and manuscript evidence from elsewhere
in Europe, as with editions of Neapolitan documents produced before 1943,
many published in the journal *Archivio storico per le province napoletane* or by
the nineteenth-century historian Matteo Camera.[82]

Due in part to their public nature, none of these sources lends itself particularly well to a biography of Johanna. Even in her own letters, she is a
construction, and while it is possible to scrutinize such sources for bias, for
prejudice, to seek out the author's attitude about Johanna or to discover
how Johanna represented herself, there is little to reveal Johanna as a private
flesh-and-blood woman. Johanna's biographers have all attempted to arrive
at some form of truth about her, selecting their sources based on their understanding of their reliability and, ultimately, based on their own agendas.
Scholars who have approached Johanna with sympathy have tended to trust
sources sympathetic to her; others have privileged sources less well disposed
toward her. Yet the sources on which they draw were rarely—particularly in
the case of chronicles—intended to convey verisimilitude. The same event
was narrated in myriad ways by chroniclers, letter writers, and even eyewit-
nesses seeking a deeper truth about what had happened who placed the stories they told within an interpretive framework meant to shed light on the
conditions of their world.

Johanna's reputation gives this book its shape and structure. Its chapters track
Johanna's career and reputation chronologically, relying as much as possible on
closely contemporary accounts that reveal how events were understood when
they happened and not how they were reevaluated and reinterpreted in hindsight. The first chapter examines responses to Andrew of Hungary's murder,
analyzing how commentators' stake in the competing claims of the Hungarian
and Neapolitan Angevins shaped Johanna's reputation in its wake. The second
chapter focuses on Louis of Taranto's reign and analyzes the transformation
of Johanna's reputation under the pens of contemporaries disillusioned with
Louis. The third and fourth chapters examine Johanna's independent reign,

---

81. Most of the archival documents on which I draw from the early part of Johanna's reign
were known to Léonard. In many cases, he provided editions in the appendices to the three volumes
he completed before abandoning his biography. I have acknowledged his prior knowledge in my
footnotes, including noting when editions can be found in his work. In each of these cases, I have
worked from my own transcriptions rather than from his editions. All translations are my own, unless
otherwise noted. Readers interested in English translations of medieval Neapolitan sources, many
of which relate to Johanna's reign, should also see Ronald G. Musto, ed. and trans., *Medieval Naples:
A Documentary History, 400–1400* (New York: Italica Press, 2013), esp. 256–97.

82. Matteo Camera, *Elucubrazioni storico-diplomatiche su Giovanna I.a, regina di Napoli, e Carlo III
di Durazzo* (Salerno: Tipografia Nazionale, 1889).

paying close attention to her strategies of self-presentation, particularly her allegiance to the papacy and her friendships with women regarded as living saints, while also assessing how Johanna's self-presentation shaped her textual reputation. The fifth reconstructs Johanna's part in the cultural imaginary of the Western Schism and describes the process by which Clementists and Urbanists created very different versions of Johanna that corresponded more to their needs than to Johanna's character or behavior. Finally, the epilogue examines Johanna's posthumous reputations in Provence and Naples. Because of the dearth of modern English-language studies, I discuss and analyze Johanna's reign as context to the talk that went on about it. I do not provide systematic consideration of Johanna's administration, or of her political and diplomatic activity, projects that I hope other scholars will take on. This is not a biography of a woman but of a reputation, of the evolving, multifaceted public image that Johanna acquired and helped to shape during her life.

In reconstructing Johanna's reputation and cultural significance, I analyze Johanna's own contributions, weighing textual descriptions of her against the image she projected through her behavior, official proclamations, friendships, and artistic and architectural commissions. Like all medieval monarchs, Johanna labored to portray herself as an ideal ruler, in part to assert her sovereign legitimacy. I do not claim to access Johanna's interiority, nor do I argue that Johanna engaged in the sort of "self-fashioning" that Stephen Greenblatt has identified as a hallmark of the Renaissance.[83] No text explicitly states how Johanna wished to be perceived, but I argue that her public self-presentation—visible in her artistic commissions, her epistolary self-styling, and her public acts of piety and friendship—constitutes a performance that can be read and analyzed for what Susan Crane has called "information on self-conception."[84]

As John Benton, Caroline Walker Bynum, and Jeffery Hamburger have argued is typical of medieval identity making, Johanna modeled her behavior and her personal iconography on types.[85] In Johanna's case, the models she

---

83. Stephen Greenblatt, *Renaissance Self-Fashioning: From More to Shakespeare* (Chicago: University of Chicago Press, 1980).

84. Susan Crane, *The Performance of Self: Ritual, Clothing, and Identity during the Hundred Years War* (Philadelphia: University of Pennsylvania Press, 2002), 3.

85. See Jeffrey F. Hamburger, "Medieval Self-Fashioning: Authorship, Authority, and Autobiography in Suso's *Exemplar*," in *The Visual and the Visionary: Art and Female Spirituality in Late Medieval Germany* (New York: Zone Books, 1998), 233–78; Caroline Walker Bynum, "Did the Twelfth Century Discover the Individual?" *Journal of Ecclesiastical History* 31 (1980): 1–17; John F. Benton, "Consciousness of Self and Perceptions of Individuality," in *Renaissance and Renewal in the Twelfth Century*, ed. Robert L. Benson and Giles Constable (Cambridge, MA: Harvard University Press, 1982), 263–95.

emulated were provided by her ancestors, as by cultural ideals of rulership. Johanna's public piety, for instance, while likely genuine, was also a performance that enhanced her reputation. To say that Johanna wished to appear pious is not to say that her behavior was cynical or her piety sham. I see no reason to doubt the sincerity of her loyalty to the papacy, her piety, or her regard for saintly friends like Birgitta of Sweden, but it would be naïve to think that her behavior, particularly given the later medieval significance of *fama*, was not also meant to be noted. Reputation and person were closely linked, and it was the duty of royals to model and perform acts of piety. I read Johanna's performance of queenship, to the extent that it is discernible in text and images, as calculated not to manifest an interior, individuated self but as an ongoing effort to demonstrate her legitimacy and shape her legacy through conformity to and adaptation of models provided by her forebears. Royal reputation was precious, its ideals laid out by conduct literature that enjoined princes to protect their reputations—indeed, the cultivation of a good reputation was often presented as one of the duties of royalty. As Johanna's younger contemporary Christine de Pizan argues in her mirror for princesses, *The Treasure of the City of Ladies*, "Prudence teaches the princess or great lady how above all things in this base world she ought to love honor and a good reputation," because a good reputation is the mirror of good morals.[86] To be a good queen required having a good reputation—something that may have been particularly salient in a century that had witnessed the disastrous repercussions for Edward II of England of reputation's loss.[87]

Johanna's behavior and her reputation bespoke her suitability for the role she had inherited and demonstrated the stability and continuity of her dynasty. Like her predecessors, who used art and patronage to communicate royal ideology, Johanna made ample use of traditional methods of self-presentation. She commissioned the copying and illumination of manuscripts, particularly religious texts; she founded churches and hospitals and patronized the artists who decorated them; she demonstrated her devotion to the papacy and saints through actions, images, and words. Such methods of self-presentation were part and parcel of how medieval kings, queens, and aristocrats disseminated ideology and built reputations and legacies for themselves. Their efforts at controlling their own images, however, always interacted with the ways that contemporaries responded to events, to gossip, and to the rumored and actual behavior of the

---

86. Christine de Pizan, *The Treasure of the City of Ladies, or the Book of the Three Virtues*, trans. Sarah Lawson (London: Penguin, 1985), 55.

87. On the role of *fama* in Edward's deposition, see Edward Peters, "*Vox populi, vox Dei*," in King and Ridyard, *Law in Medieval Life and Thought*, esp. 115.

person in question—conditioned by their own stake in the person and events under consideration. Johanna's reputation was, thus, only in part under her control, on the one hand the product of public performance and official ideology and, on the other, the product of outside forces, especially scandal and slander. It was also the product of responses to her queenship that took shape in contemporary conversations about Johanna that progressed along lines determined by cultural understandings of femininity, queenship, and sovereignty that, while Johanna could contribute to them, also shaped how contemporaries described her and even determined how Johanna sought to represent herself.

❧ CHAPTER 1

The Murder of Andrew of Hungary and the Making of a Neapolitan She-Wolf

According to Aristotle . . . woman is a failed male,
that is, the matter that forms a human being will not
result in a girl except when nature is impeded in her
actions . . . thus it has been said that woman is not
human, but a monster in nature.

Commentary on Pseudo-Albertus Magnus's *On
Women's Secrets* (late thirteenth/early fourteenth
century)

If a husband is forced to be his wife's serf, it's a terrible
calamity, for he ought to be the boss. The natural
order of things has been overturned by women in
their madness. . . . The governor was governed and
the roles of the sexes reversed, for she was active
and he passive, willing to neigh under her. Thus the
natural order of things was turned upside down. What
was normally underneath was on top, and confusion
reigned.

Jean le Fèvre, *The Lamentations of Matheolus*
(ca. 1371–72)

No woman in this world is so faithful or so
committed to any betrothal that if a lusting
lover appears and entices her with expertise and
persistence to enjoy love, she is minded to reject his
request or defend herself against his advances. . . .
A woman behaves like this because she is plagued by
oppressive lust.

Andreas Capellanus, *On Love* (ca. 1185)

On the morning of September 19, 1345, the
Regno awoke to scandal. During the night, assailants had murdered the
seventeen-year-old prince-consort, Andrew of Hungary (b. 1328). Within
days, Andrew was to have celebrated a joint coronation with his wife, Johanna of Naples, an event that he had awaited since Johanna's 1343 succession to the Neapolitan throne. The murder of a prince was scandalous
in itself. The brutality of Andrew's death compounded the scandal: He was
suffocated and strangled, mutilated, and defenestrated.

In Johanna's long reign, no scandal exceeded this one in its enduring value to her enemies and critics. The circumstances surrounding Andrew's death inspired speculation about who had murdered him and who gained the most from his death. Rumor held that Johanna and her many lovers had murdered Andrew to prevent his coronation. The crime provoked two invasions of Naples by Andrew's vengeful brother, Louis of Hungary, who insisted on Johanna's guilt and whose vendetta drew widespread military and moral support. Johanna became internationally known as a viricide—a husband murderer—a reputation that remained with her throughout her life and for posterity, even though a papal tribunal officially cleared her name in 1350. Contemporaries described her court as rife with immorality and violence, and gossip tied Andrew's death directly to Johanna's reputed infidelity, lust, and greed. These traits and her identification as a murderess became hallmarks of Johanna's public image.

Although no evidence definitively links Johanna to Andrew's murder, it has remained the defining characteristic of her reign in historical memory. Modern scholars have tended to exculpate Johanna, arguing that she gained little from Andrew's death and that there is no proof that she was involved. Others have argued that, while she may well have been complicit, nothing exists to indicate her direct guilt. Modern skepticism, however, is at variance with traditional perceptions of Andrew's murder. Within little more than a century of her death, it stood, with Johanna's own murder, as her legacy to history. A summary of her reign prepared in the late fifteenth century for Louis XII of France to demonstrate his rights to the Kingdom of Naples presents Andrew's death as the decisive moment in Johanna's life. It collapses her eventful four-decade reign into a single sequence of events that began with Andrew's death and ended almost immediately in Johanna's own justly deserved murder:

> Louis of Hungary, because Queen Johanna had strangled and killed Andrew, her husband, brother of this same Louis, went from Hungary to the Kingdom of Naples to avenge the death of Andrew, his brother, against the aforesaid Johanna . . . and, with the favor of Pope Urban VI, made Charles of Durazzo her successor and gave him possession [of the Kingdom].—Charles of Durazzo, after he had taken the aforesaid Johanna prisoner . . . suffocated her between two pillows.[1]

---

1. Dossier Bleu n° 489 (Paris, Bibliothèque nationale de France, MS fonds français 30025). Described in Émile G. Léonard, "Un abrégé illustré de la Reine Jeanne dans un tableau des droits de Louis XII sur le Royaume de Naples," Ext. des Comptes rendus et Mémoires du Congrès de Marseille 1928 (p. 72) (Marseille: L'Institut Historique de Provence, 1931), 3.

The tidiness of this account, which depicts Johanna's death in 1382 as the retributive outcome of Andrew's murder in 1345, provides eloquent testimony to how pervasive belief in Johanna's guilt became, particularly since it was from Johanna that Louis XII traced his claim to Naples.

Perhaps even more telling is the popularity of the story of Andrew's death in plays, romances, and operas in the centuries that followed. Johanna came to be remembered in some quarters as a tragic and maligned heroine, but even when this was the case, she was most famous for murdering Andrew. The Golden-Age Spanish playwright Lope de Vega's *La reina Juana de Nápoles* (written 1597–1603) is a case in point. Lope's Juana is heroic and selfless. She sacrifices her own happiness to protect her kingdom from the tyrant Andrés, who threatens to invade Naples if Juana will not marry him. When Andrés's cruelty imperils her realm and she discovers that he intends to murder her and usurp her throne, Juana again makes a sacrifice, killing Andrés to protect her people.[2] Thus, while it became a point of debate whether Andrew deserved his fate and whether Johanna was a victim or villain, Johanna's responsibility for his death remained a constant in historical memory.

The clarity with which succeeding generations perceived Johanna's guilt obscures both the uncertainty surrounding the details of Andrew's murder in its immediate aftermath and the process by which Johanna became a regicide and viricide in popular imagination. Andrew's family and supporters waged a campaign to defame Johanna that influenced how chroniclers and others described the events surrounding his murder. Johanna's enduring reputation as a she-wolf grew out of the accretion and elaboration of the story of Andrew's death, told in chronicles, letters, and other texts by commentators with varying purposes, ranging from Johanna's deposition to her exoneration. The story differed from one teller to another and became inextricably intertwined with each narrator's stake in Italian and papal politics and in Angevin history. Each rendition reflected a larger concern as well with the feasibility and meanings of regnant queenship. Among Johanna's supporters, the story became a means to present her as a victim of circumstance beleaguered by the enemies of the Church. In the hands of her detractors, Andrew's death became a cautionary tale about the dangers of female rule and proof of the illegitimacy of Johanna's claim to Naples.

---

2. Lope de Vega, *La reina Juana de Nápoles: Obras de Lope de Vega*, Marcelino Menéndez [y] Pelayo, Biblioteca de Autores Españoles 15 (Madrid: Real Academia Española, 1966), 227–80. See also Christopher B. Weimer, "The Politics of Husband-Murder: Gender, Supplementarity and Sacrifice in Lope de Vega's 'La reina Juana de Nápoles,'" *Hispanic Review* 69 (Winter 2001): 32–52.

Historical Background and Dramatis Personae

When Robert of Naples named Johanna his successor, he faced the lingering question of the Hungarian Angevin claim to Naples. Johanna's sex left her vulnerable to charges that her reign was illegitimate and reignited charges that Robert had usurped his throne from his nephew, Carobert of Hungary. With these concerns in mind, and in the interest of stability, Robert arranged a compromise with the Hungarian Angevins: Johanna's younger sister, Mary (1329–66), would marry Louis, Carobert's eldest son and the heir to the Hungarian throne, while Johanna would marry Andrew.[3] In 1333, Andrew, then only five years of age, came to Naples to be educated in what was widely understood as his future kingdom.[4] Indeed, Robert preached a sermon in honor of his arrival on Matthew 3:17, greeting the young prince with the words, "This is my beloved son, in whom I am well pleased," thus seeming to proclaim Andrew his heir.[5]

The Neapolitan court was among the most cosmopolitan in Western Europe. It was multilingual and culturally polyglot, yet Andrew and the Hungarian courtiers who accompanied him appear to have remained outsiders. Charles I's court had been substantially French, although it had included Provençal, Neapolitan, and northern Italian courtiers. French remained one of the languages of the court, but by Johanna's time, while many Provençal families—such as the des Baux, who soon became known as the del Balzo—remained, the northern French courtiers who had accompanied Charles were largely gone. In all likelihood, when Andrew first arrived at court, he spoke French with his Neapolitan cousins and was not wholly a linguistic outsider. French dynastic identity and an appreciation of chivalric literature and manners continued to shape Neapolitan court culture during Johanna's reign. Indeed, the Catalan Franciscan Francesc Eiximenis (1330–1409) reports with disgust in his *Llibre de les Dones* (1396) that while Robert's queen, the pious Sancia of Majorca, was briefly able to check the court's frivolous impulses, its ladies' fashions emulated those of the French court, as did the songs they sang and their conversation, which revolved

---

3. Kelly, *The New Solomon*, 250 and n. 34; Baddeley, *Queen Joanna I of Naples*, 5. The papal dispensation for the marriages is preserved in ADBR, B 165, fol. 49r–v.

4. Kelly, *The New Solomon*, 250 and n. 34; Baddeley, *Queen Joanna I of Naples*, 5.

5. Alessandro Barbero, "La Propaganda di Roberto d'Angiò, Re di Napoli," in *Le forme della propaganda politica nel due et nel trecento*, ed. Paolo Cammarosano (Rome: École Française de Rome, 1994), 124. Robert may initially have intended Andrew to rule Naples, but he changed his mind by 1340 at the latest.

entirely around love.[6] Over time, however, the court had come to have a distinctive culture that fused French, Occitan, and Italian—both Neapolitan and northern—elements.[7] Naples's noble culture was literate (indulging in a taste for Latin scholarship as well as French and Occitan literature), sophisticated, and cosmopolitan, but it was also increasingly and distinctively Neapolitan. During Johanna's reign a true Neapolitan literary *volgare*—a hybrid of native, Sicilian, Tuscan, and French linguistic elements—emerged that she and her court circle popularized.[8] Andrew was called upon to acculturate, to find a place for himself in a distinctive, fashion-conscious court. To some extent, he must have done so, but court records and reports by observers suggest that he never became a true member of court society, and instead that he remained separate from his Neapolitan cousins, including his future wife, who slighted and mocked him. Indeed, numerous chroniclers report that Andrew was subject to constant taunts and humiliation.[9]

In 1343, Robert died, and the throne passed to Johanna. She was seventeen; Andrew was only fifteen. The court at whose head they found themselves was split into multiple factions that vied to influence, control, or supplant the young couple. The most prominent divisions were between Provençal and Italian (primarily Neapolitan and Florentine) courtiers and the Hungarians who had accompanied Andrew to Naples and gradually won their own supporters.[10] Added to this already volatile mixture were the three Tarantini (descended from Philip of Taranto) and three Durazzeschi (descended from John of Gravina), who, as Angevin princes, had hoped to succeed ahead of Johanna or to ascend the throne through marriage to

6. Francesc Eiximenis, *Lo Libre de les Dones*, ed. Frank Naccarato (Barcelona: Curial, 1981), Ca 56, 90–91.

7. Charmaine Lee, "Naples," in *Europe: A Literary History, 1348–1418*, ed. David Wallace, vol. 1 (Oxford: Oxford University Press, forthcoming), and Lee, "Boccaccio's Neapolitan Letter and Multilingualism in Angevin Naples," *Mediaevalia* 34 (2013): 7–21, esp. 9–10.

8. Lee, "Naples." See also Francesco Sabatini, *Italia Linguistica delle Origini: Saggi editi dal 1856 al 1996*, 2 vols. (Lecce: Argo, 1996), 2:401–506, esp. 401–3, 435, 467, and Samantha Kelly, "Intercultural Identity and the Local Vernacular," *Medieval History Journal* 14, no. 2 (2011): 259–84.

9. Andrew's humiliation is reported by the closely contemporaneous chronicles of Domenico da Gravina and Giovanni Villani, among others. Donato degli Albanzani's marginal notations on his manuscript copy of Boccaccio's *Eclogues*—which deal directly with Andrew's murder—also reference widespread rumors that Andrew was mocked by the court.

10. Carlo de Frede argues that Andrew ruled over a small Hungarian court contained within the larger court but largely separate from it. On the factions and their linguistic and national makeup, see Carlo de Frede, "Da Carlo I d'Angiò a Giovanna I, 1263–1382," in *Storia di Napoli*, vol. 3: *Da Carlo I d'Angiò a Giovanna I, 1263–1382*, ed. by E. Pontieri (Naples: Edizioni Scientifiche Italiane, 1969), esp. 225–29.

Robert's granddaughters—something that likely sharpened their resentment of Andrew.[11]

It was in the interest of the Hungarians to garner as much power and influence for Andrew as possible and in the interest of the other factions—particularly the Tarantini and Durazzeschi—to prevent this. Robert had foreseen that factionalism might lead to chaos. Under the terms of his testament, neither Johanna nor Andrew was to come into their full inheritance before the age of twenty-five—long after the customary age of majority. Until then, they would be guided by a governing council appointed by Robert and overseen by Sancia. The council included Robert's closest advisors, whom he trusted to guide Johanna until she was ready to rule alone.

This state of affairs was unsatisfactory to all of the factions. Johanna, for her part, balked at the unusual provision in Robert's will that barred her from attaining her majority at eighteen. Andrew and Johanna had both already reached the age of discernment, customarily set at fourteen. Neither, therefore, was a child according to conventional definitions, and neither welcomed subjection to the governing council.[12] Pope Clement VI (r. 1342–52) was disturbed as well by the creation of the council, which usurped his suzerain rights over Naples and his prerogative as Johanna's legal guardian—something Johanna herself clearly recognized. Shortly after Robert's death, she wrote to the pope, requesting that Andrew be awarded the title (though not the power) of king, most likely with the intention of ingratiating herself with the Hungarians and shortening the term of her minority. Clement refused.[13] In papal correspondence, Johanna was entitled *regina Sicilie*, a title Sancia also retained. Clement seldom addressed the governing council, which he resented, and only rarely addressed Andrew in his letters during the period immediately following Robert's death, a clear mark of his reluctance to recognize Andrew's claim to kingship.[14]

Papal interests were best served by maintaining firm control of Johanna and checking the ambitions of the Hungarian Angevins. Clement was thus

---

11. For a detailed explanation of the various branches of the Angevin family, see Norman P. Zacour, *Talleyrand: The Cardinal of Périgord (1301–1364)*, Transactions of the American Philosophical Society (Philadelphia: American Philosophical Society, 1960), 32. Élie de Talleyrand was the brother of Agnes of Périgord, the mother of the three Durazzeschi princes, and was thus intimately involved in the politics and intrigues of the Neapolitan court.

12. Léonard, *Histoire de Jeanne Ire*, 1;198, 201.

13. Baddeley, *Robert the Wise and His Heirs*, 287; Léonard, *Histoire de Jeanne Ire*, 1:303.

14. See Eugène Déprez, ed., *Clement VI (1342–1352): Lettres closes, patentes et curiales publiees ou analysees d'après les registres du Vatican* (Paris: E. de-Boccard, 1958). Even in the earliest years of her reign, Clement gave Johanna precedence over Sancia and Andrew.

faced with overseeing a contentious dynastic situation in a valuable papal fief. This task became increasingly difficult, particularly after the rivalry between the Tarantini and Durazzeschi was exacerbated by the clandestine (and possibly forced) 1343 marriage of Mary of Naples (then only thirteen) to Charles of Durazzo (1323–48). Mary stood second in line to the throne; the marriage, which made Charles the husband of Naples's possible future queen, violated the terms of Mary's betrothal to Louis of Hungary but had tacit papal approval.[15] Naples became a hotbed of intrigue that threatened to erupt into open feuding. Clement VI was obliged to maintain constant contact with the Neapolitan branches of the Angevin family, with Johanna and her advisors, and with the increasingly irate Hungarians as he struggled to sustain the fragile peace within this most dysfunctional of families.

The Queen Regnant and Her Prince-Consort

Johanna's attempts to maintain good relations with Andrew and his family ended soon after she ascended the throne. Robert had ruled alone, refusing to share his administration with his brothers, who received the duchies of Taranto (in southern Italy) and Durazzo (in Albania) as their patrimonies. According to Robert's testament, Johanna was to rule as the sole inheritor of all of her grandfather's possessions, delegating none of her power.[16] The Hungarian Angevins might have planned to rule Naples through Andrew, but their designs were thwarted by Johanna's refusal—supported by both the governing council and the pope—to allow him to be publicly entitled king, to swear fealty to the papacy, or even to control his own finances. Andrew was commonly referred to in person and in correspondence as "king," but this was merely a mark of courtesy. Only the pope could confer the regal title, and Clement VI declined to do so.[17] Johanna treated Andrew as her consort rather than as a coruler, thus assuming her grandfather's position and consigning Andrew to that formerly held by Sancia.

---

15. See Zacour, *Talleyrand*, 32; Léonard, *Histoire de Jeanne Ire*, 1:243–45; Baddeley, *Robert the Wise and His Heirs*, 289–91. For the papal correspondence regarding Mary's marriage, see F. Cerasoli, ed., "Clemente VI e Giovanna I di Napoli—Documenti inediti dell'Archivio Vaticano, 1343–1352," *ASPN* 21 (1896): 3–41.

16. ADBR, B 168, fol. 78: "Rex . . . instituit sibi haeredem universalem Joannam, ducissam Calabriae, neptem ejus primogenitam, . . . in regno Sicilie ultra citraque Pharum necnon comitatibus Provincie et Forcalquerii et Pedimontis ac omnibus aliis terris, locis, dominiis, jurisdictionibus . . . sibi competentibus et quomodolibet competituris." Cf. Léonard, *Histoire de Jeanne Ire*, 1:218.

17. Léonard, *Histoire de Jeanne Ire*, 1:254.

While Johanna's actions and those of the governing council fulfilled Robert's wishes, they were unusual enough to draw critical notice and at variance with what Robert's intentions had seemed—at least to some contemporaries—prior to his death. Carobert had sent Andrew to be raised in Robert's court with every expectation that he would eventually rule Naples. Léonard argues that Robert "had placed Andrew, as a child, on the same footing as his grand-daughter; it could not have been to debase him before her for his entire life." Yet, as Léonard also notes, Robert's testamentary provisions incontrovertibly established just such an imbalance.[18] Indeed, Andrew—who was entitled prince of Salerno rather than duke of Calabria, the title reserved for the heir to the throne—was denied the right to succeed to the throne even if Johanna prede-ceased him.

The question of Andrew's rightful position would trouble Angevin politics long after his death. His supporters alleged that Robert had meant for Andrew to succeed him. They insisted that Robert had changed his mind about the disposition of the kingdom on his deathbed and made Andrew his heir.[19] Such claims persisted throughout Johanna's reign and intensified with Andrew's murder. According to their arguments, Johanna was not the lawful heir to the throne—she ruled only through the unnatural debasement of Naples's true sovereign, and her only claim to queenship was as Andrew's consort.

Andrew's succession, from a certain perspective, was logical: It would have adhered to the hereditary principle favoring male candidates and mirrored the

---

18. Ibid., 258. For an English translation and analysis of Robert's testament, see Musto, *Medieval Naples*, 234–54.

19. A Provençal poem written soon after Robert's death reported that he had adopted Andrew so that the kingdom would revert to the line of Charles Martel: "Nos mervilhes / Si ay revestit lo rey Andrieu c' uey es / Del realme, car dreg es e razon" (cited in Léonard, *Histoire de Jeanne Ire*, 1:219). There is no evidence to support such a claim, but the story persisted. A letter from Louis of Hungary to his Bohemian supporters shortly after Robert's death claimed that Robert had, in the last days of his life, decreed that Andrew should immediately succeed him. See Georgii Fejér, ed., *Codex diplomaticus Hungariae ecclesiasticus ac civilis*, vol. 9, pt. 7 (Buda: Typis typogr. Regiae Universitatis Ungaricae, 1829). Welbore St. Clair Baddeley was convinced that the letter was a forgery (see Baddeley, *Robert the Wise and His Heirs*, 286). Regardless, its existence reflects widespread belief that Andrew was the victim of a conspiracy. The tale was elaborated by the Neapolitan Domenico da Gravina (ca. 1300–ca. 1355), who insisted that Andrew was Robert's true heir in his *Chronicle* (finished ca. 1350). See Domenico da Gravina, *Chronicon de Rebus in Apulia Gestis [AA. 1333–1350]*, ed. L. A. Muratori, vol. 12, pt. 3 of *RIS: Raccolta degli Storici Italiani dal cinquecento al millecinquecento*, new ed. (Città di Castello: S. Lapi, 1903), 4. According to Domenico, Robert selected Andrew to marry Johanna in an effort to protect his kingdom from chaos. On his deathbed, Robert called his principal advisors and relatives together and "wished and commanded that after his death, Andrew would be king and Johanna, his consort, queen"—a desire to which all present agreed (see Domenico da Gravina, *Chronicon*, 7).

Valois succession in France. Furthermore, it reflected the common practice by which powerful men ruled territories inherited by their brotherless wives.[20] Andrew's partisans, therefore, both before and after his death, could assert his threefold legitimacy as king by descent (through his grandfather), by inheritance, *and* as Johanna's husband. These arguments would underpin narrative attacks on Johanna after Andrew's death, when Andrew's just claim to Naples's throne became the backdrop against which the story of his murder was ultimately told. Thus, in the years between Robert's death and Andrew's murder, two rival arguments circulated about Andrew's rightful position. According to the first, Andrew was Johanna's prince-consort, not entitled and not equipped (due to his youth) to rule. According to the other, he was the legitimate king of Naples, designated by Robert as his immediate and sole successor.

Setting the Scene for Murder

On May 29, 1343, Francesco Petrarch (1304–74) wrote to Robert's former secretary, Barbato da Sulmona (d. 1363), about the state of affairs in Naples. Petrarch was no dispassionate observer: Robert had formally examined him and found him worthy to be crowned with laurels, and the poet had spent considerable time at the Neapolitan court. He had developed both an enduring friendship with Barbato and an interest in the royal family. Petrarch's letter describes his grief over Robert's death and his fears about impending disaster in the divided court:

> I am really alarmed about the youthfulness of the young queen, and of the new king, about the age and intent of [Sancia], about the talents and ways of the courtiers. I wish that I could be a lying prophet about these things, but I see two lambs entrusted to the care of a multitude of wolves, and I see a kingdom without a king. How can I call someone

---

20. Indeed, it was through Beatrice of Provence (1231–67), that Charles I came to rule Provence and Forcalquier. Beatrice was the youngest of Raymond Berenger IV's daughters. Her three sisters had married the kings of France and England and the earl of Cornwall and received substantial dowries. Beatrice inherited her father's lands, and his title and power passed to Charles. A similar precedent applied in the cases of earlier regnant queens. For instance, Berenguela of Castile (1180–1246) could only be accepted as her father's heir by having a husband in whom the masculine functions of rulership, especially military obligations, were vested. During Berenguela's childhood, she was betrothed first to Conrad of Hohenstaufen and then to Alfonso IX of León in an effort to make her status as Castile's heir apparent palatable to her future subjects. See Bianchini, *The Queen's Hand*, esp. 24–32.

a king who is ruled by another and who is exposed to the greed of so many and (I sadly add) to the cruelty of so many?[21]

Petrarch paints a picture of a court riven by factionalism and ruled by rapacious, untrustworthy courtiers. Andrew was subject, seemingly, to widespread cruelty. He was not truly a king, nor was he kingly. Instead, he and Johanna were youthful lambs among lupine courtiers, without any power of their own.

Similarly grim reports of growing disorder in Naples began to reach the papal curia in Avignon: infighting in the governing council, tension between the various branches of the family, profligate spending by Johanna and Andrew, the mounting influence of a suspect group of royal retainers and nobles, and (according to Petrarch) the explosion of violence in the city of Naples, due largely to the nocturnal activities of roving gangs of noblemen. At the same time, it became increasingly clear that the Hungarian party would not be content to have Andrew merely entitled king. In consequence, Johanna wrote to Clement VI on December 1, 1343, requesting him to cease discussing Andrew's coronation and role in her administration with Hungarian envoys.[22] The letter signals a growing rift between Johanna and Andrew and the cementing of deep divisions within the Neapolitan court. Suspicion and discontent drew all of the various factions into a power struggle—sometimes overt, sometimes covert—that involved intricate schemes and alliances and culminated in Andrew's murder.

Later in 1343, Petrarch traveled to Naples on papal business and wrote to Cardinal Giovanni Colonna about his fears regarding the governing council.[23] Petrarch, whose mistrust of politicians and esteem for Robert perhaps rendered him alarmist, professed dismay at the kingdom's decline following Robert's death. He found Naples in a shocking state. The ruling council, he wrote, was in the control of a Franciscan friar, Fra' Roberto, a "homunculus" whom Petrarch describes as "a monster . . . a terrible three-footed beast, with its feet naked, with its head bare, arrogant about its poverty, dripping with pleasures."[24] Petrarch's sense of Fra' Roberto's significance was unmatched by his contemporaries—who say little of him—but his concerns

21. Francesco Petrarch, *Epistolae de Rebus Familiaribus et Variae*, vol. 1, ed. Joseph Fracassetti (Florence: F. Le Monnier, 1859), 250. Translation from Francesco Petrarch, *Rerum familiarium libri*, trans. Aldo S. Bernardo, 3 vols. (Albany: State University of New York Press, 1975), 1:228.

22. Léonard, *Histoire de Jeanne Ire*, 1:299.

23. Ernest H. Wilkins, "Petrarch's *Exul ab Italia*," *Speculum* 38 (July 1963): 453.

24. Petrarch, *Rerum familiarum*, 1:233; Petrarch, *Epistolae de Rebus Familiaribus*, V,3, 256. Fra' Roberto was Roberto di Mileto, a Franciscan friar present when Robert dictated his last testament who was subsequently one of Sancia's executors. He was rumored by his enemies to practice false poverty. See Léonard, *Histoire de Jeanne Ire*, 1:255.

about the friar reveal Petrarch's uneasiness about Naples's fate without Robert's guidance: "In the place of that most serene Robert who was recently king, this other Robert has arisen."[25] Naples, as Petrarch portrayed it, was in a state of utter disarray. The administration was vested not in the queen or her consort but in a hypocritical Spiritual Franciscan who feigned poverty while enjoying power and sensual pleasure. Petrarch's Fra' Roberto thus embodied the canker that ate at Naples and corrupted the kingdom from within.

Some days later, Petrarch wrote again to Cardinal Colonna to describe the gangs of noblemen who terrorized Naples by night and the bloody gladiatorial games staged there by day. The royal family sanctioned the games, and, according to Petrarch, on the day he accidentally happened upon them, "the Queen was present, as was Prince Andrew, a boy of noble mind, if ever he were to assume the long-deferred crown."[26] Petrarch saw a troubling connection between the nightly brigandage and daytime gladiatorial games. He presented the Regno's chief city as mired in immorality, a place where evil was tolerated and even supported by those designated to rule. Furthermore, he seems in this letter to anticipate the day when Andrew would don the "long-deferred crown" and restore order to the kingdom. His letter suggests that he hoped Andrew would grow from a noble-minded boy into a mature king who would rule alongside Johanna, whom Petrarch unquestionably recognized as the Regno's queen. His picture of her rule, however, suggests that she was as yet unfit to reign and that the governing council meant to prevent disorder had led Naples into chaos and violence.

Clement VI, at least in official correspondence, also stressed Andrew's potential even as he delayed his coronation. Carefully appeasing both sides, Clement allowed Andrew little power while still seeming to support his claims to kingship. On January 19, 1344, he wrote to Andrew for the first time since Robert's death, addressing him as his son in Christ and the illustrious king of Sicily and commanding that Andrew be given the regal title and crowned and anointed with Johanna.[27] Yet he says nothing of Andrew ruling, and the coronation appears to have been a placatory gesture. Indeed, Neapolitan emissaries obtained a papal declaration that Johanna held sole

---

25. Petrarch, *Epistolae de Rebus Familiaribus*, V,3, 256. Bernardo, *Rerum familiarum libri*, 1:233.

26. Petrarch, *Rerum familiarum*, 1:249; Petrarch, *Epistolae de Rebus Familiaribus*, V,6, 272: "Aderat Regina, et Andreas Regulus, puer alti animi, si unquam dilatum diadema susceperit." Bernardo, *Rerum familiarum libri*, 1:249. Bernardo translates *alti* as lofty, but given the context—in a letter in which Petrarch criticizes the behavior of the court—Andrew's unrecognized nobility appears Petrarch's concern.

27. Reg. 137, n° DCXL, fol. 177r, in Déprez, *Clement VI*, 1:309, no. 627.

rights to the throne and ruled by right of succession, while Andrew's title derived only from marriage.[28]

This game of concession and withholding, of careful diplomatic double-dealing, would continue almost until Andrew's death. Even as he appeased both Johanna and Andrew, Clement empowered his legate, the cardinal Aimery de Chalus (d. 1349), as administrator and governor of Naples.[29] Johanna, although she vigorously protested Aimery's presence, needed papal support and signed a proclamation making Aimery Naples's regent. Andrew signed as well, but only as a witness.[30] On February 2, 1344, Clement wrote again to Andrew as king of Sicily, saying that he wished him to be extended the title of king and to be crowned by Aimery; he wrote to Johanna, Sancia, and Andrew's mother, Elizabeth of Poland (1305–80), to the same effect and wrote to inform Johanna of Aimery's impending arrival.[31] Clement had, however, determined that only Johanna should swear fealty to Aimery, a decision that emphasized the very real difference in rank between Johanna and her consort in Clement's estimation. Under these terms, Andrew was king in name only.[32] On February 10, Clement wrote again to reassure Johanna that only she held regal power.[33] After this exchange, papal correspondence regarding the kingdom's administration continued to be addressed solely to Johanna or (rarely) to Johanna and Sancia, suggesting that the pope regarded Johanna and Aimery, rather than either Andrew or the essentially defunct governing council, as the true rulers of Naples.

As time passed and Johanna became increasingly intractable and her supporters—to whom she alienated vast amounts of territory—were increasingly reputed to control Naples, Clement began to insist that Andrew be recognized as Johanna's coruler, in name if not in fact.[34] On March 31, 1344,

---

28. Léonard, *Histoire de Jeanne Ire*, 1:339.

29. Reg. 161, *De Curia*, n° XVI, fol. 3r and n° XVII, fol. 4r, in Déprez, *Clement VI*, 1:311, nos. 631 and 632.

30. Baddeley, *Robert the Wise and His Heirs*, 322.

31. Reg. 137, n°s DCLSSII, DCSSIII–DCLXXV, DCLXXVI, fol. 185r, in Déprez, *Clement VI*, 1: 317, nos. 643, 644, 645.

32. Léonard, *Histoire de Jeanne Ire*, 1:361.

33. Baddeley, *Robert the Wise and His Heirs*, 311. Baddeley cites Arch. Vat. Secr. Clem. VI Anno i., fol. 1 E 3; Anno xi. E 676, Feb. 10, 1344: "Nihilominus a te sola recipiatur homagium et fidelitatis juramentum ad quae prestanda pro dicto regno et terris citra Farum, nobis et Ecclesiae pregatae teneris astricta."

34. Clement's growing irritation with Johanna appears to have been due largely to territorial alienations. On July 9, 1345, he ordered her to cease making territorial donations and alienations on pain of excommunication. See Reg. Vat. 139, fol. 39, n° 113, in Déprez, *Clement VI*, 3:18, no. 1822.

he wrote to the Regno via Aimery, informing its people that Andrew and Johanna were to be anointed as king and queen, thus giving Andrew public recognition as Johanna's titular equal.[35] From mid-April onward, Clement insisted that Andrew be allowed some part in the administration, and he began to address both Andrew and Johanna in official correspondence. Yet Clement's letters to Aimery about the Regno's administration continue to refer solely to Johanna as monarch.[36] In a letter of May 22, 1344, regarding Johanna's oath of fealty to her papal suzerain, no mention is made of Andrew at all.[37] Clement's letters remain addressed only to Johanna or to both Andrew and Johanna, although Andrew is included as a recipient with greater frequency.[38]

After August, the relationship between Andrew and Johanna worsened, and the pope wrote to both entreating them to overcome their differences.[39] His informants in Naples kept him apprised of the situation, and he worked assiduously to keep the peace. Writing to Andrew, he referred to Johanna as Andrew's consort (*consors tua*). Writing to Johanna, he referred to Andrew as her husband (*virum tuum*), thus seemingly placing the two on equal footing. However, although he was consulted on small matters, on major issues of government, such as making peace with the Kingdom of Aragon, Andrew was not consulted, and Clement corresponded only with Aimery and Johanna.

In November, Clement wrote to express concern about the amount of territory Johanna was alienating from the crown in the form of gifts to her inner circle, especially the Cabanni (the family of her grand seneschal and rumored lover, Roberto de' Cabanni) and Catania families—the very families whose members would ultimately be executed for Andrew's murder. Clement ordered Johanna to curtail such gifts or forfeit her power of administration and Aimery to ensure that she did so.[40] Johanna was clearly losing standing with the pope: On December 13, 1344, Clement wrote to her, demanding that she not exclude Andrew from the administration of the kingdom.[41] It is noteworthy, however, that he did not provide specific instructions as to what Andrew's part in government was

35. Reg. 137, n° DCCCXLIII, fol. 226v, in Déprez, *Clement VI*, 1:392, no. 747.

36. See, for instance, Reg. 138, n° VII, fol. 2r, in Déprez, *Clement VI*, 2:6, no. 837.

37. Reg. 138, n° XV, fol. 4, in Déprez, *Clement VI*, 2:13–14, no. 855.

38. Reg. 138, n° CXLII, fol. 47, in Déprez, *Clement VI*, 2:97, no. 968.

39. Reg. 138, n° CCXXIX, fol. 71v and n° CCXXXX, fol. 72r, in Déprez, *Clement VI*, 2:149, nos. 1057 and 1058.

40. Reg. 138, n° CCCCLXII, fol. 131 and n° CCCCLXIIII, fol. 131, in Déprez, *Clement VI*, 2:281, nos. 1261 and 1262; Léonard, *Histoire de Jeanne Ire*, 1:428.

41. Reg. 138, n° DLXXXII, fol. 161, in Déprez, *Clement VI*, 2:323–24, no. 1333.

to be.[42] He termed Andrew "our son, the illustrious king of Sicily, your husband," praising his honor and excellence and reminding Johanna that it was fitting for the husband to be the head of the wife; because of this, it was to Johanna's benefit and the benefit of the kingdom that Andrew be included in its governance.[43] Attempting to persuade Johanna of Andrew's merit, Clement described his *beata stirps* and royal lineage, insisting that he was possessed of innate goodness and virtue, with elegance, circumspection, and diligence—to the extent that his age would allow. Furthermore, the pope wrote, Andrew had inherited and exhibited the attractive ways of his forebears, which, with the aid of divine grace, must (one day) make him a vigorous man with many virtues.[44] Yet Andrew's potential lay in the future—what Clement saw in him was but the promise of the man he might become, and he seems to have had little idea of allowing Andrew to actually rule Naples.

Matters came to a head early in the summer of 1345. Aimery, despite Clement's initial determination to recall him from Naples in December 1344, had remained to monitor the explosive situation.[45] Writing to Philip VI of France on May 11, Clement explained that Johanna continued to make territorial alienations and refused to allow Andrew to participate in government business.[46] On June 10, 1345, Clement instructed Johanna in no uncertain terms to allow Andrew to be crowned, anointed, and allowed into her administration.[47] In a second letter of the same day, Clement again told her that she should allow Andrew to partake in the administration of the realm and not hinder his kingship with "contrary suggestions."[48] Yet, despite Hungarian threats, Neapolitan plots, and the growing impatience of the papacy, Johanna refused to capitulate. She wrote to Clement objecting to Andrew's elevation, expressing her determination to retain control of her administration and arguing that no one could better look after Andrew's interests and honor than she herself—suggesting

---

42. Léonard, *Histoire de Jeanne Ire*, 1:397.

43. Reg. 138, n° DLXXXII, fol. 161, in Déprez, *Clement VI*, 2:323: "filii nostri Andree, regis Sicilie illustris, viri tui"; 324: "Non enim convenit quod vir, qui caput est uxoris, ab illis, que utriusque honorem and commodum promovent . . . tuo et suo honore in had parte sevato illeso, amoris et caritatis vinculum."

44. Reg. 138, n° DLXXXII, fol. 161, in Déprez, *Clement VI*, 2:323.

45. Baddeley, *Robert the Wise and His Heirs*, 399.

46. Reg. 138, n° MXLIX, fol. 278, in Déprez, *Clement VI*, 2:532–33, no. 1705; Léonard, *Histoire de Jeanne Ire*, 1:400.

47. Reg. Vat. 139, fol. 30v, n° 92 and Reg. Vat. 139, fol. 31v, n° 94, in Déprez, *Clement VI*, 3:8, 9, nos. 1772 and 1774. Clement's instructions to both Johanna and Aimery make clear that while he wished Andrew to be entitled king, he did not intend him to supplant his wife.

48. Reg. Vat. 139, fol. 31v, n° 94, in Déprez, *Clement VI*, 3:9, no. 1774.

an interesting inversion in Johanna's understanding of gender roles within her marriage.[49]

Clement's irritation with Johanna was clearly growing. On July 9, he threatened her with excommunication if she continued to make territorial alienations.[50] He attributed the bad blood between Andrew and Johanna to the machinations of their familiars—including the very people to whom Johanna was making such large donations—who sowed discord between them to further their own interests and influence. Aimery's reports depict the Neapolitan court as the proverbial house divided against itself, its factionalism approaching mayhem.[51] Yet later in the summer, partially owing to the intervention of Guillaume Lamy, bishop of Chartres (d. 1349), who replaced Aimery as papal nuncio and Johanna's advisor in February 1345, the situation seemed to have ameliorated.[52] Clement could praise both Andrew and Johanna for having surrounded themselves with wise, God-fearing advisors.[53] It was at about this time that Johanna's pregnancy, and thus the imminent birth of an heir, was announced, and it seemed that impending parenthood might bring peace to Naples's embattled royal couple.[54]

The brief peace was not to last. On July 28, 1345, Sancia died, and with her death the ruling council Robert had established—already rendered formally defunct by Aimery—died as well. Without her influence, bedlam broke out. Johanna was reportedly engaged in numerous adulterous affairs, including with her cousin, Louis of Taranto (d. 1362).[55] Guillaume Lamy wrote to Clement in frustration that Johanna had abandoned her husband to the mockery of her retinue.[56] The Tuscan scholar Donato degli Albanzani, commenting on his friend Giovanni Boccaccio's *Eclogues*, later wrote of rumors that Johanna and her followers openly laughed at Andrew, while the

---

49. ADBR, B 176, fol. 25: "Dignetur vestra Benignitas commemorari clementer intentionem meam incommutabiliter perseverantem circa non concendam Administrationem in Reverendo Domini, viro meo; nam, sicut presuponi rationabiliter debet non est persona vivens in mundo quem tantum affectet quantum ego ipsius commodum et honorem: et quando expedire cognovero conditionibus suis et meis, id cunctis, patere poterit effectum." Cf. Baddeley, *Robert the Wise and His Heirs*, 316, n. 1.

50. Reg. Vat. 139, fol. 39, n. 113, in Déprez, *Clement VI*, 3:18, no. 1822.

51. Léonard, *Histoire de Jeanne Ire*, 1:404.

52. Ibid., 432; Baddeley, *Robert the Wise and His Heirs*, 332.

53. Letter of Clement VI to Johanna of Naples, August 5, 1345, published in Cerasoli, "Clemente VI e Giovanna I di Napoli," *ASPN* 21, n° LXXVIII, 261. Cf. Léonard, *Histoire de Jeanne Ire*, 1:432.

54. Léonard, *Histoire de Jeanne Ire*, 1:457.

55. The rumor is reported by Giovanni Villani in his chronicle, written not long afterward. See book XIII, chapter 51, in Giovanni Villani, *Nuova Cronica*, ed. Giuseppe Porta (Parma: Ugo Guanda, 1991), 3:417. Cf. Léonard, *Histoire de Jeanne Ire*, 1:440.

56. Léonard, *Histoire de Jeanne Ire*, 1:457.

Neapolitan Domenico da Gravina (d. ca. 1355) recorded in his *Chronicle* that Andrew grew incensed by his ill treatment and made childish demonstrations of military prowess as a threat of future retaliation against his enemies, should he ever come into power.[57] Further rumors of this sort reached Clement, who wrote to Johanna in May 1346 about sinister allegations regarding her conduct during Andrew's life.[58]

Late in the summer, Clement decided that Andrew must quickly be given a real role in government.[59] He instructed Aimery to crown and anoint Andrew, and plans for the coronation went forward. The legate set out for Naples from Avignon with a papal bull empowering him to perform a double coronation of the king and queen, who would be anointed together and recognized as corulers of the Regno. Clement began to send letters addressed only to Andrew regarding how he should treat papal representatives, probably because he feared Johanna would attempt to prevent the coronation. Indeed, on September 20, more than a day after Andrew's murder, he wrote to Johanna warning her not to temporize about being crowned and anointed; the next day he wrote to Andrew, telling him to delay the ceremony no longer.[60]

Even at this juncture, Andrew was not accorded specific powers; indeed, he was forced to sign a document stating that he had no rights to the kingdom. Johanna's pregnancy made the issue of who should succeed her if she died in childbirth urgent. Andrew and all of the Neapolitan clergy and nobility were required to swear a public oath that Andrew would not be declared king if Johanna died.[61] Whatever his claims about Andrew's suitability for rulership, Clement clearly believed that he would seize the throne if given the opportunity—an eventuality Clement feared and sought to prevent. Johanna was unquestionably the queen regnant, and it was she whom Clement meant to rule Naples. Up to this point, Clement had trusted Andrew only with small matters and had placated him with virtually empty concessions. Even in preparing for his coronation, Clement felt the need to ensure that Andrew could not wield power independently. The pope's caution, however, proved insufficient to calm the anxieties plaguing the factions in Naples, whose members must have feared the power that fatherhood and even nominal kingship would give Andrew.

---

57. Léonard, *Histoire de Jeanne Ire*, 1:457, discusses Donato degli Albanzani's marginal notations on his manuscript copy of Boccaccio's *Eclogues*. Cf. Domenico da Gravina, *Chronicon*, 10.

58. Domenico da Gravina, *Chronicon*, 10; Reg. Vat. 140, fol. 3v, in Déprez, *Clement VI*, 3:156, no. 2514.

59. Léonard, *Histoire de Jeanne Ire*, 1:452.

60. Reg. Vat. 139, fol. 104, n. 405, in Déprez, *Clement VI*, 3:53, no. 1974; Reg. Vat. 139, fol. 104v, n. 407 *bis*, in Déprez, *Clement VI*, 3:55, no. 1979.

61. Léonard, *Histoire de Jeanne Ire*, 1:462.

Murder in Naples

On the night of September 18, 1345, the power struggle between Johanna and Andrew ended in violence and death. Andrew, Johanna, their extended family, and their retinues had traveled to a royal hunting retreat in Aversa, a short distance from Naples, where they spent their time in sport and feasting while they awaited Aimery's arrival. After Andrew had retired to bed, his chamberlain, Tommaso Mambriccio, called him from his chamber. Then the partially clothed, unarmed prince was attacked by a group of men, beaten, suffocated, and strangled with a cord. His cries went unheard by all—including, she insisted, his sleeping wife—but his absence soon alarmed his Hungarian nurse, who went to find him. Frightened by her approaching light, Andrew's assailants threw his bruised body over the wall of the castle into the garden below, where his nurse found it and raised the alarm.

Both the royal and the papal accounts of the corpse, bloodied from desperate struggle, attest that Andrew fought violently. This much was evident from flesh found in his mouth, torn from the hand of one of his assailants. The damage to his body was extensive, revealing a degree of savagery that stunned commentators: His hair was torn out in clumps, his face lacerated, and his nostrils bloodied; his lips bore the marks of iron gauntlets and his torso those of violent pressure, while his genitals were mutilated.[62] Perhaps most troubling to commentators was the indignity of Andrew's death. Andrew was a king, even if in name only, but he had been beaten and strangled like a common criminal. The Venetian doge wrote to the count of Arbe that King Andrew was dead and had not died a good death.[63] Petrarch bewailed the "abominable and insidious savagery" ("tam nefarias et tam truces insidias") with which Andrew was slain and wished that "he had been killed by a sword or through some other form of manly death so that he would appear to have been killed at the hands of men, not mangled by the teeth and claws of beasts."[64]

---

62. Léonard, *Histoire de Jeanne Ire*, 1:471–73 and passim.

63. Arch. Venezia, Ducali et atti diplomatici, busta xi. Published by Sime Ljubic, *Commissiones et relationes venetae*, vol. 2, Monumenta Spectantia Historiam Slavorum Meridionalium (Zagreb: Sumptibus Academiae Scientiarum et Artium, 1876), 274: "rex Andreas de Apulia mortuus erat, non bona morte."

64. Petrarch, *Epistolae de Rebus Familiaribus*, V,6, 344: "aut virili morte alia, ut hominum manibus interfectus, non ferarum dentibus atque unguibus laceratus videretur." Petrarch, *Rerum familiarium*, 1:320.

In these lurid details alone, accounts of Andrew's murder agree. Theories as to the identity of the guilty party proliferated rapidly, but no consensus was ever reached. Johanna's supporters were widely held responsible. Reports differed as to the degree of Johanna's collusion, if any, and which, if any, of the Angevin princes were involved. Neapolitan factionalism shaped the stories told by chroniclers, many of whom argued that the ultimate responsibility lay with Johanna and her Tarantini cousins, led by their mother, Catherine of Valois (1303–46), titular empress of Constantinople. Domenico da Gravina asserted that Johanna and her retainers arranged the hunting trip for the sole purpose of assassinating Andrew, while others, particularly propapal authors, insisted on Johanna's complete innocence. The Hungarian faction, led by Louis of Hungary, held the entire Neapolitan royal family responsible and begged the pope to take appropriate action.[65]

Officially, however, none of the royal family was found guilty of Andrew's death. Instead, members of Johanna's inner circle, including the Cabanni and Catania families, were condemned and executed for the crime. Johanna herself insisted in a letter to Siena and Florence on September 22 that an unnamed servant (Tommaso Mambriccio, who had been executed on September 20) was one of only two assailants.[66] Charles of Durazzo, Johanna's brother-in-law, however, responded quickly to the public outrage that engulfed Aversa and Naples, and he took the lead in discovering and prosecuting Andrew's murderers—in part to prevent a Hungarian invasion of Naples—all the while portraying himself as Andrew's loyal friend and supporter. His investigation uncovered a vast conspiracy allegedly including the count of Terlizzi, Gasso de Denicy; Roberto de' Cabanni, count of Eboli and grand seneschal of the realm, as well as Johanna's reputed lover; Raimondo de Catania, knight and *maggior-domo* to the queen; Charles Artois, King Robert's illegitimate son and count of Santa Agata and Monteodorisio, along with his son, Bertrand; Niccolò di Melizzano, Johanna's chamberlain; Tommaso Mambriccio; and a number of other prominent members of the court.[67] Also charged were Johanna's nurse, Filippa

65. Léonard, *Histoire de Jeanne Ire*, 1:476.

66. Johanna's letter is Archivio di Stato di Firenza, Capitoli, t. XVI, fol. 116. An edition can be found in M. Papon, *Histoire générale de Provence*, vol. 3 (Paris: Imprimerie de Philippe-Denys Pierres, 1784), lv. Cf. Léonard, *Histoire de Jeanne Ire*, 1:474. For an English translation, see Musto, *Medieval Naples*, 274–75.

67. Camera, *Elucubrazioni storico-diplomatiche su Giovanna I.a*, 40. Giovanni da Bazzano's *Chronicon Mutinense* provides a detailed account of Charles of Durazzo's investigation. See Giovanni da Bazzano, *Chronicon Mutinense* [AA. 1188–1363], ed. Tommaso Casini, vol. 15, pt. 4 of *RIS: Racolta degli Storici Italiani del cinquecento al millecinquecento*, ed. L. A. Muratori, new ed. (Bologna: N. Zanichelli, 1917–19), 144.

Catanese—later immortalized by Boccaccio as a nefarious criminal—and her granddaughter, Johanna's childhood companion Sancia de' Cabanni.[68]

In the summer of 1346, Bertrand des Baux, who acted as papal delegate in the case, oversaw the punishment of the alleged masterminds. Bertrand Artois confessed under torture. Despite Johanna's attempts to protect them, the chief conspirators were publicly tortured and burned in a series of gruesome and well-attended spectacles.[69] Tommaso Mambriccio, executed in the immediate aftermath of the murder, was rumored to have had his tongue removed so that he could not implicate his true accomplices. There was rampant speculation that those executed were merely scapegoats or accomplices of the real murderers, who escaped punishment.[70]

Johanna herself did not escape suspicion, despite having been exonerated by the dubious investigation and despite continuing papal support. Her subjects' initial response after Andrew's death was to publicly condemn her, although the prosecution and punishment of the supposed conspirators soon calmed the public outcry.[71] Further afield, however, common report continued to condemn Johanna, and speculation about the truth surrounding Andrew's murder was fodder for discussion long after Johanna had been formally exonerated.

Johanna's behavior after Andrew's murder outraged not only his family but also observers across Europe. Her letter to Florence and Siena callously seemed to hold Andrew partially responsible for his fate, which she attributed to childish imprudence that led him to walk about at night unaccompanied despite the counsel of those who had his best interests at heart.[72] Mere weeks afterward, in the midst of open hostilities between the Angevin princes in Naples, who vied for power and sought access to the throne,

---

68. See Giovanni Boccaccio, *De casibus virorum illustrium*, ed. Pier Giorgio Ricci and Vittorio Zaccaria, vol. 9 of *Tutte le opere di Giovanni Bocaccio* (Milan: Arnoldo Mondadori Editore, 1983).

69. Léonard, *Histoire de Jeanne Ire*, 1:582–88.

70. Joseph De Blasiis, ed., *Chronicon Siculum incerti auctoris ab anno 340 ad annum 1396, in forma diary ex inedito Codice Ottoboniano Vaticano*, Società Napoletana di Storia Patria, Monumenti Storici—Serie Prima: Cronache (Naples: Francisco Giannini & Fil., 1887), 7–8; G. Villani, *Nuova Cronica*, XIII.52, 3:420; Léonard, *Histoire de Jeanne Ire*, 1:486, 582–88.

71. Léonard, *Histoire de Jeanne Ire*, 1:482–88, 582–88. The official investigation also satisfied Clement VI, who refused to consider Johanna a conspirator and wrote to Robert of Taranto in January 1346 to congratulate him for the speed with which the investigation was conducted. See Reg. Vat. 139, fol. 182, n. 777, in Déprez, *Clement VI*, 102, no. 2264.

72. Archivio di Stato di Firenza, Capitoli, t. XVI, fol. 116: "dominus vir noster tarde, horam intrandi cubiculum, descendisset ad quondam parcum contiguum Gayso aule nostri hospitii in Aversam, imprudenter & incaute imo juveniliter sicut frequenter ibi & alibi suspectam horam abire consueverat, nullius in hoc acquiescens consilio, sed tantum sequens motus precipites juventutis, non admittens socium, sed ostium post se firmans." For an English translation, see Musto, *Medieval Naples*, 274–75.

Johanna requested a papal dispensation to marry her cousin, Robert of Taranto, and then, after that was denied, permission to marry Robert's brother, Louis.[73] Both Tarantini were widely believed to have been Johanna's lovers before the murder, which they were thought by many to have orchestrated. Indeed, some, including Domenico da Gravina, saw Louis's attachment to Johanna as proof that he and his mother had schemed to murder and replace Andrew.[74] In August 1347, Louis moved into the royal residence. When Clement VI refused to allow their marriage, Johanna and Louis married secretly on August 22.[75]

Arrangements for Johanna's remarriage enraged Louis of Hungary and provided him additional justification to invade Naples. His vengeance was swift and brutal. During the winter of 1347, as Hungarian forces and their swelling ranks of supporters marched down the Italian peninsula, Johanna and Louis of Taranto fled separately to Avignon. Johanna was pregnant with her second child and abandoned Charles Martel, her son with Andrew (born Christmas Day, 1345), to a papal guardian.[76] Louis of Hungary quickly captured the Regno, and he sent Charles Martel to Buda, where he died in 1348. Louis then established himself as the ruler of Naples and continued to agitate for Johanna's condemnation and punishment, even as he avenged himself on the rest of the royal family. Among his first victims was Charles of Durazzo, whom he executed in Aversa in January 1348.[77]

---

73. Johanna requested a dispensation to marry Robert in late 1345, while she was still pregnant with Andrew's son, Charles Martel. Negotiations for the marriage with Louis were underway by the fall of 1346. See Francesco Paolo Tocco, *Niccolò Acciaiuoli: Vita e politica in Italia alla metà del XIV secolo*, Istituto Storico Italiano per il Medio Evo, Nuovi Studi Storici 52 (Rome: Nella sede dell'Istituto Palazzo Borromini, 2001), 72. Léonard points out that the documents that survive make Johanna's desires difficult to ascertain, and that the demands for dispensations came primarily from the Tarantini and their supporters. See Léonard, *Histoire de Jeanne I*[re], 1:500–502, 542–47, 614–16.

74. Domenico da Gravina, *Chronicon*, 13.

75. De Blasiis, *Chronicon Siculum*, 9; Giovanni Villani reports an alternate date of August 20 for the marriage; see G. Villani, *Nuova Cronica*, 3:511. Cf. Léonard, *Histoire de Jeanne I*[re], 1:678.

76. Charles Martel was the preferred name for Angevin crown princes. It recalled the dynasty's Carolingian lineage and invoked its ties to the Capetian house and to St. Louis (cf. Boyer, "La 'Foi Monarchique,'" 92). Thus, Johanna's choice of name underscored both her son's right to the throne and his illustrious descent. At the same time, it may have been intended to honor Andrew's grandfather and to signal that the competing claims of the senior and junior Angevin branches were reconciled in this child, the descendent of both. Given the rumors of her infidelity, Johanna may also have chosen a name that asserted her son's legitimacy.

77. Silvio Adrasto Barbi, ed., *Storie Pistoresi* [1300–1348], vol. 11, pt. 5 of *RIS: Raccolta degli Storici Italiani dal cinquecento al millecinquecento*, ed. L. A. Muratori, new ed. (Città di Castello: S. Lapi, 1907), 146, reports that Louis defenestrated Charles. The *Cronaca di Partenope* reports, "For the violent death [of his brother] the king of Hungary arrived in the kingdom with force of arms and did great damage to the kingdom. And wanting to avenge the death of his brother, he beheaded the Duke of Durazzo in the city of Aversa, the same place where King Andrew died." See Samantha Kelly, ed., *The "Cronaca di Partenope": An Introduction to and Critical Edition of the First Vernacular History of Naples (c. 1350)* (Leiden: Brill, 2011), 280–81.

Johanna arrived in Avignon accused of murder, seemingly bereft of supporters, illicitly married to a cousin whose child she was carrying, with her kingdom overrun by a mortal enemy and her already fatherless son left motherless.[78] To make matters worse, the Black Death reached Avignon not long after she did, leading Louis Heyligen (1304–61) to charge in a letter to Petrarch that Andrew's assassination had caused the pestilence.[79] Johanna's iniquity seemed to have infected all of Europe.

Perhaps if matters had stayed as bleak for Johanna as they seemed when she arrived in Avignon, her reign would have appeared less iniquitous and illegitimate to her contemporaries, even to those already disposed to be her enemies. However, Johanna's fortunes quickly improved after her arrival in Provence. Although she was taken prisoner by the Aixois and forced to wait three months at Châteaurenard because of Hungarian pressure on Clement VI, she reached Avignon on March 15, a day after the arrival of Louis of Taranto and his advisor, Niccolò Acciaiuoli (1310–65), who had fled Naples when it became clear that they could not defend the city. Clement almost immediately awarded the royal couple a dispensation for their marriage and appointed a commission to investigate the charges against them.[80] Johanna appeared before the pope and Curia in consistory to defend herself against the charge that she had been complicit in Andrew's murder. She must have had a compelling, charismatic presence; her powers of persuasion were apparently sufficient to charm the cardinals into clearing her name.[81] On March 30, the pope awarded Louis of Taranto the Golden Rose, the highest papal honor, customarily given to the most illustrious person at the papal court on the fourth Sunday during Lent. In early May, Clement arranged to buy Avignon—which Johanna ruled as countess of Provence—for 80,000 florins, which she would use to finance her return to Naples.[82] Clement forgave her indiscretions and continued to support her against her enemies.

---

78. Louis's and Johanna's marriage required a papal dispensation because of Johanna's status as papal vassal and because of consanguinity. Johanna and Louis were first cousins—their mothers had been half sisters. They were, thus, related both through the paternal line as the great-grandchildren of Charles II and through their Valois mothers.

79. Louis Heyligen, "Breve Chronicon Clerici Anonymi," in *Receuil des Chroniques de Flandre*, ed. J. J. de Smet (Brussels: Commission Royale d'Histoire, 1856), 3:17. Louis Heyligen's letter was copied into the *Chronicon*.

80. Édouard Baratier, *Histoire de la Provence* (Toulouse: E. Privat, 1969), 190.

81. Guillaume Mollat, *Les papes d'Avignon (1305–1378)*, 10th ed. (Paris: Letouzey et Ané, 1964), 292.

82. Ibid., 293; Baratier, *Histoire de la Provence*, 190. Léonard cites Archivio di Stato Napoletano, *Registri Angioini*, n. 355, fol. 128. See Léonard, *Histoire de Jeanne Ire*, 1:455.

Within a matter of months, the plague had driven Louis of Hungary from Italy. Johanna and Louis of Taranto returned to Naples on August 17, 1348, as its king and queen, their innocence and legitimacy tacitly affirmed by the papacy.

Fama and the Creation of a Royal Monster

Andrew of Hungary's murder proved pivotal in the formation of his widow's public persona. The much-discussed crime brought Johanna and the Neapolitan court international scrutiny, and chroniclers and other writers competed to define Johanna's reputation and codify their own version of the story of Andrew's murder. The ability to shape and manipulate *fama* was an invaluable political tool, one of the most potent available to those not born to power and one wielded most effectively by Johanna's opponents. Literary accounts of Andrew's death that presented Johanna as a murderess were calculated to delegitimate her, to manipulate and shape her *fama*. They worked to establish her ill repute—because *fama*, once created, took on a life of its own, exercising power and a claim to truth simply by being known—to demonstrate both her guilt and her unfitness to rule one of Europe's most important polities. At the same time, accounts that vilified Johanna acted as a means to punish her and to expose the dangers inherent in allowing a woman to rule.

Those who supported Johanna, particularly those whose sympathies lay with the papacy, attempted to portray the murder in a manner that deflected guilt and preserved her honor. The Swiss Franciscan chronicler John of Winterthur (d. after 1348) insisted that Johanna had only escaped sharing her husband's fate through hasty flight.[83] The prolific Franciscan prophet John of Rupescissa (d. 1366) defended Johanna from his prison cell in Avignon, deploring Andrew's death as a great and ominous evil while attesting to Johanna's innocence and arguing that she had been falsely implicated.[84] To

---

83. John of Winterthur, *Die Chronik Johanns von Winterthur*, ed. Friedrich Baethgen, Monumenta Germaniae Historica, Scriptores rerum germanicarum, new series, 3 (Munich: Monumenta Germaniae Historica, 1982), 260.

84. Rupescissa discusses Andrew's murder in his *Liber secretorum eventuum* (1349), *De oneribus orbis* (1354), and *Liber ostensor* (1356). See John of Rupescissa, *Liber secretorum eventuum: Edition critique, traduction et introduction historique*, ed. Robert E. Lerner and Christine Morerod-Fattebert (Fribourg: Éditions Universitaires, 1994), and John of Rupescissa, *Liber ostensor quod adesse festinant tempora*, ed. André Vauchez, Clémence Thévenaz, and Christine Morerod-Fattebert (Rome: École Français de Rome, 2005). Léonard (*Histoire de Jeanne Ire*, 1:478), cites Rupescissa's *De oneribus orbis*, Tours, Bibliothèque municipale, MS 520. Mark Dupuy comments on Rupescissa's exoneration of Johanna in his article "The Unwilling Prophet and the New Maccabees: John de Roquetaillade and the Valois in the Fourteenth Century," *Florilegium* 17 (2000): 246, n. 33.

Rupescissa, Andrew's death and the Hungarian invasion of Naples presaged the coming of Antichrist and the return to power of the Hohenstaufen following the decline of the three French kings—those of France, Naples, and Hungary—who had been the protectors of the Church. The conspiracy that felled Andrew was thus far greater and more evil than Johanna, whom Rupescissa insisted would be found blameless before God. Giovanni da Bazzano (ca. 1285–1364) contended in his *Chronicon Mutinense*, written shortly after Louis of Taranto's death in 1362, that it was not the queen but the Tarantini and their supporters who should be held responsible for Andrew's gruesome fate.[85] Giovanni's narration of Andrew's murder—which is beholden to Johanna's letter to Florence and Siena—presents a touching scene in which Johanna, sensing that something is amiss, begs Andrew not to answer the summons into the hallway. Reckless and heedless of his wife's pleas, Andrew tears his cloak from her hands and goes to meet his assailants.[86]

In these renditions of Andrew's death, Johanna is an innocent and even victimized bystander, more harmed than helped by her husband's murder. She is womanly and physically weak, condemned by her femininity to the role of helpless witness. It is her fate to be wrongfully accused and even, in the *Chronicon Mutinense*, to fall into the power of enemies who killed Andrew to gain control of her and, through her, of her kingdom. Such narratives presented Johanna as sympathetic and defenseless, even pitiable. The negative characterizations of Johanna and the damaging accounts of the murder constructed by her enemies, however, held equal and often greater currency. They would follow her throughout her life, remaining for posterity as enduring hallmarks of her reputation.

Authors antagonistic to Johanna also portrayed her as hopelessly feminine, but the definition of femininity they drew on was characterized by irrationality, violence, and lustfulness. They emphasized her malice and the dissolution of her court, portraying her as a vicious usurper who, driven by self-interest and hunger for power, had barred Andrew's ascent to the throne. Whereas Johanna's supporters either ignored the issue of Andrew's right to rule or described him after his death as implicitly equal in rank and power to his wife, those who supported Hungarian claims insisted that Johanna ruled only through violation of Andrew's legitimate (masculine) position. Among Johanna's supporters, Andrew's worth and kingliness became a given. Petrarch forgot his earlier estimation that Andrew was neither a king nor kingly and excoriated Aversa for allowing regicide to occur on its

---

85. Giovanni da Bazzano, *Chronicon Mutinense*, 142.
86. Ibid., 143.

soil. In his account, Andrew is no longer a noble-minded boy with future promise but has become a "king and just lord" who, embodying "the sacred person of a public servant," fully realized his inheritance as a holy Angevin king.[87] Giovanni da Bazzano reports that Andrew's kingship was formalized by Guillaume Lamy, who crowned his mutilated corpse.[88] Clement VI—an architect of Andrew's secondary position in Naples—wrote after the murder to Louis of Hungary and Elizabeth of Poland that he was more injured than they, because he had lost the protection of a king destined to be a champion of the Church.[89] His lamentation for Andrew's lost greatness, like Petrarch's, obscured Andrew's marginalization. Johanna's enemies, however, described Andrew's humiliation and debasement at length. Because their aim was not to glorify Andrew but to denigrate and discredit Johanna, they emphasized not the heights Andrew would have attained had he lived but the ignominy to which he was subject in life.

Johanna's sex rendered her inheritance of the throne, arguably unjust on dynastic grounds, all the more deplorable, and hostile accounts invariably strive to impugn not only her right to rule but also her morality in gendered, sexualized terms. Such accounts configure the relationship between Johanna and Andrew as predatory, portraying Andrew as the innocent victim of his licentious wife. Although Petrarch had earlier described both Johanna and Andrew as lambs among wolves, after Andrew's death, Johanna herself became the wolf in literary treatments, while Andrew was the innocent lamb led to slaughter. Giovanni Boccaccio, despite his later praise of Johanna in *De mulieribus claris* (*On Famous Women*) (ca. 1362/63), cast her in his *Eclogues* as a rabid, pregnant she-wolf, encapsulating a sense of her as monstrous and inhuman common to most accounts of Andrew's murder that sought to demonstrate her guilt.

Johanna's insistence on her right to rule and on Andrew's status as her consort inverted natural order as it was commonly understood. Johanna's critics thus accused her of failure to comport herself as a woman should, as of sexual misconduct. The very terms of her marriage to Andrew made her vulnerable to criticism: Her sovereignty subverted what Jean le Fèvre, in *The Lamentations of Matheolus*, would call "the natural order of things," upending the marital power dynamic and creating a situation in which "confusion

87. Petrarch, *Epistolae de Rebus Familiaribus*, V, 6 320–21; Petrarch, *Rerum familiarum libri*, 1:320–21.

88. Giovanni da Bazzano, *Chronicon Mutinense*, 143–44.

89. See August Theiner, ed., *Vetera monumenta historica Hungariam sacram illustrantia maximam partem nondum edita ex tabulariis Vaticanis deprompta collecta ac serie chronologica disposita*, vol. 1: *ab Honorio III. usque ad Clementem VI* (Rome: Typis Vaticanis, 1859), 687, items MXXXVIII and MXXXIX, 703, MLXVII.

reigned."[90] Since the incorporation of Roman law into canon law in the twelfth century, a husband's lordship had been legally codified and husbands seen to stand in the place of God with their wives.[91] Gratian's *Decretum* (ca. 1140) insisted on the legal and moral imperative that women be subject to their husbands (C. 33 q. 5 cc. 11–20). Gratian argues that it is the "natural order among humans that women serve men," because it is men and not women who are made in God's image (C. 33 q. 5 cc. 12, 13). Drawing on Jerome, he states that "when a Christian woman wants to command a man, the word of God is blasphemed," although even among "gentiles" women serve men, according to natural law (C. 33 q. 5 c. 15).[92] Johanna's relationship to Andrew thus existed in a state of imbalance that could be extended to apply to her assertion of sovereignty, which gave her rule not merely over one man but over many. Accordingly, Johanna's critics amplified her refusal to conform to gender norms. They presented her as devoid of appropriate womanly propriety or feeling, ruling only through an inversion of the natural order that should have made Andrew king. In retelling the story of Andrew's murder, Johanna's enemies presented the events leading up to his death and the crime itself as evidence of her unfitness to rule, framing their critiques as an indictment of Johanna's sexual morality and, implicitly, of regnant queenship.

Andrew's mother was among the first to formally accuse Johanna of murder and to use that accusation to argue for the Hungarian right to rule Naples. Writing to Clement VI after she learned of Johanna's proposed remarriage, Elizabeth of Poland excoriated her former daughter-in-law for her immorality, accused her of viricide, and demanded that the Kingdom of Naples be ceded to Louis of Hungary.[93] Those who opposed Johanna's rule

---

90. Jean le Fèvre, "From *The Lamentations of Matheolus* (c. 1371–2)," in Alcuin Blamires, ed., *Woman Defamed and Woman Defended—An Anthology of Medieval Texts* (Oxford: Oxford University Press, 1992), 178, 180.

91. Gratian, *Decretum Magistri Gratiani*, ed. A. Friedberg, in *Corpus Juris Canonici* (Leipzig: Bernard Tauchnitz, 1879–81; repr. Graz: Akademische Druck-u. Verlagsanstalt 1959), C. 33 q. 5 c 13. See also Dyan Elliott, *Proving Woman: Female Spirituality and Inquisitional Culture in the Later Middle Ages* (Princeton: Princeton University Press, 2004), 92, and Elliott, *Spiritual Marriage: Sexual Abstinence in Medieval Wedlock* (Princeton: Princeton University Press, 1993), 156–57.

92. Gratian, *Decretum*, 1, cols. 1253–56. For an English translation of these passages, see Blamires, *Woman Defamed and Woman Defended*, 85.

93. Writing to Elizabeth on August 17, 1346, Clement protested the charge and begged Elizabeth to leave matters of justice to the Holy See: "de dicta Iohanna tenente Regnum ipsum possit infra illud fieri iusticia, et super eisdem sceleribus reperiri veritas contra eam, adiciens, quod predicta Iohanna de predictis morte ac sceleribus rea et viricida signis evidentissimis et rationibus probabilibus ostendi poterat manifeste, quodque nos debemus attendere, si talis femina, sicut asseris, viricida debet iuxta consilium Romani Pontficis aluci matrimonialiter copulari." Ex Reg. orig. An. V. secr. e 255. Item MLXXXIII in Theiner, *Vetera monumenta historica Hungariam*, 716–17.

quickly took up Elizabeth's charges. Boccaccio, who had spent much of his youth in Naples and who, with his patron, Francesco degli Ordelaffi, may have joined the Hungarian troops besieging Naples in 1348, wrote about Andrew's murder in his third eclogue. In the poem, Andrew's poetic double, Alexis, is murdered by a rabid, pregnant she-wolf (*lupa*), whom most critics agree is Johanna.[94] In Latin and Italian, *lupa* means both she-wolf and prostitute. On one level, Boccaccio equated Johanna's sexuality with bestial irrationality, drawing on the Thomistic teaching that submission to bodily desires renders humans animal-like.[95] Ovid, one of Boccaccio's poetic models, ironically portrayed female sexuality as bestial, or even rabid, without bounds and far exceeding that of men, playing on tropes about female sexuality that were already timeworn when he wrote.[96] Albert the Great provided the natural philosophical corollary to this argument, representing the insatiability of female sexuality as subhuman, something that "deviates from the ideal course of nature."[97] Boccaccio amplifies this: His Johanna is not merely rabid, she is an animal. Sex and violence are wed in her, her characterization as a prostitute tied to her violent, maddened animal nature in a metaphor that Edward Muir argues Italian chroniclers often used to "explain human violence by showing how [perpetrators] had crossed the line into bestiality."[98] Boccaccio thus stripped Johanna of her humanity, discursively making her both a wolf and a prostitute and linking her to a long line of disordered queens, from

---

94. See Boccaccio's *Faunus*, line 84: "gravidam tum forte lupam rabieque." Giovanni Boccaccio, *Eclogues*, trans. and ed. Janet Levarie Smarr (New York: Garland, 1987), 27. Some scholars have argued that the she-wolf may be not Johanna but Sancia de' Cabanni, who was rumored to have been Andrew's mistress. Some chronicle accounts describe Sancia as the maker of a silken sash used to strangle her former lover. While this explanation is plausible, Boccaccio's support of the Hungarian cause and his reference to other reports implicating "lions" and "ferocious beasts" (lines 89–90) suggest that he was thinking of the queen and not of another member of her court, who should logically be counted among the lions and other beasts. See Boccaccio, *Eclogues*, 212, n. line 84, and Léonard, *Histoire de Jeanne Ire*, 1:472. On Boccaccio's short-lived support for the Hungarian vendetta, see Smarr's notes on the *Eclogues* and Vittore Branca, *Boccaccio: The Man and His Works*, trans. Richard Monges (New York: New York University Press, 1976), 73–74.

95. Thomas Aquinas, *Summa Theologiae* 1–2.73.5 ad 3. On Thomas Aquinas's treatment of sexual sin, humanity, and bestiality, see Mark D. Jorday, "Homosexuality, *Luxuria*, and Textual Abuse," in *Constructing Medieval Sexuality*, ed. Karma Lochrie, Peggy McCracken, and James A. Schultz (Minneapolis: University of Minnesota Press, 1997), 30.

96. Ovid, *The Art of Love*, I.269–343. For an English translation, see Ovid, *Ovid's Erotic Poems: Amores and Ars Amatoria*, trans. Len Krisak (Philadelphia: University of Pennsylvania Press, 2014), 122–24.

97. Cadden, *Meanings of Sex Difference in the Middle Ages*, 149.

98. Edward Muir, *Mad Blood Stirring: Vendetta in Renaissance Italy*, reader's edition (Baltimore: Johns Hopkins University Press, 1998), 149.

Empress Messalina (ca. 17–48 AD) to *The Golden Legend*'s Lupa, antagonist of James the Greater, who were also typed as wolves.[99]

Similarly, a previously unknown epistolary manifesto written in the voice of the Neapolitan people on the eve of the first Hungarian invasion laments Andrew's death and the loss of his potential for greatness, faulting Johanna's "charms" for the murder and claiming that her training as a queen had accomplished nothing beyond the impending doom of her people.[100] The manifesto, written in highly rhetorical Latin, echoes papal letters about Andrew's death in presenting the slain prince as the lost hope of the Neapolitan people—a future crusader, a just and devoted king, and a virtuous innocent whose demise signified the loss of a promising future and the commencement of a time of tragedy and suffering. In its estimation of Andrew's unrealized potential, the letter recalls Clement's description of his own loss and Rupescissa's prophetic foreboding about the significance of Andrew's death, although it diverges from these accounts in its treatment of Johanna. For this author, Johanna, as the instrument of her husband's murder, was also the cause of her people's anguish, having robbed them of the golden age that would have been under Andrew's rule only to expose them to the imminent depredations of Hungarian invaders.

All such defamatory narratives cast aspersions on Johanna's chastity. In asserting their right to the Neapolitan throne, the Hungarians and their supporters indicted Johanna not only for murder but also for sexual crimes—the charms alluded to by the Neapolitan manifesto—and proffered her licentiousness as evidence that she was unfit to rule her kingdom. Indeed, they portray Andrew's murder as yet another expression of Johanna's debased moral character, inextricably linked to her adultery and the dissipation of her court. A Hungarian manuscript of Gentile of Foligno's commentary on the prophecy *Ve mundo in centum annis*, for instance, identifies a prediction of a slain king with Andrew's murder. Gentile's commentary, likely written

---

99. According to Juvenal and Pliny the Elder, Messalina sated her sexual appetites by working in a brothel under the moniker "Wolf Girl" or "She-Wolf." See Pliny, *C. Plini Secundi Naturalis historiae libri XXXVII*, ed. Ludwig Ianus and Charles Mayhoff (Stuttgart: Teubner, 1906), X.83, and Juvenal, *Satires*, ed. Susanna Morton Braund (New York: Cambridge University Press, 1996), VI.114–35 and X.329–36. Juvenal's tenth satire tells of Gaius Silius's forced marriage to Messalina and charges that Messalina—whose lust reportedly made her cruel and violent—would have murdered Silius if he refused her. Boccaccio's *lupa* also recalls criticism of Cleopatra, whom Horace characterized as a *fatale monstrum* (*Carm.* 1. 37. 21).

100. Zwettl, Zisterzienserstift, Cod. 169 20, fol. 175v: "Ha nobilis regina Johanna tot et tantis educata deliciis unde tot poteris educere lacrimas in tuorum fidelium excidio quos secabit et incidet cruentus gladius ungarorum." This manuscript was generously called to my attention by Robert Lerner.

around 1332, links the murder of the strangled king with his long and reluctant endurance of the "abominable wantonness" of his queen, which is how Gentile interprets the prophecy's statement that the unnamed Apulian king "gulps down the menstruations of the bride."[101] Sometime around 1348, an anonymous glossator read Gentile's commentary as a reference to Johanna's notorious cuckolding of Andrew, creating a new prophetic tradition that found its way into the Hungarian manuscript. The glossator notes that the Hungarians will seize the kingdom in retribution, "because they have not anointed their lord and king, but rather have killed him with quite a terrible death." The kingdom as a whole will suffer for the queen's sins: "they will be cast down on the earth, and they will find no aid on that day . . . because she is the murderess of her lord."[102] Thus, like the author of the Neapolitan manifesto, the anonymous glossator effectively argues that Johanna's refusal to allow Andrew's anointing and her infamous sexual profligacy were the source of Naples's ruin as well as of Andrew's murder.

According to the standards of Roman law set down in the *Digest* and recognized in both common and canon law, the adultery and murder of which Johanna stood accused qualified her as legally infamous and, consequently, unfit to hold public office.[103] In legal terms, the very fact of Johanna's infamy might have invalidated her rule. While the textual campaign waged against Johanna could not depose her, it could demonstrate the consequences of her rule and expose her inappropriateness—in moral and sexual terms—as a ruler. It could also condemn her in the court of public opinion, creating a negative reputation—a *mala fama*—that rendered her morally dangerous through its very existence. Thus, the story of Andrew's murder became in the hands of many commentators a way to argue for Johanna's deposition. Andrew's unrecognized legitimacy and horrible death form the narrative substance in these accounts, but their primary function was to expose the iniquity of Johanna's reign.

Chroniclers who sought to demonize Johanna stressed Andrew's meekness and innocence to expose her wickedness. Although none went so far as to suggest Andrew's canonization, they presented him as nearly saintly, and his suffering and patience—hallmarks of fourteenth-century sainthood—serve to render him within such texts a martyr sacrificed to his wife's ambition. As a result, chroniclers often portrayed Johanna and her companions torment-

---

101. Matthias Kaup and Robert E. Lerner, eds., "Gentile of Foligno Interprets the Prophecy 'Woe to the World,' with an Edition and English Translation," *Traditio* 56 (2001): 202–3.

102. Ibid., 203 n. 20.

103. Bowman, "Infamy and Proof in Medieval Spain," 98.

ing Andrew and living dissolutely, drunk on their own misbegotten power. The author of the later fourteenth-century *Storie Pistoresi*, for example, drew on reports that Johanna had willfully exposed Andrew to mockery to cast her and her court as villains who preyed on him and took advantage of his youth.[104] Domenico da Gravina (echoing Petrarch) describes Andrew as "a little lamb among wolves," badly treated by his queen and her court.[105] He dubs Andrew "the wretched duke" (*dux miser*) and describes his blind trust in those who wished him ill, leading him to acquiesce, with childlike trust, to his murderers' invitation to accompany them to Aversa.[106] Domenico goes on to report that Johanna failed to weep for Andrew and left his corpse unattended and unmourned until a canon took mercy on it and buried it in a manner befitting a king—suggesting that the canon recognized Andrew in death as the king he had been by right in life.[107] Domenico thus highlights Johanna's unnatural, unwifely behavior and the immorality of her court, portraying Andrew as the victim and his death the symptom of Johanna's illegitimate reign.

The Florentine chronicler Giovanni Villani (ca. 1280–1348)—like his brother and continuator Matteo (d. 1363) after him—sympathized more with the Hungarian than with the Neapolitan Angevins. The Villanis' attitudes were partisan, shaped by experience of the damage done to the Florentine banking economy after Robert of Naples's withdrawal of his investments in the early 1340s and by Johanna's tendency to default on loans from Florentine banks due to the disastrous state of the Neapolitan economy early in her reign.[108] Indeed, Giovanni Villani was financially ruined by the Florentine banking disasters of the 1340s. He thus had little reason to support Johanna, who was also entangled in events that struck Villani as dangerously portentous. In the later portions of his chronicle, he took a pessimistic view of the present and saw the many disasters of the 1340s as signs of an impending "cataclysm of cosmic dimensions."[109] He interpreted events in Naples as signs of the approaching apocalypse, and Louis of Hungary's vendetta

---

104. Barbi, *Storie Pistoresi*, 216. Interestingly, this account gives Andrew quasi-miraculous qualities: the murderers chose to strangle Andrew with a silken sash because of his invulnerability to iron.

105. Domenico da Gravina, *Chronicon*, 10: "duce Andrea praefato velut agniculo inter lupos."

106. Ibid., 15: "Dux autem miser, animo juvenili acquiescens verbis fallacibus iniquorum, ad venationem eamdem se promisit iturum."

107. Ibid., 18.

108. David Abulafia, "Southern Italy and the Florentine Economy, 1265–1370," *Economic History Review* 34 (August 1981): 387.

109. Louis Green, "Historical Interpretation in Fourteenth-Century Italian Chronicles," *Journal of the History of Ideas* 28 (April 1967): 168.

against his brother's murderers must have seemed both just and justified. For Villani, history was cyclical and retributive—sin and hubris were punished by divinely designed disaster. Thus, just as the Hohenstaufen (as both Louis Green and Trevor Dean have pointed out) fell to the Angevins, the Angevins themselves had to fall when their pride and sinfulness became too great.[110] Johanna's reign was symptomatic both of the Angevin dynasty's moral decline and of the disordered, calamity-riddled time in which Villani lived.

In Villani's retributive scheme of history, vendetta, whether private or public, was one means by which wrongdoing was punished. As Dean has argued, he frequently described situations in which women caused vendettas, their "lust or quarrels" triggering male violence.[111] Louis of Hungary's invasion of Naples was such a vendetta, one that Villani attributes to Johanna's sexual immorality. However, Dean softens Villani's indictment of Johanna in his analysis. Unlike other vengeance tales Villani tells whose origins lie in female behavior, it is not only Johanna's disorderly, lustful conduct that causes Andrew's death, but also Johanna herself: Villani portrays her as a direct participant in the violence that caused Louis's vendetta.

Villani concentrates in his account on Johanna's infidelity, representing her as responsible for her husband's grisly end and speculating that Andrew was not Charles Martel's father.[112] Villani describes Andrew as cuckolded many times over by his cousins and numerous others.[113] He argues that Johanna's avarice and dissolution kept Andrew—who had been designated her coinheritor—from the throne, and that she and her lovers, all of whom hoped to gain control of the kingdom and who played on Johanna's lust to dominate her, schemed to prevent his coronation. The conspirators decided to kill the "young and innocent king" and accordingly lured him to Aversa.[114] Villani describes Andrew's death at length, dwelling both on its indignity and on Johanna's reported failure to mourn and refusal to accord Andrew the funeral

---

110. Ibid.; Trevor Dean, "Marriage and Mutilation: Vendetta in Late Medieval Italy," *Past and Present* 157 (November 1997): 13.

111. Dean, "Marriage and Mutilation," 17.

112. Villani twice alludes to Charles Martel's dubious paternity, commenting darkly that Johanna claimed that he was Andrew's son. See G. Villani, *Nuova Cronica*, 3:419, 3:421. If he were shown not to be Andrew's son—which could be indicated by his mother's *fama*—he would be considered *spurius* under canon law, and therefore illegitimate and unable to inherit the Regno's throne.

113. G. Villani, *Nuova Cronica*, 3:417: "Invidia e avarizia di suoi cugini e consorti reali, i quali vizi guastano ogni bene, collo iscellerato vizio della disordinato lussuria della moglie, che palese si dicea che stava inn avoltero con messer Luigi figliuolo del prenze di Taranto suo cugino, e col figliuolo di Carlo d'Artugio, e con meser Iacopo Capano."

114. Ibid.

of which he was worthy. Her behavior thus flouts all conventions of appropriate wifely conduct. Andrew's death, as Villani portrays it, was the result of the fractured power structure in Naples and of Johanna's desire to protect her illegitimate position against his just claims. He explicitly locates the source of this fracture in Johanna's disordered sexuality—her *disordinata lussuria*—and equates the chaos of her amorous affairs with the chaos in Naples.

The account that most virulently attacks Johanna appears in the *Chronicon Estense*, written in the latter half of the fourteenth century for the Este lords of Ferrara. The Este took a keen interest in the Neapolitan court because of the 1304 marriage of Azzo d'Este and Beatrice of Naples, Robert's sister.[115] Questions of succession and legitimacy were particularly important to the Este during this period, and the problems posed by Johanna's succession may have seemed of particular import to the chronicler. Significantly, the most pressing fourteenth-century question of inheritance in Ferrara was rooted in Azzo's marital alliance to the Angevin house. When Azzo, who had promised Charles II to bestow his goods on his oldest legitimate male heir, found himself without legitimate heirs, he was forced to bequeath his possessions to the legitimate son of his oldest bastard, thus deviating from the earlier Este practice of dividing the patrimony among sons. In the process, Azzo disinherited his two brothers. In the struggle that followed, Azzo's heir, Fresco, allied himself with the papacy for protection. When his uncles' sons wrested Ferrara from the papacy in 1317, Azzo's line lost control of the city, and the papacy lost its valuable allegiance with the Este house, traditionally the leader of the Guelfs in the March of Treviso.[116]

Like other northern Italian ruling dynasties, the Este allowed illegitimate sons rather than legitimate daughters to inherit.[117] Inheritance among the lords of Ferrara was strongly patrilineal, dividing property among men at the expense of female offspring whose succession might allow power to pass through them to other families. Johanna's inheritance of the Neapolitan throne thus ran counter to inheritance practices in Ferrara. At the same time, her insistence that she rather than Andrew—a male descended from the senior male line—was the rightful ruler of Naples conflicted with the

---

115. Beatrice married Azzo in 1304. Trevor Dean argues that the alliance between the Este and Angevins "enhanced, or rekindled, animosities in northern Italy." See Trevor Dean, "The Sovereign as Pirate: Charles II of Anjou and the Marriage of His Daughter, 1304," *English Historical Review* 11 (April 1996): esp. 353–54.

116. Jane Fair Bestor, "Bastardy and Legitimacy in the Formation of a Regional State in Italy: The Estense Succession," *Comparative Studies in Society and History* 38 (July 1996): 561.

117. Ibid., 554.

hereditary principle to which Charles II had forced Azzo to adhere, with disastrous consequences for the Este. In the *Chronicon Estense*, therefore, the story of Andrew's death, which occurred during a time of dynastic turmoil in Ferrara, where Obizzo III (1294–1352) found himself without legitimate offspring, took on a heightened importance.[118] The chronicle presents Johanna's reign and Andrew's assassination as examples of the dangers of unjust succession and deviation from the male line.

The chronicler writes that the murder occurred due to the "voluptuousness of the harlot-wife of the king."[119] Johanna is characterized as a harlot (*meretrix*) throughout the account, and Andrew's murder is explicitly linked to her sexual licentiousness. In canon law, *meretrix* could mean both "commercial prostitute" and "loose woman," a semantic range of which the chronicler was surely aware, denigrating Johanna in terms similar to those employed by Boccaccio.[120] He describes how Johanna orchestrated all of the events surrounding the murder and lured Andrew to Aversa. There, he claims, the murderers, with the "consent of the aforesaid harlot," entered the royal couple's bedchamber and struggled with Andrew, suffocating him before throwing his body from the window into the garden below.[121]

The chronicler includes a macabre conversation between Johanna and Andrew's Hungarian nurse that illustrates the queen's nefarious character. Sensing—with a nurturing feminine intuition conspicuously lacking in Johanna—that something was amiss, Andrew's nurse entered the royal bedchamber, where she found the "harlot queen" seated on the bed. She asked Johanna—who knew, the chronicler claims, all that had happened—where Andrew was. Johanna replied (echoing Johanna's letter to Siena and Florence), "I do not know where he is. Your master is exceedingly immature." Receiving this unsatisfactory answer, the nurse went in search of Andrew. She discovered his body lying in the garden, but mistakenly thought he was sleeping. She then returned to the queen and told her, "Mistress, the king is sleeping in the garden," to which Johanna, knowing already that Andrew

118. Ibid., 564.

119. Guilio Bertoni and Emilio Paolo Vicini, eds., *Chronicon Estense, cum additamentis usque ad annum 1478*, vol. 15, pt. 3 of *RIS: Raccolta degli Storici Italiani del cinquecento al millecinquecento*, ed. L. A. Muratori, new ed. (Città di Castello: S. Lapi, 1908), 131: "ibique penitus deliberare mortem predicti regis, que omnia fiebant ex volunptate meretricis uxoris dicti regis."

120. See Ruth Mazo Karras, "Prostitution in Medieval Europe," in *Handbook of Medieval Sexuality*, ed. Vern L. Bullough and James A. Brundage (New York: Routledge, 2000), 244, as well as Karras, *Common Women: Prostitution and Sexuality in Medieval England* (Oxford: Oxford University Press, 1998), 131–42.

121. Bertoni and Vicini, *Chronicon Estense*, 131.

had been slain, callously replied, "Then let him sleep."[122] This episode emphasizes Johanna's ruthlessness, juxtaposing it with the appropriate feminine behavior exemplified by Andrew's loving nurse and marking Johanna as truly monstrous.

Johanna's guilt in the *Chronicon Estense* is compounded when she returns to Naples and buries Andrew under cover of darkness. The chronicler presents her as the worst of queens, contrasting her with Andrew, whose virtue and popularity underscore her perfidy. Knowing that her people loved Andrew, Johanna and her coconspirators fortified themselves in her castle, where they were accosted by an incensed mob. Johanna's subjects, according to the chronicler, surrounded the castle, crying, "Death to the traitors who killed our lord!" and "Death to the traitors and the harlot queen!"[123] Thus, Andrew's murder illustrates Johanna's malevolent character—the chronicler's primary concern. Through his description of Johanna's behavior during and after Andrew's death, the author of the *Chronicon Estense* presents her as a cunning usurper of her husband's position, tying his description of her political treachery to her sexual debauchery and effectively arguing that her flagrant immorality and unbridled sexuality rendered her rule illegitimate in the eyes of her subjects.

Sovereignty, Gender, and Inheritance in Late Medieval Europe

Historians of medieval Europe must struggle with the question of how reliable their sources are, particularly when it comes to chronicles. Chroniclers were not historians in the modern sense, and their understandings of the purposes of history are distinctly at variance with modern academic sensibilities. As Gabrielle M. Spiegel has pointed out, it is the task of the historian to analyze "the social logic of the text, its location within a broader network of social and intertextual relations" and to "seek to locate texts within specific social sites that themselves disclose the political, economic, and social pressures that condition a culture's discourse at any given moment."[124] In so doing, we must remember that the modern distinction between historical truth and fiction was of less concern to chroniclers than was depicting a deeper truth—one easily comprehensible to contemporary readers—that transcended the facts surrounding a given event. Paul Strohm argues that "fictionality [is] a

---

122. Ibid., 131–32.
123. Ibid., 132.
124. Gabrielle M. Spiegel, "History, Historicism, and the Social Logic of the Text in the Middle Ages," *Speculum* 65 (January 1990): 84, 85.

common characteristic" of medieval chronicles and that their "fictions offer irreplaceable historical evidence in their own right."[125] The fictions chroniclers built around a particular event had to be comprehensible; in building such comprehensible fictions authors made their texts "communicative and social act[s]."[126] Texts like chronicles are "flagrantly invented on the one hand but invented within historically and socially specific structures on the other."[127] They thus offer windows on the mindset and cultural understandings of their authors, the imaginary worlds they construct reflecting chroniclers' understanding of the world in which they lived. Indeed, chronicles' fictionality was crucial to their function; as Suzanne Fleishmann has argued, medieval chronicles were the forerunners of the novel and perform "the exemplary function which certain theorists have reserved for fiction."[128] They allowed their authors to communicate a larger lesson or meaning that could be derived from events about which they heard, imagined, or witnessed and then amplified by adding dialog and dramatic embellishment. The stories told in chronicles, as by letter writers like Petrarch, could, in a sense, be truer than the truth. The historical fictions that fourteenth-century chroniclers grafted onto the story of Andrew of Hungary's murder must thus be read both as descriptions of specific events and circumstances and as commentaries about contemporary conditions that chroniclers as historians and storytellers were empowered to articulate.

Johanna's succession to the Neapolitan throne was in many ways an extraordinary event. She became a regnant queen as Naples was losing the support of many of the northern Italian communes, when the papacy was growing weaker as a territorial power in Italy and losing many of its traditional allies, and when laws of succession and inheritance were hardening to bar women from positions of dynastic power. Indeed, throughout most of Italy, women could not inherit immovable property of any sort, let alone large and influential kingdoms.[129] As Naples's monarch, Johanna became the representative of a dynasty in which primogeniture and agnatic succession had long been favored and ahead of not one but many male relatives whose

---

125. Paul Strohm, *Hochon's Arrow: The Social Imagination of Fourteenth-Century Texts* (Princeton: Princeton University Press, 1992), 4.

126. Ibid., 6.

127. Ibid., 99.

128. Suzanne Fleischman, "On the Representation of History and Fiction in the Middle Ages," *History and Theory* 22 (October 1983): 278.

129. Stanley Chojnacki, "Patrician Women in Early Renaissance Venice," *Studies in the Renaissance* 21 (1974): 178.

claims to her throne many of her contemporaries viewed as legitimate. In an age when Angevin kings had been seen as quasi-sacerdotal champions of the Church and Angevin blood was understood to confer holiness, the succession of a young and reportedly immoral woman to the Angevin royal title was in itself remarkable.

Andrew's murder was even more remarkable and outrageous. It was inevitable that the story of his death should have found its way into literature of all types. Yet how authors interpreted the murder and what they chose to say about it reveals far more about their reactions to the Angevin succession than about the circumstances of the murder itself. The men who wrote about the Neapolitan regicide were clerics or, like Villani, members of an emergent merchant class with vested interest in the political affairs of Italy and the stability of their male-dominated, patrilineal society. Johanna's queenship—which violated commonly accepted norms of inheritance and sovereignty, not to mention femininity—and the early disasters of her reign were thus frightening, threatening, and titillating by turns. Her cultural presence was powerful, and chroniclers who wrote about the early years of her reign grappled with what she represented and what her reign portended.

The anxieties many felt about regnant queenship and the doubtless genuine shock and horror that Andrew's murder inspired were joined to the political and religious concerns of those who wrote about Johanna. They had at hand a long-standing rhetorical tradition that associated women as "unredeemed flesh" with carnality and deceitfulness with which to malign her.[130] Indeed, their criticisms of Johanna both accused her of failing to embody tropes of feminine virtue and of being too female. It was a truism—one as effective in satire as in moral texts—in late medieval literature that, in the (ironic) words of Andreas Capellanus,

> Every woman in the world is . . . lustful. A woman may be eminent in distinction and rank and a man most cheap and contemptible, but if she discovers that he is sexually virile she does not refuse to sleep with him. But no man however virile could satiate a woman's lust by any means.[131]

Boccaccio's adulterous Neapolitan noblewoman, Fiammetta, like many of the women in his *Decameron*, exemplifies this tradition of oversexed literary

130. Michael A. Calabrese, "Feminism and the Packaging of Boccaccio's Fiammetta," *Italica* 74 (Spring 1997): 29.

131. Andreas Capellanus, *On Love*, translated in Blamires, *Woman Defamed and Woman Defended*, 123.

women, and it is impossible not to see contemporary textual portrayals of Johanna as part of a larger, flourishing trope. Indeed, it was an obvious trope with which to malign her, as so many of the stock antifeminist exempla in the medieval canon revolved around libidinous or unfaithful queens, such as Guinevere and Eufeme, the treacherous queen of the thirteenth-century *Roman de Silence*. In fact, queenly adultery was a cornerstone of medieval romance—as Peggy McCracken has argued, in romance, "there are only two stories to tell about the royal female body: a tale of maternity or a story of adultery."[132]

This is not to deny that Johanna may have engaged in much of the behavior of which she was accused—we cannot know whether she did or not—but the literary preoccupation with her sexuality is telling and significant, reflective of a general "preoccupation with queenly sexuality" among medieval chroniclers, but also reflective of Johanna's special circumstances.[133] On the one hand, the easiest, clearest way to defame a queen was to cast aspersions on her chastity, while on the other, exposing the perceived moral failings of a woman in a position of power was one of the few mechanisms available for punishing her transgressions. The *Decretum* classifies adultery as one of the worst sexual sins, far more egregious than mere fornication.[134] As such, its penalties were quite severe, particularly for women, who were treated in canon law as the offenders in adultery cases.[135] Most frequently, adulteresses were punished via humiliation, for instance by being paraded through city streets with their heads shaved.[136] Accounts of Johanna's adultery served in part to punish her by humiliating her and making her shame public. She went unpunished under law, but her textual shaming acted as what Muir has called a "literary substitute" for revenge.[137]

The attack on Johanna's sexual morality also served, however, as a referendum both on her rule and on the concept of regnant queenship. It drew on timeworn and commonly accepted—and therefore potent and believable—tropes to defame Johanna, providing literary proof of her *mala fama* that was also an unrealized but legally plausible argument for her depo-

---

132. Peggy McCracken, *The Romance of Adultery: Queenship and Sexual Transgression in Old French Literature* (Philadelphia: University of Pennsylvania Press, 1998), 47.

133. Parsons, "Introduction," 6.

134. James A. Brundage, "Sex and Canon Law," in Bullough and Brundage, *Handbook of Medieval Sexuality*, 40.

135. Ibid., 42.

136. Ibid.; Akehurst, "Good Name, Reputation, and Notoriety," 89.

137. Muir, *Mad Blood Stirring*, 132.

sition. The two crimes of which she stood accused—adultery and husband murder—were intimately linked, arising from and reinforcing one another. Female sexuality was commonly held to transgress natural law in ways that "attack the integrity of the family," giving rise to "adultery, incest, and the murder of parents, husbands, and children."[138] Inherent in the very concept of active female sexuality was the threat of violence against men, a fear that led the natural philosopher Pseudo-Albertus Magnus to elaborate a medieval version of the myth of the *vagina dentate*, charging that "some women or harlots"—"out of vindictiveness and malice," a commentator adds—insert metal spikes into their vaginas because "they wish to injure the penis."[139] At its most extreme, such antifeminist diatribe described women as actively predatory, preying on men because of an inborn antipathy. At the same time, as Carol Lansing notes, "the irrational appetite that is the source of violent injustice was considered feminine," while "immoderate appetite" (in the gastronomic or sexual sense) "led to violence and political injustice" in late medieval Tuscan texts.[140] In attacking Johanna's sexuality, chroniclers partook in a long-standing tradition vilifying powerful women that extended forward in time from Roman descriptions of Cleopatra and Messalina and would later be used to defame Margaret of Anjou—Shakespeare's "She-Wolf of France"—who was also smeared as monstrous and adulterous by those seeking to curtail her power.[141]

All of the narratives designed to defame Johanna ultimately act as illustrations of her unfitness to rule. They begin with the understanding that Andrew was the rightful king of Naples through descent and inheritance, making Johanna's usurpation doubly unjust. In the accounts of Andrew's murder written in the years following his death, these factors shape the narrative. Underlying these narratives is a concern with female rule—articulated in terms of uncontrollable, destructive feminine sexuality easily manipulated by Johanna's lovers—that renders these stories effectively parables about the dangers of queenship and the outcome of illegitimate power. Obscuring the historical fact of Robert's designation of Johanna as his heir, they seek to demonstrate Johanna's usurpation and incapacity by presenting her as an

---

138. Cadden, *Meanings of Sex Difference in the Middle Ages*, 223, paraphrasing Alan of Lille.

139. Pseudo-Albertus Magnus and Commentator B, in Lemay, *De secretis mulierum*, 88–89.

140. Carol Lansing, "Gender and Civic Authority: Sexual Control in a Medieval Italian Town," *Journal of Social History* 31 (Autumn, 1997): 42.

141. *Henry VI, part II*, act 1, scene 4, line 137. On Margaret's characterization as a she-wolf, see Patricia-Ann Lee, "Reflections of Power: Margaret of Anjou and the Dark Side of Queenship," *Renaissance Quarterly* 39 (Summer 1986): 183–217.

adulteress and viricide. Thus, the story of Andrew's murder was constructed as a tale about the destruction of masculine prerogative and the triumph of illegitimate female rule, described as the triumph of chaos, immorality, and injustice. In the process, Johanna herself became an archetypal she-wolf, one whose *fama* testified against her right or ability to rule.

🦊 CHAPTER 2

From She-Wolf to Radiant Queen

*The Reign of Louis of Taranto and the
Rehabilitation of Johanna of Naples*

> In the weaker sex a zeal for virtue is more laudable. . . .
> We read that plenty of women have shown the courage
> of men or have even surpassed men, and because of their
> brave heart have earned a just reward and well-deserved
> praise. . . . Eternal praise surrounds Queen Esther, for
> even though married to a cruel tyrant, like lamb to
> wolf, she did not fear, at the risk of her life, to enter the
> doorway through which no one came out who had not
> been ordered to enter. She risked her own safety for the
> sake of her own nation.
>
> Marbod of Rennes (ca. 1035–1123), *The Good Woman*,
> from *The Book with Ten Chapters*

> To the woman He said, "I will greatly multiply your
> pain in childbearing; in pain you shall bring forth
> children, yet your desire shall be for your husband,
> and he shall rule over you."
>
> Genesis 3:16

Giovanni Boccaccio begins his *De mulieribus claris* (*On Famous Women*) by saying that he initially planned to dedicate it to Johanna of Naples, "that radiant splendor of Italy, that unique glory not only of women but of rulers." In the end, he dedicated his "little book" (*opusculum*) to Andrea Acciaiuoli, countess of Altavilla and sister to Niccolò Acciaiuoli, Naples's grand seneschal. Elaborating on his first choice, Boccaccio explains that it seemed appropriate to dedicate a book about women to a woman; Johanna was the ideal candidate because of "the brilliance of her celebrated family and forebears as well as the more recent praises her own brave spirit had won." Still, a book about famous women could not ignore one of the most famous women of Boccaccio's century, and he devoted the final chapter to Johanna. In it, he extols her wisdom, strength of character, and fortitude, praising her capacity to withstand trials that were "the fault of others" and that led to her undeserved infamy. Her successes, he says, "would have been magnificent accomplishments for a vigorous and mighty king, much less for a woman."[1]

At first glance, Boccaccio's lavish praise of a woman he had earlier branded a she-wolf is incongruous. Yet time and circumstance had helped amend Johanna's reputation. Boccaccio immortalized Johanna as a virtuous queen whose misfortunes were of others' making and whose "lofty and indomitable spirit" rendered her the equal of any king—an assessment that accorded well with contemporary opinion.[2] He describes her trials in the face of war and civil strife and exonerates her of responsibility, depicting her as a paragon of virtue, both sovereign and feminine. Boccaccio was a consummate rhetorician, and his praise of Johanna should not be read simply as a change of heart. It may have been calculated, among other things, to win him court patronage.[3] Nonetheless, his voice was a significant one, and Boccaccio's portrayal of Johanna was important for her reputation, reflecting a transformed political climate and a time when attitudes toward her had changed dramatically.

The transformation of Johanna's image between 1345 and 1362 can be directly linked to the activities of two antagonists. The first was Louis of Hungary, whose vendetta against Johanna met first with the approbation and then with the strong disapproval and even horror of many observers. The other was her second husband, Louis of Taranto. Louis and his powerful advisor, Niccolò Acciaiuoli, deliberately re-created Johanna's image, absorbing her into a fictitious sovereign entity comprised of two bodies with a single voice—that of Louis, who ruled Naples in his own name between 1352 and 1362. Louis's successful bid for power, coupled with his reportedly disastrous reign, awakened sympathies for his wife. Between them, these two kings Louis transformed Johanna in the public imaginary from a usurping, power-hungry adulteress into a long-suffering, appropriately feminine, and (femininely) abused queen whose rightful position and power had been usurped.

---

1. Giovanni Boccaccio, *Famous Women*, ed. and trans. Virginia Brown (Cambridge, MA: Harvard University Press, 2001), 2/3.

2. Ibid., 2: "erecto invictoque . . . animo."

3. On Boccaccio's choice of dedicatee and quest for patronage, see Margaret Ann Franklin, *Boccaccio's Heroines: Power and Virtue in Renaissance Society* (Aldershot: Ashgate, 2006), esp. 23–30. Significantly, Boccaccio maintained his praise of Johanna in later redactions of the text, completed after he had declined her 1371 invitation to court. On the textual evolution of *De mulieribus claris*, see Vittorio Zaccaria, "Le fasi redazionali de '*De mulieribus claris*,'" *Studi sul Boccaccio* 1 (1963): 253–332.

The Consequences of the Hungarian Invasion

In 1347, as Louis of Hungary's forces marched down the Italian peninsula to avenge his brother's death, they met with widespread support. Contemporaries interpreted Louis's actions as part of a "common culture of revenge killing" that made his vendetta just and comprehensible.[4] The author of the *Chronicon Estense* writes that Louis traveled from town to town, received "with great honor," and he is echoed by most chronicle accounts of the period.[5] Moral support extended to military aid. The rulers of northern Italy either maintained neutrality (as in the case of Florence) or, like the Este lords of Ferrara and the Malatesta of Rimini, flocked to Louis's banner. Cola di Rienzo (1313–54), Rome's self-proclaimed tribune, supported the Hungarians enthusiastically in return for military aid and the county of Provence, to be ceded to Rome upon Louis's victory.[6] Beyond Italy, particularly in the empire, observers were sympathetic to Louis of Hungary as well, condemning Johanna as a murderess. The chronicler Mathias von Neuenburg reports that not only Johanna and Louis of Taranto but also the pope and some of the cardinals were widely suspected of guilt in Andrew's death.[7] He and other German chroniclers joined their voices to the chorus lauding Louis's vendetta, while German noblemen and mercenaries swelled the ranks of his army.

Boccaccio, who was in the service of Francesco Ordelaffi in Forlì at the time, initially followed his patron's example in supporting Louis of Hungary. Scholars debate whether Boccaccio actually traveled to Naples with Francesco, but he was certainly present in December 1347 when Francesco hosted Louis in Forlì.[8] His third eclogue describes Louis's (Tityrus) anger and descent into Italy:

> When Tityrus heard it
> in his hollow cliff beside the Hyster

---

4. Muir, *Mad Blood Stirring*, xxi.

5. Bertoni and Vicini, *Chronicon Estense*, 156. Chronicles of the period describe the welcome Louis received throughout Italy. For instance, in Modena, Louis and his entire retinue were treated to a lavish feast. Giovanni da Bazzano, *Chronicon Mutinense*, 141.

6. Léonard, *Les Angevins de Naples*, 353. See also Ronald G. Musto, *Apocalypse in Rome: Cola di Rienzo and the Politics of the New Age* (Berkeley: University of California Press, 2003), 166–69. Both Louis of Hungary and Johanna sent emissaries and lavish gifts to Cola, seeking his support, and their representatives argued their cases before a Roman tribunal.

7. Mathias of Neuenburg, *Die Chronik des Mathias von Neuenburg*, ed. Adolf Hofmeister, Monumenta Germaniae Historica, Scriptores Rerum Germanicarum, new series, 4 (Berlin: Weidmann, 1955), 166.

8. Branca, *Boccaccio*, 73–74.

> he wept and summoned from the Danube valleys
> innumerable dogs and toughened ploughmen,
> gnashing his teeth; and leaving flocks and woods,
> he headed out to tear down the vile forest,
> and seeks to catch the wolf and tawny lions,
> to punish those who merit it; for Tityrus
> was brother to Alexis. Do you recall
> not long ago having seen him raging,
> carrying the sharp iron hunting spear,
> and many men behind him carrying nets
> upon their shoulders as, trembling with fury,
> he crossed this way through the entire forest?[9]

As Boccaccio portrays it, Louis's mission is just and his quarry only "those who merit it"—Johanna (the wolf) and her coconspirators (the lions). He thus frames Louis's invasion as a classic revenge narrative, employing language that equates vengeance with hunting, the dehumanized prey—placed outside the bounds of civilization—represented as animals, while Louis, the hunter, is "exempted . . . from the normal responsibilities of civilized mankind" because of his quarry's bestiality.[10]

Many heralded Louis's conquest of Naples as a triumph. Domenico da Gravina reports that the Regno's subjects met Louis in Aversa to offer him the crown "with exultant spirits."[11] The *Chronicon Estense* describes Louis's passage as marked by easy victories and festivity, while Johanna "was defamed throughout the entire world."[12] According to Marco Battagli of Rimini, Louis easily "subdued the entire Regno without great violence."[13] His effortless conquest and the apparent joy of his new subjects proved the righteousness of Louis's cause.

Louis's behavior subsequent to his seizure of the Regno, however, alienated many observers. Charles, Louis, and Robert of Durazzo and Robert and Philip of Taranto rode out to meet him in Aversa, resolved to greet him as their ruler after they realized he would triumph. Numerous chroniclers describe their actions as honorable and applaud their decision. Louis seemed

---

9. *Eclogue* III. Faunus, lines 95–108, in Boccaccio, *Eclogues*, 27–28.

10. Muir, *Mad Blood Stirring*, xxvii.

11. Domenico da Gravina, *Chronicon*, 36.

12. Bertoni and Vicini, *Chronicon Estense*, 157.

13. Marco Battagli da Rimini, *Marcha di Marco Battagli da Rimini* [AA. 1212–1354], ed. Aldo Francesco Massèra, vol. 16, pt. 3 of *RIS*, new ed. (Città di Castello: S. Lapi, 1912), 53.

to receive them honorably as well, and many accounts report that he spent several days feasting with them before he had the two younger Durazzeschi and the Tarantini arrested (ultimately to be taken to Hungary as hostages) and summarily executed Charles of Durazzo.

Charles of Durazzo's execution captured many chroniclers' imaginations and represents a turning point in treatments of the Hungarian conquest. Giovanni da Bazzano describes how Louis of Hungary, wrongly believing Charles culpable for Andrew's murder, ordered the duke to show him where Andrew died and then had him decapitated on the spot.[14] A Bolognese chronicler imagined a more gruesome scene:

> The duke led the king to the place, and when they were there, the duke said: "Holy Crown, here your brother Andrew was killed." Then the enraged king drew a knife and cut off the duke's nose with his own hand, and immediately a Hungarian knight seized the duke by the hair, dragging him through all of the rooms of the palace. Another Hungarian struck the duke with a sword in the ribs in such a way that he soon died. Then the king commanded that no one move the duke's corpse, and, having done this, he and all his armed men moved toward Naples.[15]

There are numerous variants of this story. Some allege that Charles was defenestrated, others that he was decapitated or hanged. Many repeat the charge that Charles remained unburied (as Andrew was rumored to have been), and many depict Louis personally dispatching his cousin. The common theme is the violence and arbitrariness of Charles's death. Chroniclers highlighted its irregularity, stressing that it occurred not by legal process but by Louis's outraged whim.

This ominous beginning to Louis's rule set the tone for his brief ascendancy in Naples. Charles's execution made him many enemies, including the bulk of the Neapolitan nobility, who began to work for Johanna's return.[16] Louis emerges from contemporary accounts as paranoid and autocratic. He conducted investigations and meted out harsh reprisals throughout the Regno, without exercising a level of discernment that would have justified his actions.[17] He exacted extreme demonstrations of loyalty from

---

14. Giovanni da Bazzano, *Chronicon Mutinense*, 145.
15. Albano Sorbelli, ed., *Corpus Chronicorum Bononiensium*, vol. 18, pt. 1, vol. 2 of *RIS*, new ed. (Bologna: Nicola Zanichelli, 1939), 582–83 (Cronaca B).
16. Léonard, *Histoire de Jeanne Ire*, 2:111.
17. Ibid., 116.

the nobility and openly preferred his Hungarian and German supporters. Some chronicles report that nobles whose loyalty Louis suspected were horribly tortured and executed, as in the case of Corrado di Catanzaro, said to have been slowly killed by a wheel fitted with razors.[18] At the same time, nobles who remained loyal to Johanna were popularly lauded as heroes. Foremost among these was Niccolò Acciaiuoli's son, Lorenzo, who valiantly defended the castle at Melfi, the center of the revolt against Hungarian domination.[19]

For Johanna herself, one of the most important and immediate effects of Louis of Hungary's behavior was its impact on Clement VI. The pope's protection and ultimate exoneration of Johanna owed a great deal to his anger with Louis. Louis's invasion of Naples constituted an attack on the papacy, the kingdom's suzerain. Petrarch embarked on a papal mission to the northern Italian communes to demand that they deny the Hungarian army passage, prompting demonstrations of piety by Louis—under threat of imminent excommunication—calculated to counter the appearance that he was an enemy of the church.[20] His anger with Louis, combined with Johanna's long-standing relationship with Clement and her position as his ward, prompted the pope to a vigorous defense of Johanna.

In a letter to Louis dated May 7, 1348, Clement chastises him and asserts Johanna's right to the throne "ex testamento clare memorie Roberti, Regis Sicilie."[21] He takes Louis to task for crimes against Naples and the Church, citing not only the invasion but also his removal of Charles Martel from Naples, his execution of Charles of Durazzo, his behavior toward the Angevin princes, and his slurs against Cardinal Élie de Talleyrand of Périgord (uncle to the Durazzeschi) as reasons for his anger. Furthermore, the pope rebukes him for harboring both Cola di Rienzo ("excommunicate and deeply suspected of heresy") and the Swabian mercenary Werner of Urslingen (ca. 1308–54) (that "wicked man and son of perdition").[22]

---

18. The story is told by both Domenico da Gravina and Giovanni da Bazzano. Cf. Léonard, *Histoire de Jeanne Ire*, 2:117.

19. In an autobiographical letter to Angelo Soderini (written in late 1364), Niccolò Acciaiuoli boasted of his son's accomplishments. See "Appendice: Lettera di Niccola Acciaioli ad Angelo Soderini (26 decembre 1364)," in Matteo Palmieri, *Vita Nicolai Acciaioli*, ed. Gino Scaramella, vol. 13, pt. 2 of *RIS*, new ed. (Bologna: Nicola Zanichelli, 1934), 41. Cf. Léonard, *Histoire de Jeanne Ire*, 2:118.

20. Léonard, *Histoire de Jeanne Ire*, 2:10–11.

21. E. Déprez, J. Glénisson, and G. Mollat, eds. *Clement VI (1342–1352)—Lettres se rapportant à la France, publiées ou analysées d'après les registres du Vatican* (Paris: A. Fontemoing, 1925), Annus Sextus, 463, no. 3852.

22. Ibid., 463–67.

This letter represents a marked shift in Clement's attitude. He had maintained a more neutral and even affectionate tone toward Louis early in the Hungarian invasion (although he urged Johanna's subjects to remain loyal to her).[23] Over time, however, Louis's actions displaced Clement's anger from Johanna—whose conduct toward Andrew and behavior after the murder he had strongly criticized—onto himself. Increasingly, Clement expressed sympathy for Johanna, writing to Humbert, the ruler of the Dauphiné, for instance, of the poverty in which she found herself.[24] Louis's behavior also prompted Clement to vocal, public denunciation of the Hungarian king, marshaling the weight of papal approval and protection for Johanna's cause and rendering Louis, at least in papal rhetoric, the enemy of the Church.

The second consequence, more important for Johanna's reputation, was a shift in the attitude of contemporary commentators. Louis's behavior toward his relatives and the brutality with which he treated his new subjects disillusioned many of his erstwhile supporters. Disillusionment deepened into resentment with Louis's sudden departure from the kingdom during the Black Death and his subsequent campaign, which generated still more suffering in the Regno. His deeds met with stark disapproval, and many of his contemporaries viewed his treatment of the Neapolitan princes in particular as an inexcusable breach of honor. Domenico da Gravina maintained that executing Charles of Durazzo was Louis of Hungary's gravest error.[25] The author of a Sienese chronicle describes the honorable reception prepared for Louis by his cousins and says that he "did not keep faith with those princes," while Matteo Villani writes that Louis's cruelty came to be known throughout the Regno.[26] Giovanni da Bazzano deplores the king's conduct, saying that he acted "fraudulently and unjustly." He likewise condemns young Charles Martel's removal from Naples.[27] Louis's vendetta, tainted by unrighteous violence, accrued detractors, transforming Louis himself from a justly vengeful brother into a volatile and unjust usurper.

---

23. Léonard, *Histoire de Jeanne Ire*, 2:94.

24. Déprez, Glénisson, and Mollat, *Clement VI*, Annus Sextus, 447, no. 3782 (dated Avignon, March 20, 1348). Cf. Léonard, *Histoire de Jeanne Ire*, 2:93.

25. Domenico da Gravina, *Chronicon*, 36–37.

26. "*Cronaca Senese*, attribuita ad Agnolo di Tura del Grasso, detta *la Cronaca Maggiore*," in Alessandro Lisini and Fabio Iacometti, eds., *Cronache Senesi*, vol. 15, pt. 6 of *RIS* (Bologna: Nicola Zanichelli, 1931), 553–54: "non osservò la fede a li detti reali"; Matteo Villani, *Cronica, con la continuazione di Filippo Villani*. ed. Giuseppe Porta, 2 vols. (Parma: Ugo Guanda, 1995), I.12–I.13, 1:28–31, esp. 31.

27. Giovanni da Bazzano, *Chronicon Mutinense*, 145.

Commentators were most disturbed by the consequences of Louis's invasion for the Regno and its people. Petrarch—self-consciously and proudly Italian—professed horror at the thought of Hungarian soldiers marching unchecked through Italy. Writing to Barbato da Sulmona, he hoped that Louis's vendetta would "strike the guilty heads with a proper punishment," recognizing that "such a detestable deed could not remain unpunished." Petrarch goes on, however, to note that Louis's "revenge is considerably more serious than [he] feared," characterizing the Hungarians as barbarians.[28] Faced with the suffering that Louis's invasion imposed on "the innocent multitude," Petrarch could not but deplore it, a sentiment heightened by his preference for Louis of Taranto and Johanna, who were at least Italian, in Petrarch's estimation.[29] Indeed, in a 1351 letter to Acciaiuoli, he rejoiced that Louis of Taranto had driven away the barbarians, leaving the Roman heritage where it belonged: in Italian hands.[30]

Boccaccio too came to lament the impact of the invasion. Vittore Branca describes Boccaccio's opinions about the Angevin struggle as

> oscillating from positions favorable to King Louis [of Hungary] and from accusations of Jo[h]anna and the [Tarantini] . . . all the way to deprecation of Hungarian ferocity and kindly judgments of [Louis] of Taranto and his followers, to regrets for the good old times of King Robert, to eulogies of [Johanna and Louis of Taranto]. . . . From invective, he passed in turn to the palinode, to the elegy, to the paean.[31]

Boccaccio's confusion stemmed, at least in part, from the harsh realities of the invasion. If Louis's vendetta garnered widespread support in the abstract, fueled by negative perceptions of Johanna, its conclusion left little room for

---

28. *Epistolae familiares*, VII,1, trans. in Petrarch, *Rerum familiarium*, 331. The Latin reads: "non poterat tam fedum facinus impunitum esse, et est ultio hec aliquanto serior quam putavi. Verte autem, Deus, iram tuam in auctores scelerum et noxia capita digno supplicio feri" (Francesco Petrarch, *Le Familiari*, critical edition, ed. Vittorio Rossi [Florence: G. C. Sansoni, 1968], 2:95.)

29. Petrarch, *Rerum familiarium*, 331 (Petrarch, *Le Familiari*, 2:95).

30. *Epistolae familiares*, XI,13, trans. in Petrarch, *Rerum familiarium libri, IX–XXIV.* 2 vols. trans. Aldo S. Bernardo (Baltimore: Johns Hopkins University Press, 1982–1985), 115–16. On Petrarch's assessment of Louis's and Johanna's Italian character, see Patrick Gilli, "L'intégration manquée des Angevins en Italie: Le témoignage des historiens," in Istituto Storico Italiano per il Medio Evo, *L'État Angevin: Pouvoir, culture et société entre XIIIe et XIVe siècle. Actes du colloque international organizé par l'American Academy in Rome, l'École française de Rome, l'Istituto storico italiano per il Medio Evo, l'U.M.R. Telemme et l'Université de Provence, l'Università degli studi di Napoli "Federico II" (Rome-Naples, 7–11 novembre 1995)* (Rome: Istituto Storico Italiano per il Medio Evo, 1998), esp. 24–25.

31. Branca, *Boccaccio*, 74–75.

celebration. Boccaccio found himself, after the "dramatic and ferocious turn in the Hungarian expedition," unable to praise a "harsh and violent military occupation."[32]

Boccaccio describes Louis of Hungary's fury and its consequences in his fourth eclogue, *Dorus*. Louis's poetic alter ego, now called Polyphemus,

> kindled with righteous rage and wrath rushed down
> just as a torrent, swollen with winter rains,
> sweeps down the lofty mountain, far resounding,
> uproots these trees, shakes those, and proudly dragging
> mighty rocks, hurls them upon the crags.
> And not before with a ferocious vengeance
> he'd torn apart the guilty, not before
> he'd fouled the starry faces with the blood
> and mutilated corpse of guiltless Paphus,
> or heaped with chains the boys who pleased the nymphs,
> could furor dwindle in that ruthless man.[33]

Although his cause is still just, Louis has become "that ruthless man." His humanity is diminished as well: No longer a heroic hunter, Louis is now a monstrous Cyclopes. Significantly, Boccaccio uses the word *rabie*—previously used to characterize the maddened, pregnant she-wolf of Eclogue III—to describe Louis's wrath, which renders him inhuman. His rabid vengeance has encompassed those who, like Charles of Durazzo (Paphus) and the captive princes (the boys in chains), were guiltless.[34] He is "more vicious than a snake," and Boccaccio describes him stripping orchards bare, filling streams with blood, and killing livestock.[35] Even if Louis's anger was justified, its consequences for the Regno were terrible.

Boccaccio's fifth eclogue, *The Falling Forest*, elaborates on the Regno's destruction and describes his own grief. He depicts the kingdom as a burning, demolished forest: "oaks have crashed, the mighty cypress fallen, / the Italian oak is burning with set fires / in every part, no pine remains."[36] Naples,

---

32. Ibid., 76.

33. *Eclogue IV Dorus*, lines 65–75, in Boccaccio, *Eclogues*, 35. On Boccaccio's renaming of Louis of Hungary, see ibid., 216, n. 62.

34. His ascription of innocence to the Neapolitan princes already represents a change in Boccaccio's perception of events in Naples. Apparently, between writing his third and fourth eclogues, Boccaccio became convinced that they were not responsible for Andrew's death.

35. *Eclogue IV Dorus*, lines 76–83.

36. *Eclogue V Silva Cadens*, lines 78–80, in Boccaccio, *Eclogues*, 46–47.

where Boccaccio passed his youth, was irreparably altered, so that "all beauty here has perished / but grief and care remain."[37] Unready to forgive Johanna and Louis of Taranto—whose poetic counterparts, Liquoris and Alcestus, have "departed full of fear" and "left the wood in doubt / and sailed away"—Boccaccio nonetheless condemns the damage inflicted by Louis of Hungary's savagery.[38]

By the time Boccaccio wrote his sixth eclogue, probably completed around the time of Louis of Taranto's death in 1362,[39] his sentiments regarding the two kings Louis were unambiguous. Louis of Taranto in the guise of Alcestus has replaced Louis of Hungary, "savage Polyphemus," as Naples's ruler. As a consequence, Boccaccio writes, tears can cease, because "the wandering shepherds and their straying flocks / are all come back to us just as before; / with joy the woods grow green and valleys echo."[40] From a righteous vendetta, Louis of Hungary's mission of vengeance was transformed into a barbaric invasion. In the process, Louis himself was transformed into a barbarian, a monster on par with Johanna's bestial alter ego in Eclogue III, with the correlative effect that Louis of Taranto and, ultimately, Johanna, became, as his opponents, the righteous saviors of the devastated Regno.

Louis of Hungary's invasion thus had important ramifications for Johanna's position and reputation. Most immediately, it improved her standing with Clement VI. Following the Hungarian conquest of Naples, Clement regularized Johanna and Louis of Taranto's marriage and helped finance their return to Naples. He also continued to affirm Johanna's innocence, paving the way for her official exoneration. The longer-term and more intangible impact of Louis of Hungary's invasion was to diminish the pro-Hungarian sentiments of many observers. If commentators did not wholeheartedly embrace Johanna and reject Louis of Hungary, their praise of him was tempered or transformed into criticism. As support for his vendetta declined, so too did arguments against Johanna's right to rule Naples. By making Johanna and Louis of Taranto's rule preferable to his own, Louis of Hungary inadvertently facilitated their triumphant return as Naples's champions.

---

37. Ibid., 48, line 115.

38. Ibid., lines 113–14.

39. Boccaccio explains that the king is called Alcestus because "near the end of his life" he adopted the manners of "an excellent and virtuous king" (Boccaccio, *Eclogues*, 215).

40. *Eclogue VI. Alcestus*, lines 12–15 in Boccaccio, *Eclogues*, 52, 53.

The Reign of Louis of Taranto

Scenes from a Marriage

Johanna's Victorian biographer, Welbore St. Clair Baddeley, represents Louis of Taranto as the source of a "love that marriage did not previously bring to her."[41] Baddeley, who celebrated Johanna as a "proud, handsome, and courageous lady" who was, "from no fault of her own, exposed to constant and most bewildering perils," maintained that Louis of Taranto and Niccolò Acciaiuoli, who "knew not merely how to judge of these troubles, but how to deal with their contrivers," shielded her from slander and trouble during Louis's reign. He describes Louis in glowing terms, stating that "birth and wise training had made the King a master of Apulian and Angevine [*sic*] politics" and that he was "a man reliable in word and deed, fully justifying the wisdom of [Johanna's] marital choice."[42]

Baddeley interpreted Johanna's second marriage as a period of solace and peace. Louis's "love, intelligence and personal prowess . . . enabled her to support and endure the burthen of incessant trials" and to turn her attention from the distractions of rulership to "the delights of life, especially . . . of Art and Literature."[43] Baddeley's Johanna was thus allowed a Victorian ideal of feminine happiness. Freed from the onerous responsibilities of rulership to focus on more fulfilling pursuits, she formed a blissful partnership with Louis in which each performed the function most suited to his or her sex.

Baddeley could describe these years of Johanna's life as an idyllic existence of "listening to Petrarch's eloquence, to Strada's poems, or to the musical literary pictures of Boccaccio" largely because Johanna all but disappears as an independent actor from legislative records.[44] Indeed, she largely disappears as an individual from contemporary chronicles, at least as an object of ridicule and criticism. Émile Léonard, though no admirer of Louis, devoted much of the second and nearly all of the third volume of his study of Johanna's reign to Louis because of the dearth of evidence about Johanna herself from this period. However, her disappearance owed less to domestic felicity than to deliberate exclusion from government. The picture of Johanna's life that emerges from royal and papal correspondence and from some contemporary chronicle reports dating to Louis's reign is one not of happy courtly activity but rather of struggle, coercion, and, at times, virtual imprisonment.

---

41. Baddeley, *Queen Joanna I of Naples*, 60.
42. Ibid., 194.
43. Ibid., 191–92.
44. Ibid.

Official Angevin records that survive support Baddeley's fantasy. Legislation from the period following Johanna and Louis's return to Naples in 1348 through Louis's death in 1362 was almost always issued in both monarchs' names. This was exclusively the case after 1350. The need to combat Louis of Hungary gave Johanna and Louis of Taranto a common enemy, and much of their energy—along with international attention—focused on their shared endeavor of regaining the Regno. Official letters sent by Johanna after Louis died speak of her bereavement and of her husband's worth, while Louis's letters represent Johanna as a silently assenting partner in his reign. Often, this image is corroborated by contemporary chronicles, which speak of the "king and queen of Naples" as a corporate entity, working in concert.

Similarly, royally commissioned images represent a unified couple. Artistic endeavor had all but stopped in Naples between September 1345 and 1352 as a consequence of the chaos engulfing the Regno.[45] After their joint coronation in 1352, Johanna and Louis began commissioning both secular and religious art, following precedent set by earlier Angevin monarchs, who had employed patronage and cultural production to transmit royal ideology.[46] Often, Louis's and Johanna's commissions serve as visual monuments to their reign and represent them together as a coruling couple. By the same token, coins minted in both Provence and the Regno after Louis's coronation show them seated, side by side, with the inscription "Louis and Johanna, by the Grace of God King and Queen of Jerusalem and Sicily." Indeed, some of their silver coins and much of their Provençal coinage refer to both monarchs as *Rex*, or king, although the vast majority of images of the couple stress Louis's sovereignty.[47] The emphasis in such representations is on unity and cooperation. For instance, the frontispiece to the manuscript containing the statutes of Louis's chivalric order, the Order of the Knot (see below),[48]

---

45. Bologna, *I pittori alla corte angioina di Napoli*, 289.

46. Charmaine Lee characterizes the period immediately after Johanna and Louis's return to Naples as "the most productive period for Neapolitan culture," at least so far as manuscript production was concerned. See C. Lee, "Naples." Lee attributes the spike in manuscript commissions largely to Niccolò Acciaiuoli's tastes and influence. See ibid., and C. Lee, "Boccaccio's Neapolitan Letter and Multilingualism in Angevin Naples."

47. See E. William Monter, "Gendered Sovereignty: Numismatics and Female Monarchs in Europe, 1300–1800," *Journal of Interdisciplinary History* 41, no. 4 (Spring 2011): 540–41. See also Philip Grierson and Lucia Travaini, *Medieval European Coinage: With a Catalogue of the Coins in the Fitzwilliam Museum, Cambridge*, vol. 14: *Italy (III): (South Italy, Sicily, Sardinia)* (Cambridge: Cambridge University Press, 1998), 227–32, and Joëlle Pournot, "Monnaies en Provence et dans le royaume de Naples (1246–1382)," in *Marseille et ses Rois de Naples: La diagonale angevine, 1265–1382*, ed. Isabelle Bonnot (Marseille: Edisud, 1988), 51–60.

48. Paris, Bibliothèque nationale de France, MS fonds français 4274.

represents them as king regnant and queen consort, joined in matrimony and in service to God. Such commissions united Johanna and Louis in the public eye not only in marriage but also in sovereignty, portraying theirs as a harmoniously joint rule in which Robert's heiress governed in partnership with an Angevin prince whose kingship derived from both marriage and blood.

Surviving royal and papal correspondence, however, provides evidence that Johanna's marriage to Louis was, at least initially, far from happy and that her retirement from administrative duties was involuntary. This impression is borne out in contemporary chronicle accounts that portray Louis as inept, lazy, and brutal, particularly toward his wife. Chroniclers such as Matteo Villani gradually came to represent Johanna as an abused wife and condemned Louis for his mistreatment of her—an assessment echoed after Louis's death by Boccaccio's *De mulieribus claris*. By the time he died, Louis's unpopularity was such that Johanna's reputation was transformed from that of an adulterous she-wolf into that of a long-suffering victim whose birthright had been usurped and whose royal dignity had been unpardonably maligned.

Louis of Taranto's Rise to Power

The official Neapolitan investigation into Andrew of Hungary's murder targeted Johanna's closest supporters and left her isolated and vulnerable. Her aunt, Catherine of Valois, took advantage of that vulnerability to become the queen's confidant in order to make certain that one of her sons would be Naples's next king.[49] At first, it appeared that this son would be Robert, the eldest of the Tarantini, who for a time seemed to be winning the competition between the Angevin princes for power and whom Johanna requested a papal dispensation to marry. Soon, however, Louis gained the upper hand, and Johanna's requests for dispensations began to identify him as her intended.[50] Johanna's wishes, despite this paper trail—whose origin is suspect—are difficult to discern. Whatever her personal inclinations, Louis moved into Castel Nuovo, the primary royal residence, displacing his brother, on August 15, 1347, and married Johanna on August 22.[51] The marriage took place shortly before the Hungarian invasion and Johanna's and Louis's flight to Avignon, where Louis and Niccolò Acciaiuoli began the process of making Louis Naples's king. Aided by his cousin, the Florentine bishop

---

49. Catherine was Johanna's aunt twice over, first as the sister of Johanna's mother and second as the wife of her great-uncle, Philip of Taranto.

50. Tocco, *Niccolò Acciaiuoli*, 72–73; cf. Léonard, *Histoire de Jeanne I*re*, 1:604–15.

51. Tocco, *Niccolò Acciaiuoli*, 78; De Blasiis, *Chronicon Siculum*, 9.

Angelo Acciaiuoli, Niccolò used his diplomatic talents and connections to procure papal audiences for his protégé and his bride.[52] Ultimately, the efforts of the Acciaiuoli bore fruit, and Louis, far from being condemned for his irregular marriage, was awarded the Golden Rose. Indeed, he was selected for the honor ahead of the king of Majorca, then also in Avignon.[53]

In May 1348, Louis announced his determination to return to Naples.[54] Acciaiuoli traveled throughout Italy, aided by papal representatives, rallying traditionally Guelf cities to Louis's and Johanna's cause and obtaining pledges of safe conduct—all the while publicizing Louis's status as papal champion.[55] In the Regno, Lorenzo Acciaiuoli and other nobles fought to reclaim the kingdom, aided by the fickle mercenary Werner of Urslingen.[56] By late July, they controlled much of the Regno.[57] Johanna and Louis arrived outside Naples on August 17 and entered the city amid celebration, escorted by a grand procession.[58] Flushed out of the kingdom in disgrace, they returned as Naples's papally anointed champions.

Johanna's second marriage began under less than auspicious circumstances, and even after papal recognition, it drew criticism. Antifeminist polemic attacked women who remarried, arguing (in Boccaccio's words) that they "conceal their itching lust and think they are more beautiful and beloved for having pleased so often the various husbands of their frequent marriages."[59] Fueling such attacks—which could be satirical or quite genuine—was the Pauline dictum that widows are best advised to remain unmarried, which influenced clerical distaste for the idea of multiple marriages for widowed women, whose "remarriage signified shameless slavery to the voluptuous enticements of sexual passion" in the opinion of some authorities.[60] Furthermore, as chroniclers like Giovanni Villani pointed out, Johanna and Louis's

---

52. See Tocco, *Niccolò Acciaiuoli*, 77. In Avignon as in Naples, Florentine bankers were enormously influential. Acciaiuoli had close connections among the Soderini, the bankers to the Avignon popes.

53. Léonard, *Histoire de Jeanne Ire*, 2:89.

54. Ibid., 125.

55. Ibid., 138.

56. Ibid., 134.

57. Ibid., 139.

58. Ibid., 144–45.

59. Boccaccio, *De mulieribus claris* XCIV.11 (Pompeia Paulina), in Boccaccio, *Famous Women*, 403.

60. James Brundage, "Widows and Remarriage: Moral Conflicts and Their Resolution in Classical Canon Law," in *Wife and Widow in Medieval England*, ed. Sue Sheridan Walker (Ann Arbor: University of Michigan Press, 1993), 17.

relationship amounted to concubinage before they received the papal dispensation that regularized it.[61] Even afterward, there were questions as to its validity. *Fama* constituted evidence in adultery cases;[62] Johanna was a convicted adulteress in the court of public opinion. According to some authorities, adulterous wives should forfeit their dowries,[63] a line of reasoning that may have underlain Hungarian insistence on Johanna's infidelity. Aside, however, from its implications for her right to rule, Johanna's reputation as an adulteress made the marriage problematic: Some decretists after Gratian held that adulterers could not marry their partners in adultery, particularly when the adultery was publicly known.[64] Rumor charged Louis as Johanna's coadulterer, rendering their ability to marry suspect while also raising questions as to the legitimacy—and hence viability as heirs to the throne—of their children.

In Provence in particular, Johanna's marriage to Louis occasioned unrest. The Provençals protested long-standing Tarantini pretensions to the county and upheld their right—established in the oath exchanged at the accession of each new monarch—to be governed only by the Angevin ruler.[65] Charles II had left a testamentary provision that his son Philip of Taranto should succeed him in Provence, the Piedmont, and Forcalquier if Robert's heir were female.[66] Angevin subjects in the counties heartily resented this stipulation, which was ignored by Robert. Although Philip initially resisted swearing fealty to Johanna for Provence, he eventually capitulated, but this did not stop him or his sons from periodically renewing their claims.[67] Louis's marriage to Johanna awakened anxieties that the Tarantini would gain control of Provence, and Johanna's subjects pressed her for assurance that she would not cede the counties to her husband.[68]

---

61. Villani described their relationship as *iscellerato matrimonio* (G. Villani, *Nuova Cronica*, XIII.99, 3:511). Cf. Léonard, *Histoire de Jeanne Iʳᵉ*, 3:75.

62. Brundage, *Law, Sex, and Christian Society in Medieval Europe*, 411–12. Brundage, drawing on Bernard of Pavia and Johannes Teutonicus, explains that, from the thirteenth century, "if the situation was notorious and plainly evident to everyone in the community, a bishop was justified in proceeding against the offender without proving specific acts of intercourse" (412).

63. Ibid., 408.

64. Ibid., 307–8. This position was argued by Rolandus in his *Summa*, as by the author of *In primis hominibus*, who added the stipulation that notorious adulterers should be prevented from marrying one another.

65. Johanna's oath to safeguard Provençal liberties was made in Naples at the time of her coronation. The official, notarized copy of the pledge is preserved in AMM, AA 76 1.

66. Cf. Léonard, *Histoire de Jeanne Iʳᵉ*, 2:62, and de Feo, *Giovanna D'Angio*, 15–16.

67. Philip's oath of fealty for his Provençal holdings is preserved in ADBR, B 483.

68. Léonard, *Histoire de Jeanne Iʳᵉ*, 2:66.

Although papal favor did not dispel all doubts about him, the changes in Louis of Taranto's status after his return to Naples enabled him to assert military and administrative control over the Regno. Louis would be the only one of Johanna's husbands to rule in his own name. His success owed much to his role as papal champion, which recalled that of his ancestor, Charles I. Louis was able, as neither Andrew nor Louis of Hungary had been, to command the loyalty of both the Neapolitan nobility and the papacy's Italian allies. He likewise benefited from widespread anger with the Hungarians. The other crucial ingredient to his success was Niccolò Acciaiuoli, who worked to make Louis Naples's king in the fullest sense of the word.

Acciaiuoli was a member of one of Florence's most illustrious banking families. He moved to Naples in 1331 and joined a circle of Florentine bankers and merchants that included Giovanni Boccaccio.[69] Like Boccaccio's, the young Acciaiuoli's ambitions tended in other directions, and he gravitated toward the royal family, eschewing business for politics and military pursuits. He forged a relationship—rumored to be romantic, although his most recent biographer doubts this—with Catherine of Valois.[70] With Catherine's patronage, he became a royal chamberlain in 1335, when he also became Louis's *magister hospitii*.[71] He made himself generally indispensable to the Tarantini, taking over their affairs in the Morea and parlaying his successes there into vast wealth and holdings.[72] By the time of Johanna's succession, Acciaiuoli was one of the foremost men in Naples. Louis's marriage to the widowed queen made him the confidant and advisor of the new king of Naples and, from 1348, the Regno's grand seneschal. His fortunes were indelibly tied to the Tarantini, especially Louis, and he fought tenaciously and successfully for their advancement.

After returning to Naples, Acciaiuoli turned his attention to regaining control of the Regno and ensuring that Louis would rule it. His task would prove difficult. The first order of business was to demonstrate Louis's regal character and secure his throne by defeating the Hungarians. As a military leader, however, Louis met with little success. By November 1348, he was in desperate need of reinforcements, but his appeals to Florence for aid went unheeded.[73] His misguided trust in Werner of Urslingen led to the burning of Lucera and the massacre of its people when Werner retransferred his

---

69. Tocco, *Niccolò Acciaiuoli*, 19.
70. Ibid., 23.
71. Ibid., 24.
72. Ibid., 28, 38–39.
73. Léonard, *Histoire de Jeanne Ire*, 2:154.

allegiance to Hungary. The Hungarians retained control of the sea routes to Naples, and Louis made few advances in the key areas he sought to recover.[74] To make matters worse for his image, Neapolitan victories most often came under the command of Johanna's loyal allies.[75] When, after a five-month absence, Louis returned to Naples, he found the city victorious.

Despite such setbacks, Louis and Acciaiuoli gradually gained the upper hand. While Louis was away from Naples between mid-August 1348 and mid-February 1349, Johanna's immediate entourage, including her close confidant, the count-chamberlain Enrico Caracciolo, witnessed all acts.[76] During the same period, acts concerning Provence and Forcalquier, with few exceptions, were issued in Johanna's name alone.[77] Significant changes began with Louis's return. He began to call himself king of Sicily and Jerusalem, and he and Johanna issued legislation jointly, with Louis's name first.[78]

Over time, Louis eroded Johanna's monopoly over Provence, whose magnates had previously remained staunchly loyal to her. Her Provençal counselor was sidelined and replaced.[79] Then, Johanna faced opposition in Provence after she named her ally, the Neapolitan Giovanni Barrili, as seneschal. The appointment was meant to ensure Provence's loyalty, but the nobles preferred his native predecessor, Raymond d'Agoult. Johanna's political misstep cost her dearly. Louis saw an opening to embarrass his wife. He wrote letters supporting Raymond, winning the favor of many Provençal nobles, even as Johanna herself issued letters demanding accommodation of Barrili.[80]

In Naples, Louis and Acciaiuoli filled government posts with their own supporters, gaining control over important positions such as that of the master of seals, awarded to Angelo Acciaiuoli, who was also named Louis's chancellor. Ultimately, Florentines occupied every level of the Neapolitan administration.[81] On April 25, Louis arrested Enrico Caracciolo and his son,

---

74. Ibid., 156.
75. Ibid., 157.
76. Ibid., 167.
77. Ibid., 168.
78. Ibid., 166.
79. Ibid., 169–70.
80. Louis's letter is AMM, BB 20, fol. 142. Louis wrote in both his own name and Johanna's. Cf. Léonard, *Histoire de Jeanne I*ʳᵉ, 2:179. Johanna's demands that the Provençals admit Barrili are preserved in AMM, AA 64, 1–3, and BB 20, fols. 92–94. AMM, BB 20, fol. 86 contains a letter to the people of Marseille explaining Johanna's reasons for appointing Barrili. Cf. Léonard, *Histoire de Jeanne I*ʳᵉ, 2:171–74.
81. Tocco, *Niccolò Acciaiuoli*, 100.

confiscated their goods and titles, and executed Enrico.[82] Another blow to Johanna fell in May, when twenty-five counts and barons and seventy-four other nobles—most of whom favored Johanna—were taken captive by Hungarian forces.[83] The defeat proved disastrous for Neapolitan security (and finances, given the need to ransom the captured nobles), but it was catastrophic for Johanna's ability to rule, as it deprived her of many powerful supporters. She was left isolated, effectively her husband's hostage.[84] By mid-June, Louis was acting in his own name.[85] On June 27, he procured letters from his wife entitling him duke of Calabria, a position last held by Johanna's father that indicated his ascendancy.[86] Although not officially recognized as king, Louis for all intents and purposes ruled Naples.

The cardinal legate Annibale de Ceccano arrived in early July to negotiate with the Hungarians, and he quickly took Johanna's part against Louis.[87] The legate and queen conspired to return the kingdom to papal rule.[88] This was an expedient measure for Johanna, as it would end the Hungarian occupation and liberate her from her husband's control, but it did little to ingratiate her with Louis of Hungary, who expressed outrage that a viricide should be shielded by the papacy.[89] Johanna, meanwhile, waged a secret epistolary campaign, using covert channels to communicate with her Provençal supporters. On August 7, 1349, Louis of Taranto sent letters to Provence instructing its people to ignore all communications bearing Johanna's name alone and reminding them that she and he ruled jointly, effectively arguing that any action Johanna took independently was illegal.[90]

Further clues to the struggle unfolding between Johanna and Louis lie in a letter from Clement VI to Louis of September 10, 1349. Rumor held Louis guilty of usurping his wife's position and charged that he kept her a

82. Léonard, *Histoire de Jeanne Ire*, 3:184–85, 185 n. 3. Probably in retaliation, Enrico's kinsman Filippo Caracciolo stabbed Acciaiuoli in June 1350. Acciaiuoli survived, while Filippo escaped into exile. It is a testament to Johanna's lasting anger with Louis and Acciaiuoli that she pardoned Filippo and restored his property after Acciaiuoli's death. She also restored the county of Gerace to Enrico Caracciolo's son. See Léonard, *Histoire de Jeanne Ire*, 2:247; Tocco, *Niccolò Acciaiuoli*, 105.

83. Léonard, *Histoire de Jeanne Ire*, 3:191.

84. Ibid., 185; cf. Tocco, *Niccolò Acciaiuoli*, 104.

85. Léonard, *Histoire de Jeanne Ire*, 3:193.

86. De Blasiis, *Chronicon Siculum*, 14; cf. Léonard, *Histoire de Jeanne Ire*, 3:194.

87. Léonard, *Histoire de Jeanne Ire*, 3:196.

88. Ibid., 220.

89. Ibid., 200.

90. Ibid., 209.

virtual prisoner. Clement's angry letter provides evidence of contemporary gossip:

> If one can believe a nearly universal report, not only are you failing to treat the queen as a wife and queen, you are also not far from holding her in open contempt. You have reduced her to appearing more your servant than your wife. Led—or rather seduced—by your counselors, on the order of whom, to repeat what nearly the whole world says, you do and you undo everything, you have despoiled the queen of the administration of the kingdom, into which she admitted you for love. You have deprived her of homage and conversation with her faithful subjects, to the point that without your will and permission and that of your counselors, no one may speak to her. Through the care and under the order of your advisors, you have taken the royal seals from the queen—the great seal, the small, and that for fiscal affairs—and you have entrusted them to the bishop of Florence [Angelo Acciaiuoli] and other people. If one is to believe what is said, without making anything known to the queen, despite both her refusal and her protestation of her rights and in prejudice to her interests, they seal letters bearing her name and titles that, notably, contain great and excessive donations, as well as other business. It is also said that you have restricted her from companionship and her servants in such a way that both your and her honor and propriety are greatly diminished.[91]

Clement's letter reveals that, despite official representations of unity, Louis was said to mistreat and to have marginalized Johanna. The pope's insistence that "nearly the whole world" repeated such charges indicates that the situation in Naples was more discussed and more turbulent than official court records suggest.

At issue were conflicting definitions of what it meant for Johanna to be queen, as of what Louis's role as her consort entailed. Clement saw sovereignty—both inherited and wielded—as Johanna's. Louis's position was the product of Johanna's love, and his kingship derived solely from his status as her consort. Louis, however, asserted direct personal control over both Johanna and the administration. Like Clement, he cited his marriage as integral to his role as king, but his representation of what it meant for Johanna to be his wife stood in stark opposition to Clement's. Countering efforts to return his wife to power, Louis put forward his own vision of what marriage to a

---

91. Reg. Vat. 143, fol. 68v, reproduced in Déprez, *Clement VI*, 3:21, no. 4245.

royal heiress entailed, drawing on his rights as a husband rhetorically as he defended himself and his reign.

Throughout 1349, Johanna struggled to free herself from Louis's dominance, even as Louis forced her to write letters and issue legislation that insisted that she was happy and well cared for.[92] Clement, unconvinced, began to fear for Johanna's life. He sent letters to the Neapolitan nobility and other prominent figures, appealing to them to protect her.[93] At the same time, Johanna and Annibale enlisted the aid of Bertrand Rudolphe, formerly Johanna's advisor regarding Provence, and the count of Avellino, Hugh des Baux, to aid them. In mid-July, six Provençal galleys under Hugh's command arrived in Naples.[94] They flew the papal colors, a statement of loyalty to the pope and to Johanna and refusal to accept Louis's lordship.[95]

Hugh demanded that Louis annul all alienations of Provençal territory and recognize that Johanna ruled the counties alone. Hugh's galleys blockaded the harbor, barring ships from entry in an unambiguous statement of the consequences of refusal.[96] To make matters worse for Louis, Johanna became ill, generating rumors that he had attempted to poison her. Letters to this effect were read in public, and Hugh announced that he was prepared to storm Castel Nuovo to liberate the queen, whom he represented as an abused captive.[97]

Louis wrote to Clement (in both his own and Johanna's names) to protest this treatment on August 5, 1349.[98] His letter insists that there was no discord between Louis and his wife, with whom he shared one flesh and one body ("una caro et unum corpus vivunt").[99] Louis's argument reflects canon law's treatment of marriage as an "indissoluble" bond that creates a "corporate

---

92. Among the evidence of Johanna's resistance is an act of January 15, 1350 (ADBR, B 539) disavowing letters in which she appealed to Clement not to make subsidies to Louis and to take immediate control of the Regno. It likewise withdraws earlier claims that she was not in possession of her seals. Significantly, Louis's closest supporters, including Angelo Acciaiuoli, witnessed the act, giving credit to Clement's fears that Louis and his advisors prevented Johanna's independent action. Léonard provides an edition, along with an edition of the official act notifying Hugh des Baux of the revocations (ADBR, B 539 4). See Léonard, *Histoire de Jeanne Ire*, 2:458–64, nos. LIII and LIV. The passage disavowing Johanna's complaints is on 461.

93. Léonard, *Histoire de Jeanne Ire*, 2:221.

94. Ibid., 256, 261.

95. Ibid., 257.

96. Ibid., 265.

97. Ibid., 265–66.

98. ADBR, B 550. Léonard provides an edition; see *Histoire de Jeanne Ire*, 2:469–73, no. LVII.

99. ADBR, B 550. See Léonard, *Histoire de Jeanne Ire*, 2:470.

couple" fused in one flesh.[100] He asserted his authority as the sharer of Johanna's body to speak for her, averring that their wills were identical. Refuting representations of Johanna as dispossessed and victimized, Louis argued that she did not wish and had not sought Hugh's intervention. Behind his argument was an insistence that, as Johanna's husband, he had every right to direct Naples's administration, control his wife's movements, and make decisions on her behalf.

It briefly appeared that Hugh might prove Johanna's salvation. After treating with Louis of Hungary, he announced that, if Johanna were freed, he could guarantee the liberty of the captive Angevin princes, that the Hungarians would retreat, and that peace would be restored. All the while, his ships circled the harbor, where Louis's banner was displayed in a location usually reserved for the colors of criminals condemned to death.[101] When Louis prevaricated, Hugh arrested his supporters. Finally, defeated, Louis capitulated. Johanna promptly reassumed governance of Provence, began issuing legislation independently, and appointed her own seneschal.[102] She wrote to Marseille on September 2, thanking its people for their loyalty and announcing that she and Louis had made peace and that she alone would govern the county. She repeated her husband's earlier assertion that they shared one flesh ("in sacri conjugii federe existimus una caro"), but her letter makes clear that the voice of that shared body is her own, just as the authority it claims over Provence belongs to her.[103] She thus embraced Louis's image of a corporate couple, but she absorbed Louis into herself.

Johanna's victory was brief. In the fall of 1349, Hugh helped to negotiate a truce with Louis of Hungary, then encamped at Aversa. Johanna and Louis of Taranto were to sail with Hugh to Provence, while Louis of Hungary traveled to Rome and then to Buda, until a tribunal empaneled by the papacy had ruled on the matter of Johanna's culpability (or lack thereof) for Andrew's death. If found guilty, Johanna would be removed from power and punished; if she were found innocent (as she was, in 1350) Hungary would make peace with Naples.[104] When Johanna and Louis sailed, however, Hugh

100. Jo Ann McNamara, "Women and Power through the Family Revisited," in *Gendering the Master Narrative: Women and Power in the Middle Ages*, ed. Mary C. Erler and Maryanne Kowaleski (Ithaca: Cornell University Press, 2003), 26.

101. Léonard, *Histoire de Jeanne Ire*, 2:266.

102. Ibid., 267.

103. AMM, BB 21, fol. 50. Léonard provides an edition; see *Histoire de Jeanne Ire*, 2:474–75, no. LIX.

104. Léonard, *Histoire de Jeanne Ire*, 2:278.

remained behind. He gained the confidence of Johanna's sister, Mary—who was engaged in a long-running standoff with Louis over control of her dowry—only to force her to marry his son, Robert, by whom she was most likely raped.[105] Hugh's ship, with Mary and her children on board, rejoined the flotilla in Gaeta. Acting as an outraged brother, Louis boarded Hugh's galley, stabbed him, threw his corpse overboard, and arrested his sons.[106] For Mary, Hugh's actions ended any hope that marriage would free her from Louis, since she was now married to Robert des Baux, fated to languish in prison for the rest of his life (until Mary herself, years later, apparently had him killed). For Johanna, they meant the loss of her kingdom for the remainder of Louis's life. Louis promptly appointed a new seneschal in Provence and forced her to yield all concessions made to her.[107]

Two letters preserved in Marseille record Johanna's defeat.[108] On October 29, Johanna wrote to the city to disavow all reports about Louis's cruelty. Her letter speaks volumes about the power of rumor and attests—in its very need to quell them—to how many and how dire were the reports circulating about her welfare:

> By the contrivance of some sons of iniquity and scandal, a certain report has been running through our counties of Provence and Forcalquier, and especially in the city of Marseille, that holds that the glorious prince, our reverend lord and husband, the illustrious King of Jerusalem and Sicily, has been detaining us in prison and had both stolen our seal and prepared various horrible fates for us.[109]

She goes on to allege that forged letters have been sent in her name to the city that asked for assistance and galleys to "remove us from the hands and power of the aforesaid lord, our husband."[110] She professes ignorance of them and affirms that Louis has never mistreated her, protesting her wifely affection (*affectu uxorio*) for him. The next day, she wrote again to the people of Marseille, informing them that Hugh had acted independently, without her knowledge or encouragement.[111] In closing, she returns to the image of the

---

105. Matteo Villani charges that Hugh "forced her to consummate the marriage." See M. Villani, *Cronica*, I.96, 1:180–81.

106. Ibid.; cf. Léonard, *Histoire de Jeanne Ire*, 2:283.

107. Léonard, *Histoire de Jeanne Ire*, 2:285.

108. AMM, BB 21, fol. 76v, and AMM, BB 21, fol. 77r. Léonard provides editions of both. See *Histoire de Jeanne Ire*, 2:477–79, nos. LXII and LXIII.

109. AMM, BB 21, fol. 76v.

110. Ibid.

111. Ibid., fol. 77r.

sovereign body shared with Louis, saying that Hugh's actions hurt her reputation and honor as much as Louis's, because she and Louis were "inseparable." She thus subsumed herself within Louis, abiding by the fiction that his voice spoke for them both and that his actions were her own.

That Niccolò Acciaiuoli was behind Louis's triumph is without doubt. Johanna clearly held him responsible. She wrote another capitulatory missive to Clement on January 18, 1350, this time to disavow earlier criticism of Acciaiuoli.[112] She writes that she has come to appreciate Acciaiuoli, whom she commends to the pope's paternal affection, and fears that her earlier letters may have inspired hatred for him in the pope.

Thus, by the beginning of 1350, Johanna had been forced into cooperation. Louis and Acciaiuoli then undertook the task of recrafting her public image into that of a docilely assenting consort. Johanna was represented as Louis's silent, loving wife, while Louis's was the public, official face of the corporate couple. She and Louis were jointly crowned during Pentecost in 1352. Although Louis was legally defined as her consort and could not succeed Johanna if she died, he was the Regno's sole ruler.[113]

Louis's Independent Reign

Acciaiuoli commenced a concerted campaign to restore the Regno to its former glory. He hoped to realize in Louis the fulfillment of two empty titles: king of Jerusalem and king of Sicily.[114] Foremost among his aims was the reconquest of Sicily. While he never fully achieved this—in large measure because he lacked royal support—he retook the city of Messina, into which Louis and Johanna marched in triumph in October 1356.[115] He also worked to restore the Angevin dynasty's position as the leader of the Guelfs, forging alliances with traditionally Guelf cities in northern Italy and seeking a close association with the papacy. Acciaiuoli's ambitions for the Angevin monarchy—which appear to have far outstripped Louis's—were thus in keeping with tradition, and he drew on traditional means to communicate them. Among other things, he turned to patronage as a tool to legitimate Louis's reign. He commissioned the

---

112. ADBR, B 3, fol. 20. Léonard provides an edition in *Histoire de Jeanne Ire*, 2:479–80, no. LXIV.

113. Louis was empowered to act independently throughout the Regno, and he claimed that Johanna had given him Provence as her dowry. Cf. Léonard, *Histoire de Jeanne Ire*, 2:294. Emperor Charles IV, to whom Johanna owed fealty for Provence, confirmed the gift, receiving Louis's homage (ADBR, B 205, fol. 3r).

114. Tocco, *Niccolò Acciaiuoli*, 148.

115. Léonard, *Histoire de Jeanne Ire*, 3:242.

copying of historical works, including a manuscript now in Paris that includes Isidore of Seville's *Chronicon*, Paul the Deacon's histories of the Romans and Lombards, and the *Historia Sicula*, which describes the conquest of Sicily.[116] As Charmaine Lee points out, these texts, which chart the history of the Regno, work together "as an example of *translatio imperii* specifically associated with the Angevins in their southern Kingdom."[117] Acciaiuoli's campaign to restore the Regno was thus both ideological and military.

Unfortunately for Acciaiuoli's plans, Louis alienated Clement's successor, Innocent VI (r. 1352–62).[118] Louis proved a bitter disappointment to contemporary observers as well. His reign was marked by military disaster and crippling financial crisis. Mercenaries, including the Great Companies, against whom Louis's contemporaries judged him spectacularly ineffectual, overran Naples and Provence.[119] Acciaiuoli himself characterized the Regno's financial state as disastrous, writing later in life that Louis and Johanna found themselves so destitute that they were obliged to eat young grain—living hand to mouth, with nothing set by for the future.[120] While Acciaiuoli earned the respect of popes and statesmen,[121] Louis won few admirers, ultimately estranging even Acciaiuoli, who spent the last years of his reign in northern Italy and Provence.

Johanna must have found Louis's reign stifling, but little evidence remains of how she responded to it. A letter to her from Innocent VI, dated November 17, 1353, suggests that she was far from happy.[122] In response to

---

116. Paris, Bibliothèque nationale de France, MS fonds français 756–57.

117. C. Lee, "Boccaccio's Neapolitan Letter and Multilingualism in Angevin Naples," 13.

118. Léonard, *Histoire de Jeanne Ire*, 3:37.

119. Free companies terrorized Europe during the fourteenth century. They were particularly active in Italy, both in the north (especially Umbria and Tuscany) and in the south, although they were also key players in the battles of the Hundred Years' War in France. On the activities of the free companies in Italy, see William Caferro, "Slaying the Hydra-Headed Beast: Italy and the Companies of Adventure in the Fourteenth Century," in *Crusaders, Condottieri, and Cannon: Medieval Warfare in Societies around the Mediterranean*, ed. L. J. Andrew Villalon and Donald J. Kagay (Leiden: Brill, 2002), 285–304. In the Regno, the Great Companies (often in allegiance with Louis of Durazzo) devastated agriculture and terrorized the population. Mercenaries were also active in Provence, which was overrun in 1357 by the "Archpriest" Arnaud de Cervole (ca. 1300–66). See Léonard, *Histoire de Jeanne Ire*, 3:298. Cf. Jonathan Sumption, *The Hundred Years War: Trial by Fire* (Philadelphia: University of Pennsylvania Press, 2001), 2:562.

120. "Lettera di Niccola Acciaioli ad Angelo Soderini," in Palmieri, *Vita Nicolai Acciaioli*, 51: "che loro è convenuto mangiare lo grano in erba."

121. Acciaiuoli was honored with the Golden Rose in March 1360. See Tocco, *Niccolò Acciaiuoli*, 224.

122. Reg. Vat. 235, fol. 218v, published in F. Cerasoli, "Innocenzo VI e Giovanna I di Napoli. Documenti inediti dell'Archivio Vaticano," *ASPN* 22 (1897), no. XXVIII, 507–9.

Johanna's complaints, Innocent counseled her to face adversity serenely and emulate Christ's handmaid (*ancilla Christi*) by overcoming the fragility of her sex, confronting calamity with patience, and bearing terrors with magnanimity.[123] The letter is silent as to what terrors and calamities Johanna faced, but Innocent advises her to maintain her trust in God. Unlike his predecessor, he was not prepared to intervene on her behalf, aside from offering spiritual consolation. Johanna's role was to suffer patiently, and Innocent helped to give her the appearance of a martyr by lending her endurance a religious hue.

Indeed, Innocent differed from Clement VI in his lack of interference in Neapolitan affairs. He quarreled repeatedly with Louis, but he did little, other than to periodically excommunicate him, to alter the course of events in the Regno. The excommunications were short-lived and without military or financial repercussions. With Louis, such threats held little sway.[124] The pontiff accordingly withdrew from the Angevins, intervening only periodically on behalf of Mary's daughters and the remaining Durazzeschi princes, whose interests Talleyrand continued to promote.

The captive princes returned to Naples in 1352. The Durazzeschi remained at odds with Louis throughout his reign. Louis of Durazzo openly rebelled, allying himself with the mercenaries who roamed the Regno and with Spiritual Franciscan dissidents.[125] At times, he portrayed his struggle against Louis of Taranto and Johanna as a holy war, and when they were excommunicated in 1355 for failing to pay the census owed annually to the pope, Louis of Durazzo announced that he fought them on behalf of the Church.[126] The intermittent war between the cousins was costly and took a heavy toll on the Regno. Robert of Durazzo also led a rebellion in Provence that was said to have the backing of much of the papal Curia, before he was killed fighting for France at Poitiers in 1356.[127]

By any measure, Louis of Taranto's reign was turbulent. Shortly before his death, however, commentators reported that matters seemed to be improving.

---

123. Ibid.: "fragilitatem sexus feminei supergressa calamitates patientia . . . calcas terrores magnanimitate superas."

124. Léonard, *Histoire de Jeanne Ire*, 3:38–42.

125. Ibid., 474. Louis's alliances with so-called *fraticelli* ultimately led to investigation by the Church. His association with the Spiritual dissidents is well known and has been discussed in H. C. Lea, *A History of the Inquisition in the Middle Ages* (New York: MacMillan, 1901), 2:284, and Gordon Leff, *Heresy in the Later Middle Ages: The Relation of Heterodoxy to Dissent, c. 1250–c. 1450* (Manchester: Manchester University Press, 1967), 234–35.

126. Léonard, *Histoire de Jeanne Ire*, 3:124, 144. The interdict was announced by an open letter of Innocent VI on January 13, 1355.

127. Ibid., 142–43. Jean Froissart tells the story of Robert's death in his chronicle (chapter 161).

Louis of Durazzo was captured in 1362 and died soon after. Repeated ill-ness was said to have changed Louis of Taranto's character for the better; his renewed amicability with Acciaiuoli, as well as seemingly improved relations with his wife, boded well.[128] Boccaccio, at any rate, saw improvement and commented on it in both his sixth eclogue and in the introduction to *De casibus virorum illustrium* (*On the Falls of Famous Men*), which he initially in-tended to dedicate to Louis or Acciaiuoli.[129] Matteo Villani reports that Louis was overcome by remorse for his wicked life and went on a pilgrimage just before he died in May 1362.[130] Johanna affirmed to the pope that Louis died full of faith and she hoped for his salvation.[131] Louis's reign was over, and hers was set to begin in earnest.

Crafting Louis of Taranto's Regal Identity

In representations of Louis as king, two different men emerge. One is the official image of him as an ideal Angevin king, while the other is the image of him as incompetent and negligent disseminated by contemporary com-mentators. The first was the result of carefully crafted propaganda that de-picted Louis as the legitimate Angevin monarch. The second is a measure of the failure of the first, at least insofar as Louis's reputation was concerned, and it provides evidence of the discrepancies between court ideology and the realities of Louis's reign.

Louis faced a difficult struggle to become accepted as Naples's king. First, in order to be king in more than name, he needed the support of the papacy and the compliance of his wife. Second, he needed to combat his reputation as a regicide and adulterer. In part, this would entail transforming Johanna from a harlot queen into a supportive, demure consort. Third, Louis needed to defend his legitimacy by resuscitating the reputation of the Angevin mon-archy. Whereas Andrew had been perceived as a victim, Louis, wishing to be a king rather than a consort, had to establish his mastery over his wife and kingdom by showing himself regal in birth, in bearing, and in ability, in part by asserting the inherently masculine nature of kingship.

The official image of Louis as king—and the related image of Johanna as his consort—was advanced by Louis's 1353 founding of the Ordre du

---

128. Léonard, *Histoire de Jeanne Ire*, 3:472.

129. C. Lee, "Naples." On the textual evolution of *De casibus*, see Vittorio Zaccaria, "Le due redazioni del '*De casibus*,'" *Studi sul Boccaccio* 10 (1977–78): 1–26.

130. M. Villani, *Cronica*, X.100, 2:578.

131. Léonard, *Histoire de Jeanne Ire*, 3:479.

Saint-Esprit au Droit Désir, also known as the Ordre du Nœud or Order of the Knot. The order's statutes survive in a unique, sumptuously illuminated manuscript now in the Bibliothèque nationale de France.[132] They fill seventeen folios, are in French, and very closely resemble those of the Order of the Star, founded by John II of France (1319–64) in 1351.[133] They describe the duties of the three hundred Knights of the Knot: to aid and counsel the king, show him honor and loyalty, and protect the Church. Ostensibly, the order's objective was to liberate the Holy Sepulcher and retake Jerusalem, whose titular sovereignty Louis claimed, while also defending Naples.[134] More remarkable than the text are the manuscript's illuminations, which provide a sophisticated, meticulously constructed argument about Louis's identity as an Angevin king that likely originated with Acciaiuoli.[135]

The first illumination provides a clear statement about Louis's and Johanna's monarchical identities (see figure 5).[136] The text reads, "Louis, by the grace of God King of Jerusalem and Sicily." It does not mention Johanna. The image depicts Louis and Johanna venerating the Trinity, suspended above them in a mandorla. Within the mandorla, the crucified Christ rests in the lap of God the Father, over whose heart the dove of the Holy Spirit flies.

---

132. Paris, Bibliothèque nationale de France, MS fonds français 4274, contains the only known copy of the Order of the Knot's statutes. A nineteenth-century reproduction exists; while the images are not nearly of the quality of a modern facsimile, they give a good general sense of the manuscript's program. See Horace de Viel-Castel, ed., *Statuts de l'Ordre du Saint-Esprit au Droit Desir ou du Noeud, institue a Naples en 1352 par Louis d'Anjou, premier du nom, roi de Jérusalem, de Naples et de Sicile—Manuscrit du XIVme siècle, conservé au Louvre dans le Musée des Souverains Français. Avec une notice sur la peinture des Miniatues et la description du manuscrit par M. le Comte Horace de Viel-Castel, conservateur du musée des souverains français au Musée Impérial du Louvre* (Paris: Engelmann and Graf, 1853).

133. Léonard, *Histoire de Jeanne Ire*, 3:13; cf. Maurice Keen, *Chivalry* (New Haven: Yale University Press, 1984), 190–91.

134. For a brief analysis of the statutes of the Order of the Knot, see the doctoral thesis of Sylvie Pollastri, "La noblesse napolitaine sous la dynastie angevine: L'aristocratie des comtes (1265–1435)" (Université Paris X-Nanterre, 1994), 301–5.

135. Léonard, *Histoire de Jeanne Ire*, 3:15. Léonard argues persuasively that the order's statutes bear Acciaiuoli's intellectual stamp and reflect his ambitions. His argument rests on the wealth of classical and contemporary literary allusions in the statutes, as in their illuminations: A correspondent of Petrarch and Boccaccio and patron of Zanobi da Strada (1312–61), Acciaiuoli aspired to membership in the fledgling humanist movement of which they were part and to associate the Neapolitan court with it. Among other things, the order's knights were to be crowned with laurels. On Acciaiuoli's literary pretensions, see Boccaccio's letter to Francesco Nelli: Epistola XIII in Giovanni Boccaccio, *Epistole e Lettere*, ed. Ginetta Auzas, vol. 5 of *Tutte le Opere di Giovanni Boccaccio*, ed. Vittore Branca (Milan: Arnoldo Mondadori, 1992), 596–629.

136. Paris, Bibliothèque nationale de France, MS fonds français 4274, fol. 2v. Bologna briefly discusses the manuscript and provides a black-and-white reproduction of this illumination and others in *I pittori alla corte angioina di Napoli* (see esp. 305–7), as does Bräm, *Neapolitanische Bilderbibeln des Trecento*, 1:443–45, and vol. 2, pls. XXXVII and XXVIII.

Figure 5.   Louis of Taranto and Johanna of Naples venerate the Trinity. Frontispiece to the Statutes of the Order of the Knot—Paris, Bibliothèque nationale de France, MS fonds français 4274, fol. 2v. Bibliothèque nationale de France.

Blood pours from the wounds in Christ's side, hands, and feet, flowing along his arms and down the cross. Above the mandorla, an angelic host adores the Trinity. Louis and Johanna kneel below this celestial panoply on either side of the cross, each aligned with a banner-carrying angel. Louis's golden hair and beard and large crown mirror those of Christ and God the Father above. He is dressed as a knight, in a short gold-and-white tunic ornamented with blue fleurs-de-lys (a French motif present in the Angevin coat of arms since the time of Charles I), a sword at his side. He hovers somewhat above the ground to the right of the cross. He clasps his hands in prayer, face raised to the Trinity. An attendant carrying a standard topped by a crown stands behind him. The standard partially overlaps the angel who flies above Louis; the angel floats behind and is closely associated with the crown, which is winged and to which is attached a veil emblazoned with a cross and a knot. Further asserting Louis's French identity, one of the crown's wings is covered in fleurs-de-lys. The composition of this trio creates an unbroken connection between Louis and the heavenly host, emphasizing his divine appointment.

Johanna kneels to the Trinity's left—the secondary position. She, like Louis, hovers above the ground (although closer to it). Her posture mirrors Louis's, but her face is less raised; it is difficult to determine whether she looks at the Trinity or at her husband. If she is looking at the Trinity, her gaze is directed at Christ's pierced, bleeding feet. Her golden hair is topped with a tall crown similar to but smaller than Louis's. Behind her, a smaller woman stands with clasped hands. An expanse of blue separates the two women from the angel above, the distance between them emphasized by their juxtaposition with the trio on the other side of the cross.

This frontispiece lays out Louis's and Acciaiuoli's plans for Naples's governance and their conception of the relationship between Johanna and Louis. Johanna's presence underscores Louis's right to the throne. Yet the image makes an unambiguous statement about the balance of power between them. Both are crowned and richly attired, their shared Angevin blood signaled by their close physical resemblance. Both claim earthly crowns and majesty, but only Louis—the male inheritor of Angevin sacral power—claims a crown associated with the Holy Spirit, one that physically connects him to the heavens and is reserved for the champion of the Church.

For all but two of the remaining sixteen folios, Johanna is absent while Louis figures prominently, receiving the homage of his knights, officiating at tournaments, dispensing justice, and presiding at banquets. His majesty is emphasized throughout. Folio 3r, for instance, stresses Louis's divine calling and lends his kingship celestial and even apocalyptic overtones (see figure 6). The text explains that Louis founded the order "for the honor of the Holy Spirit, on the day [Pentecost 1352] on which, by His grace, we were crowned." It contains two vertically oriented bordered miniatures surmounted by a triangular pinnacle, echoing the architecture of a church. In the upper register, the dove of the Holy Spirit flies within a mandorla surrounded by angels. Stars

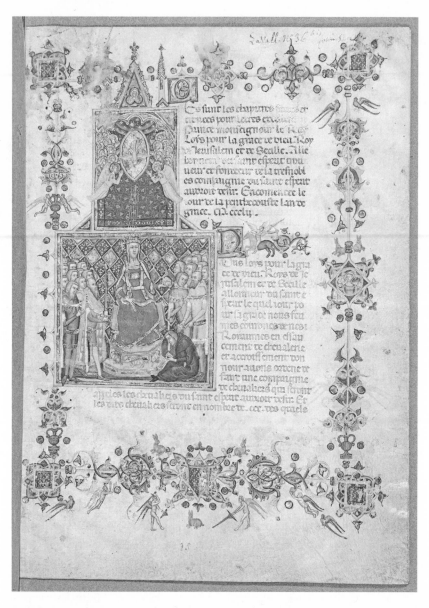

Figure 6. Louis of Taranto honored by the Knights of the Knot and blessed by the Holy Spirit. Statutes of the Order of the Knot—Paris, Bibliothèque nationale de France, MS fonds français 4274, fol. 3r. Bibliothèque nationale de France.

radiate from the mandorla's top, while golden rays shoot into the miniature below. In the lower register, Louis sits enthroned, surrounded by knights, just as the dove is by angels. The rays emanating from the dove touch his head, linking the two. Three small dogs play at his feet as he sits enthroned, the embodiment of nobility and kingship, holding an orb and scepter as a scribe records the statutes of his order.[137]

Many of the remaining miniatures are framed to resemble churches or tabernacles containing Louis, and many stress his sacral kingship. Of particular note is folio 7v, which contains five miniatures. In one, knights hold aloft Louis's winged crown. In another, a dove flies surrounded by rays of light above an altar prepared for the Eucharist. Within an inner border, Louis stands like a celebrant on a dais behind a table that mirrors the Eucharistic table and offers a chalice to three kneeling knights. At the bottom of the folio, Louis feasts with his knights and three crowned women, who may be Johanna and their daughters, neither of whom survived childhood.[138] This folio thus gathers together all of the components of Louis's identity as king, highlighting his relationship to the Holy Spirit, divine election, quasi-sacerdotal position, largesse as a giver and partaker of feasts, and role as father and husband to Angevin princesses.

To emphasize Louis's connection with the Holy Spirit, the date chosen for the order's inception was that of Johanna and Louis's joint coronation: Pentecost 1352. There is no documentary evidence for its existence until a year later, but the founding date assigned to the order is significant, stressing Louis's kingship and its blessing by the Holy Spirit, as well as his Angevin descent.[139] In romance, Pentecost was the day for the gathering of the Arthurian court—an association that implicitly presented Louis's kingship as heroic. At the same time, Louis's coronation date and evocation of a personal connection to the Holy Spirit followed Angevin precedent.[140] François de Meyronnes had argued that Robert was confirmed in his realm as the champion of the Church and appointee of the Holy Spirit; Louis's role as champion of the Holy Spirit identified him as Robert's successor.[141] Thus, the order's founding date, like its devotion to the Holy Spirit, underscores Louis's spiritual and familial links to his predecessors, and it associates his reign with

---

137. Paris, Bibliothèque nationale de France, MS fonds français 4274, fol. 3r.

138. Louis and Johanna's daughter Françoise died in 1352. Their elder daughter, Catherine, died sometime after 1362.

139. Léonard, *Histoire de Jeanne Ire*, 3:12.

140. Charles II's coronation was also on Pentecost. The forms for Angevin coronations are preserved in Cardinal Jacques Cajétan's Roman ceremonial (Avignon, Bibliothèque Ceccano, MS 1706, fols. 17r–19v), editions of which can be found in Franz Ehrle, "Zur Geschichte des papstlichen Hofceremoniells in 14 Jahrhundert," *Archiv für Literatur und Kirchengeschichte des Mittelalters* 5 (1889): 567–71, and L.-H. Labande, "Le cérémonial romain de Jacques Cajétan," *Bibliothèque de l'École des Chartes* 54 (1893): 45–74. See also Boyer's "La 'Foi Monarchique,'" 87–89.

141. See Kelly, *The New Solomon*, 116–17.

one of the holiest days in the liturgical calendar, appropriating the powerful associations of Pentecost for his image.[142]

His role as the founder of a chivalric order equated Louis with the monarchs of England and France, who had just founded their own orders.[143] In an age when lavish expenditure and largesse were markers of political power, the public pageantry that accompanied the order's foundation demonstrated his regal character. On the most basic and obvious level, the founding of the Order of the Knot was an assertion of a particular kind of aristocratic masculinity. According to the chivalric ethos, "ancestors define descendants because blood is not simply one's own but is continuous through time" and "deeds consolidate identity because chivalric standing must be continually reasserted."[144] Louis's role as a chivalric king was inherited from his male forebears—something which, given the "gendered transmission" of knightliness, Johanna could not inherit.[145] Her sex barred her from the very activities by which Acciaiuoli and Louis defined Louis's kingly persona, and the definition of sovereignty they expounded excluded her.

The manuscript's artistic program conveys far more on a symbolic and ideological level. It re-created Louis of Taranto—the second son of a junior

---

142. Émile Léonard believed that the stress on the Holy Spirit reveals Louis of Taranto's heterodox religious sentiments, and he maintained that Louis emulated the supposed Spiritual Franciscan leanings of Charles II and Robert (Léonard, *Histoire de Jeanne Ire*, 3:21). Both Louis and Johanna actively supported the Franciscan order, and it is significant that they named their younger daughter Françoise. Louis sought to associate himself with Louis of Toulouse (surely in part because of their shared name), the revival of whose cult he encouraged during his reign. He probably commissioned a now-lost series of frescoes depicting the life of St. Louis in a chapel annexed to the Duomo in Naples (see Bologna, *I pittori alla corte angioina di Napoli*, 322–23). Samantha Kelly has argued persuasively that Robert's "religious involvements were almost wholly orthodox, and were oriented toward more classic royal goals" (Kelly, *The New Solomon*, 74). The Order of the Knot suggests that Louis's goals were similar. It signifies his desire to represent himself, according to contemporary ideals, as a pious king, following the examples of his forebears. Louis's chancellor, Angelo Acciaiuoli, was a Dominican and would likely not have advanced so far in the Angevin administration had Louis been committed to a Spiritual agenda. Ultimately, the conception of the order was a statement of orthodoxy and allegiance to the papacy, a reminder of the favor shown Louis by Clement VI. Not all scholars agree with Kelly's arguments about Robert's orthodoxy; both Caroline Bruzelius and Ronald G. Musto have argued that the court had Spiritual leanings and Joachite tendencies. See Bruzelius, "Queen Sancia of Mallorca"; and Ronald G. Musto, "Franciscan Joachimism at the Court of Naples, 1309–1345: A New Appraisal," *Archivum Franciscanum Historicum* 90 (1997): 419–86.

143. Although the Order of the Knot was one of the earliest orders to be founded—after Alfonso XI of Castile's Order of the Band (1330), Edward III of England's Order of the Garter (1348), and John II of France's Order of the Star (1351)—its close parallels to John II's order and, perhaps, the disasters of Louis's reign have garnered it less attention than its more famous antecedents. See Keen, *Chivalry*, 179.

144. Crane, *The Performance of Self*, 107.

145. Ruth Mazo Karras, *From Boys to Men: Formations of Masculinity in Late Medieval Europe* (Philadelphia: University of Pennsylvania Press, 2003), 35.

prince—as the legitimate inheritor not only of the Angevin throne, but also of the sacred power it conferred. The illuminations portray him as a courtly monarch, as the scion of the Capetian and Angevin lines and heir of their *beata stirps*, and as the champion of the Church. He thus claimed all of the characteristics of Angevin rulership denied to his wife because of her sex. The statutes effectively proclaim Louis the inaugurator—despite the lamentations of those who believed Naples's hopes had died with Andrew—of a new golden age for the Regno.

Louis's role as champion of the Church made him the natural leader of the Guelfs—a position claimed by earlier Angevin monarchs—and aligned him with the French monarchy, as with contemporary eschatological expectations that a French prince would combat Antichrist.[146] Many of Louis's contemporaries—including Boccaccio and Matteo Villani—mocked the Angevin court's francophone proclivities, finding the order's use of French and courtly pageantry pompous;[147] French was the language of courtly culture, and fluency was one mark of Louis's chivalry.[148] Yet the reassertion of the Angevin monarchy's French identity was even more significant. The order's statutes explicitly associate Louis with the Capetian bloodline, as does its visual program. Numerous lions appear in the illuminations' margins (see figure 5). The lions recall Louis VIII, "the Lion of France," who was the progenitor of Louis of Taranto's *beata stirps*, his link to the Capetian line, and his namesake.[149]

---

146. It may also have constituted a rebuttal to Cola di Rienzo, self-proclaimed Knight of the Holy Spirit, who had sought to position himself as Italy's temporal leader and the champion of both the pope and, later, the emperor Charles IV (1316–78). On Cola as *candidates Spiritus Sancti miles*, see Musto, *Apocalypse in Rome*, 180; cf. Giovanni da Bazzano, *Chronicon Mutinense*, 137. Cola had presented an open, if not particularly serious, challenge to the Angevin regime as recently as 1350 by offering the Regno to Charles IV if he would take up the temporal sword usurped by the papacy. Cola, who developed Spiritual Franciscan sympathies after spending time in exile among *fraticelli* in the north of the Regno, wrote to both Charles IV and the archbishop of Prague of a coming renewal to begin on Pentecost and referred to the disordered state of the Regno, which was "more agitated than ever" ("quod regnum fluctuat plus quam unquam"), as one thing that would be corrected. See Cola di Rienzo, *Epistolario di Cola di Rienzo*, ed. Annibale Gabrielli, Fonti per la storia d'Italia 6 (Rome: Forzani, 1890), nos. XXXI (96–111) and XXXV (144–79), esp. 166; cf. Musto, *Apocalypse in Rome*, 284. Amanda Collins has made the extraordinary and implausible claim that Louis's order was a continuation of a similar order that originated with Cola. See Amanda Collins, *Greater than Emperor: Cola di Rienzo (ca. 1313–54) and the World of Fourteenth-Century Rome* (Ann Arbor: University of Michigan Press, 2002), 77.

147. See M. Villani, *Cronica*, III.83, 1:428–29, and Boccaccio's letter 1362 letter to Francesco Nelli (Epistola XIII in Boccaccio, *Epistole e Lettere*, 596–629); cf. Léonard, *Histoire de Jeanne Ire*, 3:20.

148. Karras, *From Boys to Men*, 47.

149. The association between Louis and lions is also a chivalric trope. Lancelot, Galahad, and Yvain—"the knight with the lion"—were all associated with lions, signifiers of their valor and nobility.

Another possible referent comes from Arthurian romance. The popular, widely circulated *Prophecies of Merlin*—first described by Geoffrey of Monmouth—include a prediction that a Lion of Justice will arise, "and at its roar the towers of Gaul shall shake and the island Dragons tremble," inaugurating an age when "gold shall be squeezed from the lily-flower and the nettle, and silver shall flow from the hoofs of lowing cattle."[150] Louis's identification as lion and papal champion reveals him as the founder of an impending golden age after the trials of war and plague, one who will vanquish the foes of Naples and the Church—claims particularly salient immediately following the Hungarian invasions. On the frontispiece, a lion vanquishes a dragon—possibly Louis's Sicilian rivals—while in the margin of folio 4r, a lion wearing Louis's crown and veil sits in a vine scroll. A crowned woman—probably Johanna—completes the visual argument about Louis's kingship. Seated in the marginal vine scroll, she holds a scepter and looks toward the lion, suggesting that Johanna has earthly power, while Louis's power is spiritual as well as temporal. He is, thus, the promise of a new age and of his bloodline, assuming a role defined by his illustrious progenitors that Johanna, a woman, could not fill.

The order's importance for the historian lies in its conceptual refashioning of Naples's monarchy on the model of the earliest Angevin kings. Acciaiuoli's ambition was to create a strong Regno that dominated Italy, was allied to the papacy, and commanded respect across Europe. He made the most of Louis's heritage and portrayed his marriage so as to diminish its importance in giving Louis his throne. Acciaiuoli's ambitions for Louis and for Naples precluded Johanna's participation. His design of the Order of the Knot reveals the full extent of his plans and ambition, including how he meant for the world to see Louis and Johanna. They were not adulterous usurpers but a divinely called king and queen whose union presaged Naples's new political ascendancy. Likewise, the order's ideological program demonstrates how slight Johanna's role was to be in the new order Acciaiuoli envisioned. He recast her as a queen consort happy to give way to her husband and content to act as his silent and supportive partner, to give him access to the throne without wishing to occupy it herself.

---

150. Geoffrey of Monmouth, *The History of the Kings of Britain*, trans. Lewis Thorpe (London: Penguin Books, 1966), 174. It is tempting as well to see in the lions and dragons echoes of the *Oraculum Cyrilli*, on which Rupescissa had just written a commentary. There is no evidence, however, to suggest that the *Oraculum Cyrilli* was known to Louis, Acciaiuoli, or the artist who painted the miniatures.

Contemporary Treatments of Louis of Taranto

Early in his reign, Louis succeeded in playing the roles royal rhetoric claimed for him. Observers anxious about Naples's fate hoped that his kingship might correct the erratic course of Neapolitan politics. Matteo Villani, for instance, was among the many observers shocked by the brutal Hungarian treatment of the Regno's people, which made him kindly disposed toward Louis of Taranto early in his reign. Villani's narrative of Louis's reign begins with triumph, as Louis and Johanna return victorious to Naples as king and queen. He describes the procession that led them into the city, providing details about its pomp and grandeur.[151] Similarly, Rupescissa initially described Louis as "the Church's rampart," appealing to Innocent VI to aid Louis in his efforts to reclaim Sicily, which he saw as vital to the struggle against Antichrist.[152]

Public opinion soon turned against Louis, however. Literary and chronicle descriptions of his reign are almost uniformly negative. He emerges from them as weak, cowardly, lazy, selfish, and mean-spirited. Generally beginning by speculating on Louis's involvement in Andrew of Hungary's murder, chroniclers who wrote about him concentrated on his military inadequacy and reported mistreatment of his wife. Petrarch and Boccaccio lamented his shortcomings and the defects of his character, joining a chorus of chroniclers who shifted the blame for Naples's decline squarely onto Louis's shoulders. While Johanna's early rule was adjudged disastrous, Louis's assumption of her powers was no palliative, and his right to rule and skill in governance came to be regarded as inferior to her own—with the result that Johanna herself came to be seen in a more positive light.

By the time Louis died in 1362, many of his contemporaries found him so despicable that they actively welcomed Johanna's return to power. Early in Louis's reign, Johanna maintained her reputation as a viricide, and she was frequently treated in hostile chronicle accounts as Louis's accomplice—or even, as in the chronicle of Marco Battagli of Rimini, as his leader—in iniquity.[153] By the end of his reign, even formerly antagonistic commentators

---

151. M. Villani, *Cronica*, I.21, 1:41–42.

152. Tours, Bibliothèque municipale, MS 520, fol. 20v. The comment comes in Rupescissa's 1354/55 commentary on the prophecy *Veh mundo in centum annis*, known as *De oneribus orbis*, in which he discusses his fear that Peter of Aragon will attack Louis in defense of Sicily, which Rupescissa warns will "allow the introduction of the next Antichrist." On Rupescissa's commentary and prophetic system, see Jeanne Bignami-Odier, "Jean de Roquetaillade (de Rupescissa): Théologien, polémiste, alchimiste," *Histoire littéraire de la France* 41 (1981): 75–209.

153. Battagli, *Marcha di Marco Battagli da Rimini*, 51–54.

represented Johanna as noble and righteous and, most importantly, as Naples's rightful sovereign. In large measure, this change stemmed from the hatred Louis inspired and the sympathy his mistreatment of her awakened.

Louis provided ample fodder for hostile commentators. The perceived intrigue and sordidness surrounding his marriage to Johanna and suspicions of their adultery before Andrew's death outraged commentators. Bartolomeo Sacchi, writing a century later, remembered Louis simply as "Louis the adulterer."[154] Giovanni Villani comments on Louis and Johanna's "wicked marriage" and says that many people calumniated the pope for regularizing it.[155] The *Chronicon Estense* disapprovingly notes the royal couple's consanguinity but contends that their marriage was performed with papal sanction, implicating Clement VI in its irregularity and immorality.[156] Similarly, the *Chronicon Siculum* equates their relationship with concubinage.[157]

Domenico da Gravina in particular expressed scandalized horror at the competition between the Tarantini for Johanna's bed and hand. He alleges that Catherine of Valois and Robert of Taranto took up residence in Castel Nuovo within days of Andrew's death and "remained with [Johanna] day and night in order to persuade her to enter into . . . marriage."[158] The royal drama became increasingly scandalous after Louis decided that he too wanted to marry Johanna. Domenico presents Louis's victory as possibly tantamount to rape:

> Louis suddenly entered the castle, and having raised its drawbridge, he ordered the castle's entrance to be diligently guarded so that no one could enter. And, having gone in to his mother and conferred with her, he immediately gained access to the queen's chamber and had intercourse with her.[159]

If Domenico was anxious to depict Johanna as responsible for Andrew's murder, he was less concerned to demonstrate her willingness to marry Louis. He portrays her as Louis's and Catherine's victim, a pawn maneuvered for their ends. Like Domenico, Matteo Villani also focused on the scandal with which Louis's marriage to Johanna began. Villani, however, charges

154. Bartolomeo Sacchi, *Platynae Istorici—Liber de vita Christi ac omnium pontificum* [AA. 1–1474], ed. Giacinto Gadia, vol. 3, pt. 1 of *RIS*, new ed. (Città di Castello: S. Lapi, 1913), 274.

155. G. Villani, *Nuova Cronica*, XIII.99, 3:511.

156. Bertoni and Vicini, *Chronicon Estense*, 150.

157. De Blasiis, *Chronicon Siculum*, 9.

158. Domenico da Gravina, *Chronicon*, 19.

159. Ibid.

that Acciaiuoli forced both Johanna and Louis into it, manipulating them to serve his own ends:

> And without the dispensation, because he was her kinsman in the third degree, the young man feared to enter the chamber to comfort the queen; and dragged by the arm by his tutor [Acciaiuoli], he married the aforesaid lady in secret.[160]

Villani's Louis, initially, is young and unpracticed, thrust into a situation to which he is not equal. He soon finds himself menaced by the inexorable Hungarian vendetta, against which he cannot defend the Regno, and begins a steady decline into inadequacy.

For Domenico da Gravina, the moment when Louis took possession of both Johanna and the reins of power was a catastrophic turning point in Neapolitan history. Andrew's murder set off a chain reaction. Johanna provided the catalyst, but Louis's victory heralded disaster from which the kingdom could only be relieved by divine intervention:

> Oh, how wretched is that kingdom because reduced to the rule of women and children! Oh, how it behooves each subject to mourn who formerly rejoiced in the bygone years of tranquil peace under the rule of King Robert and his forebears! Now, however, . . . they are each led into war and sadness. Who includes them in the grievous calamity, so that for one woman's crime the entire wretched kingdom is harassed? And, oh, if only through harassment they might be made at peace! But it is feared that only the dispersal of goods and personal danger will follow. . . . Oh, how much evil the cunning demon knew how to manage when he managed the betrayal of [Andrew]! He cunningly foresaw that such great evil must follow from that cause. But yet my hope, while I live, always resides with Christ; I firmly hope to be liberated from such dire straits by He *who heals the contrite of heart* (Ps. 146:3) and *raises up all who are bowed down* (Ps. 144:14).[161]

Domenico thus foresaw calamity for Naples of biblical proportions, echoing the prophet Isaiah's predictions (Isaiah 3:4) about naïve rulers who would misgovern Judah and comparing Naples's degradation to that of Jerusalem, reduced to anarchy under inept rule.

---

160. M. Villani, *Cronica*, I.11, 1:28. Acciaiuoli's fifteenth-century biographer, Matteo Palmieri, offered a similar rendition of events. See Palmieri, *Vita Nicolai Acciaioli*, esp. 8–9.

161. Domenico da Gravina, *Chronicon*, 19–20.

For a time, Domenico believed Louis of Hungary would be the divine scourge that restored order to Naples. His description of Louis and Johanna's flight from the Hungarians emphasizes the inevitability of their defeat:

> Therefore the aforesaid Lord Louis, seeing that his men could not resist the enemy in any way, especially once the king [of Hungary]'s forces had arrived, thought it advisable to leave the kingdom rather than remain in Naples or Capua. . . . Oh, if only someone had seen the unhappy queen wailing in tears with raised voice, her hair disheveled, when from her great castle she descended to the sea, where the galley was prepared for her retreat, boarding the galley without companion, but abandoned by everyone![162]

Domenico thus revels in Johanna and Louis's defeat and humiliation, stressing the ignominy of their retreat. Their flight is proof of their illegitimacy and inadequacy, and Johanna's friendless exile is fitting punishment for her misdeeds.

Louis's flight from Naples is pivotal in many chronicle accounts, most of which focus on his cowardice. His flight provided evidence that he lacked fortitude and courage, shortcomings disastrous in a king. Matteo Villani states that Louis fled in haste and poorly provisioned, primarily because of his inexperience.[163] Other accounts are more inclined to blame Louis's flawed character. Flight was contrary to late medieval standards of masculine honor, shaming a man and creating "a social calamity more disastrous than any other for a man's relations with his fellows, as shameful for him as impurity for a woman."[164] The author of the *Chronicon Estense* states baldly that Louis fled because he was afraid (*timuit*).[165] The Sienese *Cronaca Maggiore* charges that he ran from Naples out of fear of the Hungarian king ("per paura di lui").[166] The chronicler also contemptuously charges that Louis remained in hiding for the duration of his three-day stay in Siena.[167]

Yet, despite Louis's craven flight, fate favored him. Domenico da Gravina was dismayed when Louis of Hungary departed, ending his hopes for a renewed, morally cleansed Regno. He laments that all of the kingdom's

---

162. Ibid., 34–35.
163. M. Villani, *Cronica*, I.11, 1:28.
164. Muir, *Mad Blood Stirring*, xxiv.
165. Bertoni and Vicini, *Chronicon Estense*, 159.
166. "Cronaca Senese, attribuita ad Agnolo di Tura del Grasso, detta la *Cronaca Maggiore*," in Lisini and Iacometti, *Cronache Senesi*, 553. Agnolo confuses Louis of Taranto and Louis of Durazzo.
167. Ibid.: "il detto misser Luigi stè nell'albergo in Siena 3 dì e non uscì mai fuore."

subsequent troubles derived from Johanna's and Louis of Taranto's return.[168] He refuses to recognize Louis of Taranto as king: Throughout his narrative, with few exceptions, "King Louis" is Louis of Hungary, while Louis of Taranto remains "Lord Louis" (*dominus ludovico*). Nonetheless, Domenico was forced to admit that Louis of Taranto ruled Naples. He comments on Johanna's activities immediately after her return, but she fades from his narrative as Domenico describes Louis's determination to be recognized as king and to rule alone.[169] The same pattern appears elsewhere, as in the *Chronicon Estense*. While the chronicler remains pro-Hungarian throughout his narrative, his characterization of Johanna as a harlot ends with Charles of Durazzo's execution, and she is simply the queen of Naples (*regina Neapolim*) for the remainder of the chronicle.[170]

In displacing Johanna, Louis removed her from the scrutiny of hostile commentators; he replaced her both as ruler and as the focus of contemporaries' ire. Domenico da Gravina accordingly recrafted his critique of the royal family to focus on Louis, describing how misplaced was his subjects' trust in him. His narrative continues through Louis of Hungary's second Neapolitan campaign, detailing Louis of Taranto's defeats and dwelling on his failings as a ruler. When called on for aid by his subjects, who believed that he would succor them, Louis responded that "no one could have aid from the king," leaving them, terrified, to see to their own defenses.[171] Indeed, many chroniclers charge Louis with military laxness and incompetence, although some contemporary Sienese chronicles describe him as an active and valued ally.[172]

Matteo Villani's chronicle continues beyond 1350, when Domenico da Gravina's ends, and he reviews Louis's reign as a whole. As a result, he provides the most thorough assessment of Louis's reign and character to be found in contemporary sources, if one penned at a substantial geographic remove and largely based on rumor that made its way to Florence. He followed Louis of Taranto's activities closely, reporting regularly on his reign and cataloging his faults as he progressed from cautious optimism about Louis to the conviction that he was corrupt. As his chronicle progresses, Villani begins to soften his stance on Johanna, whom he increasingly portrays as mistreated and

168. Domenico da Gravina, *Chronicon*, 36.
169. Ibid., 48.
170. The transition begins on 154 of Bertoni and Vicini, *Chronicon Estense*.
171. Domenico da Gravina, *Chronicon*, 53.
172. See Lisini and Iacometti, *Cronache Senesi*, 155, 569–97.

disenfranchised. Johanna, he writes, wished to be more honored by her husband ("volea essere da lui piu reverita") and to have her queenship acknowledged. While he describes Hugh des Baux's duplicity and opportunism, Villani does not fault her for Hugh's dishonorable behavior, and he depicts Johanna as his victim.[173] Indeed, he often returns to the theme of Johanna's victimization.

Villani discusses Johanna's exoneration for Andrew's murder shortly after he describes Hugh's failed attempt to return her to power. Villani's characterization of Johanna at this point is strikingly different from earlier in the chronicle. He began his continuation of his brother's chronicle by reviewing material already recounted by Giovanni, including Andrew's assassination. Matteo's version of the tale differs from Giovanni's in important ways. First, he acknowledges Johanna's right to the throne, even as he laments that Robert's love for his bloodline inspired errors of judgment that led to great misfortune.[174] As a regnant queen, according to Villani, Johanna was a disaster, largely owing to the defects of her sex:

> Dying, [Robert] left the young queen enriched by great treasure, governor of her own realm, but impoverished of mature counsel, both master and lady of her baron, who, as her husband, should have been her lord. And in this was Solomon's dictum verified, which says that if the wife has primacy she becomes contrary to her husband. Johanna, finding herself with dominion, and having immature, vain counsel, showed little honor to her husband and ruled and governed all of the Regno with great wantonness and largesse that was more vain than virtuous. And, through the ambitions of the nobility and by the instigation of perverse and wicked counsel, matrimonial love did not flourish, but rather deteriorated. And so it was, they say, that by wicked machination the Queen became estranged from her husband's love.[175]

Villani traces Andrew's murder to this inversion of right matrimonial order and to the intrigues of Johanna's court. He is less ready than his brother to brand Johanna a viricide or speculate on her extramarital affairs, but he nonetheless sees her as culpable. Her greatest offense may lie in her propensity to be swayed by her advisors and companions, but she shares their guilt.

---

173. M. Villani, *Cronica*, I.94, 1:175.
174. Ibid., I.11, 1:26: "che commisse errori i quali furono cagione di molti mali."
175. Ibid.

Around the time of Johanna's papal exoneration in 1350, Villani moderated his treatment of her. When the papal commission decreed that she was not responsible for Andrew's death, she was a consort who, like Andrew before her, was dishonored by her spouse and barred from power. Marginalized by Louis, Johanna was no longer as threatening or as reprehensible. Thus, while Villani questions the commission's integrity and comments on its ruling sardonically, he does not condemn it or Johanna:

> [Finally,] seeing that if this affair were not concluded it would produce infamy and danger for the queen, everyone desired that the process be concluded. And even though the absolute truth of the matter could not excuse the queen to the extent that the affair was cleansed of its dubious reputation [*fama*], they proposed that if any suspicion of less than perfect matrimonial love could be suggested, or proved, it had not come about through corrupt intention, or by the Queen's desire, but through the force of the evils or deeds which were done to her, which her fragile feminine nature had neither the wisdom nor the ability to redress. And it was proved through many testimonies as though that were true. Having discreet and well-disposed auditors, she was adjudged innocent of this evil deed and absolved of every charge that for some time had been laid on her.[176]

The passing years and her changed circumstances had rendered Johanna more traditionally feminine; the assertion that her "fragile feminine nature" placed her at the mercy of unscrupulous advisors seemed plausible in a way it had not earlier. If the Johanna of 1345 had seemed monstrous, the Johanna of 1350 was more acceptably feminine, her public persona transformed by her assumption of the role of queen consort and beleaguered wife.

Villani's reevaluation of Johanna coincided with growing dislike for her husband. Like many commentators, he was disillusioned by Louis's inability to bring peace to the Regno and appalled by the years of famine, rapine, and violence caused by the struggles within the Angevin family. Villani argues that even before his coronation, Louis was out of his depth, dismayed to find himself "impoverished and poorly obeyed" without any idea of "what to do."[177] He portrays Louis's coronation in ominous terms, describing two portentous events:

---

176. Ibid., II.24, 1:235.
177. Ibid., II.41, 1:265.

And after the coronation, the king rode through the city of Naples in royal vestments, mounted on a large and ponderous warhorse and escorted by his barons. As they were passing through the Petrucci gate on the street to the harbor, certain women, to do him honor and to celebrate, threw roses and perfumed flowers down to him through a window. The horse took fright and reared, and, while the noblemen who guided it struggled to bring it to the ground, the horse, which was heavy, broke the reins. King Louis, finding himself without reins astride the frightened horse, immediately leaped deftly to the ground. And the crown fell from his head and broke into three pieces, losing three points. . . . On this same day, one of his daughters died, the last of his children with the queen. Many people for this reason predicted dire things for the royal majesty.[178]

Villani's description—likely an after-the-fact textual revision—suggests that he, too, predicts dire things for the royal majesty (indeed, he states that the material to follow will reveal Louis's corruption). The dark portents with which Louis's official reign began presaged the new king's destined failure and the calamities to befall the Neapolitan crown.

Villani was harshly critical of Louis as a crowned king. As in Domenico da Gravina's chronicle, Johanna all but disappears as an actor in the royal drama for a time. When she does appear, she is an unnamed member of the royal couple. In general, however, only Louis—*il re Luigi*—is mentioned, and it is to his credit that Villani lays his charges that the Regno was misgoverned, poorly defended, and in a state of near anarchy. He attributes to Louis the unbridled sexual appetite that he saw as common among royalty and by which his brother had earlier characterized Johanna, and he links Louis's lust to his seigniorial failings.[179] In Villani's opinion, the activities of the rebels

---

178. Ibid., III.8, 1:335–36. Villani is incorrect that Françoise, who died in 1352, was the last of Louis's and Johanna's children. Their daughter Catherine died at an indeterminate date after 1362.

179. Villani's chronicle abounds with characterizations of Europe's nobles as immorally libidinous. For instance, he accuses the "king of Spain" (Peter "the Cruel" of Castile) of having put away his wife because of his "disordered" ("disordinato") sexual appetite (ibid., IV.18, 1:497). He charges that Peter "copulated with greatly disordered carnal concupiscence" ("si copulò con tanta disordinata concupiscenza carnale") with his mistress, with whom he did "many dissolute and shameful things" ("molte dissolute e sconce cose") (ibid., 1:498). The prologue to book 6 expands on Villani's antinoble, antiroyal sentiments, as the chronicler muses on the "tyrannical nobility" ("tirannesca signoria"), whose "unbridled libidos take no satisfaction from the act" ("la loro sfrenata libidine non prende saziamento dal fatto") (ibid., VI.1, 1:713–14). The prologue to book 7 continues this theme, considering "the horrible sins committed through the unbridled license of princes and worldly lords" ("lli orribili peccati che ssi commettono per la sfrenata licenzia de' prencipi e de' signori mondani") (ibid., VII.1, 2:13).

and mercenaries who overran the Regno reflected Louis's negligence, and he argues that their victories stemmed from the fact that "the king would not supply himself against them," despite ample warning. Instead, "the provision he made . . . was to remain continually in dance and celebration with women."[180] The Neapolitans suffered greatly due to the mercenaries' depredations, which, Villani argues, took place precisely because the companies knew that "King Louis had not made a single provision for defense against them."[181] Villani also heaps scorn on Louis's eventual decision to pay the mercenaries to leave the Regno, stating that the king "had no power other than with money" and that his exaction of the required funds from his subjects elicited "great complaint against the Crown by the men of that land."[182]

According to Villani, the Regno's people soon longed for Johanna's return to power. He describes a riot in November 1355 by her partisans, strengthened in number by those disgusted by Louis's behavior: "By common accord," Villani tells us, "everyone took up arms, and they armed all of the foreign merchants and artisans in the city. And they raised the riot, shouting: 'Long live the queen, and death to her council!'"[183] The riot illustrates Villani's developing argument that Louis's iniquitous rule constituted usurpation of his wife's position, and he begins to use Johanna symbolically to emphasize Louis's failure as a king.

Under Louis's care, the kingdom was devoured by war ("era d'ogni parte in guerra") and chaos ("tempesta"), so that "not a single road of it was safe."[184] The Regno's people suffered due to the "bad providence of the king, their lord, who demonstrated himself to care for little outside of his own pleasures."[185] As Louis becomes an indolent, selfish failure, Johanna reemerges as his foil. Whereas Villani represented her independent rule as a travesty, as a queen consort, Johanna becomes the epitome of chivalric queenliness. When Louis's forces took Messina, they captured the Sicilian infantas; Villani describes how Johanna took the princesses into her retinue. She behaved graciously: "having received the ladies with great honor, the queen placed them in her company, treating them charitably in all things."[186] By contrast, Villani

---

180. Ibid., IV.58, 1:557–58.
181. Ibid., V.56, 1:680.
182. Ibid., V.76, 1:699.
183. Ibid., V.88, 1:711.
184. Ibid., VI.74
185. Ibid., VI.74, 1:799: "per gran colpa della mala provedenza de rre loro signore, che fuori di suoi diletti poco d'altro si mostrava di curare."
186. Ibid., VII.44, 2:64.

accuses Louis of having ordered the death of Count Simon of Chiaramonte, who had been his agent in Sicily and who wished to marry Infanta Bianca.[187] He portrays Louis as ungrateful and juxtaposes his ignoble behavior with Johanna's greater courtliness where Bianca was concerned.

By the end of Louis's reign, "the barons, especially the princes, were not at peace and in concord with the king," whom Villani represents as increasingly irrational.[188] Villani charges him with burning the city of Venafri in a violent rage: "The king, in the heat of his fury, not reflecting that the city was his and had long been part of the kingdom, had it burned and destroyed, because he could not rid it of rebellious bandits."[189] Louis's irrationality was all the more pronounced because of his alienation of Acciaiuoli, without whose guidance he was, Villani says, "impoverished of wise counsel"—language that, significantly, echoes his earlier assessment of Johanna's reign.[190] His appeal was so limited and his power so diminished that it fell to Johanna to accomplish affairs of state. When they refused to fight against Louis of Durazzo, Louis disbanded his knights from Nido and Capovana, whose loyalty he suspected, and would have executed them but for Johanna's influence. Intervening with the knights, she "prayed and commanded those from Capovana and from Nido that they carry out the king's desire, and this was done without argument out of reverence for the queen."[191] Louis then proceeded to ransack Capovana and Nido in fury, until his brother, Robert, calmed him. Villani thus presents Louis as hotheaded and impulsive, and he implies that he would have committed even greater evils were it not for the intervention of his wife and brother.

Villani represents Johanna as having a powerful influence with her people; reverence for her held greater sway with them than did fear of her husband. She fills the traditional queenly role of intercessor, endowed with an almost maternal interest in her subjects' welfare. He also depicts her as an ideal consort, drawing on the image of queens as softening influences with their tougher husbands: it was the understood function of the queen to exemplify "the virtues of sanctity, healing and prayer, intercession for the guilty, and charity for the weak."[192] Thus, as a consort, Johanna became for Villani the embodiment of queenly virtue.

---

187. Ibid., VII.54, 2:76.
188. Ibid., IX.12, 2:298.
189. Ibid., VI.49, 1:769.
190. Ibid., IX.95, 2:421.
191. Ibid., IX.94, 2:420.
192. McNamara, "Women and Power through the Family Revisited," 26.

After Louis died, Villani was unsparingly critical in contemplating his reign: He was a "lord of rather shameful and dissolute life."[193] Villani's final reflections on Louis are damning:

> He was a lord of little weight and less authority. . . . He showed little love for his own blood; he . . . treated his cousins poorly, driving them through his aggression to rebel. He was a liar when it came to promises. . . . Those among his barons who were the most wicked sinners were closest to him and shared the most secret counsel and the greatest power, and with them he lived dishonorably. He was fickle, timid and cowardly in cases of adverse fortune. . . . He was greedy to make money and maintained justice half-heartedly, and he made himself little feared by his barons. . . . To the queen he gave little honor, whether by his own fault, which was great, or by the queen's. As though she were a common woman and in great insult to the crown, he beat her often, and in that which was her own, he did not let her do either for herself or for others what honor required.[194]

Tellingly, Villani directly associates Johanna with the Neapolitan crown: By beating his wife, Louis insulted not his position or his responsibility, but the crown itself. A common woman, Villani suggests, could be beaten by her husband, but Johanna was no common woman. Villani thus endorses Johanna's inherited position, so that she embodies the crown even as she is also Louis's abused wife, both sovereign and female. As Ernst Kantorowicz has demonstrated, later medieval kings had two bodies, an individuated, mortal one and an immortal one that embodied, inherited, and transmitted sovereignty.[195] Johanna, the inheritor of Angevin sovereignty, also had two bodies, one mortal and female and one immortal and sacrosanct, against both of which Louis sinned. His failings as a husband thus extended to and encompassed his failings as a king.

Villani's narration of Louis's career plots a trajectory as well for Johanna's reputation. Early in his career, she is Louis's coconspirator; then she becomes the personification of the evil from which his rule might rescue the Regno. When he gains the upper hand and reigns alone, she disappears from the narrative, appearing only occasionally as *la reina*, his often

---

193. M. Villani, *Cronica*, X.100, 2:578: "signore d'assai sconcia e disoluta vita."

194. Ibid., 2:579–80. The passage about Johanna reads, "Alla reina facea poco onore, e o per suo difetto, ch'assai n'avea, o per fallo della reina, molte volte come una vil femina in grande vituperio della corona la battea, e di quello ch'era suo no lle lasciava fare né a sé né altrui il debito onore."

195. Ernst Kantorowicz, *The King's Two Bodies: A Study in Mediaeval Political Theology* (Princeton: Princeton University Press, 1997).

nameless consort, devoid of agency or personality. When Louis's iniquitous rule negates the memories of her own, Johanna reappears as the legitimate queen for whom her people long. When he is arbitrary and violent, she is the intercessor who protects her subjects. And finally, at the end of his calamity-riddled reign, she is the queen who embodies sovereignty, Naples's rightful ruler—perhaps flawed in her female humanity, but also one with the crown.

Villani's account of Louis's reign and character amplifies comments made by other commentators, before and after Louis's death, that suggest that his reassessment of Johanna—which must have been based largely on reports about Naples and about the royal couple that traveled to Florence—reflects broader trends. Rupescissa remarks in his *Liber ostensor quod adesse festinant tempora* (1356) that an Italian visitor to Avignon had told him that all "the holy men and devoted people of Italy" knew that Louis would not produce an heir. For, Rupescissa says, commenting on a prophecy known as *Cum necatur flos ursi*, which includes a passage about a rooster and hen, Louis is the cock who does not spring up, and his wife the hen who does not seek the nest in order to produce chicks.[196] In so describing Louis, Rupescissa drew on rumors that Louis was an abusive husband. He says that Louis's hardness has "greatly wearied" Johanna, prompting her to avoid his "nest" and deny him children.[197] His description suggests that he was privy to current gossip about the royal couple, as to widespread criticism of Louis. Indeed, during Louis's reign, Rupescissa abandoned his earlier conviction that the Neapolitan Angevins were destined to play a pivotal role in the Apocalypse as the champions of the Church.

Early in Louis's reign, Petrarch had been cautiously optimistic about him. He wrote to Acciaiuoli in February 1352 that, when the Hungarians finally left Naples, "the worst side ha[d] been conquered . . . and the best side ha[d] triumphed."[198] He welcomed Louis's coronation, anticipating the day when he would restore "desired tranquility to the ravished kingdom and to the people."[199] Petrarch's optimism derived almost entirely from faith in Acciaiuoli's "well-known talent," which he trusted to ensure "rule . . . with just moderation."[200] He proffered Robert as a model and hoped that Louis

---

196. John of Rupescissa, *Liber ostensor*, 165, §IV.48. Rupescissa's identification of Louis as the cock (*gallus*) plays on the dual valence of the word, which here means both Frenchman and rooster.

197. Ibid., 150, §IV.28.

198. *Epistolae familiares*, XII,2, in Petrarch, *Rerum familiarium*, 2:132 (Petrarch, *Le Familiari*, 3:6).

199. Petrarch, *Rerum familiarium*, 2:132 (Petrarch, *Le Familiari*, 3:6: "ereptam restituens regno pacem, tranquillitatem populis exoptatam").

200. Petrarch, *Rerum familiarium*, 2:132 (Petrarch, *Le Familiari*, 3:6).

would emulate "his illustrious and divine uncle."[201] Disappointment soon led Petrarch to reassess the situation in Naples. In April 1352, he lamented that the Regno "within and without its boundaries . . . is shaken and belabored."[202] Around the time of Louis's death, he wrote a letter praising Johanna for her "generous, noble, and beneficent mind," saying that he was "sorry for her, . . . and . . . for Italy," and pledging his support for her as Robert's blood descendent—and thus as the legitimate heir to the Neapolitan throne.[203] His final, regretful analysis of Louis appears in a letter to Acciaiuoli, written just after Louis died. He mourns that the seneschal had not been as able to "instill the royal virtues in [Louis] as [he was] able to facilitate his path to the throne."[204] He observes that, had Louis been responsive and allowed Acciaiuoli to guide him, he would have left behind a more renowned name.[205]

Boccaccio portrayed Louis as Alcestus, which he claimed derives from *alce*, meaning "virtue," and *estus*, meaning "fervor,"[206] although it may also echo the myth of Alcestis, who gave her life so that her husband, who had offended the gods, could live (just as Louis of Taranto fought to protect his spouse from Louis of Hungary's vengeance). His sixth eclogue represents Louis, even at the end of his checkered career, as Naples's champion against the forces besieging the Regno. Yet, even as he poetically extolled Louis's virtue, Boccaccio criticized him in *De mulieribus claris*. Alcestus may have acquired "the manners of an excellent and virtuous king" toward the end of his life—when Boccaccio hoped to win his patronage and planned to dedicate *De casibus* to him—but they are not on display in Boccaccio's nearly contemporaneous biography of Johanna.[207] His paean to Johanna praises

201. Petrarch, *Rerum familiarium*, 2:139 (Petrarch, *Le Familiari*, 3:16.)

202. Letter to Stefano Colonna: *Epistolae familiares*, XV,7 in Petrarch, *Rerum familiarium*, 3:268 (Petrarch, *Le Familiari*, 3:150).

203. Letter to Hugo, Count of San Severino: *Epistolae familiares*, XXIII,17 in Petrarch, *Rerum familiarium*, 4:296 (Petrarch, *Le Familiari*, 4:200: "illustrem . . . reginam, . . . generosum illum serenumque ac benificum animum . . . Doleo propter ipsam . . . denique propter Italiam"). Petrarch writes Johanna was born of Robert's blood—"sanguine ortum erit." The date and provenance of *Epistolae familiares*, XXIII,17 are unknown (cf. Ernest H. Wilkins, *Petrarch's Correspondence* [Padua: Antenore, 1960], 87). In most collections, it comes immediately before a letter to Niccolò Acciaiuoli that discusses Louis's death as a recent event. The letter deals mostly with "the court dogs" and references Johanna's struggles within the court. This discussion and Petrarch's statement of sympathy and support for Johanna may make most sense if one assumes Louis still to be living.

204. *Epistolae familiares*, XXIII,18 in Petrarch, *Rerum familiarium*, 4:299 (Petrarch, *Le Familiari*, 4:203).

205. Petrarch, *Le Familiari*, 4:203: "profecto diutius vixisset, felicius obiisset, nomen clarius reliquisset."

206. Boccaccio, *Eclogues*, 219.

207. Ibid.

her, among other things, for withstanding "the grim ways of her husbands," listed—along with flight, exile, and "papal threats"—among the evils she has endured.[208] Given that the portion of *De mulieribus claris* that describes Johanna was written in 1362 and *coniugum* (husbands) is plural, this must refer to Andrew of Hungary and Louis of Taranto, both of whom Boccaccio had earlier praised. Here the tables are turned, and he portrays Johanna as the victim and eventual victor in struggles against her husbands.

This discrepancy may be linked to a decisive break between Boccaccio and Acciaiuoli, which occurred in 1362.[209] It may also reflect Boccaccio's efforts to secure Johanna's patronage after Louis's death. Either way, Johanna's transformation within Boccaccio's work—one that survived in subsequent redactions of *De mulieribus claris*—accords with changes in her public persona and the political realities of the time when she resumed independent rule. In 1345, no one would have described Johanna as valiant for having tolerated Andrew. By 1362, Andrew and Louis were listed among Johanna's burdens, and their conflicts with her form a background of martyrdom and forbearance against which she is transformed into the magnificent queen Boccaccio describes. Boccaccio's reevaluation of Johanna was gradual. In 1355, when he penned the first redaction of *De casibus*, although he still characterized Johanna as a whore, he shifted the blame for Andrew's death from Johanna to her nurse, Filippa Catanese (whom he also charges acted as Johanna's procuress).[210] Boccaccio would later excise his criticism of Johanna from *De casibus*, and his celebration of her as a radiant queen would become his lasting assessment of her. Silenced and marginalized by Louis, Johanna emerged victorious in 1362, cleansed of her past reputation by suffering. The harlot queen had gestated during Louis's reign to be reborn a paragon of feminine virtue acquired through patience and endurance. As a queen consort, Johanna cast off the trappings of sovereignty that her contemporaries objected to, with the irony that in the process her sovereignty itself became acceptable and even desirable.

In large measure, Johanna's popularity and rehabilitated reputation at the end of Louis of Taranto's reign were byproducts of his unpopularity. Reacting

---

208. Boccaccio, *Famous Women*, 471–72.

209. Boccaccio's grievances against Acciaiuoli, whom he would lampoon as Midas in his eclogues, are laid out in an extensive letter to Acciaiuoli's steward, Francesco Nelli. See Epistola XIII in Boccaccio, *Epistole e Lettere*, 596–629.

210. Giovanni Boccaccio, *De casibus virorum illustrium*, ed. Pier Giorgio Ricci and Vittorio Zaccaria, vol. 9 of *Tutte le opere di Giovanni Bocaccio* (Milan: Arnoldo Mondadori Editore, 1983), "Appendici," 1107.

first against Louis of Hungary and then against Louis of Taranto, many of her contemporaries transferred their sympathies to Johanna, preferring her to opponents who, by contrast, reflected well on her. However, her more traditionally queenly conduct and even her temporary marginalization were also important factors in her transformation. The patience that Innocent VI urged on her, whether displayed by her own will or forced on her, did, in fact, equate her with the *ancilla Christi*. Her suffering, as imagined by contemporaries, rendered her more virtuous.

Indeed, the perception that she patiently endured abuse at Louis's hands feminized Johanna in ways with which her contemporaries could sympathize. Contemporary medical discourse described women as naturally "passive and sedentary," and Johanna's enforced passivity thrust her into a role perceived as more natural than that of sovereign queen.[211] She became like Griselda, the patient wife Johanna's contemporaries Petrarch, Boccaccio, and Chaucer praised for withstanding her husband's intolerable cruelty without complaint. If medieval polemic demonized powerful, independent women, it praised women who were meek and often valorized their suffering. Chaucer's *Legend of Good Women*, for instance, identifies female virtue with mildness, pity, and patient suffering. His Hypermnestra—who also appears among Boccaccio's famous women—is "pitouse, sadde, wyse, trewe as steel," enduring reproach and imprisonment rather than betray her husband.[212] For Boccaccio, Hypermnestra was an example of womanly virtue because she refused to fall "into shameful infamy," modeling "righteous conduct" instead.[213] As Jill Mann has observed, in Chaucer's (as in Petrarch's and Boccaccio's) literary world, "power is male, submission and suffering are female."[214] In *The Man of Law's Tale*, Constance notes that women's lot is "thraldom to oure bodies and penance." Like Hypermnestra, Constance "suffers her fate with stoic dignity," modeling behavior that, Mann argues, is for Chaucer "the only acceptable feminine ideal"—namely, "passive resignation" and "silent endurance."[215]

Chaucer's Italian contemporaries shared his view of passive feminine suffering. Boccaccio describes it as virtuous, praising Johanna for enduring the "grim ways" of her husbands. Like Boccaccio's Polyxena, whose "sublime

211. Cadden, *Meanings of Sex Difference in the Middle Ages*, 176.

212. Geoffrey Chaucer, "The Legend of Good Women," line 2582, in *The Complete Works of Geoffrey Chaucer*, ed. Walter William Skeat (Oxford: Oxford University Press, 1903), 6:393.

213. Boccaccio, *Famous Women*, XIV.

214. Jill Mann, *Feminizing Chaucer* (Cambridge: Boydell & Brewer, 2002), 101.

215. Ibid., 102, 107.

spirit" could not be crushed "under the sword of a victorious enemy," Johanna survived defeat at Louis's hands and emerged a model of patience and forbearance.[216] According to Christine de Pizan, who was heavily invested in royal performance and comportment, princesses should aspire to such feminine virtue, displaying "humility . . . pity, charity, chastity, and patience," the last exemplified by "being long-suffering, turning the other cheek" when offended.[217] During Louis's reign, Johanna exemplified such patience and humility. Stripped of the power she had wielded over Andrew, as over her realm, she was consigned to a more traditional womanly (and wifely) role, and her suffering—a realization of the medieval dictum that woman signifies Christ's humanity and was born to suffer—redeemed her.[218] At the same time, seeming weak and being dominated made Johanna a better woman. Matteo Villani's description of Johanna's first marriage reveals his anxiety about gender inversion, and it reflects concerns discernible in other contemporary accounts of Johanna's early reign. Her marriage to Louis corrected that inversion; she was no longer "both master and lady of her baron." Once balance had been restored and she was relegated to a more traditionally feminine role—because being the object of violence made her the epitome of femininity—Johanna ceased to trouble commentators in the same way. Indeed, the abuse she was believed to have endured endeared her to them.

The literary and epistolary Johanna of 1362 differed radically from that of 1345. In contemporary accounts, she figures not as a harlot and adulteress but as a humbled, wronged queen consort. Louis's correction of the inversion that had so concerned observers obscured her earlier, monstrous persona. His redefinition of her position—literally visible in the frontispiece to the Order of the Knot's statutes—ultimately proved too successful. Her new persona, when juxtaposed with Louis's own reputation for cruelty and dissipation, reflected poorly on him. Ironically, her silence and humiliation, like her relegation to the role of consort, ennobled her, in some measure validating her return to power. She became the maternal, feminine alternative to Louis's disordered, lax kingship, and her blood descent from Robert—celebrated as the personification of a lost golden age—legitimated her return to power.

---

216. Boccaccio, *Famous Women*, XXXIII.

217. Christine de Pizan, *Le Livre de Trois Vertus: édition critique*, ed. C. C. Willard and Eric Hicks, Bibliothèque du XVe siècle 50 (Paris: H. Champion, 1989), 30; Karen Pratt, "The Image of the Queen in Old French Literature," in *Queens and Queenship in Medieval Europe*, ed. Anne Duggan (Bury St. Edmunds: Boydell Press, 1997), 238.

218. Caroline Walker Bynum, "'. . . And Woman His Humanity': Female Imagery in the Religious Writing of the Later Middle Ages," in *Fragmentation and Redemption: Essays on Gender and the Human Body in Medieval Religion* (New York: Zone Books, 1992), esp. 171–79.

The reactions of his contemporaries toward Louis's treatment of Johanna reveal that she, despite her sex, was perceived as the rightful inheritor of Angevin sovereignty. Robert's reign was remembered, during the turbulence of Louis's, as a time of peace and order, and Johanna, his direct descendent, represented hope for the restoration of order. Once Louis of Hungary had undermined his own claims to Neapolitan sovereignty and Louis of Taranto had proved a spectacular failure, Johanna's return to power seemed both right and desirable. Indeed, her husband's mistreatment of her—which Villani tellingly equated to abuse of the crown—amounted to an act of lèse-majesté, because she was Naples's true ruler.

❦ CHAPTER 3

A Most Loving Daughter

Filial Piety and the Apogee of Johanna's Reign

> You may have found . . . writings of pagan authors
> . . . criticizing women, [but] you will find little said
> against them in the holy legends of Jesus Christ and His
> Apostles; instead, even in the histories of all the saints,
> just as you can see yourself, you will find through God's
> grace many cases of extraordinary firmness and strength
> in women. Oh, the beautiful service, the outstanding
> charity which they have performed with great care and
> solicitude, unflinchingly, for the servants of God!
>
> Christine de Pizan, *The Book of the City of Ladies*
> (ca. 1405)

After Louis of Taranto's death, Johanna re-emerged as an actor on the stage of European politics. She did so with the benefit of the improved reputation won by her long absence from public scrutiny and her perceived patience and resilience in the face of suffering. She stood poised to enter a new phase in her career, one in which she would actively reign as a sovereign queen.[1] Giovanni Boccaccio lauded her at the time as the "radiant splendor of Italy, that unique glory not only of women but of rulers," but it remained to be seen whether she would or even could live up to his revised assessment of her.[2]

During the period book-ended by Louis's death and the beginning of the Western Schism in 1378, Johanna worked to redefine herself as a sovereign queen. She asserted herself as such, ruling alone, without the interference of her two subsequent husbands—who were not associated in her reign[3]—or a papal legate while she pursued a policy of widely recognized support for

---

1. The scholarly consensus is that while Johanna benefited from the counsel of skilled advisers, she directed the Regno's government. See Gaglione, *Donne e potere a napoli*, 51, 249–51, and Monter, *The Rise of Female Kings in Europe*, 62.

2. Boccaccio, *Famous Women*, 2–3.

3. William Monter has noted that Johanna's coins after 1362 represent the queen alone, without either her third or her fourth husband. See *The Rise of Female Kings in Europe*, 67; cf. Monter, "Gendered Sovereignty," 540.

the papacy and pious action modeled on the examples of her Angevin forebears. Her artistic commissions reflect her ambitions: In the miniature for
sext in the *Book of Hours of Johanna of Anjou*, completed in the latter half of
the 1360s, Johanna's portrayal echoes and refutes the frontispiece to Louis's
statutes for the Order of the Knot (see figure 7).[4] Johanna, once again clad
in a red dress with long white sleeves, again kneels before the Trinity, here in
pious study. She is alone, without her consort, and God the Father extends
a golden scepter directly to her. Other images in the manuscript also stress
Johanna's singularity, her piety, and divine approbation of her queenship, as
on folio 234v, in which the Trinity blesses Johanna, and folio 240v, in which
Johanna shelters beneath the Virgin Mary's cloak as the Virgin presents her to
Christ (see figure 8). The visual program of the manuscript, commissioned
for Johanna's own use, thus encapsulates her conception of her sovereignty.
She carried that understanding of her sovereignty into her political, diplomatic, and religious activities. If only temporarily, she shrugged off both the
mantle of the "harlot queen" and that of the long-suffering wife, emerging
instead as a true Angevin sovereign, a divinely appointed monarch who was
a prominent member of the league that fought to protect papal prerogatives
in Italy and laid the groundwork for the papacy's return to Rome. Freed
from Louis's dominance and the shadow of the scandals that had dogged her
early career, Johanna was able, for the first time in her already long reign,
to steer her kingdom and participate in shaping her own image, crafting for
herself a modified form of Angevin sovereignty tailored to her position as a
regnant queen.

While the exercise of sovereignty and not the reshaping of her reputation must have been Johanna's prime concern, the two were intimately linked. Johanna's public actions and self-presentation portrayed
her as a very different woman from that described by contemporaries
earlier in her career. Princely reputation was highly prized in medieval
Europe, something stressed in court commissions, in mirrors for princes,
and in criticism of disreputable monarchs. Medieval society's "exter-
nally oriented honor ethic" meant that a woman in Johanna's position
was always "on display, subject to the judgment of others, and continually reinvented in performance"—something of which Johanna and her
advisers must have been well aware.[5] Accordingly, in her rhetorical and
behavioral self-presentation, as in cultural commissions, Johanna stressed

4. Vienna, Österreichische Nationalbibliothek, MS Cod. 1921, fol. 231v. Cf. Duran, "The
Politics of Art," 88–89, and Bräm, *Neapolitanische Bilderbibeln des Trecento*, 1:183, 451–52.

5. Crane, *The Performance of Self*, 4.

Figure 7. Johanna of Naples at study, receiving a golden scepter from the Trinity. *Book of Hours of Johanna I*—Vienna, Österreichische Nationalbibliothek, Cod. 1921, fol. 231v.

her legitimacy as a regnant queen whose persona was defined by piety and virtue. As Thelma Fenster and Daniel Lord Smail have argued, in a culture that placed *fama* at the center of legal, ethical, and moral discussion, "*fama* as talk had to be fed." It was of vital and inescapable importance, requiring

FIGURE 8.   The Virgin Mary presents Johanna of Naples to Christ. *Book of Hours of Johanna I*—Vienna, Österreichische Nationalbibliothek, Cod. 1921, fol. 240v.

"conscious manipulation."[6] If her *fama* had earlier been the product of talk about her, Johanna now had the opportunity, because *fama* was constantly

---

6. Thelma Fenster and Daniel Lord Smail, eds., "Introduction," in *Fama: The Politics of Talk and Reputation in Medieval Europe* (Ithaca: Cornell University Press, 2003), 4.

renegotiated, to reshape her reputation, tailoring her public performances of sovereignty to create a new, positive *fama* that was a potent political tool. While her actions may well have reflected genuine religious and political commitments, they also did the cultural work of legitimating her position and enhancing her public image.

Johanna's reputation during the period of her renewed rule was characterized by loyal, even obedient papal allegiance, religious endowments, and patronage of and friendship with living saints (see chapter 4). Like most ruling dynasties, the Angevins had long cultivated a reputation for piety. As Samantha Kelly points out, "The ideal of the pious king was a commonplace in medieval mirrors of princes, and an image most kings sought to embody: regular prayer and confession, patronage of religious houses, almsgiving, and similar activities were all standard practice."[7] Angevin monarchs—particularly Robert and Sancia—had gone beyond standard practice, performing acts of public piety that stressed their dynasty's special grace. Robert had preached sermons, avidly collected religious texts, and taken part, alongside Sancia, in the vexed dispute over apostolic poverty, while Sancia had gained fame for her commitment to Spiritual Franciscan ideals and ardent desire to live as a Clarissan nun.[8] The traditional modes of sacral Angevin kingship were inaccessible to Johanna by virtue of her sex. Yet by cultivating a reputation for piety—the virtue most associated with femininity, as with righteous rulership—and by rhetorically subordinating herself to the papacy as its loving, loyal daughter, she articulated an active, devout queenship that trod the middle ground between Robert's quasi-sacerdotal kingship and the less worldly, more overtly spiritual piety favored by her dynasty's princesses, most recently Sancia.[9] Too feminine to be a sacral king and, by necessity, too active in the world to be a saintly princess, Johanna drew on and adapted both models. She sought high-profile associations with people of unimpeachable reputation, and she publicized and performed her loyalty to the pope rhetorically and in military action. Humbling herself before saints and popes while assuming the role of papal champion, she modified the traditional role of the

---

7. Kelly, *The New Solomon*, 73.

8. On Robert's self-presentation, see Kelly, *The New Solomon*, and Darleen Pryds, *The King Embodies the Word: Robert d'Anjou and the Politics of Preaching* (Leiden: Brill, 2000). On Sancia's piety, and particularly her relationship to the Franciscan order, see Musto, "Queen Sancia of Naples," and Bruzelius, "Queen Sancia of Mallorca."

9. See Klaniczay, *Holy Rulers and Blessed Princesses*, esp. 295–319. Klaniczay argues for a thirteenth-century transition, discernible in the French, Hungarian, and Neapolitan royal houses, from promoting saintly kings to saintly princesses who, like Elizabeth of Hungary, cultivated close relationships to the mendicant orders and retired from public life and court festivity (ibid., 295).

Angevin monarch to emerge, for a time, as the papacy's staunchest supporter and a celebrated queen regnant.

Johanna's labors bore fruit: The negative *fama* of her early reign receded, although it never entirely disappeared. Association with and obedience to figures with recognized spiritual power and authority helped to legitimate her exercise of earthly sovereignty—not merely within her own kingdom but also as a leading figure in European politics. Her new reputation as an active, successful queen for a time trumped her competing reputation as an illegitimate wanton, and contemporaries were all but silent in the 1360s and 1370s regarding scandals in Naples. Instead, they concentrated on Johanna's service to the papacy and demonstrations of piety. Their willingness to do so suggests that she succeeded in sublimating the aspects of her queenship that rendered her so threatening, replacing them with a more palatable model of regnant queenship.

Fama and Historical Memory

Émile Léonard described the period after Louis of Taranto's death as the apogee of Johanna's reign. Yet modern scholarship often ignores or dismisses her independent reign (ca. 1362–80) or treats it—often without offering justification—as a failure.[10] Geoffrey Barraclough, for instance, characterizes Johanna as "infamous, dissolute and incompetent," describing her succession to the Neapolitan throne as disastrous for the papacy (although he presents no evidence to support these assertions).[11] To Suzanne Noffke, Catherine of Siena's editor, Johanna appears "licentious, violent, and fickle, an opportunist of the first degree," while Ronald G. Witt, in a biography of Coluccio Salutati, describes her similarly as "a licentious and indolent queen, committed to bedroom intrigues."[12] David Abulafia sums up the period as "a constant record of court intrigues," although he concedes that Johanna succeeded, at long last, in negotiating a settlement over Sicily.[13]

---

10. A recent, notable exception is Monter, who identifies Johanna's rule as pivotal for the history of female sovereignty. See *The Rise of Female Kings in Europe*, 62, 64–67.

11. Geoffrey Barraclough, *The Medieval Papacy* (Norwich: Harcourt, Brace & World, 1968), 162; cf. Bridget Morris, *St. Birgitta of Sweden* (Woodbridge: Boydell Press, 1999), 122.

12. Catherine of Siena, *The Letters of Catherine of Siena*, ed. and trans. Suzanne Noffke (Tempe: Arizona Center for Medieval and Renaissance Studies, 2000), 1:98; Ronald G. Witt, *Hercules at the Crossroads: The Life, Works, and Thought of Coluccio Salutati* (Durham, NC: Duke University Press, 1983), 127.

13. Abulafia, "The Italian South," 511–12.

Such dismissive attitudes stretch back through time to the biographical summary of Johanna's life prepared for Louis XII of France (see chapter 1), which truncated her lengthy reign to encompass only Andrew of Hungary's assassination and her own murder, and beyond that to rhetoric associated with her role in the schism (see chapter 5), altogether ignoring the intervening decades. They spring from a perception of Johanna's reign that depends solely on hindsight and the distortion of historical memory, and they grow out of uncritical acceptance of her detractors' appraisals of her. Her long career is refracted through the prism of the schism, so that only its scandals—Andrew's murder, rumors of adultery and court intrigue, her own murder, and her role in the schism, as interpreted by her opponents—can be seen in sharp focus.

Even scholars and authors who have dealt directly with Johanna's reign in the years since Léonard's monumental but incomplete biography have treated its second half only cursorily, often focusing on its scandals at the expense of its successes. In large measure, they do so because of reliance on contemporary sources that are politically biased (as in the case of Pierre d'Ameil's correspondence, discussed below) or taken out of context (as in the case of Birgitta of Sweden's *Revelations*, discussed in chapter 4). By the same token, modern scholars are blinded by knowledge of Johanna's role in the Western Schism as an early, prominent supporter of the Avignon pope Clement VII. Johanna's part in the schism transformed her reputation (see chapter 5), effacing the pious persona that dominated accounts of her reign between 1362 and 1378.

Reading Johanna's reign through sources aware of her role in the schism obscures how differently she was perceived before the cataclysm of the schism. If one excludes sources that treat her reign through that prism, concentrating instead on accounts penned before the schism, a decidedly different picture emerges. If she did not earn the accolades contemporaries reserved for her ancestors, neither was Johanna commonly judged a failure. Contemporary assessments, even when voiced by political opponents, are most remarkable not for their attacks on Johanna but for their expressions of admiration. Witt's curt dismissal of Johanna notwithstanding, Salutati provided a sympathetic epitaph for her that acts as the sad counterpoint to Boccaccio's triumphal introduction to her independent reign. Writing in 1381 to congratulate Charles III of Durazzo (1345–86), who had just deposed and imprisoned her, Salutati reminded Naples's new king that Johanna provided a model of wise, just rule:

> You will discover no woman among the feminine sex who can compare
> with this one, your Johanna, daughter of Charles, duke of Calabria,

whether in magnitude of spirit or in virtues or in glory. Consequently, that woman of such great benevolence and mercy, who had been opposed from the time of her accession—after the removal of the celebrated King Robert—now in the fortieth year of her reign, having amply secured the government, governed with mildness of character and the bridle of justice, with remarkable consolation and effectiveness for all of her subjects, whose well-being she always consulted; and if virtue of leadership, mercy, justice, and benevolence were able to stabilize the king's throne, her scepter would necessarily have been preserved most firmly and with the deserved goodwill of her subjects.[14]

That Salutati, who supported the Roman pope Urban VI, should offer such praise of Johanna in the early years of the schism testifies to her positive reputation during her independent reign. Her strategies of self-presentation, like her political and diplomatic strategies, were remarkably effective. Despite the negative light that time and hindsight have cast on her, Johanna's reputation on the eve of the schism was markedly different from what it would become. It stands as testimony to her success and, indeed, to the success of sovereign queenship as she helped to define it.

Renegotiating Sovereignty

Happy Accidents

To some degree, Johanna's perceived success as a sovereign and the comparative tranquility of her independent reign were accidents of history and survival. Louis of Durazzo, the last Durazzeschi prince of Johanna's generation, died in 1362, leaving a young son, Charles (Johanna's eventual deposer), whom Johanna brought to be raised in the royal household.[15] Louis's death constituted the removal of one of the last great impediments to her rule, so that only Philip and Robert of Taranto remained of the princes who had challenged Johanna early in her reign. Philip had married Johanna's sister, Mary, in 1355, and their frustrated ambitions remained substantial obstacles. Mary's four daughters—Johanna, Agnes, Clementia, and Margaret

---

14. Coluccio Salutati, *Epistolario di Coluccio Salutati*, ed. Francesco Novati, 4 vols. (Rome: Forzani E. C. Tipografi del Senato, 1891), 2:24–25.

15. Léonard, *Les Angevins de Naples*, 402. In addition to essentially adopting Charles (the future Charles III), who had been living in the royal household as a hostage, Johanna also posthumously pardoned Louis of Durazzo (ibid., 392, 405), clearing his name and pardoning his family for their rebellion.

of Durazzo—were Johanna's likely heirs, and their family's bids for power, as well as those of their des Baux (or del Balzo) cousins, provided much of the intrigue of the latter half of Johanna's reign. Their interests remained entangled with those of the papal Curia, where Cardinals Élie de Talleyrand of Périgord (uncle to the Durazzeschi) and his archrival, Guy de Boulogne, continued to press their competing interests with the new pope, Urban V (r. 1362–70).[16] Factionalism continued, but when there was violence—as when Francesco del Balzo and Philip of Taranto went to war against one another in the 1360s—Johanna was not directly involved and freer to pursue her own interests and those of the kingdom than she had been before. Time and mortality continued to remove her opponents: Robert of Taranto and Talleyrand both died in 1364, Mary in 1366, Guy de Boulogne in 1373, and Philip in 1374, while her nieces married and left the Regno.

The second key to Johanna's success was equally fortuitous and far more significant. As the Angevin sovereign of Naples, her interests were inherently tied to the papacy. Her sex made that relationship all the more crucial. As such, papal personality and inclinations had a direct bearing on Johanna: Whereas Clement VI had championed her interests against both Louis of Hungary and Louis of Taranto, Louis of Taranto's success in marginalizing her was largely due to Innocent VI's reluctance to intervene forcefully on her behalf (see chapter 2). When Innocent died in September 1362, he was succeeded, after a contentious election, by Guillaume de Grimoard, the Benedictine abbot of St. Victor in Marseille, who took the name Urban V. Urban and his successor, Gregory XI (r. 1370–78), would pursue an entirely different relationship with the Neapolitan court. Guillaume de Grimoard had been a papal legate in Naples, sent by Innocent VI to oversee the transition after Louis of Taranto died. In that capacity, he had been Johanna's ally and confidant. Indeed, Johanna had gratefully handed the administration over to him on June 5, 1362, buying herself time to reassert her position on Naples's throne.[17] Upon his call to accept the papacy, Urban continued—largely

16. Ludwig Vones, *Urban V. (1362–1370): Kirchenreform zwischen Kardinalkollegium, Kurie und Klientel*, Päpste und Papsttum 28 (Stuttgart: Anton Hiersemann, 1998), 161. The delicate curial politics of Urban's early pontificate were inextricably entangled with Neapolitan politics. Indeed, Urban's election was a direct result of the split between the supporters of Talleyrand and Guy de Boulogne, and the pressures placed on him by these rivals were considerable. See Part II of Vones's study, especially 160–207, and Zacour, *Talleyrand*, esp. 31–43, 64–68.

17. Vones, *Urban V.*, 161. Johanna concealed Louis's death for several days to protect herself from her cousins' designs on the throne. It briefly seemed that one of the Tarantini might succeed in deposing Johanna. Guillaume de Grimoard's intervention, like that of Niccolò Acciaiuoli, was instrumental in securing Johanna's throne. Cf. Léonard, *Histoire de Jeanne Ier*, 3:487; Léonard, *Les Angevins de Naples*, 405.

because of competing interests within the Curia—to be a close participant in Neapolitan politics, more often than not protecting Johanna's interests, even against the Curia itself.

His successor, Pierre Roger II, who became Gregory XI, had ties to Naples as well. The nephew of Clement VI, Pierre Roger was also related to Francesco del Balzo and Robert des Baux (Mary's alleged rapist and late husband). During the territorial struggles between Philip of Taranto and Francesco that followed Mary's death, Urban appointed him to arrange a settlement, thus allowing him to gain expertise in the tangled mess of Angevin dynastic politics.[18] He was in contact with Archbishop Pierre d'Ameil throughout the latter's tenure of Naples's see, communicating with him about lands disputed between the Roger family and the Tarantini and adjudicating a case brought by Pierre over the partition of archiepiscopal revenues with his successor.[19] His familiarity with Angevin politics may have garnered Johanna his sympathy, and, as their interests coincided throughout his pontificate, Gregory XI came to rely upon her.

Sovereignty and Marriage

It took time for Johanna to capitalize on these fortuitous developments. The first years of her independent reign were stormy, her success by no means a foregone conclusion, in part because of the continuing problem of marriage. After Louis of Taranto's death, one of Johanna's first concerns was necessarily dynastic. Although her children had died—Catherine, the last, sometime around 1362—she was in her midthirties and might still bear an heir. It was necessary, therefore, for her to marry quickly and wisely. A husband—the right husband—might provide a shield, protecting Johanna from political rivals and her reputation from the hazards of single womanhood by containing her sexuality and checking the independence that had so worried earlier commentators. At the same time, remarriage brought the dangerous ambiguities attendant on the problem of kings consort to the fore. Opening the

---

18. Paul R. Thibault, *Pope Gregory XI: The Failure of Tradition* (Lanham, MD: University Press of America, 1986), 25–26. Philip and Francesco were locked in continual struggle. Both Urban and Gregory intervened in their quarrels, as when Philip accused Francesco of using the evil eye to make Mary barren. Cf. Léonard, *Les Angevins de Naples*, 417. See also nos. 2332 (Reg. Vat. 248, fol. 130v) and 2333 (Reg. Vat. 248, fol. 131v) in Paul Lecacheux, ed., *Lettres secrètes et curiales du Pape Urbain V (1362–1370) se rapportant à la France, publiées ou analysées d'après les registres du Vatican* (Paris: Fontemoing, 1902), 1:406–7, and F. Cerasoli, "Urbano V e Giovanna I di Napoli—Documenti inediti dell'Archivio Vaticano, 1362–1370," *ASPN* 20 (1895): 390, n. 96.

19. Thibault, *Pope Gregory XI*, 20–21.

Regno's administration to a second Louis of Taranto was one threat, while the controversy surrounding Andrew of Hungary's marginalization threatened to arise again as well. For Johanna's safety and for posterity, remarriage was necessary; for her exercise of sovereignty, it was imperative she form a union that would not result in her remarginalization. Johanna's concerns were compounded by those of her male relatives, eager not to be dominated by her next consort and jealous of their power and influence. The Tarantini, both of whom were married, could not access the throne through her, but while Mary and her daughters remained Johanna's heirs, Philip stood in close proximity to it and was determined to protect his position.

The papacy was also intimately involved in the question of Johanna's remarriage. Urban V, in one of the first political intrigues of his pontificate, sought at the French court's behest to convince Johanna to marry Philip of Touraine (1342–1404), the future duke of Burgundy and John II's youngest son.[20] She refused, possibly because she feared once again ceding her sovereignty to a powerful husband, and pleaded the excuse that, for posterity's sake, she could not marry anyone with whom she shared such close kinship. Writing to John, she explained that she had vowed to God never again to marry someone to whom she was closely related, having learned through bitter experience that consanguineous unions resulted in the deaths of her children ("ad privandum Nos posteritate").[21] Pressed by Urban, she remained firm in her resolve, insisting that because of her religious and dynastic scruples she could not alter her response.[22]

Instead, she married James IV of Majorca. The great nephew of Sancia of Majorca, James was substantially younger than Johanna and had the added attraction of being largely unconnected and politically inexperienced. Born

---

20. Urban wrote to Johanna to broach the topic on November 29, 1362, advising her "ut cum dilecto filio nobili viro Philippo, duce Turonii, carissimi in Christo filii nostri Johannis regis Francie illustris nato, matrimonio copuleris." He promoted Philip as the wisest choice financially and militarily for the Regno, reminding her of her substantial spiritual and material debt to the Church ("in tuis etiam debet esse devotionis affectibus ut illi jungaris connubio qui et sui progenitores eidem ecclesie, tue matri et domine"). See Lecacheux, *Lettres secrètes et curiales du Pape Urbain V*, 1:13, nos. 122 (Reg. Vat. 245, fol. 18r) and 123 (Reg. Vat. 245, fol. 17v).

21. Register of Nicola d'Alife, fols. 260–61, published in Camera, *Elucubrazioni storico-diplomatiche su Giovanna I.a*, 246: "nunquam cum coniuncto ita de propinquo nobis sanguine inire matrimonium." Nicola (or Niccolò) d'Alife was Robert's secretary and continued in that capacity during Johanna's reign. When Camera completed his study, he had access to Nicola's register, which has since been destroyed, making his editions invaluable. Some of the register has been published as well by Dante Marrocco, working from an early modern transcription. See Dante Marrocco, *Gli Arcani Historici di Nicolò di Alife* (Naples: Ariello, 1965).

22. Reg. Nicola d'Alife, fols. 262–63, pub. in Camera, *Elucubrazioni storico-diplomatiche su Giovanna I.a*, 247.

in about 1336, James had spent much of his childhood and young adulthood imprisoned—reportedly in an iron cage—at the court of his uncle, Peter IV "the Ceremonious" of Aragon (1319–87), after his father, James III (1315–49), died attempting to regain Majorca from Peter.[23] In May 1362, James escaped from Barcelona and fled to Naples, where he was welcomed and harbored.[24] He seemed a suitable choice to be Johanna's third husband, and her counselors advised her to marry him.[25] His sad history elicited great sympathy, particularly because of his relationship to Sancia, and, given the emptiness of his royal title—which meant nothing, since Peter ruled Majorca—and his lack of resources, his marriage to Johanna presented few obvious difficulties for her exercise of sovereignty. Their marriage contract, which denied James any Neapolitan title besides that of duke of Calabria (which made him theoretically the foremost nobleman in Naples), was finalized in December 1362, and the marriage took place early the following year.[26] As a matter of course, he was excluded from the succession and legally defined—like Andrew and Louis before him—as Johanna's consort. He presented little threat either to Johanna's autonomy or to papal interests, and Urban accepted the match with equanimity.[27] James's role as consort was limited and minimal; he played only a scant part in the papal politics with

---

23. On the disputed claims by the Aragonese and Majorcan kings to the Balearic Islands and other formerly Majorcan territory, see David Abulafia, *A Mediterranean Emporium: The Catalan Kingdom of Majorca* (Cambridge: Cambridge University Press, 2002), 35–36. On James, see J. N. Hillgarth, *The Spanish Kingdom, 1250–1516*, vol. 1: *Precarious Balance* (Oxford: Oxford University Press, 1976), 365–66; J. Ernest Martínez Ferrando, *La Tràgica Història dels Reis de Mallorca* (Barcelona: Ed. Aedos, 1960), 247–73; and Ferran Soldevila, *Història de Catalunya*, 3rd ed. (Barcelona: Editorial Alpha, 1972), 463–64. In addition, much of Peter IV's official chronicle concerns the struggle between Peter and James (or Jaume/Jayme) III. The chronicle comments, briefly, on James IV's marriage to Johanna, although it is notably silent about his incarceration. See Pere III of Catalonia (Pedro IV of Aragon), *Chronicle*, trans. Mary Hillgarth, ed. J. N. Hillgarth, 2 vols. (Toronto: Pontifical Institute of Mediaeval Studies, 1980), III.8–III.9, 1:236–37.

24. Baddeley, *Queen Joanna I of Naples*, 199. Cf. Alberto Boscolo, *Saggi di storia Mediterranea tra il XIV e il VI secolo*, Fonti e Studi del Corpus Membranarum Italicarum, Prima Serie: Studi e Richerche 19 (Rome: Il Centro di Ricerca, 1981), 77–109, esp. 97.

25. Baddeley, *Queen Joanna I of Naples*, 200.

26. Ibid.; Camera, *Elucubrazioni storico-diplomatiche su Giovanna I.a*, 248. The conventions ratified by the pope regarding the marriage are reproduced in full by Lecacheux. See no. 385 (Reg. Vat. 261, fol. 29v, n. 57) in Lecacheux, *Lettres secrètes et curiales du Pape Urbain V*, 1:49–52.

27. Vones, *Urban V*, 206. Indeed, rather than chiding Johanna for her disobedience, he wrote to congratulate her on February 8, 1363. See no. 205 (Reg. Vat. 245, fol. 84v) in Lecacheux, *Lettres secrètes et curiales du Pape Urbain V*, 1:24. He wrote as well to various members of the Neapolitan court and nobility, entreating them to accept the marriage and to treat James with respect. See nos. 243–342 in Lecacheux, *Lettres secrètes et curiales du Pape Urbain V*, 34–40. In April, he also wrote to Louis of Hungary, instructing him to respect the marriage and accept James as a brother; see no. 376 (Reg. Vat. 245, fol. 133r) in Lecacheux, *Lettres secrètes et curiales du Pape Urbain V*, 1:48.

which Urban and Johanna were concerned. Indeed, in official correspondence with the Neapolitan court, Urban excluded James, addressing Johanna as the sole ruler of Naples, while James, if addressed at all, was referred to only by his Majorcan title.

Johanna's third marriage, despite these precautions, proved initially as tumultuous as her previous two. While she did conceive, she suffered a miscarriage in 1365 and never bore another child.[28] James was sickly and—perhaps unsurprisingly, given his history—reportedly mentally unstable.[29] Archbishop Pierre d'Ameil wrote to Urban during the summer of 1363 that Johanna was afraid of her husband, and both he and Johanna wrote alarmed letters to the pope about James's behavior.[30] He was purportedly paranoid, and his humiliation over his marginalization at court made him irrational and even violent. According to Pierre, he was willfully stubborn and prone to rages, which were particularly intense when he drank wine.[31] He insisted on being admitted to meetings on affairs of state and threw frightening tantrums when his will was thwarted. At times he was lucid, but periodically—according to Johanna, during certain cycles of the moon—he became maddened, and anything that might be used as a weapon had to be removed from his chamber.[32]

Johanna reported to Urban that she was forced to placate James to keep him calm in public, soothing him by allowing him into secret councils

---

28. Urban wrote to console Johanna on July 19, 1365. See no. 1886 (Reg. Vat. 247, fol. 131v) in Lecacheux, *Lettres secrètes et curiales du Pape Urbain V*, 3:329. Cf. Cerasoli, "Urbano V e Giovanna I di Napoli," 203, n. 55.

29. In a letter to Urban, Johanna attributed James's instability to the circumstances of his youth ("ex juventute") and the wretchedness of his long imprisonment ("ex squallore diuntini carceris") (Reg. Nicola d'Alife, fol. 65, in Camera, *Elucubrazioni storico-diplomatiche su Giovanna I.a*, 83). Early in James's residence in Naples, Pierre d'Ameil wrote many letters about his delicate mental and physical condition. See Letters 14, 15, 72, and 77 in Henri Bresc, ed., *La Correspondance de Pierre Ameilh, Archêveque de Naples puis d'Embrun (1363–1369)*, Sources d'Histoire Médiévale 6 (Paris: Centre nationale de la recherche scientifique, 1972), 40–42, 154, 159; cf. Kenneth M. Setton, "Archbishop Pierre d'Ameil in Naples and the Affair of Aimon III of Geneva (1363–1364)," *Speculum* 28 (October 1953): 655, n. 38.

30. Letter 19 in Bresc, *La Correspondance de Pierre Ameilh*, 56–57. In response, Urban instructed James to distance himself from insidious followers who disrupted his marriage and to avoid causing scandal ("ad obviandum scandalis") by attempting to modify the terms of his marriage agreement; cf. no. 593 (Reg. Vat. 245, fol. 244v) in Lecacheux, *Lettres secrètes et curiales du Pape Urbain V*, 1:80. He also attempted to enforce peace between the spouses from afar, writing them letters of counsel. See Lecacheux, *Lettres secrètes et curiales du Pape Urbain V*, 219, nos. 1342 (Reg. Vat. 246, fol. 376r) and 1343 (Reg. Vat. 246, fol. 376r).

31. Letter 19 in Bresc, *La Correspondance de Pierre Ameilh*, 56–57.

32. Ibid.

against the better judgment of her advisors.[33] He refused, she wrote, to be content with the "honorable status" accorded him in their marriage contract. When reminded of the legality of his position, James raged scandalously:

> He had frequently remarked in public, while making certain vile gestures, that, if he were able to rule, he would not renounce it either for the pope or for the Church, because he did not care to obey them. Indeed, I urged him not to say such words publicly, but he replied to the contrary that he should have revealed it openly, to which I demanded what he would dare to do. Then he hurled back that he would even pierce the body of Christ with a knife. What is certain, Sustaining Father and Lord, is that he had already made fifty pledges of donation to his familiars, some for three thousand florins, some for two thousand, some for a thousand, some for more, some for less.[34]

When Johanna reprimanded him for pledging sums to his followers from the royal treasury to which he had no right, James became violent and slanderous:

> And with fury he threw himself toward me and seized me by the arm in the presence of many people, who almost believed that I would fall to the ground. And although there might then have been many exceedingly impatient to prevent actual injury to my person, I, lest due to mischief something worse occur, ordered explicitly that no one should dare to move to punish him, giving them to understand that he had done what he did not from wicked intention, but in order to comfort himself, not believing that he had dragged me so forcefully. And turning toward me, he descended into disgraceful words to defame my reputation, saying in a loud voice that I was a viricide, a vile harlot, and that I collected pimps around me who brought men to me

---

33. Johanna's limited inclusion of James in the government is mentioned both by herself and by Pierre d'Ameil, who reported to Urban that her council was concerned that James would oust Johanna from power just as Louis of Taranto had. He also informed the pope that the rumor that James, who had threatened to leave Naples, was about to be appointed reformer general of justice had deepened tensions between Johanna and the Tarantini princes and was causing scandal throughout the Regno. See Letters 17, 18, 20, 24, 26, 28, and 30 in Bresc, *La Correspondance de Pierre Ameilh*, 51, 53, 58, 69, 71, 71, 76. Pierre was obliged to intervene directly—with Johanna's consent—and point out that only the pope could make such an appointment. See Letters 24 and 30 in Bresc, *La Correspondance de Pierre Ameilh*, 68–69, 76; cf. Setton, "Archbishop Pierre d'Ameil in Naples," 653–54.

34. Reg. Nicola d'Alife, fols. 65–69, printed in Camera, *Elucubrazioni storico-diplomatiche su Giovanna I.a*, 83–84.

during the night, and that he would exact an exemplary vengeance on them.[35]

She goes on to relate that James's erratic behavior and defamatory charges became common knowledge, causing public scandal.[36] The Tarantini sent their wives to comfort and spend the night with her, presumably to shield her both from James and from suspicions that pimps were procuring her lovers; Mary even brought a number of armed guards.

James's crazed behavior cemented his marginal position. In deliberation with her cousins and her council, Johanna (out of necessity, she stressed to the pope) decided that she should limit contact with her husband, spending time with him alone only when her advisors deemed it safe. All of this, she insisted, depended on Urban's approval, and she would adhere to his counsel like a good daughter ("filialiter inherebo").[37] There is very little doubt, given the archbishop's corroboration, that this episode did occur, but it worked ultimately to Johanna's benefit. Everyone was eager to limit James's influence. Johanna, to this end, presented herself to Urban as a loving wife who defended her husband, expressing compassionate understanding for the tribulations that had led to his insanity. As she had in her refusal to marry Philip of Touraine, she cast her assertion of independence in a pious light, presenting it not as insistence on her own will but as the only responsible course of action. James's behavior was dangerously sacrilegious and scandalous, while hers in checking him revealed her devotion to the papacy, to the Church, and to God, whose transubstantiated flesh she charged James had threatened. Affirming the necessity of her actions, Johanna marginalized James, ruling alone and free of his interference even as she averred her love and concern for him.

Johanna thus won her independence. She was married, but without the potential pitfalls that marriage could present to regnant queens. James spent

---

35. Ibid. Following an error in the register also replicated by Marrocco (*Gli Arcani Historici di Nicolò di Alife*, 105–10), Camera, who believed it referred to Louis of Taranto, mistakenly dated the letter to 1347. His dating makes no sense, and the corroborating stories related by Pierre d'Ameil make it clear that this letter is about James. Subsequent scholars, including Léonard, have relied on Camera's edition while dating the letter to early 1364 (Léonard, *Les Angevins de Naples*, 407). Pierre d'Ameil describes the scene, which took place in January 1364, in very similar terms, saying that James was "in excessu turbatus" and spoke "obprobrissa verba plurima." See Letter 76 in Bresc, *La Correspondance de Pierre Ameilh*, 158; cf. Setton, "Archbishop Pierre d'Ameil in Naples," 655, n. 37.

36. Reg. Nicola d'Alife, fol. 68, in Camera, *Elucubrazioni storico-diplomatiche su Giovanna I.a*, 84: "tota Civitas per ora omnium huius modi universaliter material revolvebatur."

37. Ibid.

little of what remained of his life in Naples, focusing instead on regaining Majorca. His relationship with Johanna continued to be uneasy, marked by short periods of reconciliation and longer periods of estrangement. For a time, he fought with the papal league against the Visconti in northern Italy. When Peter IV "the Cruel" of Castile went to war against Aragon in 1365, James offered his services. He was captured and held for ransom at Valladolid in late 1367. Johanna, after some prodding by Urban V, helped James's sister, the marchioness of Montferrat, to ransom him.[38] Continuing to eschew the Neapolitan court, where Johanna reigned alone and unchallenged, James continued his military endeavors—and he was sane enough to be taken seriously by Castilian chroniclers—fighting in the Hundred Years' War as an ally of the Black Prince until he died of a fever at Soria in January 1375.[39]

The Affair of Johanna of Durazzo and Aimon of Geneva

The early years of Johanna's independent reign were, thus, far from tranquil. Pierre d'Ameil's letters—the most detailed source about royal affairs for this period—portray her court as scandal-ridden and rife with infighting that prevented effective governance, although they also present Johanna as determined to safeguard her sovereignty. The archbishop's interpretation of events is by far the best-known source for this period of Johanna's life, and his voice has been given disproportionate weight. His letters have been consulted for numerous studies, including Henri Denifle's monumental study of the Hundred Years' War, and they have long been a resource for scholars of

---

38. Urban wrote to Johanna on January 30, 1368, to urge her to ransom James. See no. 2667 (Reg. Vat. 249, fol. 53v) in Lecacheux, *Lettres secrètes et curiales du Pape Urbain V*, 3:463. James's situation caused his wife considerable difficulty. She was, as ever, in dire need of funds, especially given the added exigencies of papal wars on the Regno's treasury. She was obliged to seek a loan from her Provençal subjects to pay the ransom. The financial agreement she reached with a Provençal knight, Galhard Tornier, for a loan of 26,000 florins "pro liberationis Serenissimi Principis domini Jacobi . . . Carissimi viri nostri" is preserved in ADBR, B 5, fols. 83r–84v.

39. Ferrando, *La Tràgica Història dels Reis de Mallorca*, 265–74. James's exploits and captivity figure in both Aragonese and Castilian chronicles. See *Crónica del Rey Don Pedro* and *Crónica del Rey Don Enrique, Segundo de Castilla*, in Cayetano Rosell, ed., *Cronicas de los Reyes de Castilla, desde Don Alfonso el Sabio hasta los Catolicos Don Fernando y Doña Isabel*, Biblioteca de Autores Españoles, desde la Formacion del Lenguaje Nuestros Dias 66 (Madrid: Ediciones Atlas, 1953), 1:578–79, and 2:34–36. More recent editions can be found in Pero Lopez de Ayala, *Crónica del Rey Don Pedro y del Rey Don Enrique, su hermano, hijos del rey don Alfonso Onceno*, ed. Germán Orduna (Buenos Aires: Incipit-Ediciones Criticas, 1994). See esp. 1:5 and 2:163, 165, 241–43, 373. See also Pere III of Catalonia, *Chronicle*, 588–89.

Neapolitan history, including Kenneth M. Setton, Eugène Martin-Chabot, and Antonino Mango.[40]

Pierre's correspondence paints a picture of a court in turmoil. During his nearly three-year tenure of Naples's archiepiscopal see (1363–65), Pierre was an agent of Guy de Boulogne and Guy's nephew, Robert of Geneva (1342–94), who would go on to be first a cardinal and then the Avignon pope Clement VII. In that capacity, Pierre was continually locked in combat with Johanna and Niccolò Acciaiuoli (who became Johanna's advisor after Louis of Taranto died), as well as other members of the royal family. He described Johanna as an entirely unsatisfactory ruler, although he was admittedly somewhat intimidated by her. He complained repeatedly that she, often in cooperation with her sister, threatened and sought to impede him, and he argued vociferously that she was unfit to rule, despite her determination to do so.[41] Writing to Guy on October 29, 1363, Pierre reported on the early period of Johanna's renewed rule and revealed that she had informed him that she would have nothing to do with a papal legate if one were sent to help her govern:

> The lady queen, as she told me, does not wish any legate, no matter who, fearing that the administration—in which she delights and wants to do everything, because she had so long looked forward to this time—will be removed from her. However, her administration is not effective—on the contrary, it is useless—even if it is very sensible, and ultimately it will be necessary that this kingdom be ruled otherwise than by her.[42]

---

40. See Setton, "Archbishop Pierre d'Ameil in Naples," 644, n. 1; Henri Denifle, *La Guerre de cent ans et la désolation des églises, monastères et hôpitaux en France* (Paris: A. Picard et Fils, 1899), 2:514–15; Eugène Martin-Chabot, "Le Registre des lettres de Pierre Ameil, archevêque de Naples (1363–1365), puis de Embrun (1365–1379)," *Mélanges d'archéologie et d'histoire* 25 (1905): 279–92; and Antonino Mango, *Relazioni tra Federico III di Sicilia e Giovanna I di Napoli: Documenti degli Archivi de Vaticano*, Documenti per servire alla storia di Sicilia, Series 1: Diplomatica 22 (Palermo: Società Storia Patria Palermo, 1915). Norman Zacour, for his study of Talleyrand, and Léonard, for the portion of Johanna's life described in *Les Angevins de Naples*, have also drawn on Pierre's letters.

41. See Letter 33 (after June 23, 1364) in Bresc, *La Correspondance de Pierre Ameilh*, 258. Johanna and Mary both emerge from Pierre's letters as truly formidable women. Mary, it seems, was a dangerous opponent: In July of 1364, Pierre accused her of threatening him and ordering her followers to attack the archiepiscopal palace, where they captured two of his servants. See Letter 161 (July 27, 1364) in Bresc, *La Correspondence de Pierre Ameilh*, 291–93. He also complained repeatedly that Johanna's rule was ineffectual and argued that a legate should be sent to the Regno. See Letters 41, 46–49 in Bresc, *La Correspondence de Pierre Ameilh*, 89–91, 101–9.

42. Letter 48 (October 29, 1363) in Bresc, *La Correspondance de Pierre Ameilh*, 106.

From the outset, Pierre opposed Johanna's independent rule. Yet if Johanna, in her insistence on ruling alone, was stubborn, Acciaiuoli, in his capacity as grand seneschal, was far worse. He was an ally of Talleyrand, Guy's arch-nemesis, and Pierre thought Acciaiuoli's influence too great, arguing that he effectively ruled the Regno.[43] He and Pierre were openly at war, and Johanna more often than not sided with Acciaiuoli.[44] As such, Pierre's judgments of Johanna, her administration, and her court are tinged by partisanship, and they reflect the frustrations he felt trying to accomplish his agenda rather than an objective relation of affairs at what must, during the transition from Louis of Taranto's rule, have been a turbulent time at court.

Pierre's dislike of Johanna derived primarily from the other memorable Neapolitan scandal of the period. He came to Naples intent to help Philip of Taranto forge an alliance with Guy through the marriage of his stepdaughter, Johanna of Durazzo (1344–87), to one of the cardinal's relatives.[45] Johanna was Mary's eldest daughter and, as such, the childless queen's likely successor, not to mention one of the richest heiresses in Europe. Talleyrand, her great uncle, took a keen interest in her welfare and future, while Philip, in keeping with the long-standing rivalry between the Durazzeschi and Tarantini, had conflicting interests. When Philip approached Guy and asked that he choose a relative to marry Johanna of Durazzo and live in the Regno (where he could be of use to Philip), Guy selected his nephew, Aimon of Geneva (d. 1367), the eldest son of Amadeus III, count of Geneva, and the brother of Robert of Geneva.[46] Talleyrand (who feared what it signified for young Charles of Durazzo) strongly opposed the marriage, as, after an initial period of approval, did both Johanna and Mary.[47]

---

43. Letter 82 (January 18, 1364) in Bresc, *La Correspondance de Pierre Ameilh*, 166.

44. Letter 66 (January 1364) in Bresc, *La Correspondance de Pierre Ameilh*, 144: "Quoniam contra magnum senescallum bellum apertum michi est nec ipse vult pacificari."

45. Pierre proposed the match between Johanna of Durazzo and Aimon of Geneva a mere five days after arriving in Naples (Setton, "Archbishop Pierre d'Ameil in Naples," 652). In addition to Setton's comprehensive article about the scandal surrounding Johanna of Durazzo's ill-fated love for Aimon of Geneva, the affair has been discussed by Zacour, *Talleyrand*, 64–68, and Vones, *Urban V.*, 212–36. See also Pietro Fedele, "L'amore di Giovanna di Durazzo per Aimone III di Ginevre," in *Miscellanea di Studi Storici in onore di Antonio Manno* (Turin: Officina Poligrafica Editrice Subalpina, 1912), 2:635–53.

46. Zacour, *Talleyrand*, 65.

47. Letter 10 (June 1363) in Bresc, *La Correspondance de Pierre Ameilh*, 25–28: "Sane circa matrimonium quod scitis . . . consenciunt et summe volunt dominus Philippus et mater; placet etiam domine regine"; cf. Zacour, *Talleyrand*, 67. Pierre took Mary's abandonment of his cause personally, particularly when she protested to Urban V that she had never supported it in the first place. See Letter 112 (April 29, 1364) in Bresc, *La Correspondance de Pierre Ameilh*, 229.

Pierre d'Ameil acted in the ensuing battle as the young duchess's confidant and go-between with Aimon of Geneva, whom she came to prefer to her other suitor, Louis of Navarre (1341–76), the younger brother of Charles "the Bad," after Pierre (according to his own account) convinced her that Aimon was the handsomer of the two.[48] Matters became considerably more complicated, however, when Johanna and Acciaiuoli found an opportunity to negotiate peace with Sicily, ending an unpopular war waged for generations that placed great strain on the always stretched Neapolitan treasury. Not long after Pierre's arrival at court, the news reached Naples that the wife of Frederick III of Sicily (1341–77) had died, creating the possibility that peace could be made via marriage. The most suitable bride was Johanna of Durazzo, which jeopardized Guy's and Philip's plans.[49] Johanna and Acciaiuoli determined to pursue the Sicilian peace, dashing Johanna of Durazzo's hopes. The pope and Talleyrand supported their efforts, which, among other things, held the promise of returning Sicily to papal obedience.[50] Pierre became hopelessly entangled in the intrigue that followed. He wrote voluminous correspondence—often in cipher—excoriating Johanna and Acciaiuoli and attempting to discredit them, even as he revealed his own role in the schemes to marry Johanna of Durazzo as suited Guy de Boulogne.

The negotiations dragged on for months. Pierre contrived to have Aimon visit Naples en route to Jerusalem as a pilgrim, worrying and angering Johanna while convincing her niece of her love for Aimon. The struggle heightened tensions between the queen and Philip; the Tarantini allied themselves with Guy de Boulogne—who was proposed as an ideal papal legate—against Johanna and Acciaiuoli.[51] Johanna insisted—with the agreement of Urban and Talleyrand—that the Sicilian marriage was vital to the Regno's stability.[52] Talleyrand, fearful that Durazzeschi lands would pass

---

48. Letter 14 (July 5, 1363) in Bresc, *La Correspondance de Pierre Ameilh*, 38; cf. Setton, "Archbishop Pierre d'Ameil in Naples," 653.

49. Letters 40 (September 3, 1363), 44 (September 21, 1363), and 48 (October 29, 1363) in Bresc, *La Correspondance de Pierre Ameilh*, 87–88, 98–99, 104–6; cf. Setton, "Archbishop Pierre d'Ameil in Naples," 656. Johanna tried to negotiate a marriage between Frederick and Johanna of Durazzo's sister Margaret, but Frederick insisted that he preferred Johanna of Durazzo. Cf. Boscolo, *Saggi di storia Mediterranea tra il XIV e il VI secolo*, 97–99.

50. Zacour, *Talleyrand*, 68.

51. Letter 49 (November 6, 1363) in Bresc, *La Correspondance de Pierre Ameilh*, 106–9; cf. Setton, "Archbishop Pierre d'Ameil in Naples," 659.

52. Letters 60 (November 23, 1363), 61 (January 4, 1364), and 62 (January 1364) in Bresc, *La Correspondance de Pierre Ameilh*, 130–39; cf. Setton, "Archbishop Pierre d'Ameil in Naples," 660–62. Pierre so annoyed Johanna that she became opposed to Aimon on principle, informing Pierre that Louis of Navarre's suit would be preferable should negotiations with Frederick III fail.

into foreign hands, entreated the pope to forbid such a transfer and to ensure that Louis of Durazzo's son, Charles, inherited the lands alienated during the Hungarian invasion.[53] Accordingly, Urban instructed Johanna to bar her niece from ceding any territory to her future husband and implicitly suggested that she should prevent the duchess from marrying Aimon by requiring that she request his permission and inform Talleyrand before Johanna of Durazzo married anyone other than Frederick III.[54]

The situation came to a head in December 1363, when Johanna of Durazzo absolutely refused to marry Frederick III, driving her aunt to a show of force. On December 22, Johanna detained her niece in Castel Nuovo, apparently causing great scandal in Naples.[55] In so doing, she effectively burned any bridges remaining between herself and Guy de Boulogne, who had supported her early in her reign. The situation escalated as suitable terms were reached with Frederick while Johanna of Durazzo continued to resist. Pierre, the Tarantini, and James of Majorca opposed the marriage, leading Johanna to move her niece to stricter confinement and threaten even harsher punishment. Pierre was also in a difficult position because of his role in the debacle, and he complained in a letter to Urban that Acciaiuoli had incited the Neapolitans against him for thwarting the peace they so desperately desired.[56]

By mid-January, Johanna of Durazzo had capitulated, agreeing to marry either Frederick of Sicily or her previous favorite, Louis of Navarre. Pierre suggested that Guy should present her marriage to Frederick as coerced and even attempted to argue that she might be considered—through consent—legally bound to Aimon.[57] Guy rushed to her defense, insisting that a forced marriage would be uncanonical and that, if Johanna of Durazzo

---

53. Zacour, *Talleyrand*, 67.

54. Ibid.; Setton, "Archbishop Pierre d'Ameil in Naples," 664. Talleyrand's stipulations were likely designed to bring about Johanna of Durazzo's marriage to Frederick III and dispossession of her Italian lands, which would then pass to Charles (Zacour, *Talleyrand*, 67).

55. Letter 61 (January 4, 1364) in Bresc, *La Correspondance de Pierre Ameilh*, 136–37: "Sane ista detentio, sicut dixi nuper domine regine, licet sit scandalosa et injuriosa detente." Pierre reported as well, in a memoir probably prepared for the pope, that "in tota civitate Neapolitana fuit de hiis publica vox et fama" (Letter 90 [February 1364] in Bresc, *La Correspondance de Pierre Ameilh*, 195); cf. Setton, "Archbishop Pierre d'Ameil in Naples," 665, 685. Pierre reports that Johanna of Durazzo's incarceration was so strict that she was forbidden to hear mass on Christmas and one of her servants, imprisoned with her, died because she was denied medical care.

56. Letter 64 (January 5, 1364), in Bresc, *La Correspondance de Pierre Ameilh*, 143. See also Setton, "Archbishop Pierre d'Ameil in Naples," 669.

57. Letter 68 (January 6, 1364) in Bresc, *La Correspondance de Pierre Ameilh*, 146–50.

had already pledged herself to his nephew, the queen could not prevent their union.[58]

Although he had earlier supported the planned Sicilian marriage, Urban came to share Guy's perspective. The force in the Curia that opposed Johanna of Durazzo's marriage to Aimon died with Talleyrand in 1364, and Urban began to insist that she be freed. At the end of February, when the queen had not complied, Urban issued bulls against her, sending them to Pierre to publish.[59] Pierre, however, was too frightened of Johanna and Mary to obey. Writing to Guy, he portrayed them as terrifying, insidious women:

> And you should know that the queen and [the duchess's] mother said many wicked things about me in the presence of that same duchess, and they have made many threats to my person. . . . And because there is no iniquity greater than the iniquity of women, particularly of those two, in truth I now begin to be most powerfully afraid because of the kind face they present me with. Since Easter, the queen has invited me to dine four times, and I always have to excuse myself.[60]

Apparently, Pierre feared angering Urban less than he did arousing the sisters' wrath. He delayed publishing the bulls, leading the pope to issue them again in May.[61] Pierre wrote to explain himself in June, revealing that the bulls' rumored existence had caused the situation to worsen for the duchess after Johanna and Mary learned of them and responded by detaining many of her followers and increasing the guard placed on her.[62]

58. Bresc reproduces two letters from Guy, one to Acciaiuoli and the other to Johanna, in which the cardinal reminds them that "juxta sancta Ecclesie ordinationem matrimonia debent ideo esse libera quod nullus ex quacumque causa mundi cogendus est ad matrimonium contrahendum . . . si violenter contraheretur matrimonium, nullum esset." See Letters 94 and 95 (February 19, 1364) in Bresc, *La Correspondance de Pierre Ameilh*, 202–4. See also Setton, "Archbishop Pierre d'Ameil in Naples," 686.

59. Urban argued that Johanna of Durazzo and Aimon had entered into a union of consent and ordered that the duchess be freed and allowed to travel to a place where she could make her will known without fear. The bull is reproduced as Letter 115 (February 28, 1364) in Bresc, *La Correspondance de Pierre Ameilh*, 233–34, and also in Cerasoli, "Urbano V e Giovanna I di Napoli," 181–82. Setton, "Archbishop Pierre d'Ameil in Naples," discusses it on 689. Urban wrote to entreat the aid of Cansignorio della Scala, the ruler of Verona, for the imprisoned duchess, complaining that Johanna held her niece "sub arta custodia" and explaining the need to move Johanna of Durazzo to a neutral location. See no. 1163 (Reg. Vat. 246, fol. 288v) in Lecacheux, *Lettres secrètes et curiales du Pape Urbain V*, 2:185.

60. Letter 111 (April 23, 1364) in Bresc, *La Correspondance de Pierre Ameilh*, 227.

61. Setton, "Archbishop Pierre d'Ameil in Naples," 689.

62. Letter 136 (June 26 – July 12, 1364) in Bresc, *La Correspondance de Pierre Ameilh*, 263. See also Setton, "Archbishop Pierre d'Ameil in Naples," 689–90.

In the meantime, a treaty was negotiated between Sicily and Naples by which, among other things, Frederick could only style himself ruler of Trinacria—recognizing Johanna's right to call herself monarch of the Kingdom of Sicily—and would respect Johanna's sovereignty in Messina, captured by Acciaiuoli in 1356.[63] Then, in June, Frederick invaded Messina, rendering months of negotiation wasted. Public opinion in the Regno held Pierre responsible, and a group of nobles sent Urban an outraged letter accusing the archbishop of destroying their hopes for peace.[64] Guy de Boulogne, now the most influential member of the Curia, was so incensed that he convinced Urban to send a legate to publish the bulls against Johanna and Mary. The legate read the declaration against them in Naples on July 11, driving Mary and Johanna to send angry letters to the Curia denouncing Pierre, who was forced to defend himself to the cardinals.[65] He then fled to Benevento. When, on August 21, Johanna and Mary had not released Johanna of Durazzo, Urban placed the Regno under interdict. Pierre (doubtless to his relief) was removed from his post, while the sisters persisted in their steadfast refusal to comply with papal directive and a new archbishop, Bernard du Bousquet—with whom Johanna would enjoy a substantially better relationship—was sent to the Regno in his stead.[66]

Urban lifted Johanna's excommunication on November 15, with the caveat that she must free her niece and allow her to marry as she pleased within one year's time.[67] She was again under interdict when, after Urban refused to grant a dispensation for consanguinity, Johanna of Durazzo married Louis of Navarre. It appears that this excommunication was merely pro forma and that Urban was not seriously perturbed by the end to the long and scandalous affair.[68] If anything, its conclusion fulfilled Talleyrand's wishes, for Johanna of Durazzo, disinherited because of her illicit marriage, could no longer bar Charles of Durazzo's inheritance of the duchy.[69] Indeed, it became increasingly apparent that Charles would likely succeed Johanna as Naples's ruler,

---

63. Setton, "Archbishop Pierre d'Ameil in Naples," 674–75. On Acciaiuoli's conquest of Messina, see chapter 2.

64. Letter 132 (June 18, 1364) in Bresc, *La Correspondance de Pierre Ameilh*, 255–57. See also Setton, "Archbishop Pierre d'Ameil in Naples," 690.

65. See Letter 145 (July 12, 1364) in Bresc, *La Correspondance de Pierre Ameilh*, 272–73. Pierre argues that all he had done was in fulfillment of his pastoral duty to uphold canon law.

66. Setton, "Archbishop Pierre d'Ameil in Naples," 691.

67. Vones, *Urban V.*, 216.

68. Léonard, *Les Angevins de Naples*, 418.

69. Urban formally excluded Johanna of Durazzo from the Neapolitan succession in January of 1370. See no. 3020 in Lecacheux, *Lettres secrètes et curiales du Pape Urbain V*, 3:522.

particularly as he enjoyed the support of the childless Louis of Hungary, who seemed likely to name him his own successor as well.[70]

These two scandals—James of Majorca's madness and the imprisonment of Johanna of Durazzo—are among the few episodes of Johanna's independent reign to be studied in any depth. Because of the detail of Pierre's letters, and a paucity of competing sources, they have shaped perceptions of this period of Neapolitan history. Pierre's blatant prejudices make this problematic. His letters reveal how he represented Johanna while in struggle with her; they reveal little about how others might have seen her or understood their conflict, although they suggest an alternative interpretation of events in their allusions to widespread outrage with Pierre. His characterization of Johanna as dangerous, fickle, and obstinate, and above all as an ineffectual ruler, tallies with other estimations of her and her reign, corroborating the harsh judgments of chroniclers like Domenico da Gravina and the author of the *Chronicon Estense*. But Pierre's stake in events and his open partisanship render his account suspect. Johanna certainly attempted to wield her niece as a political pawn, resorting to harsh measures when opposed. Yet Johanna—who had herself been forced into a politically expedient marriage at a young age—adhered to what had originally been papal objectives in trying, with the apparent approval of her subjects, to end a long, expensive war. Pierre's insistence on manipulating affairs in Naples to suit Guy, rather than for the good of the kingdom, must justifiably have angered Johanna, and his reports should be read in context, keeping in mind both his role and his bias, as well as how very differently the affair must have appeared to others. The archbishop was no impartial observer, and his letters should be read and interpreted critically.

Daughter of the Papacy

Pierre d'Ameil's scandalous tales and criticism of Johanna notwithstanding, most observers of Johanna's independent reign were either ignorant of or uninterested in the dramas of the Neapolitan court. Their references to her during this period counterbalance Pierre's descriptions, offering an alternative view of her style of rule and conduct. Freed from the marital power struggles in which she had spent her early reign and supported by capable advisors—most notably Acciaiuoli and the Neapolitan jurist Niccolò

---

70. By Louis's invitation, Charles went to live at the Hungarian court. Although Louis's presumed heir was his niece, Elizabeth, it became apparent by 1370 that he intended Charles to succeed him.

Spinelli (1325–1406)—Johanna took a much more active role in international politics. It was in fulfillment of this role that she most often drew her contemporaries' notice. She involved herself more closely in the government of the counties, she worked to expand Angevin influence in the eastern reaches of her far-flung territory—particularly in what are now Albania and the Peloponnese peninsula—and she took firm hold of Naples's administration.[71]

Even as Johanna consolidated her power, she worked to align herself with the papacy, as when she intervened in 1364 at Urban's request after Raymond des Baux, prince of Orange, imprisoned Catherine des Baux, lady of Courthezon, seizing her lands and castles. Johanna launched an epistolary campaign against Raymond, and she instructed her Provençal seneschal to intercede militarily on Catherine's behalf. Moments like this gave Johanna an opportunity to assert her sovereignty and evoke her special relationship to the papacy. In her letters against Raymond, Johanna represented herself as outraged both as countess of Provence—and thus Catherine's suzerain—and as the Church's representative, defending Catherine's rights both rhetorically and militarily during a two-year war in which she ultimately triumphed.[72] Johanna did not preach sermons or fight personally in wars, but she lent her pious and enthusiastic support to papal projects, thus fulfilling her duties as a

---

71. On Johanna's efforts in the east, see Anthony Luttrell, "The Principality of Achaea in 1377," *Byzantinische Zeitschrift* 57 (1964): 340–45. Angevin rule in Albania and the Morea was tenuous throughout the period. Native rulers, like Karlo Thopia, who conquered Durazzo in 1368 (only to briefly lose it to Johanna of Durazzo's husband, Louis of Navarre, in the late 1370s), resisted and often overthrew Angevin suzerainty. Johanna successfully challenged Philip of Taranto's rule in the Morea, which she leased to the Hospitallers in 1377. See John V. A. Fine, *The Late Medieval Balkans: A Critical Survey from the Late Twelfth Century to the Ottoman Conquest* (Ann Arbor: University of Michigan Press, 1994), esp. 371–402, and Peter Topping, "The Morea: 1311–1364" and "The Morea: 1364–1460," in *A History of the Crusades*, gen. ed. Kenneth Meyer Setton, vol. 3: *The Fourteenth and Fifteenth Centuries*, ed. Harry W. Hazard (Madison: University of Wisconsin Press, 1975), 104–40 and 141–66, respectively, esp. 143–48.

72. Johanna wrote to Raymond in April 1366 that she intervened "non solum de nostris ymo etiam appostilicis iustivotu iusticie." A copy of the letter is contained in a fifteenth-century collection of René of Anjou's letters (Aix-en-Provence, Bibliothèque Méjanes, MS 771 [1064], 219–23, at 219). Urban wrote to request Johanna's support for Catherine on July 22, 1364 (cf. no. 1118 [Reg. Vat. 246, fol. 258r] in Lecacheux, *Lettres secrètes et curiales du Pape Urbain V*, 2:176). Catherine's situation worsened in 1365, when Raymond took her captive. Johanna, increasingly active in the administration of the counties, instructed her seneschal, Raymond d'Agoult, and the nobility of Provence to fight to free Catherine and restore her rightful holdings (ADBR, B 559 2, B 559 3). The struggle was still ongoing in February 1366, when Urban asked Raymond to come to Avignon for negotiations and asked Johanna to permit him to travel through her lands (cf. nos. 2126 [Reg. Vat. 248, fol. 48v] and 2127 [Reg. Vat. 248, fol. 49r] in Lecacheux, *Lettres secrètes et curiales du Pape Urbain V*, 3:372). It was not until 1367 that Raymond d'Agoult succeeded in dispossessing Raymond des Baux, charging him with cruelty and insolence against both Catherine and Johanna (cf. L. de Laincel, "Sault," *Revue de Marseille et de Provence* 5 [1869]: 72).

papal vassal and Angevin sovereign. In the process, she began to assume the traditional Angevin role of papal champion.

Johanna and Urban V

Urban V's election augured well for Johanna. She wrote him an effusive letter of congratulation, telling him that she rejoiced within and her spirit was filled with immense joy.[73] Despite their disagreement over Johanna of Durazzo's marriage—which, Pierre's insistence on its scandalous nature notwithstanding, did little to impede Johanna's ability to cast herself as the obedient servant of the papacy—she and Urban worked closely together throughout his pontificate, their cooperation enhanced by his resolve to return the Apostolic See to Rome. He assumed the papacy not as a cardinal but as an abbot and outsider, and as such, his priorities and those of the Curia frequently diverged. Perhaps more literally than his predecessors, he saw Rome as the center of Christendom and a source of vital renewal and strength for the Church, and he was determined to the return the papal court to the city in spite of the cardinals' nearly unanimous desire to remain in Avignon.[74] This was a goal that required winning over the resistant ultramontane cardinals and pacifying the northern Italian tyrants. The latter project was already underway, under the command of Cardinal Gil Albornoz (1310–67), but Urban sought to intensify the Church's efforts. Accordingly, he moved against Bernabò Visconti of Milan—whom he declared a heretic and against whom he called a crusade in 1363—rallying a league of allies, including Bernabò's own former supporters, offered absolution if they partook in the crusade.[75] The struggle escalated in 1367 and 1368, when Urban's brother, Anglic Grimoard, preached the crusade in Italy, while Perugia and English mercenaries led by John Hawkwood (1320–94) joined the fight against the papacy in 1370.[76]

The kings of France and Cyprus were among the most prominent papal allies at this time, but Johanna lent her support to the fight as well. Coins minted during the period portray her as a sovereign who performed all of the functions of rulership, including military ones, which were conventionally

73. Reg. Nicola d'Alife, fol. 186, in Camera, *Elucubrazioni storico-diplomatiche su Giovanna I.a*, 245.

74. Vones, *Urban V.*, 477.

75. Norman Housley, *The Avignon Papacy and the Crusades, 1305–1378* (Oxford: Oxford University Press, 1986), 77, 156–57.

76. Ibid., 78–79; cf. Thibault, *Pope Gregory XI*, 89–90.

understood as masculine. Beginning in 1370, her *reines d'or* show her holding both a sword and scepter, while those from 1372 on portray her not in a dress but in a coat of mail.[77] Contemporaries took Johanna's part in the struggle seriously. Indeed, Urban represented her as his active partner, writing, for instance, to invite the Florentine commune to take up arms alongside Albornoz and Androin de la Roche, the papal legates, "and also Johanna, the illustrious Queen of Sicily, and the great cities of Tuscany."[78] His rhetorical recognition of Johanna's contribution was not mere window dressing. Urban's registers reveal a growing dependence on her, and he was forced to request her aid—financially and militarily—with increasing frequency as the battle wore on, setting a precedent that would continue under Gregory XI, who inherited the war against the Visconti along with the papal tiara.[79] Indeed, with time, this dependence became more pronounced, as Charles V of France funneled more resources into his campaigns against the English, Cyprus was torn by dynastic strife after the death of Peter I in 1369, and Louis of Hungary, an early ally in papal efforts, became increasingly unreliable. Johanna remained loyal, and papal pronouncements rewarded her constancy.

It is a common misperception that Johanna wished the papacy to remain in Avignon,[80] one that owes as much to her adherence to Clement VII

---

77. Monter, "Gendered Sovereignty," 541.

78. No. 1298 (Reg. Vat. 246, fol. 346v) in Lecacheux, *Lettres secrètes et curiales du Pape Urbain V*, 209.

79. Urban requested military aid ("subsidio gentis armigere") from Johanna on June 13, 1366 and again on June 24, this time against John Hawkwood. See nos. 2288 (Reg. Vat. 248, fol. 99v) and 2302 (Reg. Vat. 248, fol. 112r) in Lecacheux, *Lettres secrètes et curiales du Pape Urbain V*, 3:399, 401; cf. Cerasoli, "Urbano V e Giovanna I di Napoli," 387, n. 92. He wrote again to hasten the arrival of the promised troops in September (see Lecacheux, *Lettres secrètes et curiales du Pape Urbain V*, 3:418, no. 2393) and October (ibid., 3:426, no. 2422). In November, he wrote to ask Johanna to send fifteen armed galleys to Marseille (ibid., 3:431, no. 2451). In August 1367, he asked her to send armed troops under the command of Gomez Albornoz—the legate's nephew—against their enemies (ibid., 3:436, no. 2482). The battle had by now moved into the Regno itself, necessitating a greater dependence on its subjects. Urban wrote to the people of Naples at large that December, asking them to answer the call to arms (ibid., 3:456–57, no. 2617). In August 1368, he requested a galley and one thousand gold florins for its upkeep from Johanna to support her subjects fighting for the papacy (ibid., 3:487, no. 2814 *bis*). He made further requests for men and arms in March (ibid., 3:507, no. 2919), April (this time destined for Spoleto; see ibid., 3:509, no. 2936), and June 1369 (for troops and money to support Anglic; see ibid., 3:512, no. 2953). In January 1370, Urban asked Johanna to support Cyprus against Turkish invasion and requested that she aid the people of Rome by supplying them grain (see ibid., 3:523, nos. 3026, 3029). Rome still needed grain in March, when Urban wrote to request further aid from Naples (ibid., 3:527, no. 3053). Finally, in August 1370, Urban asked Johanna to supply six galleys to escort his household back to Provence (ibid., 3:547, no. 3182) so that he could oversee negotiations between France and England.

80. Bridget Morris, for instance, argues that Birgitta of Sweden—an ardent advocate of the papacy's return to Rome—did not "agree with [Johanna] on political matters, especially with regard to the papacy" (Morris, *St. Birgitta of Sweden*, 124).

during the schism as to her sale of Avignon to Clement VI. In fact, quite the opposite was true: Johanna enthusiastically supported and sought to associate herself with Urban's efforts, although perhaps not solely out of devout conviction that the Apostolic See belonged in Rome. Indeed, in 1367, she offered Urban residence in the Regno, over which he already held dominion as its suzerain:

> Most Blessed Father and Most Clement Lord, it has been reported by many, and it has been written, that Your Blessedness is seen to intend to come to Italy. . . . I therefore entreat God that he will mercifully deign to grant that, before the day appointed for my end, I might deserve to see this. And indeed it is to be considered, if it pleases, that this city of Naples might itself be described as a suitable location for your residence. Because although it is granted by all kingdoms universally that the Apostolic See should preside with divine power, it holds sole presidency over that kingdom, with even earthly dominion, from which it might follow suitably enough that Your Holiness should cross over the sea into his city in order that he might come to visit this people peculiarly his own.[81]

Johanna's motives in extending such an invitation were surely not purely altruistic. Rather, they conformed to her forebears' strategies in their own relationships with the papacy. The "Gallican model" of monarchical–papal relationships had developed under Johanna's Capetian relatives, particularly Louis IX and Philip IV.[82] Angevin monarchs cultivated the same dynamic after Charles I's emergence as the papal champion against the Hohenstaufen. As the counts of Provence, theoretical leaders of the Guelfs, and papal vassals and champions, the rulers of Naples had long enjoyed considerable influence over popes.[83] Johanna's invitation to Urban should be read in this context. Her letter reminded him of his unique relationship to the Regno, as to her as its sovereign, and she portrayed herself as a loyal vassal while simultaneously seeking to gain influence over him via proximity. In her tenuous position as a queen whose legitimacy was constantly under negotiation, a close, protective relationship with the papacy was imperative to shield her from her relatives' pretensions to her throne, as from international hostility, lending her sovereignty the special grace accorded to her ancestors by their relationships to the papacy.

---

81. Reg. Nicola d'Alife, in Camera, *Elucubrazioni storico-diplomatiche su Giovanna I.a*, 262.
82. Klaniczay, *Holy Rulers and Blessed Princesses*, 296.
83. Ibid., 297; cf. Boyer, "La 'Foi Monarchique,'" 85, 93.

Urban, however, refused her invitation, just as he deflected Charles V's efforts to adhere to the "Gallican model" by keeping him in Provence. He elected instead to return to Rome, regardless of the disordered state of affairs in Italy. After he declined Johanna's offer, she pledged her assistance for his return to the Eternal City—telling him that, but for her sex, she would rush to throw herself at his feet, covered in ashes—and sent ten galleys to escort him from Provence to Italy.[84] Matteo Camera notes that Johanna's show of support outdid that of the other Italian naval powers: Whereas Naples sent ten ships, Pisa, Venice, and Genoa sent only thirteen between them.[85] Urban left Avignon at the end of April 1367 and arrived in Viterbo on June 9. He rode into Rome on October 16 amid joyous festivities, escorted by the Este and Malatesta lords and the count of Savoy, his entrance, as Guillaume Mollat has observed, calculatedly that of an Italian, and not a French, prince—a gesture of conciliation that signaled his resolve to restore the papacy, now removed from French influence, to Italy.[86]

Yet, while Urban rebuffed Johanna's attempts to lure him to Naples, he took care to favor her publicly. In fact, the honors he bestowed on her were extraordinary. During Lent in 1368, Johanna traveled to Rome to honor her suzerain. Urban was in the midst of a renewal of Rome, as of the Church, and her entry into the city was greeted by a grand public procession and lavish feast.[87] She was present for that year's presentation of the Golden Rose, traditionally awarded by the pope to the most eminent person—usually a king, although Niccolò Acciaiuoli had been so honored in 1360—at his court on the fourth Sunday of Lent.[88] On that particular Sunday, in addition to Johanna, Peter I of Cyprus and his son (the future Peter II) were both present. Urban defied protocol—and the cardinals, who were reportedly horrified—by presenting Johanna with the Rose, which should by custom have gone to Peter.[89] She was the first queen and first woman to receive the Golden Rose. The slight against Peter was particularly pronounced not only because of Johanna's sex but also because he was a crusader king who had fought against the Turks and in Alexandria even as Urban was renewing his call for foreign crusades during a lull in the Visconti war.[90] He

---

84. Léonard, *Les Angevins de Naples*, 419, n. 2.

85. Camera, *Elucubrazioni storico-diplomatiche su Giovanna I.a*, 262, n. 1.

86. Mollat, *Les papes d'Avignon*, 263.

87. Ibid.

88. Ibid., 506–7. The Golden Rose was shaped like a blooming rose branch and studded with sapphires, pearls, and garnets. Its value exceeded one hundred florins, making it a truly princely gift.

89. Ibid.; Vones, *Urban V.*, 454.

90. Housley, *The Avignon Papacy and the Crusades*, 246.

was the chief representative of the crusading mentality Urban sought to foster and, as such, the obvious recipient of the Rose.[91] The insult was compounded by the fact that, at least on a rhetorical level, the two monarchs were rivals. Peter—a descendent of Hugh III of Lusignan—and Johanna both claimed titular sovereignty over Jerusalem, and both were the descendants of dynasties whose members portrayed themselves as great crusaders who stood at the apex of Christendom's secular aristocracy. Peter was even crowned Jerusalem's king in 1359.[92] Thus, Urban's demonstrated preference for Johanna could be interpreted both as tacit recognition of her claims—as Jerusalem's ruler and as a leading papal ally—and as an expression of greater gratitude for her service. The moment was crucial, and it signaled that Johanna was one of the pope's most valued supporters.

Urban's reliance on and expressed affection for Johanna were constant throughout his pontificate. He actively furthered her interests and those of the Angevin monarchy, for instance canonizing Elzéar of Sabran (1285–1323) amid great pomp in Rome on April 15, 1369.[93] Elzéar, a Provençal nobleman and the count of Ariano, was a Franciscan tertiary celebrated for his deep, self-abnegating piety who had been among Robert's and Sancia's most trusted vassals and advisors.[94] He was also Urban's uncle and godfather. His canonization was a testament to the degree to which Urban's and Johanna's interests coincided, as to the continuing cooperation between the papacy and the Angevin sovereign. As Gábor Klaniczay has noted, Angevin monarchs had long enjoyed an influence over the papacy that "place[d] the papal prerogative of canonisation at the service of the Angevins' ambition to capitalise on the cult of saints for purposes of dynastic propaganda."[95] Elzéar's recognition as a saint was in keeping with this tradition and honored both Johanna and her grandparents. At the same time, his canonization in Rome associated the Angevin dynasty with Urban's restoration and renewal of the Church. Johanna, in turn, supported Urban's projects throughout his pontificate, sending him soldiers and financing his wars, while her galleys escorted him across the sea to Viterbo and back again when, in 1370, Urban returned to Avignon with the intention of brokering a truce between the warring French and English kings.

---

91. Vones, *Urban V.*, 477.

92. Housley, *The Avignon Papacy and the Crusades*, 39.

93. Mollat, *Les papes d'Avignon*, 124; Klaniczay, *Holy Rulers and Blessed Princesses*, 297, n. 7.

94. Kelly, *The New Solomon*, 141.

95. Klaniczay, *Holy Rulers and Blessed Princesses*, 297. See also André Vauchez, *Sainthood in the Later Middle Ages*, trans. Jean Birrell (Cambridge: Cambridge University Press, 2005), 78–80.

Johanna and Gregory XI

Johanna continued to enjoy this close, cooperative relationship with Gregory XI after Urban's death in December 1370. During his pontificate, she represented herself as driven by faith and zealous for papal projects, including foreign crusades, her expressions of "glowing, fervent devotion to Christ's service" leading Gregory to request that she succor Constantinople, then under Turkish threat, rather than embarking, as she proposed, on a crusade.[96] She was his ally in the Italian campaigns of the papal league and assisted him in his return to Rome. Her galleys escorted him from Marseille in September 1376 just as they had Urban in 1367, while many members of her court were in his entourage as he entered Rome the following January.[97] One of the notable successes of Gregory's papacy, as of Johanna's reign, was a result of their cooperation. Working in concert, Niccolò Spinelli, Johanna, and Gregory negotiated a lasting peace between Naples and Sicily—thenceforth to be called Trinacria—in 1372, returning the island, its rulers now formally defined as Angevin vassals, to papal obedience and finally ending the long war between the two kingdoms.[98] Sicily was not truly reincorporated into the Angevin domain, but Johanna and Gregory won a rhetorical triumph, and Johanna realized—at least in part—one of the primary ambitions of Angevin rulers since the Sicilian Vespers.

Their alliance, like Johanna's alliance with Urban, owed much to her support for the papacy's Italian wars. Urban's decision to leave Italy had caused tensions within the papal league; enthusiasm for his crusade against the Visconti waned with his departure, and the league had signed a truce in November 1370.[99] Gregory, however, shared his predecessor's goals, and he commissioned Gomez Albornoz (d. 1377) to renew the league in

---

96. F. Cerasoli, "Gregorio XI e Giovanna I di Napoli—Documenti inediti dell'Archivio Vaticano, 1370–1378," *ASPN* 25 (1900): 22, no. 182, 6–7, no. 167; cf. Housley, *The Avignon Papacy and the Crusades*, 117. No crusade against Turks in the Aegean materialized, although Johanna's 1376 lease of the principality of Achaea to the Order of Hospitallers may have been intended to aid crusade efforts in the region. See Raymond-J. Loenertz, O.P., "Hospitaliers et Navarrais en Grèce, 1376–1383: Regestes et documents," *Orientalia christiana periodica* 22 (1956): esp. 330.

97. Gregory fixed his departure date for September 1, 1376, thanking Johanna in June for her pledge of six galleys and requesting that they be prepared to leave Marseille at the appointed time. Cerasoli, "Gregorio XI e Giovanna I di Napoli—Documenti inediti," 22, no. 182. See also Léonard, *Les Angevins de Naples*, 452.

98. On the terms of the peace and Gregory's role in the treaty, see "Appendix D: Gregory XI and the Sicilian Settlement," in Thibault, *Pope Gregory XI*, 215–17; cf. Léonard, *Les Angevins de Naples*, 433.

99. Thibault, *Pope Gregory XI*, 90.

June 1371.[100] Much as Urban had before him, Gregory relied on Johanna. Her loyalty bolstered his position in Italy, as when he used her territorial feud with Amadeus of Savoy (1334–83) in the Piedmont to leverage the count's support, and when he called for her financial assistance for a counterattack against the Visconti, who marched on Bologna in April 1372.[101] She supplied and maintained three hundred lances for the papal armies, while Spinelli, now the seneschal of Provence, fought alongside the league's military commanders, pursuing Angevin interests in the Piedmont even as he fulfilled Johanna's duty as Gregory's vassal and champion.[102] He emerged as one of the most successful captains of the renewed campaign, making the Angevin contribution even more significant than during Urban's time. Even Johanna's final marriage, to Duke Otto of Brunswick (1320–98), a scion of the Welf dynasty from which Italy's Guelfs took their name and whom Mollat aptly describes as "a baron of minor lineage but a valorous leader of mercenaries," in 1376 was in keeping with her filial devotion to the papacy.[103] Otto was one of the most celebrated warriors fighting on the papacy's behalf.[104] It was a pragmatic marriage that honored one of the pope's most important allies, associating Johanna even more intimately with the pope's war. Otto, barred from the succession, received no powers in Naples; his importance lay not in his wealth or connections but in his ability to personally perform the military role Johanna had claimed for herself.[105]

This is not to say that Johanna was slavishly or uncritically obedient to the papacy. Quite the opposite was true when the welfare of her kingdom or her own interests failed to coincide with those of the pontiff. This was most

---

100. Ibid., 93.

101. Ibid., 97–98. In cooperation with Spinelli, Gregory used the territorial dispute between Naples and Savoy to secure Amadeus's cooperation: G. Mollat, ed., *Lettres secrètes et curiales du pape Grégoire XI (1370–1378), intéressant les pays autres que la France, publiées ou analysées d'après les registres du Vatican* (Paris: E. de Boccard, 1962), 1:266, no. 1906 (Reg. Vat. 269, fol. 292r–v). As Thibault notes, the situation played to Gregory's advantage, because the pontiff was "in a position, by virtue of his war with the Visconti as well as his status as suzerain of the Kingdom of Naples, to offer definite advantages to the Count of Savoy" (Thibault, *Pope Gregory XI*, 96).

102. Thibault, *Pope Gregory XI*, 107, 111, 114; cf. Léonard, *Les Angevins de Naples*, 436. Ultimately, Spinelli used his activities in the Piedmont to reclaim Angevin territory, although Amadeus was not required to cede the territory Spinelli occupied as long as the league was in force and the count remained loyal (Thibault, *Pope Gregory XI*, 107–8).

103. Mollat, *Les papes d'Avignon*, 189.

104. Léonard, *Les Angevins de Naples*, 302; Thibault, *Pope Gregory XI*, 100, 114.

105. Otto became the Regno's military commander. He was entitled prince of Taranto, a title Johanna could bestow after confiscating it, along with the principality of Achaea, from Francesco del Balzo. Francesco and his wife, Margaret of Taranto, who had inherited the Tarantini lands after Philip's death, rebelled against Johanna, who put down their insurrection in April 1374 and seized all of their lands and titles. ADBR, B 181, fols. 3r–5r; cf. Léonard, *Les Angevins de Naples*, 449–50.

obviously the case when she ignored Urban V's orders to free Johanna of Durazzo, but she asserted her will at other times as well. Gregory repeatedly chided her for failure to cooperate with the inquisitors he sent to extirpate heresy in the Regno. He accused her of impeding their efforts and ordered her to instruct her officials to cease interfering with them.[106] During the War of the Eight Saints (1375–78) between Florence and the papacy, as well, Johanna adhered to her own interests rather than to papal directives. Gregory wrote to Johanna on December 26, 1375, instructing her to suspend trade with Florence and eject Florentine merchants from her kingdom.[107] While Johanna was one of few monarchs to comply with this order,[108] she did not fully obey the papal command. Because her administration had relied on Florentines since the late 1340s and because of the long-standing economic relationship binding the Regno to Florence, the order caused Johanna great difficulty. She delayed publishing the papal bull ordering the merchants' banishment until August 1376, and Richard C. Trexler has argued that she "did all in her power to protect the Florentines."[109] While she expelled Florentine merchants from the city of Naples in early August, she did not enforce their banishment in the rest of the Regno, and she turned a blind eye to Florentine goods in Neapolitan waters.[110] Thus she complied with the letter of Gregory's directive without obeying its spirit, preserving her relationship with the Florentine commune even as her papal suzerain waged war against it. Indeed, the Florentine chronicler Gregorio Dati later observed that, "the queen, being a Florentine at heart . . . never wanted to consent" to the harsh decree, leading her to flout the papal command by postponing the bull's publication.[111] However, such assertions of independence notwithstanding,

---

106. Gregory wrote to both Johanna and Bernard du Bousquet on this topic in March and October 1373. See F. Cerasoli, "Gregorio XI e Giovanna I, regina di Napoli," *ASPN* 24 (1899): 14, 19, and Mollat, *Lettres secrètes et curiales du pape Grégoire XI*, 2:3120, nos. 2230 (Reg. Vat. 269, fol. 97) and 2231 (Reg. Vat. 269, fol. 87v; Reg. Vat. 244-D, fol. 119, n. 263); cf. Thibault, *Pope Gregory XI*, 190–91. Gennaro Maria Monti notes that, allegations of Spiritual Franciscan leanings notwithstanding, Angevin monarchs generally cooperated with inquisitors. Johanna was less cooperative, and inquisitors were weaker during her reign than they had been previously—so weak as to often be without effect. See Gennaro Maria Monti, *Dal Duecento al Settecento: Studi Storico-Giuridici*, Biblioteca di coltura meridionale 1 (Naples: I.T.E.A., 1925), 105–24, esp. 115–19.

107. Mollat, *Lettres secrètes et curiales du pape Grégoire XI*, 2:175, no. 3682 (Reg. Vat. 244 I, fol. 132, n. 309).

108. Léonard, *Les Angevins de Naples*, 451.

109. Richard C. Trexler, *The Spiritual Power: Republican Florence under Interdict*, Studies in Medieval and Reformation Thought 9 (Leiden: E. J. Brill, 1974), 84, 86.

110. Ibid., 85, 105.

111. Gregorio Dati, *L'Istoria di Firenze dal 1380 al 1405*, ed. L. Pratesi (Norcia: Tonti Cesare, 1902), 34, cited and translated in Trexler, *The Spiritual Power*, 85–86.

Johanna's preferred diplomatic stance was one of rhetorical obedience—even if that obedience was only ostensible—and she proved, but for few exceptions, an unwavering ally to both popes.

By 1372, the papal league was in dire financial straits. Louis of Hungary and Frederick III of Sicily resisted Gregory's efforts to levy funds; he was forced to pawn the papal jewels, and he became increasingly reliant on Johanna for loans to sustain the campaign in Lombardy.[112] Even as the papacy's financial situation deteriorated, so too did relations between the papal administrators—many of them Limousins—and the Italian communes. Florence, in particular, grew concerned about papal incursions on its power and into its territory. Its chancellor, Coluccio Salutati, complained that "Gallic devourers" were ravaging Italy. By 1375, Florence and the papacy were at war, and the commune was placed under interdict on March 31, 1376. Rebellions spread throughout the north; forty cities revolted against the papacy in the early months of 1376.[113]

As the papal league crumbled, Gregory appealed, once again, for Johanna's help.[114] His letters during the last years of his pontificate lavish praise on her. She was his "filia peramantissima," his most deeply loving daughter, and he depended on her, because she was "the Church's own singular daughter" ("peculiarem ejusdem ecclesie filiam"), upon whom it could rely for protection from its enemies.[115] Johanna's support was constant amid the turmoil of the pope's return to Italy, and as he entered Rome in 1377, only the Neapolitan court could be looked to for devoted service.[116] Writing to inform Johanna of Florence's excesses, Gregory expressed his confidence that she, its "most devoted daughter" ("devotissime filie"), would share in her mother Church's "most bitter bitterness."[117] It was a given of their relationship that she would.

---

112. Thibault, *Pope Gregory XI*, 112. In July of 1373, Gregory requested that Johanna send six thousand florins to Bologna, while she was a partner in a Florentine subsidy of twenty thousand florins for the campaign in the Piedmont in August of that year. See Mollat, *Lettres secrètes et curiales du pape Grégoire XI*, 1:280, no. 2007 (Reg. Vat. 269, fol. 193-Bv) and 297, no. 2138 (Reg. Vat. 265, fol. 69v); cf. F. Cerasoli, "Gregorio XI e Giovanna I di Napoli," *ASPN* 24 (1899): 308, no. 103, and Cerasoli, "Gregorio XI e Giovanna I, regina di Napoli," 498, no. 34.

113. Thibault, *Pope Gregory XI*, 146–47; Alison Williams Lewin, *Negotiating Survival: Florence and the Great Schism, 1378–1417* (Madison, NJ: Fairleigh Dickinson University Press, 2003), 45.

114. Unwilling to enter into conflict with Florence, Johanna prevaricated, but she still aided the papacy to the extent that she could without making war on Florence. In June of 1376, for instance, Gregory wrote to thank her for the six galleys she agreed to supply for his passage into Italy, requesting that they be ready in Marseille on the first of September (Cerasoli, "Gregorio XI e Giovanna I di Napoli—Documenti inediti," 22, no. 182).

115. Ibid., 23, no. 183.

116. Léonard, *Les Angevins de Naples*, 452.

117. Cerasoli, "Gregorio XI e Giovanna I di Napoli—Documenti inediti," 9–10, no. 70: "amaritudinem amarissimam sancte Romane Ecclesie matris tue."

Although Klaniczay has observed that the "Gallican model" followed by Angevin monarchs never entailed subordination to the papacy, that, despite "exemplary piety," they never "yield[ed] to the Church when it came to affairs of state," Johanna's adaptation of their model entailed a show of piety through subordination.[118] She cultivated a reputation for obedience and filial devotion to the papacy to which she clung even when she asserted her own will. Part of her singularity lay in the paradox of her position—she was the most obedient, most devoted daughter of the Church, a position that empowered her as the Church had need of and, indeed, depended on what Gregory called her powerful arm ("tue potentie brachium"), returning her rhetorically to the position of papal champion held by earlier Angevin sovereigns.[119]

Textual *Fama* and Queenly Performance

Johanna appears in contemporary chronicle accounts as a papal ally, rather than as the stubborn and incompetent queen described by Pierre d'Ameil. She figures in chronicles from Bologna, Rome, Orvieto, Mantua, and Siena—all, at least initially, members of the league against the Visconti—as a prominent member of the papal league. In the *Cronaca Senese* of Donato di Neri and his son, for instance, Johanna enters the narrative when her galleys escorted Urban to Pisa en route to Rome.[120] She is the only person mentioned by name when the chronicler recounts how the Italian communes sent troops to support the pope against the Visconti.[121] He goes on to narrate her troops' victories, describing the rout of Ambrogio Visconti's forces at their hands and the death and imprisonment of his men in Apulia.[122] Year by year, through the pontificates of both Urban V and Gregory XI, the papal league's activities against the Visconti and mercenary bands are described and Johanna's contributions tallied along with those of the other leaders—many of whom were actually present, but whose contributions are weighed similarly—of the papal forces. Her efforts against Ambrogio and alliance with Emperor Charles IV (r. 1355–78) and the pope are also noted by two Bolognese chronicles in which she figures as one among many papal allies.[123]

---

118. Klaniczay, *Holy Rulers and Blessed Princesses*, 296.

119. Cerasoli, "Gregorio XI e Giovanna I di Napoli—Documenti inediti," 13, no. 72.

120. *Cronaca Senese di Donato di Neri e di suo figlio Neri* (1352–81), in Lisini and Iacometti, *Cronache Senesi*, 565–685, at 614.

121. Ibid., 616.

122. Ibid., 617.

123. *Cronaca A* and *Cronaca B* in Sorbelli, *Corpus Chronicorum Bononiensium*, 216 (A); 220 and passim, 242–43, 294 (B).

Johanna features similarly in the *Discorso Historico degli Accidenti di Orvieto*, in which she and the Church are portrayed as partners in northern Italy in 1365, particularly vis-à-vis the fluctuating allegiances of the mercenaries led by John Hawkwood, whose services the league bought.[124] Her activities in the north are commented on as well in the *Breve Chronicon Monasterii mantuani sancti Andree*, which notes that Urban called upon Johanna for aid as he was forming the papal league and describes her efforts in support of Lodovico Gonzaga in 1368.[125] Her grand reception in Rome is mentioned in the *Discorso Historico degli Accidenti di Orvieto* just after the fact of Urban's return to the city, the two sets of festivities closely associated by the chronicler.[126] An anonymous *Diario Romano* (1370–1410) also comments on Johanna's grand entrance into the city, noting her reception of the Golden Rose.[127] Contemporary German chroniclers who recorded the activities of the papal league follow the same pattern. Albert Bezani identifies Johanna as a prominent member of the league, listing all of its members but singling her out as a central figure ("speciliater cum domina et nobili domina Iohanna regina Neapolitana et Provincie"), while the author of the *Chronicon Moguntinum* remarks on her close relationship to Gregory XI and discusses her reception of him in Naples as he traveled to Rome.[128]

These chronicle accounts have in common an absence of interpretation and analysis, which sets them apart from the elaborate, imaginative

---

124. *Discorso Historico degli Accidenti di Orvieto* in Luigi Fumi, ed., *Ephemerides Urbevetanae, dal Cod. Vaticano Urbinate 1745*, vol. 15, pt. 5 of *RIS*, ed. Ludovico Muratori, new ed. (Città di Castello: S. Lapi, 1903), 1–98, at 87–88: "Et anco soldaro la Chiesia et la reina Giovanna di Napoli la compagnia de l'inglesi, che fussero contra la compagnia di Anecchino: chè questa compagnia de l'inglesi erono molta gente et bene armati et fortissime genti et era molto riccha compagnia."

125. Orsini Begani, ed., *Breve Chronicon Monasterii mantuani sancti Andree ord. Bened. di Antonio Nerli* (AA. 800–1431), vol. 24, pt. 13 of *RIS*, ed. L. A. Muratori, new ed. (Città di Castello: S. Lapi, 1910), 143. Antonio Nerli, the monastery's abbot from 1380, probably began his chronicle around the turn of the fifteenth century, making his account somewhat after the fact but still relatively contemporary. On Nerli, see Pietro Torelli, "Antonio Nerli e Bonamente Aliprandi cronisti mantovani," *Archivio storico Lombardo*, 4th series, 15, no. 38 (1911): 209–10, 218–24.

126. *Discorso Historico degli Accidenti di Orvieto*, 92–93.

127. "Appendix: Diario Romano (1370–1410) attribuito a Gentile Delfino," in Francesco Isoldi, ed., *La Mesticanza di Paolo di Lello Petrone (XVIII Agosto MCCCCXXIV – VI Marzo MCCCXLVII)*, vol. 24, pt. 2 of *RIS*, ed. Ludovico Muratori, new ed. (Città di Castello: S. Lapi, 1910), 71.

128. Albertus de Bezanis, *Cronica pontificum et imperatorum*, ed. Oswald Holder-Egger, Monumenta Germaniae Historica, Scriptores rerum Germanicarum in usum scholarum separatim editi 3 (Hannover: Hahn, 1908), 113; Karl Hegel, ed., *Chronicon Moguntinum*, Monumenta Germaniae Historica, Scriptores rerum Germanicarum in usum scholarum separatim editi 20 (Hannover: Hahn, 1885), 41. The author of the *Chronicon Moguntinum* was most likely a vicar of the Mainz cathedral chapter named Johannes Kungstein (d. 1404/5) (cf. Jennifer Kolpacoff Deane, "Archiepiscopal Inquisitions in the Middle Rhine: Urban Anticlericalism and Waldensianism in Late Fourteenth-Century Mainz," *Catholic Historical Review* 92 [2006]: 202).

stories of Andrew of Hungary's murder and Louis of Taranto's rule told by chroniclers such as Matteo Villani and Domenico da Gravina. They conform instead to the model of historical writing that Louis Green identifies as typical of medieval chronicles, which "claimed to do no more than set down the facts that had come to their notice in the strict order of their occurrence."[129] Their authors' purposes are different from those of Giovanni or Matteo Villani, who were more concerned with "the interpretation of the significance of historical development."[130] Johanna is not their subject but merely a player in a larger historical drama. The events they describe are not meant to illuminate a larger moral point, so that no narrative embroidery or authorial commentary about her character or role in events is necessary. This silence is in itself telling, however: Johanna ceased during this period to be a figure of intrigue and scandal, drawing notice for her military and political contributions rather than for the sordidness of her personal life or the morals of her court. Indeed, even Matteo Villani, who offered lengthy, detailed commentary regarding the earlier part of her career, notes only the fact of her relationship with Urban V due to the pope's legatine duties in Naples.[131] Further afield, as in Iberia, where the activities of the papal league drew less notice, Johanna became just one among many rulers noted by chroniclers who took stock of Europe's monarchs, an unremarkable figure in a list of kings.[132]

Chroniclers were not the only observers to reflect the change in Johanna's public persona. Her role as papal daughter—which both Urban V and Gregory XI did much to publicize—redefined how Johanna's contemporaries perceived her. That role was a precondition for the image of herself as a sovereign queen that she cultivated in the latter half of her reign. It made her a valuable ally, and it made her a valued associate for other women—most notably Birgitta of Sweden and Catherine of Siena—eager to align themselves with the papacy and gain fame for piety. As chapter 4 will discuss, Johanna's new identity allowed her to add a new spiritual dimension to her public persona that wholly transformed her reputation.

---

129. Louis Green, *Chronicle into History: An Essay on the Interpretation of History in Florentine Fourteenth-Century Chronicles* (Cambridge: Cambridge University Press, 1972), 3.

130. Ibid., 7.

131. M. Villani, *Cronica*, XI.26, 2:625.

132. See, for instance, Ayala, *Crónica del Rey Don Pedro y del Rey Don Enrique, su hermano, hijos del rey don Alfonso Onceno*, 1:5; 2:122. An exception to this trend is the odd claim made in the appendix—whose author is unknown—to Peter IV of Aragon's chronicle that Johanna attempted to contract marriage with either Peter or his son after James of Majorca's death, an unsubstantiated story that must hinge on Johanna's reputation for multiple marriages. See Pere III of Catalonia, *Chronicle*, 2:592–93.

By 1378, Johanna of Naples, no longer widely perceived as the she-wolf of Boccaccio's *Eclogues* or the "harlot queen" of the *Chronicon Estense*, had succeeded in remaking her public image. Thanks to her high-profile support for papal projects, she had come, at least rhetorically, to occupy the position of papal champion traditionally reserved for the Angevin monarch. She was a partner in the popes' return to Rome and a ready source of troops, finances, and ships. Urban V and Gregory XI were themselves partially responsible for her transformation. She and they strove to represent her as the *filia devotissima* and *peramantissima* of the Church, legitimating her problematic sovereignty. As the papacy's other traditional allies—particularly France, Hungary, and Cyprus—became less reliable, Johanna's importance in the arenas of Italian and papal politics was on the ascendant, and her participation in the papal league was noted by contemporary chroniclers who singled out her contributions as particularly significant. Her active role in politics and warfare—even if she did not, as Spinelli and Otto of Brunswick did on her behalf, actually lead her armies into battle—ensured that she functioned in contemporary histories not as an example of royal iniquity or living proof of the dangers of feminine power but as an active, effective monarch whose sovereignty her contemporaries nearly ceased to question openly.

Johanna's strategies of self-presentation drew on those of her predecessors, as she sought to return the status of the Angevin monarchy to the heights it had enjoyed before the calamities of her early reign. Her task was complicated by contemporary ambivalence about female succession, as about femininity, so clearly articulated in the wake of Andrew of Hungary's death. Louis of Taranto's reign and unpopularity had redressed the gender imbalance lamented by commentators like Matteo Villani, in part by containing Johanna's power and sexuality within a more traditional marriage. With Louis's death, she was able to reassert her sovereignty, taking care to associate herself with her glorious ancestors and *beata stirps*, whose memory and legacy legitimated her position even as she labored to maintain the sense that she was, to some degree, still contained and constrained by marriage.

Johanna's relationship to the papacy aided in both projects. On the one hand, her protection by and championing of the papacy legitimated her position. On the other, her insistence on her humble obedience to the pope—emphasizing her position as his vassal—rendered her exercise of sovereignty less threatening to contemporary commentators, her power contained by being harnessed for papal projects and sanctioned by papal approval. Indeed, the papacy could be said to stand in the place of Johanna's husband. As Dyan Elliott has observed, late medieval holy women—in constant danger of seeming to overreach the bounds of feminine power—submitted themselves to their confessors, who enjoyed a "quasi-matrimonial prerogative" that echoed canon law's insistence on wives' obedience to their husbands.[133] Johanna's rhetorical obedience to the pope mirrored this relationship, placing her under papal control like a wife under a husband's control or a female penitent under her confessor's. Matteo Villani, describing the power imbalance between Johanna and Andrew of Hungary, had argued that the problems of her court stemmed from the fact that Johanna was "both master and lady of her baron, who, as her husband, should have been her lord."[134] Louis of Taranto's reign had demonstrated the infeasibility for Johanna's sovereignty of a marital relationship that corrected that imbalance. Accordingly, she subordinated her subsequent two husbands to secondary status in the Regno while she subordinated herself to the papacy, stressing its lordship over her. The popes were her fathers and suzerains; she was not a woman acting independently, but a daughter acting on behalf of her father. Thus rhetorically contained, Johanna actually became more powerful: She portrayed herself as obedient even when asserting her will, whether in resisting the papal order to expel Florentines from the Regno during the War of the Eight Saints or in marginalizing James of Majorca. The position of sovereign queen as Johanna articulated it was, thus, paradoxically both powerful and subservient, active and humble. Contemporary chronicle accounts, like Johanna's burgeoning friendships with famous holy women, suggest that she succeeded in winning observers' acceptance and, indeed, approval.

---

133. Elliott, *Proving Woman*, 92–93.
134. M. Villani, *Cronica*, I.11, 1:26.

✖ CHAPTER 4

An "Especially Good Friend" to Saints

Friendship, Politics, and the Performance of Sovereignty

> She truly loved God and was most highly wary of herself so no one might speak badly of her and that she might not give occasion for anyone to disparage her. Therefore she fled levities and places or persons for which she could be branded; and she had in her company honest handmaids and well-mannered companions.
>
> Prior Peter of Alvastra and Master Peter of Skänninge, *Vita* of Birgitta of Sweden (1373)

> Oh, what a very great treasure a princess or any other lady has who possesses an honourable reputation! Certainly there is nothing so great in this world that she could have and nothing she should so much love to accumulate. . . . She will get to know people of good and upright lives who are devoted to God, and she will want them to be her friends. She will receive them humbly and speak to them confidentially and very willingly hear them and ask them to pray for her. In this way the virtue of sobriety will rule the good princess.
>
> Christine de Pizan, *The Treasure of the City of Ladies* (ca. 1405)

In the later fifteenth century, a Swedish abbess named Margareta Clausdotter sat down to write a biography of Birgitta of Sweden (1303–73), the founder of the Birgittine order, whose motherhouse at Vadstena Margareta had ruled since 1473. Birgitta's daughter, Katherine of Vadstena (1332–81), was under examination for sainthood. Margareta recorded her family's history as part of the canonization effort, fleshing out a holy genealogy for the saintly dyad of mother and daughter whose biographies lie at the center of Birgittine hagiography. Her narrative journeyed south with Katherine and Birgitta as they sojourned in the Kingdom of Naples en route to Jerusalem in the early 1370s. Their pilgrimage was of central importance for Birgitta's life story, and the saint's time in Naples was a vital—if problematic, from Margareta's perspective—chapter in her life. Birgitta and Katherine had been the guests of Johanna of Naples, who, when

Margareta wrote, was best remembered in Sweden as a notorious adulteress, murderer, and schismatic. Margareta needed to find a way to account for the association between two such different women. She wrote, "The queen, who was a widow and ruled over the kingdom, was named Johanna. And she was an especially good friend to Saint Birgitta and loved her a great deal."[1] Yet, despite her assertion that Johanna and Birgitta were friends, Margareta goes on to hold Johanna responsible, through her lust and willfulness, for the death of Birgitta's eldest son. The resulting tale is contradictory and confused, at once presenting Johanna as pious and committed to Birgitta and as a sinful wanton disastrously lacking in self-control.

Margareta confronted a puzzle: Birgitta, a celebrated ascetic and visionary deeply concerned about propriety and about her reputation, "fled levities and places or persons for which she could be branded," yet she also associated with and was dear to one of the most infamous women of her age. Why? Margareta's confusion stems from the problematic duality of Johanna's reputation. On the one hand, she was the "harlot queen" derided by her political opponents, while on the other, she was a paragon of queenly virtue and friend to saints.

The Political Uses of Sanctity

The latter reputation was the one Johanna herself cultivated. Her firm political adherence to the papacy and rhetorical self-styling as the pope's loyal vassal reshaped Johanna's reputation, so that in papal rhetoric, she had become the *filia peramantissima*—the most deeply loving daughter—of the Church. Johanna's support for the papacy was but one aspect of her efforts to demonstrate herself an ideal Christian queen. Her friendship with Birgitta of Sweden added a new dimension to her reputation for piety, allowing her to represent herself as the friend and protector of saintly women even as she came to be sought out by women striving to demonstrate their sanctity.

Johanna's efforts to associate herself with sanctity adhered to established Angevin models of self-presentation. Indeed, her reputation as a legitimate sovereign hinged on her assertion of a distinctively Angevin identity that drew on and adapted her forebears' legacy of sacral kingship and active piety. Like her ancestors, she cultivated a reputation marked by her relationship to her *beata stirps*, and like them, she realized her role as the secular defender

---

1. Margareta Clausdotter, *Chronicon de genere et nepotibus S. Birgittae, auctore Margareta Clausdotter, abbatissa Vadstenensi*, in *Scriptores Rerum Svecicarum Medii Aevi*, ed. Claudius Annerstedt (Graz: Akad. Dr.-u. Verlag-Anst, 1966), 3.2:211–12.

of the Church through military support, as through patronage of religious projects, cults, institutions, and figures. To an even greater extent than they, however, she fostered and publicized friendships with living saints whose reputations for sanctity redounded to her credit.

Emulating her forebears, Johanna sought *fama* for works of piety. Many scholars have argued that late medieval women, particularly in Italy, turned to religion as a source of power "that was otherwise denied to them," finding methods to work within and around the Church that legitimated that power.[2] For a queen, whether a consort or a reigning queen, piety was the cardinal virtue, and Johanna presented herself as pious in ways understood as distinctively feminine even as she drew on both Angevin precedent and aristocratic models of patronage. As Samantha Kelly has noted, Robert of Naples had employed patronage as the "engine of royal propaganda," setting a precedent on which his granddaughter drew.[3] Johanna's self-presentation through religious patronage is perhaps best seen in the Church of Santa Maria dell'Incoronata in Naples, near the royal residence at Castel Nuovo—a location that explicitly tied the new foundation to royal power and presence.[4] Johanna, who founded the church in the mid-1360s as part of a larger hospital complex she gave to the Carthusian order to oversee, commissioned lush frescoes portraying scenes from the Old and New Testaments, the Triumph of Faith, and the Seven Sacraments by the Neapolitan painter Roberto d'Odorisio (d. after 1382).[5] The traditional explanation for the frescoes—now, sadly, badly damaged—is that they commemorate Johanna and Louis of Taranto's 1352 coronation. "Dell'Incoronata" refers, however, not to their coronation but to the Crown of Thorns, a thorn of which was given to the church by Johanna, who requested it as a gift from the reliquary of Sainte Chapelle in Paris.[6] The church's visual program revolved around the crown of thorns, which it paired with the temporal crown of the Angevin rulers. Paola Vitolo suggests that the style of the frescoes, which mimics that of Giotto—even going so far as to copy the clothing styles of the 1340s—was intended to honor Robert, Giotto's patron, and to signal the

2. Daniel Bornstein, "Women and Religion in Late Medieval Italy: History and Historiography," in *Women and Religion in Medieval and Renaissance Italy*, ed. Daniel Bornstein and Roberto Rusconi, trans. Margery J. Schneider (Chicago: University of Chicago Press, 1996), 2.

3. Kelly, *The New Solomon*, 12.

4. On the significance of the Incoronata's frescoes and location for Johanna's self-presentation, see Vitolo, *La Chiesa della Regina*, 29–30.

5. Vitolo suggests that Johanna chose the Carthusians to honor the memory of her father, who was devoted to the order (Vitolo, *La Chiesa della Regina*, 34).

6. Bologna, *I pittori alla corte angioina di Napoli*, 2:293. Cf. Vitolo, *La Chiesa della Regina*, 15.

dynastic bond between Robert and Johanna.[7] Santa Maria dell'Incoronata thus celebrated Johanna's dynasty and the blood shared by the Angevins and St. Louis—Sainte Chapelle's builder and the king who acquired the crown of thorns—drawing on Capetian and Angevin models of dynastic legitimation to identify Johanna with both and stress the stability and continuity her reign represented.[8] Indeed, Louis is among several of Johanna's *beata stirps* represented. The visual program within the church functions as a monument to Angevin piety: The sacrament of Ordination is illustrated by the ordination of St. Louis of Toulouse, while Robert of Anjou and Charles of Calabria—the two men through whom Johanna traced her claim to her throne—appear in a fresco representing the Triumph of the Church.[9]

Johanna financed numerous other religious foundations, including the church of Sant'Antonio Abate in Naples (founded to care for those afflicted with ergotism, or St. Anthony's fire), a Celestine house at Casaluce in 1365, and both a Franciscan monastery in Naples and a charterhouse on Capri in 1371, all of which received decorative programs celebrating her dynasty's piety.[10] Ferdinando Bologna has remarked on the artistic fecundity of this period in Neapolitan history, during which Johanna invited foreign artists, especially Tuscans, into the Regno and fostered a rapidly maturing artistic movement that included native-born artists and whose fruits are still visible in the illuminated *Book of Hours of Johanna I of Anjou* (see figures 7 and 8), as in the paintings that adorned her new churches.[11] During Johanna's reign, Neapolitan production of illuminated bibles was at its height; a number of the most sumptuous manuscripts were produced for the court.[12] Painters Johanna patronized represented her demurely at prayer and depicted the famous piety of her forebears, using their skill in the service of what Andreas Bräm has characterized as the most significant expression of Johanna's self-presentation during her independent reign.[13] At the same time, Johanna

7. Vitolo, *La Chiesa della Regina*, 48, 63, 79.

8. Ibid., 25, 27–28.

9. Ibid., 29; Bologna, *I pittori alla corte angioina di Napoli*, 2:293.

10. Bologna, *I pittori alla corte angioina di Napoli*, 2:326, 329. See also Hans Aili and Jan Svanberg, *Imagines Sanctae Birgittae: The Earliest Illuminated Manuscripts and Panel Paintings Related to the Revelations of St. Birgitta of Sweden*, 2 vols. (Stockholm: Royal Academy of Letters, History and Antiquity, 2003), 1:90–92, 97, in which Svanberg discusses the artistic programs of Johanna's religious foundations.

11. Vienna, Österreichische Nationalbibliothek, MS Cod. 1921; Bologna, *I pittori alla corte angioina di Napoli*, 2:323, 325.

12. Bräm, *Neapolitanische Bilderbibeln des Trecento*, 1:12.

13. Ibid., 183–84.

actively patronized religious orders, for instance hosting the general chapter of the Franciscan order in 1370 and throwing a lavish banquet at Castel Nuovo to which the friars marched in solemn procession through the streets of Naples.[14]

Perhaps the most important feature of Johanna's public piety, however, and that most clearly in line with Angevin dynastic propaganda, was her effort to patronize and connect herself to sanctity. As Jean-Paul Boyer and Gábor Klaniczay have both argued, Angevin monarchs had long promoted an association between themselves and saints, the most prominent examples (outside of their vaunted kinship to Louis IX) being Charles II's miraculous discovery of Mary Magdalen's relics at St. Maximin in Provence and the family's promotion of Louis of Toulouse, Johanna's great uncle.[15] As André Vauchez notes, aristocratic prestige during the medieval period derived as much from "an almost supernatural quality" aligned with high birth as from political power and riches.[16] Saintly relatives conferred this supernatural quality, legitimating the exercise of worldly power and endowing rulers so genealogically blessed with an aura of holiness. Thus, the royal family publicized its kinship to both Louis of France and Louis of Toulouse, as to Elizabeth of Hungary, its *beata stirps* sanctifying its blood and sacralizing its kingship.[17] Yet Angevin patronage of saints extended beyond their bloodline. The dynasty's members promoted the canonizations of many saints with whom they were associated, such as Elzéar of Sabran and his wife, Delphine (see chapter 3), Nicolaus of Tolentino (canonized 1325), and even Thomas Aquinas, whose 1319 canonization trial Robert supported financially and whose canonization he attended.[18] Indeed, along with their Valois kin, the Angevins exercised a near monopoly over canonization during the period of the Avignon papacy; only three canonization processes carried out between 1305 and 1378 were not heavily influenced by what Vauchez has called

14. Léonard, *Les Angevins de Naples*, 431.

15. On Angevin promotion of the cult of Louis IX, see Cecilia Gaposchkin, *The Making of Saint Louis: Kingship, Sanctity, and Crusade in the Later Middle Ages* (Ithaca: Cornell University Press, 2009). On Charles II and the cult of Mary Magdalen, see Katherine Ludwig Jansen, *The Making of the Magdalen: Preaching and Popular Devotion in the Later Middle Ages* (Princeton: Princeton University Press, 2000), esp. 18–19, 41–45. On the cult of Louis of Toulouse in Angevin dynastic propaganda, see Klaniczay, *Holy Rulers and Blessed Princesses*, 305–16, and Kelly, *The New Solomon*, esp. 122–29.

16. Vauchez, "'Beata Stirps,'" 68.

17. Boyer, "La 'Foi Monarchique,'" 87–90.

18. See Vauchez, *Sainthood in the Later Middle Ages*, 78–80; Klaniczay, *Holy Rulers and Blessed Princesses*, 297, n. 7; Kelly, *The New Solomon*, 98–100.

"the Franco-Angevin lobby."[19] Angevin ideology thus stressed the family's proximity to the holy; its promotion of and kinship with saints linked it to the divine and fostered "the quasi-religious veneration of the prince in the Angevin political system."[20]

While her sex prevented her from exercising quasi-sacerdotal kingship, Johanna could and did tap into sainthood as a source of power and legitimation. She emphasized her *beata stirps*, keeping her family's most prominent links to sanctity at the forefront of popular memory. She publicized her successful prayers to Mary Magdalen, a saint long said to favor the Angevin dynasty. Her gratitude for the Magdalen's protection prompted Johanna to make lavish donations to her shrine at St. Maximin and to the Magdalen convents for reformed prostitutes Sancia of Majorca had founded in Naples.[21] She continued as well to actively promote the cult of Louis of Toulouse. When the friars at the Franciscan convent of St. Louis of Toulouse in Marseille attempted to sell jewels belonging to the saint, Johanna angrily forbade them, refusing to countenance any dishonor to her holy relative through the alienation of his relics.[22] She sought too to add to the ranks of her family's *beata stirps* by promoting Sancia's beatification. Indeed, she wrote to Innocent VI in 1352 to reveal that, upon opening her grandmother's tomb in order to transfer her body to another, more ornate tomb at the Church of Santa Chiara—founded by Sancia—she had discovered her body whole and miraculously uncorrupted.[23]

Even as she emphasized her links to confirmed and potential saints who had already crossed death's threshold, Johanna created a network of friendships that connected her to saints with whom she had personal relationships.

---

19. Vauchez, *Sainthood in the Later Middle Ages*, 81. Vauchez includes Thomas Aquinas's among the three canonizations not sponsored by the Angevins or Valois, because it was initially requested by the Dominican province of Sicily. Robert of Naples was an early supporter, however. The process was conducted in Naples, and a prominent Angevin official, Bartholomew of Capua, was a principal witness, while Robert himself was present in Avignon on the day of Aquinas's canonization (ibid., 78–79). It might be argued, then, that even Thomas Aquinas's canonization was closely associated with Angevin patronage.

20. Boyer, "La 'Foi Monarchique,'" 86.

21. Jansen, *The Making of the Magdalen*, 324–25.

22. Johanna's letter is preserved in AMM, AA 5, fol. 47v, in which she refers to the saint as "beati Ludovici confessoris egregy avunculi nostri graciosa."

23. Musto, "Queen Sancia of Naples," 189; cf. Aislinn Loconte, "Constructing Female Sanctity in Late Medieval Naples: The Funerary Monument of Queen Sancia of Majorca," in *Representing Medieval Genders and Sexualities in Europe: Construction, Transformation, and Subversion, 600–1530*, ed. Elizabeth L'Estrange and Alison More (Farnham: Ashgate, 2011), esp. 112–13; Klaniczay, *Holy Rulers and Blessed Princesses*, 319; Boyer, "La 'Foi Monarchique,'" 98.

After the beginning of the papal schism in 1378, she and her Valois cousins urged Clement VII, who depended absolutely on their support, to canonize Urban V.[24] For Johanna, the project was perhaps not disinterested; Urban's unstintingly generous praise closely associated her with his cult, and she became his champion in death as in life. Her most important contacts with sanctity, however, were with potential female saints. A public woman in a world in which female celebrity was problematic—and one whose reputation had suffered from the more tawdry implications of public womanhood—Johanna befriended women whose celebrity derived not from high birth or scandal but from their status as living saints. Johanna's political and dynastic need for marriage and children, not to mention the exigencies of sovereignty, made accepted ideals of feminine piety, even for royal women—chastity, asceticism, voluntary poverty—impracticable for her.[25] Yet she could and did patronize women who embodied and gained fame for their realizations of these ideals. The most significant of these relationships was her friendship with Birgitta of Sweden, which in turn facilitated later friendships with Birgitta's daughter, Katherine, and Catherine of Siena (1347–80).

Johanna's celebrated role in the religious politics of her day drew these women to her, while she positioned herself as their partner and patron in religious projects. The resulting friendships were mutually beneficial, bolstering Johanna's claims to pious queenship and Christian leadership and her friends' to sanctity and political influence. Examining how and why Johanna became a useful ally in holy women's quests for sanctity reveals how public friendship underpinned *fama*, as well as how both sainthood and pious queenship were constructed by women seeking political and spiritual power in the later Middle Ages.

An Unlikely Friendship: Johanna of Naples and Birgitta of Sweden

Among scholars of late medieval spirituality, Johanna is perhaps best known for her relationship with Birgitta. For many modern scholars—as for Margareta

---

24. Vauchez, *Sainthood in the Later Middle Ages*, 80, n. 68. Urban was formally beatified in the late nineteenth century.

25. The royal women among Johanna's *beata stirps*, such as Sancia and Isabelle of France (Louis IX and Charles I's sister), modeled these ideals. On Isabelle, see Sean Field, *Isabelle of France: Capetian Sanctity and Franciscan Identity in the Thirteenth Century* (Notre Dame: University of Notre Dame Press, 2006), and Agnes of Harcourt, *The Writings of Agnes of Harcourt: The "Life of Isabelle of France" and the "Letter on Louis IX and Longchamp,"* ed. and trans. Sean L. Field (Notre Dame: University of Notre Dame Press, 2003). Cf. Klaniczay, *Holy Rulers and Blessed Princesses*, esp. 237–38.

Clausdotter—the friendship between the fastidious Swedish prophetess and Naples's purportedly lascivious queen has long presented a conundrum. Birgitta's rich, prolific career intersected Johanna's at crucial junctures, and there is abundant evidence for their friendship. Birgitta's biting prophetic invective against Naples's queen, as well as her apparent affection for her, are often remarked on in Birgittine scholarship. Despite Birgitta's visions of Johanna (discussed below), there is overwhelming evidence of their mutual regard. Johanna was a prominent supporter of early efforts to canonize Birgitta and promote her cult, and she played an important role in the saint's later years.[26] Birgitta's cult flourished in the Regno—so much so that her supporters collected depositions there to present to the canonization commission—even before her canonization in 1391, due largely to the Angevin court's patronage.[27] Conversely, Birgitta's followers, most notably her editor and advisor, Alfonso of Jaén, and her daughter, Katherine, identified Johanna as Birgitta's friend and a partner in their quest to canonize her. Johanna's patronage of Birgitta had its reward: In the Regno and elsewhere, especially in early Birgittine literature, Johanna was memorialized as the saint's "especially good friend."[28]

Johanna's friendship with Birgitta began in 1365, when Birgitta visited the tomb of St. Thomas at Ortona.[29] After she miraculously healed the son of Lapa Buondelmonte, Niccolò Acciaiuoli's sister, Birgitta entered court circles and met Johanna.[30] She stayed in Naples until 1367 and returned in 1371 on her way to the Holy Land with Katherine and two of her sons, Birger and Karl, whom she presented to the Neapolitan queen. Karl fell ill and died while in Naples; Johanna and her household were mourners at his funeral. Birgitta stopped again in Naples as she traveled from Jerusalem back

---

26. Morris, *St. Birgitta of Sweden*, 124.

27. Tore Nyberg notes, "Birgitta's Italian environment, especially Naples, was required in collecting material for the canonization process. . . . Eighteen incidents of divine help and assistance either through Birgitta in life or upon asking in prayer for her intercession were put on record here during October and November [1376], covering different areas of daily life, from relief in sickness and toothache to the recovery of stolen objects." See Tore Nyberg, "The Canonization Process of St. Birgitta of Sweden," in *Procès de canonisation au Moyen Âge / Medieval Canonization Processes*, ed. Gábor Klaniczay (Rome: École française de Rome, 2004), 77–78.

28. Clausdotter, *Chronicon de genere et nepotibus S. Birgittae*, 212.

29. Thomas's relics were transferred to Toulouse in 1369 but were still in Ortona when Birgitta visited.

30. Birgitta's miraculous healing of Lapa's son, Esau, was mentioned by witnesses during the first canonization hearing. See Isak Collijn, ed., *Acta et Processus Canonizacionis Beate Birgitte*, 2 vols, Samlingar utgivna av Svenska Fornskriftsällskapet. Series 2: Latinska Skrifter (Uppsala: Almqvist and Wiksells, 1924–31), 1:272.

to Rome, where she had lived since 1350, remaining for several months as Johanna's guest while she recovered from the arduous journey. She gained fame in Naples for her public attacks on the city's immorality—prompted by Johanna herself, who asked Birgitta to pray and prophesy for her people and arranged for a panel of theologians to examine her prophecies—and for the healing miracles she performed. Birgitta spoke out against what she perceived as Neapolitan depravity and gave Johanna herself a long, detailed vision about the precarious condition of her soul. After Birgitta's death, Johanna promoted her canonization, lobbying Gregory XI to recognize her friend's sanctity and sponsoring the gathering of witness testimony in Naples. She even testified that Birgitta worked a posthumous healing miracle for her, evoking a relationship that continued beyond the grave.

Birgitta's Criticism of Johanna

Scholars have traditionally treated the relationship between the Neapolitan queen and the Swedish saint as contentious and even hostile, expressing puzzlement that Birgitta, given her criticism of Johanna, never disavowed her friendship. Drawing primarily on Margareta Clausdotter's chronicle and the final textual redaction of Birgitta's *Revelations*, modern biographers have constructed a fraught relationship between the saint—pious, abstemious, chaste (since her widowhood), and inflexibly moral—and Naples's infamous, dissolute queen. According to this narrative, Birgitta disapproved of Johanna's lifestyle and condemned her excessive sensuality, leading her to rebuke the queen severely. Common among historians' claims regarding their relationship is the charge that Birgitta did not "agree with [Johanna] on political matters, especially with regard to the papacy," whose continued residency in Avignon many erroneously assume Johanna encouraged.[31]

Based solely on the evidence in her *Revelations*, Birgitta considered Johanna an inadequate ruler. She was horrified when she first traveled in the Regno by the disrepair into which its holy sites had fallen and scandalized by its subjects' lax morals and shameless habits (*Rev.* VII.4:9; *Rev.* VII.28). Her *Revelations* reveal Birgitta's disgust with Neapolitan dress and customs, as with the city's sexual permissiveness and the consequent frequency of abortions (*Rev.* VII.27: 18–23, 26–27). She likewise objected to the practice of

---

31. Morris, *St. Birgitta of Sweden*, 124. One of the most recent studies of Birgitta's visions makes this mistake, noting "Birgitta was several times Johanna's guest . . . despite Johanna's ecclesiastical politics and orientation as a follower of Avignon popes." See Pavlína Rychterová, *Die Offenbarungen der Heiligen Birgitta von Schweden: Eine Untersuchung zur alttschechischen Übersetzung des Thomas von Štítné (um 1330–um 1409)* (Cologne: Böhlau Verlag, 2004), 58.

keeping Muslim slaves who were not made to convert to Christianity and often forced into prostitution, and she deplored superstitious tendencies that led Neapolitans to employ witches and fortunetellers (*Rev.* VII.28:9, 12–13, 18–22).

As the Regno's sovereign, Johanna was implicated in its sins, and Birgitta urged her to reform herself and her people. She criticized her directly as well. Even before Birgitta met Johanna, she critiqued the Angevin dynasty for its irregular marriages, which, she learned in a vision, detracted from the worth of its religious bequests, regardless of whether such marriages received papal approbation (*Rev.* VII.4:15–16). Birgitta directed her criticism as much toward the papacy as toward Johanna, but Johanna's marriage to Louis of Taranto exemplified such irregularity, earning Birgitta's censure. Birgitta also received two revelations (probably on behalf of Lapa Buondelmonte) regarding Niccolò Acciaiuoli's suffering in purgatory, where he endured torment for his role in arranging Johanna and Louis's consanguineous union.[32]

A harsh critic of her times and contemporaries, Birgitta reserved some of her harshest criticism for Johanna. Chapter eleven of book VII of her *Revelations* details visions Birgitta received in Naples around the time of her pilgrimage to the Holy Land. Given to Johanna at Birgitta's request by the archbishop of Naples, it contains biting castigation of the queen. Birgitta chastises her for sexual immorality, claiming that God has told her that Johanna "lived all her life like a wanton woman, rather than a queen" and enjoining her to truthfully confess and atone for her sins.[33] She directs her to seek better counselors and distance herself from flattery, as well as to strive to honor God by living with greater contrition, charity, modesty, and humility. Birgitta goes on to predict that Johanna will die childless ("non habebit prolem de utero suo") and advises her to work to safeguard her kingdom from chaos after her death and to be more mindful of justice (and less of wealth) during the time remaining to her.[34] She offers guidance on the Regno's administration as well, particularly regarding its finances, counseling Johanna to lighten existing taxes and not impose new ones, to serve her poor subjects and alleviate their poverty, and to establish peace and concord among them (*Rev.* VII.11:10, 13, 14).

---

32. *Rev.* IV.7:46, *Rev.* IV.9:24–26. See Birgitta of Sweden, *Sancta Birgitta Revelaciones, Book IV*, ed. Hans Aili, Samlingar utgivna av Svenska Fornskriftsällskapet, Series 2: Latinska Skrifter (Stockholm: Almqvist & Wiksell, 1992), 82, 89.

33. *Rev.* VII.11:19, in Birgitta of Sweden, *Sancta Birgitta Revelaciones Lib. VII*, ed. Birger Bergh, Samlingar utgivna av Svenska Fornskriftsällskapet, Series 2: Latinska Skrifter (Uppsala: Almqvist & Wiksell, 1967), 142.

34. *Rev.* VII.11:15–17, 142.

The revelation continues with dire commentary on the state of Johanna's soul. Birgitta describes a vision that exposes Johanna's true character and predicts calamity if she should continue on her present course:

> **23.** . . . A lady was seen standing in a shift spattered with semen and mud. And a voice was heard: "This lady is a monkey smelling its own reeking backside, which has poison in its heart, is noxious to itself, and rushes into traps that make it fall." **24.** Likewise, she was seen to have a crown made of twigs spattered with human feces and mud from the streets and to sit naked on a wobbling beam. **25.** And immediately a most beautiful virgin was seen, who said: "This is that impudent and bold woman reputed by men to be a lady of the world, but she has been cast out from before God's eyes, as you discern." **26.** And the virgin added: "Oh, woman, think of your beginning and attend to your end, and open the eyes of your heart and see that your counselors are such men as hate your soul!"
>
> **27.** *Likewise, about a certain queen.* A woman was seen to sit upon a throne of gold, with two Ethiopians standing before her, one, as it were, to her right and the other to her left. **28.** And the one to the right cried out, saying, "Oh, leonine woman, I bear blood. Receive it and pour it out, because it is fitting for the lioness to thirst after blood." **29.** And truly, the one to the left said, "Oh woman, I bring you fire in a dish. Receive it, because you are of a fiery nature, and pour it into the waters, so that your memory might be in the waters as on the land." **30.** And after this, there appeared a virgin of wondrous splendor, at the sight of whom the Ethiopians fled. She said, "This woman is dangerous. If she succeeds in her will, many will be in tribulation. **31.** Yet truly, if she herself is troubled, it will be of use to her toward eternal life; but she does not wish to abandon her will or to experience tribulation in accordance with God's will. Therefore, if she is abandoned to her own will, she will be no consolation either to herself or to others."[35]

Despite this unflattering portrait, the revelation ends with the hope that Johanna—whose pious works, Christ tells Birgitta, have won divine favor—will mend her ways, escaping the opprobrium of both God and humanity (*Rev.* VII.11:32). Her sinfulness, though extraordinary, is not absolute; the revelation functions as a jeremiad, exhorting Johanna to repentance and reformation.

---

35. *Rev.* VII.11:23–31, 143.

Given the virulence of Birgitta's description of Johanna, the continued friendship between the two women throughout what remained of Birgitta's life, not to mention Johanna's efforts to secure her canonization, has perplexed many scholars. Johannes Jørgensen, the author of a colorful biography of Birgitta, characterizes Johanna as licentious and destructively willful, commenting bemusedly that, "in spite of everything [Birgitta] never broke off the connection with [Johanna]."[36] Bridget Morris notes that while the Regno was once great, "Neapolitan prosperity and culture started to disintegrate" under Johanna's rule, while her court was "notoriously full of corruption."[37] She reflects,

> It is of interest, therefore, why Birgitta should apparently have become such good friends with the queen, and why the queen should have taken her part in the canonisation process. In spite of Birgitta's harsh words about the queen . . . [Johanna] appears to have paid heed to Birgitta, and there seems to have been a strong bond of respect and friendship between the two women.[38]

According to most biographers, including Jørgensen and Morris, the inspiration for Birgitta's scathing depiction of Johanna was an adulterous affair between Johanna and Karl Ulfsson, the saint's eldest son. Both Jørgensen and Tore Nyberg accept as fact that Karl "had a liaison with the queen of Naples," while Albert Ryle Kezel argues that Johanna's "worst offense was her questionable relationship with Birgitta's dying son [Karl] in the winter of 1371–1372."[39] Thus the common conclusion is that maternal outrage and anxiety shaped Birgitta's treatment of Johanna.

The affair is said to have occurred when Karl accompanied his mother, sister, and brother to Naples. Karl—conventionally treated as the most worldly of Birgitta's eight children—had left his wife behind in Sweden with the intention of returning after fulfilling his pilgrimage vow. When he met Johanna, the story goes, their mutual attraction proved so overwhelming that he determined to abandon his wife and pilgrimage to remain with her, imperiling both of their souls and thoroughly scandalizing his mother.

---

36. Johannes Jørgensen, *Saint Bridget of Sweden*, 2 vols, trans. Ingeborg Lund (London: Longmans, Green, 1954), 2:234.

37. Morris, *St. Birgitta of Sweden*, 122.

38. Ibid., 124.

39. Tore Nyberg, "Introduction" to, Marguerite Tjader Harris, ed. *Birgitta of Sweden: Life and Selected Revelations*, Classics of Western Spirituality, trans., Albert Ryle Kezel (Mahwah, NJ: Paulist Press, 1990), 38; Kezel, *Birgitta of Sweden*, 288, n. 585.

According to Jørgensen, Karl "became [Johanna's] lover. For both of them it was a late summer's idyll" that lasted until Karl's death.[40] Birgitta, however, could not allow her son to live in such sin; through prayer, she brought about his death. Morris, who questions the story but incorporates it into her biography nonetheless, sees "Birgitta's stern judgment in preferring the death of her favourite son to the ignominy of his adulterous relationship with the queen of Naples" as an expression of Birgitta's moral inflexibility, sharply contrasted by Johanna's irresponsible sensuality.[41]

The story originates with Margareta Clausdotter. Writing a full century after Birgitta's death, she described Karl as "a very lascivious and lustful man" and offered his dalliance with Johanna as an illustration of his character. For Margareta, Karl was Birgitta's burden, and his salvation was her pressing task. Karl's relationship to Birgitta fit within what Barbara Newman has called the "maternal martyr paradigm," a common late medieval trope in the *vitae* of saints who were also mothers. The trope was already well established in the Birgittine tradition, which often describes Birgitta's suffering on account and on behalf of her children.[42] According to Margareta, Birgitta instructed her children in the etiquette of the court before presenting them to the queen. In typical fashion, Karl only half heeded his mother's instructions: "When Karl came before the queen, he [first] did obeisance to her as he should according to her rank, and then he kissed her on the mouth."[43] Margareta relates that Johanna—now in her midforties—was instantly smitten with Karl, who was some years older:

> As a result of [Karl's behavior], the queen conceived a great love for him, because he dared to do this, and she did not want to let him depart, but said rather that she wanted to keep him with her and have him for her husband. Saint Birgitta said that must not be, because his wife lived and was at home in Sweden, but the queen said that she did not care about that and that things should be as she wished.[44]

Birgitta, deeply distraught, prayed for divine aid and was quickly answered by Karl's sudden illness and death. In so doing, she conformed to the type of the maternal martyr, whom Newman describes as willing, in "extreme cases," to

---

40. Jørgensen, *Saint Bridget of Sweden*, 234.
41. Morris, *St. Birgitta of Sweden*, 125.
42. Barbara Newman, *From Virile Woman to WomanChrist: Studies in Medieval Religion and Literature* (Philadelphia: University of Pennsylvania Press, 1995), 77. For Newman's analysis of Birgitta's self-presentation as a maternal martyr in her *Revelations*, see 84–85, 89.
43. Clausdotter, *Chronicon de genere et nepotibus S. Birgittae*, 212.
44. Ibid.

"consent to [her children's] deaths," emulating the Virgin Mary's acceptance of Christ's death.[45] While Johanna mourned her dead lover—burying him "with as great expense as if he had been her husband"—Birgitta remained stoic and continued on to Jerusalem.[46]

Scholars have read Birgitta's *Revelations* against Margareta's tale of Karl's doomed affair with Johanna. After the onset of the schism, her Urbanist opponents (whose part Birgitta's followers took) resurrected Johanna's reputation for sexual misconduct (see chapter 5); Margareta, like Birgitta's modern biographers, would likely have known far more about Johanna's identity as a "harlot queen" than about her fame for piety. Mindful of Johanna's reputation for immorality and previous adultery and ignoring the fact that Margareta's story serves more to exemplify the tension between Karl and Birgitta than to vilify Johanna, Birgitta's biographers have interpreted the harshness of her visionary treatment of Johanna in light of Margareta's tale. That Birgitta's invective against Johanna was rooted in maternal indignation is seemingly supported by another revelation (*Rev.* VII.13), which Birgitta received regarding the fate of Karl's soul soon after his death. She experienced a vision that continued intermittently for several days in which the Virgin Mary assured her that she had intervened on Karl's behalf before the divine tribunal convened to examine his soul. The demon sent to prosecute Karl miraculously forgets his sins, and the Virgin, speaking for the defense, convinces Christ—Karl's judge—that Birgitta's years of tears on Karl's behalf, his lifelong devotion to Mary, and his determination to travel to Jerusalem as a pilgrim should wipe clean his moral slate.

If one accepts Margareta's tale of Karl's romance with Johanna, Birgitta's apparent anxiety regarding Karl's salvation can be read as confirmation of the perilous moral state in which he found himself immediately before his death. Following this line of reasoning, Birgitta, comforted by the knowledge that Karl's soul was saved, was willing to see Johanna again and even remain in Naples for many months as her guest. When she departed from Naples, she was angry enough to send Johanna the revelation cited above, but her rage had calmed enough after her pilgrimage to allow her to maintain her relationship with Johanna and hope for her repentance.

Johanna and Birgitta Reconsidered

There are many reasons not to credit Margareta's story and to revise the established narrative of Birgitta's relationship with Johanna, not the least

---

45. Newman, *From Virile Woman to WomanChrist*, 77.

46. Clausdotter, *Chronicon de genere et nepotibus S. Birgittae*, 212.

of which is her substantial temporal distance from the events she describes. While Margareta may conceivably have recorded an oral Birgittine tradition, there is no suggestion in earlier material of an extramarital affair between Johanna and Karl. (And, it is worth noting, Margareta does not report that an affair actually took place, only that Johanna desired it.) That the story first appeared so long after Birgitta's death is suspicious, as is its clear adherence to a common late medieval hagiographic trope. Furthermore, a glaring inaccuracy in her narrative calls the veracity of Margareta's story into question: her contention that Johanna intended to marry Karl. Margareta says that Johanna was a widow, but at the time of Karl's death, Johanna was married to James of Majorca and could hardly have married someone else.

Indeed, the descriptions of Karl's death provided by witnesses during the canonization trial reveal that James was among the mourners at his funeral. Alfonso of Jaén, an eyewitness, testified that after Karl died,

> Lady Johanna, the queen of Sicily, and other illustrious persons and many of the lady's nobles, and also the lady queen's husband, King James, along with many people of the aforesaid city, accompanied Lady Birgitta with lamentation and many tears in bearing her dead son to the monastic church of Santa Croce.[47]

The noble procession Alfonso describes matches Margareta's description of Karl's funeral in grandeur, but his narration of events makes clear that it was the entire royal household—and not merely Johanna—that mourned Karl's passing. His funeral was appropriate for a visiting nobleman and honored guest, and Alfonso's testimony gives no hint of impropriety or unusual attachment on Johanna's part.

The witnesses who recalled Karl's death during the canonization process offered it as an illustration not of Johanna's sinfulness but of Birgitta's saintly patience. Alfonso, for instance, described Birgitta's serene demeanor at Karl's deathbed:

> Lady Birgitta herself, his mother, sat far from him, as it were eight or ten paces from where her son lay dying, and at that time she neither rose from her place nor sent forth cries or tears, but raising her hands, she blessed God, thanking Him and conforming herself humbly to the divine will.[48]

---

47. Collijn, *Acta et Processus*, 370.
48. Ibid.

Birgitta's restraint continued after Karl's death, when her fortitude and serenity were, Alfonso revealed, widely discussed. As the funeral procession made its way to the church, its members weeping, Birgitta alone remained unmoved:

> She, however, was like an immobile pillar of patience; she made neither lament nor complaint like the others, but rather blessed God and said words to this effect: "Go, my son, pilgrim blessed by God and by me." And all of this is well known today . . . and was publicly spoken of and famous in the city of Naples.[49]

Birgitta paid no heed to murmurs about her ostensible lack of grief, silencing them by responding, "I do not care who speaks ill of me, as long as I still do the will of God."[50] Thus, even in the accounts of her contemporaries, Birgitta was a maternal martyr who humbly accepted God's judgment that her child should die.

For Birgitta's followers (as for subsequent biographers), her patience was of central importance to her identification as a saint. Magnus Petri (or Peterson), one of her longtime companions, like Alfonso, recalled her patience (*paciencia*) and testified that at Karl's tomb she "neither appeared to be nor was able to seem moved, nor emitted cries or tears, but with the greatest patience she gave thanks to God." Magnus also places Johanna at the funeral, along with "many of the princes of Apulia and nearly the entire city." He offers their lamentation and the magnitude of the public grief as counterpoints to Birgitta's stoicism, calling on Johanna as a witness to the saint's remarkable fortitude. The court's presence serves to underscore the exceptional, saintly nature of Birgitta's *paciencia*, so that "the queen, like all the others seeing this, was exceedingly amazed at such great patience."[51]

Thus, the story of Karl's death is significant in early Birgittine hagiography not because Birgitta saved her sinful son from the perils of an adulterous liaison with Johanna but because it reveals the extent of Birgitta's holy patience. Indeed, "patient endurance" was, as Richard Kieckhefer points out, "a motif that dominates the era's hagiography."[52] The impassibility described by witnesses at the canonization trial conformed to contemporary ideals of

---

49. Ibid., 370–71.
50. Ibid, 371.
51. Ibid, 261.
52. Richard Kieckhefer, *Unquiet Souls: Fourteenth-Century Saints and their Religious Milieu* (Chicago: University of Chicago Press, 1984), 50.

saintly behavior, Birgitta's *paciencia* demonstrating "the outward passivity and inward conformity of will" that were hallmarks of the fourteenth-century saint.[53] Patience was the virtue for which Birgitta was most praised and the trait that, as the "key virtue in fourteenth-century spirituality," most clearly signaled her sanctity.[54] Thus, the circumstances of Karl's death are not significant in witness testimony; Birgitta's meek acceptance of it is.

Johanna's presence at Karl's funeral functions in witness testimony both to honor Birgitta and her family—who warranted such a splendid procession—and to emphasize Birgitta's saintly forbearance. Johanna's amazement at her patience helps to establish Birgitta's reputation. She acts as a foil to the saint and as an additional and noteworthy witness to Birgitta's stoicism. Johanna is never mentioned as the sole mourner, and the outpouring of communal grief Magnus and Alfonso describe serves the narrative purpose of calling attention to Birgitta's exceptional patience while allowing them to comment on how publicly it was displayed and discussed. To be a saint meant, in large part, to have the *fama* of a saint, and their testimony establishes that Birgitta had just such a reputation in Naples.

If one were committed to the story of Johanna's affair with Karl, it might be countered that the long revelation Birgitta received about Karl's soul suggests she was particularly concerned for him. Conceivably, Karl's adultery (whether actual or intended) might be among the sins his demonic prosecutor miraculously forgets, but there is no suggestion within the text that he died in a state of mortal sin. The only argument for the veracity of Margareta's story comes from the Virgin's opening statement to Birgitta, when she reveals that she stood by Karl's deathbed "so that he would not have such carnal love (*carnalem amorem*) in his memory" that he would die at odds with God.[55] Mary's reference to carnal love does not necessarily imply sexual love, and she may simply be referring to worldly love more generally. In essence, the Virgin stands in for Karl's confessor at the last rites, preparing his soul to meet its maker by helping him sever his earthly ties.

There is nothing in what remains of the revelation to suggest that Birgitta's anxiety had anything to do with Johanna. Birgitta was anxious throughout her life about the fate of souls—she received visions about other souls, such as Niccolò Acciaiuoli's—and there is nothing uncharacteristic about her concern for her son. Birgitta was consumed with care for the afterlife

---

and questions of salvation and damnation, and it is not surprising that she should worry about Karl. The text contains no hint that Birgitta was uneasy about a specific sin or that Karl was unworthy of salvation. Indeed, the Virgin explains to Birgitta that Karl's worth and unstinting love for her as God's mother brought her to his deathbed. An angel then explains that Birgitta's tendency to pray for him and perform good works when she saw him falling into sin helped to save him, since he learned from her a proper fear of God and remembered to confess whenever he sinned. Despite this testimony to Karl's good qualities, the prosecuting demon insists on enumerating the sins for which he failed to make amends, only to find that his list has burned up and his memory of what it contained been erased (*Rev.* VII.13:36–37). The sins he can recall are venial (*venialia peccata*), while adultery is a mortal sin.

The debate that follows concerns minor sins. The angel counters the demon's arguments by pointing out that Karl was a pilgrim to the Holy Land and had willingly left his home and friends, thus earning a pilgrimage indulgence. Moreover, Karl did not wish to be sinful, but rather sought to please God by atoning for his sins (*Rev.* VII.13:45–47). Had Karl died in a state of mortal sin and abandoned his pilgrimage for Johanna, none of these statements would be true.[56] At no point, unless the true miracle is that the heavenly tribunal is content to ignore a mortal sin, or that Birgitta's intervention and Karl's illness came about so swiftly that no sin ever occurred, is there any suggestion that Karl died as Margareta claims. Nowhere does the text support the idea that Karl had a relationship with Johanna. Rather, the message of the revelation is that even a soul stained by venial sins can be redeemed, and that Karl and Birgitta's shared faith and pious intentions ensured Karl's salvation.

Thus, there is no compelling contemporary evidence to support Margareta's story. Regardless of whether there was an affair between Johanna and Karl concealed by what Kezel describes as "the scrupulous discretion of the Birgittine circle" (a feat that would have required a conspiracy of silence that continued even beyond the advent of the schism and the subsequent break between Johanna and Birgitta's followers), there is no trace of contemporary gossip about it.[57] The affair was unknown and thus not part of Johanna's

---

56. Even if Birgitta's prayer took effect before the affair began, Karl's intentions would still have been sinful, especially considering Christ's admonition (Matt. 5:28) that to look on a woman lustfully is to have committed adultery with her. Indeed, under canon law, adultery was the result not of action but of lustful intent, so that, according to Gratian, men so sinned when they looked at women with shameful desire (*turpiter concupiscitur*). See Gratian, *Decretum*, causa 32, q. 5.13, 14.

57. Kezel, *Birgitta of Sweden*, 288, n. 585.

reputation or Birgitta's biography during their lives, only becoming part of their literary and historical personae after being grafted onto their histories by historians familiar with Margareta's story, Johanna's postschism reputation, and Birgitta's prophetic invective against her.

Johanna's Relationship with Birgitta in Contemporary Context

Indeed, during Birgitta's life and for several years after her death in 1373, only a select group of people knew of most of the evidence cited by historians who characterize her relationship to Johanna as troubled. While Birgitta received and shared with her closest followers (including her Swedish companions, scribes, and translators, Prior Peter of Alvastra and Master Peter of Skänninge) revelations highly critical of Johanna, the saint and her companions considered them private, and they only entered the Birgittine canon after 1380. The most damning of Birgitta's revelations concerning Johanna is *Revelations* VII.11. In addition to the visions cited above, the revelation takes her to task as a "wanton woman" and deficient ruler. Its tone is unquestionably stern, but neither Birgitta nor her followers wished to publicize its contents or shame Johanna. Birgitta intended it for Johanna alone, to inspire personal reform and not to denounce or discredit her. Even in modern editions of Book VII, the chapter heading (supplied by Alfonso of Jaén) states that the full revelation included information about Johanna that is secret and not to be disseminated with the text of the *Revelations*.[58]

Accordingly, the visionary material in *Revelations* VII.11 specific to Johanna did not appear in the earliest textual redactions of Birgitta's *Revelations*. Alfonso began editing Birgitta's visionary material late in 1372 and had produced a coherent work divided into seven thematic books with his own critical apparatus when Gregory XI convened the first canonization commission in 1377. This "first Alfonsine redaction" of the *Revelations* was submitted to the commission for examination and met with great approval. It most likely formed the core of the text—known as the "second Alfonsine redaction"—submitted to the second examining commission, called by Urban VI after Gregory's death in 1378.[59] Neither redaction contained the

---

58. The heading reads: "Hic est principium cuiusdam reuelacionis, quam domina Birgitta habuit pro domina regina Neapolitana in eadem ciuitate, *sed alia, que ibi continentur, non ponuntur hic, quia secreta sunt*, que pertinent ad statum et personam dicte domine regine" (italics mine). See Birgitta of Sweden, *Revelaciones Lib. VII*, 140.

59. Birgitta of Sweden, *Sancta Birgitta—Revelaciones, Book I, with Magister Mathias' Prologue*, ed. Carl-Gustaf Undhagen, Samlingar utgivna av Svenska Fornskriftsällskapet, Series 2, Latinska Skrifter, 7.1 (Uppsala: Almqvist & Wiksell, 1978), 14; Aili and Svanberg, *Imagines Sanctae Birgittae*, 1:12.

material most critical of Johanna. In Alfonso's first and second redactions, Book VII.11 ended with verse 6, omitting all material lambasting Johanna.[60] In some early manuscripts, the text ends with the statement, "Listen to what the queen did to me. I allowed her to be exalted in the kingdom, etc.," while others lack any mention—overt or oblique—of Johanna at all.[61]

The earliest extant manuscripts of Birgitta's *Revelations*, which likely reflect the first and second of Alfonso's textual redactions, are now located in New York's Pierpont Morgan Library (MS M. 498), Warsaw's Biblioteka Narodowa (MS 3310), and Palermo's Biblioteca Centrale della Regione Siciliana (MS IV.G.2). These three sumptuously illuminated manuscripts, clearly members of the same family, were executed in a Neapolitan workshop—although apparently not at Johanna's behest—between 1375 and 1390.[62] Because Birgitta lacks a halo in all of the miniatures, they must have been completed before her canonization in 1391.[63] Hans Aili and Jan Svanberg date all three to between 1377 and 1381, arguing based on the style of the miniatures and evolution of the text that the Warsaw manuscript (which reflects the first Alfonsine redaction) was completed in 1377, the New York manuscript (which represents the second redaction) between late 1377 and

---

60. Birgitta of Sweden, *Revelaciones Lib. VII*, 77.

61. *Rev.* VII.11:6: "Audi, quid regina fecerat michi. Ego permisi eam exaltare in regnum etc." (cf. Birgitta of Sweden, *Revelaciones Lib. VII*, 141). The comment about Johanna, which has no relevance to the revelation as it was first disseminated, was omitted by some scribes. The Middle English version in London, British Library, MS Cotton Claudius B. I, probably translated from a Latin manuscript of the first Alfonsine redaction, mentions Johanna in neither the heading nor the end of verse 6, with which VII.11 ends. See Birgitta of Sweden, *The Liber Celestis of St. Bridget of Sweden: The Middle English Version in the British Library MS Claudius B I, together with a Life of the Saint from the Same Manuscript*, ed. Roger Ellis, 2 vols., Early English Text Society 291 (Oxford: Oxford University Press, 1987), 1:xi–13, 475.

62. On the dating of the manuscripts, see Carl Nordenfalk, "Saint Bridget of Sweden as Represented in Illuminated Manuscripts," in *De Artibus Opuscula XL: Essays in Honor of Erwin Panofsky*, ed. Millard Meiss (New York: New York University Press, 1961), esp. 379–82; Birgitta of Sweden, *Revelaciones Lib. VII*, 36 and passim; Birgitta of Sweden, *Revelaciones, Book I*, 150; and Aili and Svanberg, *Imagines Sanctae Birgittae*, 1:21, 23, 26, 31. Ferdinando Bologna proposed that Johanna commissioned New York, Pierpont Morgan Library, MS M. 498 (Bologna, *I pittori alla corte angioina di Napoli*, 329). Subsequent scholars—with the recent exception of Andreas Bräm—have not accepted this argument. As Joan Isobel Friedman points out, "neither the curators at the Morgan Library nor other specialists of Neapolitan illumination have accepted Bologna's attribution, and there is no inscription, coat-of-arms, or colophon to indicate either the original patron or the original owner." See Joan Isobel Friedman, "MS Cotton Claudius B.I.: A Middle English Edition of St Bridget of Sweden's *Liber Celestis*," in *Prophets Abroad: The Reception of Continental Holy Women in Late-Medieval England*, ed. Rosalynn Voaden (Cambridge: D. S. Brewer, 1996), 98, n. 39. For Bräm's association between Johanna and the early Birgittine manuscripts, see Bräm, *Neapolitanische Bilderbibeln des Trecento*, 1:183.

63. Nordenfalk, "Saint Bridget of Sweden as Represented in Illuminated Manuscripts," 379; Birgitta of Sweden, *Revelaciones Lib. VII*, 36; Birgitta of Sweden, *Revelaciones, Book I*, 157.

early 1378, and the Palermo manuscript (which reflects the second redaction but has supplemental material) in 1381.[64] Their style is consistent with that developed in Naples under Johanna's patronage during the 1370s, and their artistic similarities indicate that they were the product of one workshop and only one or two artists and scribes.[65]

Their richness of ornamentation suggests that the manuscripts were commissioned for prominent royal and ecclesiastical figures who might support Birgitta's canonization. Aili identifies these three manuscripts with the "thirty to fifty manuscript codices, the majority of them destined for royal or church libraries or universities in the Mediterranean area and Central Europe" produced in response to widespread demand.[66] The codices are mentioned in a letter written in the later 1380s by Magnus Petri, by then the first confessor general of Vadstena Abbey, in which he describes the requests for such manuscripts by monarchs, including Johanna herself.[67] All three extant manuscripts include only the first six verses of Book VII.11.[68] Therefore, assuming that they are representative of the codices Magnus describes, the text as it was first and widely disseminated did not include the private revelations to Johanna.

In the summer of 1380, soon after Johanna's break with Urban VI, Peter of Alvastra compiled a new redaction of the *Revelations* in Sweden that incorporated material left out of the previous redactions.[69] Among his additions was the full text of Book VII.11 as we now know it. Apparently, Peter no longer felt it necessary to shield Johanna, and he published Birgitta's damning vision for posterity. His supplementary source material—entrusted to the monks of Vadstena—continued gradually to enter the canon, leading to the creation over the course of the next century of a "Vadstena redaction" that ultimately included still further material about Johanna, including a revelation (*Rev.* IV.141:4) that modern scholars have read—without warrant—as

---

64. Aili and Svanberg, *Imagines Sanctae Birgittae*, 1:57.

65. Ibid., 58.

66. Ibid., 16.

67. See Carl-Gustaf Undhagen, "Une source du prologue (Chap. 1) aux Révélations de Sainte Brigitte par le cardinal Jean de Turrecremata," *Eranos* 58 (1960): 214–26. In the letter, Magnus names the most prominent figures to request the manuscripts, including the queens of Cyprus, Castile, and Sicily (i.e., Naples). See ibid., 225, lines 23–24.

68. New York, Pierpont Morgan Library, MS M. 498, which I had the opportunity to examine, ends Chapter 11 thus: "Audi quod regina fecerat michi. Ego permisi eam exaltare in regnum, etc." A later hand has added a marginal notation directing the reader to Chapter 13 of the *Epistola ad Reges* for information about Johanna omitted from the manuscript.

69. Birgitta of Sweden, *Revelaciones, Book I*, 28.

proof of Birgitta's disapproval of Johanna's papal politics.[70] Thus many of the critical revelations about Johanna entered the Birgittine canon during the summer of 1380 at the earliest.[71]

Therefore, Johanna's contemporaries had no access to Birgitta's harshest criticism of her. It is unlikely that the contents of Birgitta's secret revelation to Johanna, deemed inappropriate by her followers for inclusion in the *Revelations*, would have been widely known. The rest of her visionary criticism of Johanna (and, indeed, much of that contained in Book VII.11) is more impersonal and in line with her other critiques of Europe's nobility, especially queens, such as Magnus Eriksson (1316–74) of Sweden's wife, Blanche of Namur (1320–63), and Eleanor of Cyprus (1333–1417), both of whom receive considerable attention in Birgitta's *Revelations*.

If one removes from consideration the visionary material added to the *Revelations* after 1380, the relationship between Johanna and Birgitta looks far different. As mentioned above, Birgitta condemned Johanna's marriage to Louis of Taranto (*Rev.* IV.4:15–16). *Revelations* VII.27 reveals that, at Johanna's behest and that of Naples's archbishop, Bernard du Bousquet, Birgitta prayed for the city's people in 1372.[72] The ensuing revelation was delivered before a large audience. This chapter, which exhorts the Neapolitans to be more mindful of the Passion, and the subsequent one—in which Birgitta criticizes them for the sins, including sexual immorality and recourse to abortions, enumerated above—describe visions about the Regno's shortcomings that were made public and implicate Johanna by association. Her sins are those common to her realm, however, and she is not criticized or condemned by name. Rather, she appears in a favorable light for having sought Birgitta's instruction and intercession on her subjects' behalf.

Thus, Birgitta and her followers' presentation of the saint's relationship with Johanna differed greatly from that modern historians have described. Her disciples, especially Alfonso and Katherine, referred to Johanna

---

70. Ibid., 27; Birgitta of Sweden, *Revelaciones, Book IV*, 18; Kezel, "Translator's Foreword," in Harris, *Birgitta of Sweden*, 61. *Rev.* IV.141 is about Birgitta's efforts to convince Gregory XI to return to Rome. The section about Johanna, *Rev.* IV.141:4, reads: "Tunc autem respondit domina Birgitta: 'O, Domine Deus meus! Regina Neapolis et multi alii dicunt michi, quod impossibile est eum venire Romam, quia rex Francie et cardinales et alii quamplurima ei ponunt impedimenta ad veniendum'" (Birgitta of Sweden, *Revelaciones, Book IV*, 394). Thus, the text says not that Johanna wished the pope to remain in Avignon, but that she and others had told Birgitta that Gregory could not travel to Rome because of the opposition of the French king, the cardinals, and unnamed others.

71. Birgitta of Sweden, *Revelaciones, Book I*, 27.

72. Heading for *Rev.* VII.27. The vision was also recalled by Alfonso, who remarked on its public nature, during the canonization process (Collijn, *Acta et Processus*, 373).

throughout the canonization process, depicting her as a valued friend and ally and wielding her reputation as a tool to enhance Birgitta's. That Birgitta had given Johanna a personal revelation was known and remarked on—as by Alfonso, who revealed during the canonization hearing that Johanna had received from Birgitta "in secret a certain divine revelation made to her by Christ containing great threats, terrors, and the wrath of God," but also stated that it was "extremely secret."[73] The revelation's existence was known, while its particulars were not. Given Johanna's already well-established reputation for past sinfulness, it cannot have been surprising that Birgitta would urge her to repent. And, significantly, the revelation of a private visionary communication suggests an intimacy that linked Johanna and Birgitta as penitent and spiritual advisor—even evoking the seal of confession in the secrecy of their communications—as well as friends.

A Prophet to Monarchs

Rather than distancing herself from Birgitta because of her criticism, Johanna cultivated their relationship of penitent and advisor/confessor. And, indeed, if the terms of Birgitta's criticism were harsh, the criticism itself was not unprecedented. Birgitta made a habit of critiquing the lives and reigns of monarchs. She attempted unsuccessfully to intervene in the conflict between the French and English kings, and she felt compelled by God to guide and instruct kings, as to admonish queens. In their *vita* of Birgitta, presented under oath to witnesses at Montefalco in December of 1373 and submitted for examination by the canonization commissions,[74] Prior Peter and Master Peter describe how she was called while still in Sweden to warn Magnus Eriksson against levying unjust taxes—counsel she would later give Johanna as well. Birgitta's *Revelations* chide Magnus and Blanche of Namur severely. As the wife of one of Magnus's advisors, Birgitta was given the task of educating Blanche when she came to Sweden in 1335. She established herself as a mother figure to both Magnus and Blanche.[75] Over time, she became increasingly critical of Blanche, a pattern that Morris describes as typical of Birgitta's relationships:

> Later in her revelations, however, she develops an ambiguous attitude to the queen, but one that is part of a discernible pattern when there is a cycle of revelations directed at particular individuals: she describes,

---

73. Collijn, *Acta et Processus*, 373.
74. Nyberg, "The Canonization Process of St. Birgitta of Sweden," 69, 80.
75. Jørgensen, *Saint Bridget of Sweden*, 2:71, 83.

criticises and upbraids the person in question in one revelation, in another she gives practical advice as to how people should mend their ways, and if there are any further ones they contain reprimands and condemnations for not taking her guidance.[76]

In many ways, Birgitta's critiques of and advice for Blanche resemble those she would later address to Johanna. Blanche, like Johanna, is accused of being overly fond of luxury and leisure. And, as would be the case with Johanna, Birgitta turned her scrutiny on Blanche's sexual life, scolding her for taking a vow of celibacy with Magnus for the wrong reasons: Birgitta argued that it was not love of celibacy but desire to escape childbirth that set Blanche on this course, one determined by what Birgitta describes as Magnus's unnatural sexual desires (*Rev.* VIII.11–12).

Birgitta also offered counsel to Eleanor of Cyprus. As she later would in Naples, Birgitta publicly revealed in Famagusta a vision she had received about the city while in Jerusalem. The revelation to Famagusta, which includes a personal revelation to Eleanor, was among Prior Peter's additions, and thus, as with the personal revelation to Johanna, would not have been widely known to a contemporary audience. Yet its public delivery suggests that it would have been discussed, at least locally. In it, in addition to offering advice about crowning a new king, Birgitta advised Eleanor, as she had Johanna, to distance herself from sycophantic advisors and to curb the habit among Cypriot women of wearing revealing clothing and perfume (*Rev.* VII.16:22–30).

As Claire Sahlin has noted, Birgitta assumed "the role of prophet of moral reform, one who announces to the world God's grave displeasure with the spiritual condition of the people and points out the way to salvation," directing her attention particularly to "corrupt secular and spiritual leaders who led their subjects away from Christ."[77] Birgitta's followers frequently commented on this aspect of her calling. They saw her as a divine messenger to Europe's rulers and described Birgitta's frankness and fearlessness before powerful men and women as indicators of her sanctity. Witnesses at the canonization hearings stressed both the high status of those she approached and her unflinching honesty about her visions. Magnus Petri described how Birgitta gave revelations to Johanna, Eleanor, and others, exposing their faults and threatening divine retribution, even though she "could very rightly have feared death or captivity or other afflictions."[78] Katherine likewise recalled

76. Morris, *St. Birgitta of Sweden*, 58.

77. Claire L. Sahlin, *Birgitta of Sweden and the Voice of Prophecy* (Woodbridge: Boydell Press, 2001), 42.

78. Collijn, *Acta et Processus*, 84–85, 262.

her mother's missions to Naples and Cyprus, echoing Magnus's assertion that Birgitta did not fear for her life or safety, despite the dangers she faced in criticizing such powerful people.[79]

Birgitta's criticism of Johanna was, therefore, consistent with her calling to carry messages of rebuke and instruction to monarchs, as with her behavior toward these monarchs in general. Birgitta was particularly concerned with the morals and comportment of the nobility and with the marriages and sexual practices of the kings and queens she addressed. Johanna's position as queen and sovereign exposed her to instruction on two fronts, and she received advice and admonition both about what Birgitta considered queenly concerns—dress, sexual behavior, modesty—and kingly ones, such as taxation and justice. But, rather than singling Johanna out for criticism, Birgitta critiqued her much as she did the other monarchs of her acquaintance.

The Politics of Friendship

For their contemporaries, what would have set Birgitta's and Johanna's relationship apart from Birgitta's other royal associations was the length and warmth of their friendship. When Birgitta left Sweden, she was disillusioned with Blanche and Magnus Eriksson, and she did not renew her ties to the Swedish court. Her overtures to Edward III of England and John II of France were rebuffed, while her relationship with Eleanor of Cyprus was confined to her pilgrimage. Her friendship with Johanna was more lasting, and it included long periods of contact and intimacy. Perhaps most significant, as regards Johanna's reputation, was the degree to which Johanna publicized their friendship and positioned herself as Birgitta's spiritual daughter, her devoted friend, and her avid patron.

Friendship is not a historical constant. Its meanings fluctuate and evolve. Scholarly confusion about Birgitta's friendship with Johanna stems, at least in part, from a misunderstanding of what their friendship meant and how it was interpreted by those who observed it. There is a rich and growing literature on medieval friendship.[80] Stephen Jaeger, for instance, has written about what he calls ennobling love, arguing that "love, even in its most passionate

---

79. Ibid., 315.

80. See, for instance, Julian Haseldine, ed., *Friendship in Medieval Europe* (Stroud: Sutton, 1999); Eva Österberg, *Friendship and Love, Ethics and Politics: Studies in Mediaeval and Early Modern History* (Budapest: Central European University Press, 2010); Albrecht Classen and Marilyn Sandidge, eds., *Friendship in the Middle Ages and Early Modern Age: Explorations of a Fundamental Ethical Discourse* (Berlin: De Gruyter, 2011); and Suzanne Stern-Gillet and Gary M. Gurtier, eds., *Ancient and Medieval Concepts of Friendship* (Albany: SUNY Press, 2014).

manifestation, is a form of show"—that is, it is a performance.[81] Friendship, the most disinterested form of love, was both a sign and a conveyer of virtue, ennobling both participants. Friendship was thus a component of reputation, one intended—regardless of the genuine affection it may have entailed—to enhance the standing of those who partook in it. Friendship was not merely a performance; it was also understood to have an emotional component. Indeed, it was the emotional component that gave it power. Medieval theorists drew on Cicero, Aristotle, and Augustine to define ideal friendship. They described a hybrid between Ciceronian friendship, which could only exist between two equals (which for Cicero meant high-minded men), and Augustinian friendship, based on Christian charity. It entailed selfless love, esteem, and admiration, but it also had clearly defined duties: a true friend was honest, rather than a flatterer, and virtuous. As a result, only certain truly excellent people—kings, abbots, scholars, knights—were capable of true friendship as defined and glorified in medieval literature. Women hardly ever enter into the medieval discourse of friendship, because friendship was an inherently masculine virtue, one primarily found in women who transcended their femininity by becoming saintly.

What did it mean for Birgitta and Johanna to be friends? Birgitta saw the world in black and white, starkly distinguishing between good and evil. Eva Österberg has argued that Birgitta's essentially dualist worldview made her see "temporal friendship as evil and disastrous."[82] In Birgitta's thought, friendship was a snare, a possible seduction away from God. The only acceptable friendship was based on faith in God, one in which friends turned to one another for spiritual comfort.[83] As a spiritual advisor, Birgitta offered such friendship to her followers, including Johanna, to whom she was in some sense both friend and mother. It was an edifying relationship, one built around divine service and predicated on Birgitta's moral and spiritual superiority. This was not a Ciceronian friendship between two equals but rather one that united a spiritual advisor and an acolyte in an unequal partnership governed by conformity to God's will. Yet, in the case of Birgitta and Johanna, it also played the classical role of enhancing the virtue and standing of both.

Johanna appears to have happily accepted the role of Birgitta's spiritual daughter and friend, receiving Birgitta's rebukes and instruction and allying

---

81. C. Stephen Jaeger, *Ennobling Love: In Search of a Lost Sensibility* (Philadelphia: University of Pennsylvania Press, 1999), 5.

82. Österberg, *Friendship and Love, Ethics and Politics*, 39.

83. Ibid., 39–40.

herself with others who welcomed the saint's maternal role in their lives. It is in this light that we should read Birgitta's prophecy for Johanna: It was a sign of her friendship and concern, the opposite of the flattery Birgitta warned queens against. Her reception of Birgitta's harsh maternal criticism aligned Johanna with Birgitta's biological daughter, Katherine, whom Birgitta also guided with a stern hand and for whom she also received critical visions and instructions. Katherine's fifteenth-century biographer reveals that when, as a young widow in Rome, Katherine began to long for Sweden and married life, Birgitta had her literally whipped her into acceptance of a life devoted to divine service, so that her sanctity was in large measure due to her mother's discipline.[84] Birgitta was a harsh taskmaster, and those who accepted her maternal guidance had to accept her strict, sometimes painful, instruction.

Medieval friendship, like friendship as theorized by Cicero or Aristotle, might be private—a potentially risky enterprise fraught with moral danger—or public. The latter type of friendship applies to the case of Johanna and Birgitta, who, whatever their personal feelings and whatever real intimacy or familiarity they shared, performed their friendship in public. If we step back and look at their friendship as contemporaries would have perceived it, what we see is the performance. Birgitta's prophetic diatribe against Naples, for instance, was delivered in a public forum provided by Johanna, who asked her to pray and prophesy for her people—in whose best interest Johanna thus publicly acted. It was delivered to a panel of theologians called by Johanna to examine Birgitta, giving her friend a public platform to earn the theological approval that would be crucial to securing her canonization. Birgitta's saintliness reflected well on Johanna, because it suggested that she was worthy of Birgitta's concern, while Johanna's status as both reformed sinner and pious queen reflected well on Birgitta, who inspired some of Johanna's most public acts of piety.

It was not merely Birgitta's prophetic voice and judgment that Johanna helped to publicize, but also a vision of Christ's birth that Birgitta received in Jerusalem. Birgitta's vision was central to her Marian piety, and Johanna's decision to help disseminate it demonstrates her determination to foster Birgitta's cult and to be associated with it. Sometime between 1372 and 1376, Johanna commissioned the Florentine painter Niccolò di Tommaso (d. after

---

84. Ulf Birgersson, *Vite Katerine*, ed. Tryggve Lundén (Uppsala: Almqvist & Wiksell, 1981), 209. For an English translation and analysis of Ulf's text, see Thomas Andrew DuBois, "St. Katerina in Her Own Light," in *Sanctity in the North: Saints, Lives, and Cults in Medieval Scandinavia*, ed. Thomas Andrew DuBois (Toronto: University of Toronto Press, 2008), 271–306; Katherine's whipping is described at 291. For a consideration of Birgitta as a mother, see Birger Birg, *Heliga Birgitta: Åttabarnsmor och profet* (Lund: Historiska Media, 2002), esp. 143–46.

FIGURE 9. Niccolò di Tommaso, St. Birgitta's Vision of the Nativity, ca. 1375–1376. Philadelphia Museum of Art (John G. Johnson Collection, 1917).

1376) to paint Birgitta's serene vision of a painless Nativity (*Rev.* VII.22) for the new Church of Sant'Antonio Abate in Naples. Niccolò's painting of Birgitta's vision, in which the Virgin kneels in prayer at the moment of Jesus's birth rather than lying recumbent, established a "new iconographic formula" for depicting the Nativity that spread from Naples via Florence throughout Europe in the late fourteenth and early fifteenth centuries (see figure 9).[85]

85. Chiara Frugoni, "Female Mystics, Visions, and Iconography," in Bornstein and Rusconi, *Women and Religion in Medieval and Renaissance Italy*, trans. Schneider, 148.

The painting directly associates the vision it depicts with Birgitta, who kneels to the right of the Nativity scene. As such, it promotes Birgitta herself as much as the content of her vision. Niccolò also painted two other representations of Birgitta's vision in Naples, one for Gregory XI's private chambers and one that he sent to Florence.[86] Thus, it was through Johanna's patronage that Birgitta's influential Marian vision was made known and popularized.

Numerous scholars have noted the increase in religious foundations during the years of Johanna's friendship with Birgitta and hypothesized that her contrition for the sins Birgitta exposed drove her to make such bequests. Johanna's decision to display Birgitta's vision of the Nativity in the new royal foundation of Sant'Antonio Abate certainly suggests a connection between her religious patronage and her friendship with Birgitta. Whether or not she was prompted by contrition, Johanna took pains to appear to heed Birgitta, demonstrating her reception of the saint's message and the depth of her religious commitment. Of particular note is a clear instance of Johanna following a public directive given by Birgitta. As mentioned above, Birgitta railed during her public revelation against the practice of keeping Muslim slaves who were not forced to convert to Christianity and sold as prostitutes. In response to this criticism, Johanna freed an enslaved Turkish woman and sent her to Birgitta in Rome. Birgitta died before meeting her, but the woman—who became Katerina Magnusadottir, combining the names of Birgitta's daughter, Katherine, and Magnus Petri—accompanied Birgitta's family and companions when they took her relics to Sweden. Vadstena Abbey's memory book reveals that she remained there as a nun until her death some years later.[87]

After Birgitta's death, Johanna continued to assert her personal devotion by insisting on Birgitta's sainthood. Katherine traveled to the Regno as part of her campaign to canonize her mother, while Bernard du Bousquet, Johanna's firm ally, began taking depositions about Birgitta's miracles there in 1376.[88] Royally commissioned paintings of Birgitta and her vision of the Nativity were being produced in Naples as the canonization process began in 1377, when Katherine presented her own petition and those of Johanna and Emperor Charles IV to Gregory XI in Rome, to be entered as material evidence regarding Birgitta's sanctity.[89]

86. Aili and Svanberg, *Imagines Sanctae Birgittae*, 1:93–101, 155.

87. Claes Gejrot, ed., *Vadstenadiariet* (Stockholm: Kungliga Samfundet för utgivande av hand-skrifter rörande Skandinaviens historia, 1996), 142. Cf. Morris, *St. Birgitta of Sweden*, 141.

88. See note 27, above; Morris, *St. Birgitta of Sweden*, 145–46.

89. Morris, *St. Birgitta of Sweden*, 1, 146.

Johanna's support was crucial to the early stages of the effort to canonize Birgitta. Katherine brought Gregory two letters from Johanna attesting to her knowledge of Birgitta's sanctity. In them, she represents herself as the friend and advocate of both Birgitta and Katherine, appealing to Gregory as his humble and reverent daughter ("humilis et reverens filia vestra").[90] She calls Gregory's attention to Birgitta's *fama*, established through the prayer, good works, and vigils for which she became known during her travels, calling her friend the "grace of all virtues."[91] Birgitta's sanctity was evident, Johanna argues, through the innumerable visions she received in her capacity as Christ's bride, as through her determination not to remain in Sweden but to illuminate the world—including Naples—with her piety. Johanna insists that Birgitta's blessedness was beyond all doubt and calls upon Gregory to hear the supplication of his "devoted daughter" that Birgitta be entered into the catalog of saints.[92] In so doing, she stresses her own links to the saint and evokes her special relationship to the pope, simultaneously asserting the veracity of her experience of Birgitta's holiness and the value of her voice in extolling it. She thus became in a sense, through her patronage as through her experience, a partner in Birgitta's sanctity.

Johanna's share in Birgitta's sanctity was also revealed by a miracle that the saint performed at her behest for the son of James of Majorca's sister, Isabella, marchioness of Montferrat (1337–1406). Proof of Birgitta's posthumous miracles was crucial to demonstrating her sainthood, and it is significant that Johanna herself provided that evidence. During the canonization trial, Katherine described a letter she received from Johanna as proof of her mother's posthumous intercessory power. The letter, which survives in a Swedish manuscript, is very straightforward. Johanna wrote to inform Katherine of the miracle, saying that she knew her friend was always eager to hear "happy news" (*leta nova*). She explains that her nephew, William of Montferrat (1365–1400), was so ill that the doctors despaired of his life, prompting Johanna to pray to Birgitta for help. Shortly thereafter, the boy returned to health.[93]

Katherine's account of the letter, however, is more complex. She embroidered Johanna's narrative in a way that redounded to Johanna's credit as well as to Birgitta's, heightening the drama and expanding Johanna's role in it. In her deposition, Katherine revealed

90. Collijn, *Acta et Processus*, 54.

91. Ibid., 54–55: "decus omnium virtutum."

92. Ibid., 55.

93. Uppsala, Universitätsbibliothek, MS C 15, fol. 135v. Robert Lerner generously called this manuscript to my attention.

a letter by the lady Johanna, queen of Sicily, which she sent to Lady Katherine giving witness, in which was contained a miracle for a certain son of the marchioness of Montferrat, whom the doctors judged to be nearly departed from life. And then the aforesaid lady queen touched him with a certain small golden cross, which the Blessed Birgitta had given her, and called upon her in prayer, and the aforesaid boy was immediately well. This lady queen entrusted the news of this miracle in that same letter, sealed with her secret seal, and said therein that quite thirty persons were present, who abundantly filled the place, when the aforesaid boy rose up, healed.[94]

In the initial act of sending such a letter, Johanna created a partnership between herself and Katherine, the two women united to prove the sanctity of the woman who was the spiritual mother to one and the earthly mother of the other. Johanna portrayed herself to Katherine—who subsequently portrayed Johanna to the canonization commission—as enjoying a friendship with Birgitta that continued after the saint's death, ensuring her Birgitta's intercession and protection. Katherine's expanded account emphasizes the two women's closeness, which inspired Birgitta to give the queen a gift—the golden cross—that, Katherine suggests, Johanna carried with her thereafter. Katherine also evoked a domestic, maternal Johanna, a devoted queen and loving aunt who kept vigil at the sick child's bedside. Reaching for the golden cross given to her by a woman already renowned for her sanctity, Katherine's epistolary Johanna is pious and compassionate, demonstrating her faith in her friend's power, as in Christ's, when hope in medicine had failed.

Katherine's rendition of events emphasizes Johanna's piety, relying on it to underscore Birgitta's sanctity. Birgitta's holiness suffuses Johanna, who is a fitting conduit for Birgitta's healing power. Thus, the Birgittine investment in Johanna's reputation was great, tying Birgitta's miracle directly to Johanna's behavior and building the case for Birgitta's sanctity, at least in part, on Johanna's role as her devoted follower and friend.

Saintly Friendship and the Politics of Reputation

Johanna's friendship with Birgitta provided a new avenue by which to reshape her reputation and enhance her image as a pious queen. At the same time, it provided spiritually ambitious would-be saints with a means to assert both their piety and their relevance in the unsettled religious politics of

---

94. Collijn, *Acta et Processus*, 349.

the later fourteenth century. In the years following Birgitta's death, Johanna continued to seek associations with saints, a project in which her now redoubtable reputation and the precedent set by her friendship with Birgitta aided her. Johanna clearly wished to be seen as one of Birgitta's successes. As Sahlin has noted, Birgitta used her prophetic voice to urge reform on her age's most powerful figures. Johanna was not merely powerful, she was a notorious sinner, one whose conversion stood as a testament to Birgitta's efficacy as a spiritual guide and mouthpiece of divine displeasure. The two women used their fame to one another's advantage. Johanna's reputation benefited from the pious persona her devotion to Birgitta allowed her to demonstrate, and Birgitta's benefited from Johanna's meek acceptance of her instruction and willingness to promote Birgitta's reputation for sanctity. With Birgitta's death, her followers, most notably Katherine, incorporated her friendship with Johanna into their narratives of the saint's life and works, making Johanna a key witness to Birgitta's sanctity and promoting her as an example of Birgitta's spiritual influence. The precedent that cooperation set made Johanna an ideal friend to other saintly women.

Birgitta's death in 1373 created a vacuum. Her spiritual and political roles were vacant, as was her position as Johanna's friend. By the middle 1370s, Johanna's reputation for piety and papal allegiance was well established. As the pope's *filia peramantissima* and a noted patron of religious causes, Johanna was a valuable potential ally to anyone hoping to fill the void left by Birgitta's death. Two successors presented themselves: Birgitta's daughter, Katherine, and Catherine of Siena.

Her Mother's Daughter: Katherine of Vadstena as Friend and Ally

Katherine of Vadstena became, for Birgitta's followers, the saint's clear successor. Johanna herself sought to establish Katherine as the inheritor of her mother's virtue soon after Birgitta's death. Johanna had already made overtures of friendship to Katherine, most notably by sending the letter describing Birgitta's healing miracle to her rather than to Alfonso of Jaén. In her second letter appealing to Gregory XI to canonize Birgitta, Johanna positioned herself as Katherine's patron and Katherine as Birgitta's successor. Katherine, Johanna assured the pope, followed her mother's holy example as a living testament to her sanctity.[95] Katherine was Birgitta's heir, and by spearheading the quest to have her mother sanctified, she declared herself

---

95. Ibid., 55.

the continuator of her mother's work, claiming a leading role that eclipsed that of Alfonso or Birgitta's other followers. Johanna supported and praised Katherine's mission, asking Gregory to take note of the woman who begged for her saintly mother's "exaltation" (*exaltacionem*).[96] In so doing, Johanna portrayed herself as a good judge of saintly character, using her rapport with Gregory to advance Katherine in his good graces.

Johanna and Katherine were more than partners in the project to canonize Birgitta. They were spiritual sisters, the recipients of Birgitta's harsh but loving guidance. Seen in this light, Katherine's enhancement of Johanna's story about Birgitta's posthumous miracle takes on added significance. Johanna hosted Katherine in Naples as depositions were taken there regarding Birgitta's miracles, and Katherine petitioned for Birgitta's canonization armed with letters from Johanna. Each identified the other as a witness to and evidence of Birgitta's sanctity, and each praised the other for virtue and piety. Indeed, Johanna's identity as a pious, repentant queen devoted to Birgitta became central to the early Birgittine narrative of the saint's life, and Katherine's flattering portrait was both recognition and assertion of Johanna's crucial role in Birgitta's life and sanctity. Johanna, in turn, praised Katherine, suggesting as early as the mid-1370s that her role as Birgitta's successor extended to sainthood, that Katherine was a living copy and continuation of her mother. Johanna and Katherine were thus partners in the making not only of Birgitta's reputation but also of one another's. Their cooperation was fated to be short lived—interrupted by the beginning of the papal schism—but the friendship and partnership they worked together to shape illuminates the potential each saw in association with the other.

Sisters in Arms: Johanna and Catherine of Siena

While Katherine was the Birgittine successor to her mother, the Tuscan ascetic and visionary Catherine of Siena inherited the politico-religious role left vacant by Birgitta's death. With it, she too stepped into the role of Johanna's friend and ally. The Neapolitan queen's status as papal champion drew Catherine to her, leading to an epistolary friendship that highlighted both women's piety and papal devotion. If Katherine was Johanna's spiritual sister, Catherine of Siena was her political sister: she and Johanna shared the role of papal daughter. Johanna called herself the pope's devoted daughter; Catherine addressed him as *Babbo*, "Daddy." A generation younger than Johanna,

---

96. Ibid.

Catherine positioned herself as the queen's partner, calling her both sister and mother.

Catherine burst onto the scene of Italian politics in 1374, her emergence as a force in regional and papal politics orchestrated by high-ranking members of the ecclesiastical hierarchy to fill the void left by Birgitta's death.[97] Birgitta's prophetic voice had, F. Thomas Luongo argues, provided Gregory XI with valued insight and the "prophetic authority to buttress policies the pope favored," most notably the papacy's return to Rome. Catherine's voice functioned similarly, and her emergence as a public figure coincided closely with the break between the pope and the northern Italian communes, especially Florence, which gave her a vital role in mending strained relations between her papal father and his Tuscan allies.[98]

It was in this context that Catherine first approached Johanna, writing to her in late June 1375 to urge her to support papal projects, particularly a crusade against the Turks that Catherine believed was imminent. Addressing Johanna as her "dearest sister," Catherine implored her "to come to the aid of Christ's bride in her need, with your possessions, your person, your counsel."[99] Suzanne Noffke, Catherine's editor and translator, argues that this letter represents Catherine's pursuit of Johanna, as she "tr[ied] in vain to win her steady loyalty to the Church."[100] Noffke sees Johanna as a notorious sinner whose conversion Catherine attempted. This assessment, however, particularly during the period when Gregory himself identified Johanna as his staunchest supporter, makes little sense. Both Gregory and Johanna deliberately represented Johanna as the papacy's obedient daughter, defining her as a papal champion.

It is in this context that Catherine's letter makes the most sense. Luongo has argued that Catherine began her letter-writing campaign—taking on the role of publicist for papal projects—by "systematically addressing the key players on the political stage," including Johanna.[101] She approached such figures as a friend, using her epistolary medium to communicate with greater informality and intimacy than would have been possible in person

---

97. F. Thomas Luongo, *The Saintly Politics of Catherine of Siena* (Ithaca: Cornell University Press, 2006), 57–58, 71. On Catherine's role in ecclesiastical politics, see also Blake Beattie, "Catherine of Siena and the Papacy," in *A Companion to Catherine of Siena*, ed. Carolyn Muessig, George Ferzoco, and Beverly Mayne Kienzle (Leiden: Brill, 2012), 73–98.

98. Luongo, *The Saintly Politics of Catherine of Siena*, 57.

99. Catherine of Siena, Letter T138/G314/DT41, in *Letters*, 1:98–102, at 101.

100. Catherine of Siena, *Letters*, 98.

101. Luongo, *The Saintly Politics of Catherine of Siena*, 89.

and to claim a place in high political and ecclesiastical circles.[102] Catherine's first letter to Johanna constitutes an attempt to form an alliance with a figure central to papal efforts, adding her voice to Gregory's exhortations and inserting herself into a dialog already ongoing between the queen and her papal suzerain/father.

Catherine wrote again to Johanna the following month to entreat her support for the crusade, which she began to envision as a crusade to the Holy Land. This letter begins, as do most of Catherine's letters, with an expression of concern for the recipient's (Johanna's) spiritual well-being followed by "theological excursus, mystic apostrophe, and practical advice or admonition" that "amplifies" the letter's theme.[103] In this particular instance, the lesson is on loving God and performing divine service. Noffke wrongly describes the letter, with its expressions of concern for Johanna's spiritual state, as Catherine's appeal for both "[Johanna's] personal conversion and for her support of Gregory XI and the crusade effort."[104] Johanna's conversion from a life of sin and disobedience does not appear Catherine's prime concern; indeed, she closes the letter with the wish that Johanna will "keep living in God's holy love."[105] Catherine's focus was not Johanna's spiritual welfare but the projected crusade, for which she wanted Johanna's pledge of participation. She describes a bull sent by Gregory to the Franciscan and Dominican provincials for publication in Tuscany. It was, Catherine says, a call to arms, seeking devout Christians "to go to war against the unbelievers and to die for Christ overseas." Catherine hoped to enlist Johanna's support:

> I beg and urge you then, in the name of Christ crucified, to fire up your desire and get ready, so that whenever that sweet moment comes you may give whatever aid or force is needed to deliver our gentle Savior's holy place from the unbelievers' hands, and their souls from the devils' hands so that they may share in the blood of God's Son as we do. I beg you humbly, my venerable mother, not to refuse me an answer concerning your position and your good desire in regard to this holy endeavor.[106]

She closes by asking the queen to communicate her readiness to the pope. Thus Catherine was really asking her to demonstrate to Gregory "a holy readiness

---

102. Ibid., 76.

103. Ibid., 72; see Letter T133/G312/DT32, in Catherine of Siena, *Letters*, 1:122–26.

104. Catherine of Siena, *Letters*, 1:122.

105. Letter T133/G312/DT32, in Catherine of Siena, *Letters*, 1:126.

106. Ibid., 125.

and burning desire" for the crusade in the hope that Johanna—whom Gregory was simultaneously calling his *filia peramantissima*—would lend the project her support, winning Gregory's pledge of "strength and aid" as well.[107]

Johanna readily complied, sending Catherine the answer she desired. On August 4, Catherine wrote to Johanna again and referred to a letter, now lost, the queen had sent her:

> I want you to know, my revered lady, that my soul is jubilantly happy after receiving your letter. It gave me great consolation because, it seems to me, you have a holy and wholesome readiness to give both your possessions and your life for the glory of the name of Christ crucified. You can show no greater sacrifice or love than to be ready to give even your life, if necessary, for him. Oh what a great joy it will be to see you giving blood for blood! May I see the fire of holy desire so growing in you at the remembrance of the blood of God's Son that you may be leader and patroness of this holy crusade just as you bear the title of queen of Jerusalem. Thus the holy place will no longer be held by these evil unbelievers but honorably possessed by Christians, and by you as something of your own.[108]

Catherine thus flattered Johanna, playing on her status as Jerusalem's queen. As Noffke notes, Johanna must have replied very quickly indeed; Catherine's two letters were most likely composed within a month of each other.[109] She also did as Catherine asked and wrote to express her enthusiasm for the crusade to Gregory, who responded with gratitude for her zeal but suggested that her energies might be better spent aiding Constantinople against the Turks.[110]

Gregory's response notwithstanding, Catherine assured Johanna that "the holy father wants this very badly" and asked that she assure him of her own desire for the crusade.[111] It appears that Catherine's enthusiasm for the project outweighed Gregory's, and that she sought to galvanize Johanna's support—as the pope's ally and as the queen of Jerusalem—in order to influence him. Johanna was a logical leader, and Catherine hoped to harness her piety and her political and spiritual prestige for her cause. Indeed, she even

---

107. Ibid.
108. Letter T143/G313/DT39, in Catherine of Siena, *Letters*, 1:147–49, at 148.
109. Catherine of Siena, *Letters*, 148, n. 8.
110. Cerasoli, "Gregorio XI e Giovanna I di Napoli—Documenti inediti," 6–7, no. 167.
111. Letter T143/G313/DT39, in Catherine of Siena, *Letters*, 1:149.

presented Johanna as an exemplar of royal virtue to other royals, writing, for instance, to Elizabeth of Poland to inform her of Johanna's commitment to the crusade and urge Hungary's dowager queen to emulate her—a suggestion that one can only assume Elizabeth found extremely distasteful.[112]

Johanna's support for Catherine's cause, like her encouragement of and correspondence with her, speaks volumes about her desire to befriend Catherine. Catherine's friendship allowed Johanna to publicize her piety and commitment to papal ideals. It also provided her an additional opportunity to champion and partner with a saintly woman. As Luongo has pointed out, most of Catherine's "letters to prominent secular and ecclesiastical rulers never made it past the filter of court secretaries (assuming they were delivered at all)."[113] Given the rapidity of Johanna's response to Catherine, she likely sought the association. Catherine's relationship with Gregory and her rising fame for piety and prophetic insight made her a natural ally for Johanna. Johanna's support was repaid by the praise Catherine heaped on her in her letters, which her *familia*—her disciples—circulated abroad. Her friendship and approval reflected well on Johanna, as did any fame the Neapolitan queen gained through Catherine's letter-writing campaign as a queen zealous for the honor of Christendom and the reconquest of the Holy Land. The two women amplified each other's reputations for filial piety to the papacy, forming a friendship constructed around the ideal of service to the Church. Their correspondence cast Johanna in the role of crusader, papal champion, and Christian sovereign of Jerusalem, thereby portraying her as a true Angevin monarch who defended the Church and enjoyed a remarkable affinity to sanctity.

Taken together, Johanna's friendships with Katherine of Vadstena and Catherine of Siena suggest that she saw saintly friendship as integral to her royal persona. Her performance of pious queenship rested on a foundation of typical Angevin patronage, but public friendship enhanced that performance. Both friendships were of relatively brief duration and terminated with the onset of the schism—which led Katherine to distance herself from Johanna and Catherine to actively denounce her (see chapter 5)—but their very existence provides evidence of how useful such friendships were for the creation of both saintly and queenly identities. Both personae were, in the context of late medieval culture, artfully constructed and highly politicized—a reality of which Johanna and her friends were clearly aware. Friendship had political and public uses: The people with whom one was known to associate shaped

---

112. Letter T145/G311/DT40, in Catherine of Siena, *Letters*, 1:165.
113. Luongo, *The Saintly Politics of Catherine of Siena*, 77.

one's *fama* and defined one's virtue. Birgitta, Prior Peter and Master Peter tell us, understood this well enough to avoid being linked to those for whose society she could be "branded." If inappropriate or ill-reputed friends could be the undoing of a reputation, friendships with the right people—be they pious queens or saintly women—could be the making of a reputation.

Johanna's relationship to the papacy and fame for piety attracted women like Catherine and Birgitta to her, rendering her patronage invaluable and providing her with the opportunity to publicize her piety along with their friendship. Friendship with saints was an invaluable tool in reshaping her reputation, particularly given how fastidious the saints Johanna befriended were about the people with whom they associated. Birgitta, as Österberg has pointed out, felt that "the 'right' friends . . . were [those] with whom you shared a devotion to God."[114] To be recognized as Birgitta's or Catherine's friend was to have earned a saint's approbation, which reflected an upright moral character. Johanna thus harnessed their reputations for sanctity in the service of her own, seeking to present herself, according to the model of her ancestors, as a sovereign graced by both a special relationship with the papacy and an intimate link to sanctity. Her pious bequests during her independent reign are tangible evidence of Johanna's public devoutness, while her obedient devotion to holy women, as to popes, drew her into the most important religious movements of her time. She acceded to saintly requests as she did to those of the papacy; she championed the crusade promoted by Catherine of Siena just as she disseminated Birgitta's vision of the Nativity and fulminations against Naples, sending her a Turkish slave as a direct and unambiguous statement of her obedience. Had the schism not radically altered her standing with the prominent religious of her day, there is every indication that Johanna would have continued to foster her relationships with Catherine of Siena and Katherine of Vadstena.

The filial obedience that Johanna asserted in relation to the papacy applied to her relationship with Birgitta as well. Holy women such as Birgitta and Catherine, like Johanna herself, turned traditional female roles on their heads, earning power and influence by manipulating feminine subordination. Johanna and her saintly friends may have understood one another as women who sought influence through religion, but Johanna's power came in part through her submission not only to a spiritual father—the pope—but also to a spiritual mother. Johanna's value to Birgitta's supporters lay as much in her

114. Österberg, *Friendship and Love, Ethics and Politics*, 39.

reverence for and obedience to the saint as in patronage of her cult. Their relationship was intimate and lasting, and Birgitta's celebrity, particularly in the Regno, reflected well on Johanna, her humility before Birgitta's wrath serving to amplify her reputation for piety.

In part, in seeking friendships with celebrated holy women, Johanna emulated the examples of her female forebears, particularly Sancia. Yet Sancia's self-abnegation and later-life retirement from the world were impossible for a sovereign queen; Johanna had to remain on the public stage, where her image was enhanced by close association with holy women who embodied the spiritual ideal Sancia had emulated. Johanna may also have been seeking redemption—both public and spiritual—through association with saintly women. Their shared femininity obviated the suggestion of impropriety that might have greeted Johanna's friendship with a male saint. Johanna created a sacred family for herself, patronizing holy women and receiving their instruction, perhaps striving to be worthy to enter their ranks, just as the fifteenth-century English matron Margery Kempe hoped one day to be admitted to the ranks of the holy virgins. Dyan Elliott has described Margery as "spiritually upwardly mobile"; Johanna was as well, though her efforts were, perhaps, more directed toward this life than the next.[115] Her friends' virtue reflected on her, and her promotion of them gave her a share in their sanctity. At the same time, their desire for association with Johanna suggests that she had become someone whose reputation could enhance the reputation of spiritually ambitious women.

Yet, despite her success in remolding her public persona, Johanna's new image was fragile. Catherine of Siena's biographer, Raymond of Capua (d. 1399), wrote that she had noted the fragility of a virgin's reputation.[116] The same might be said for the reputations of queens. Even before the beginning of the schism, which was to prove disastrous to Johanna's reputation, her rehabilitated public image was easily damaged. It threatened to shatter when she angered her contemporaries, her old reputation—that defined by chroniclers and poets after Andrew's death—reemerging to demonstrate the delicacy of her new image. In 1365, after Niccolò Acciaiuoli died, Johanna attempted to recoup from the late seneschal's heirs lands granted to him by Louis of Taranto. It is perhaps ironic that she did so in response to a papal directive. She arrested Acciaiuoli's son, Angelo, and his nephew, divesting

115. Dyan Elliott, *Fallen Bodies: Pollution, Sexuality, and Demonology in the Middle Ages* (Philadelphia: University of Pennsylvania Press, 1999), 49.

116. Raymond of Capua, *The Life of St. Catherine of Siena*, trans. George Lamb (Rockford, IL: Harvill Press, 1960), 143.

them of their holdings and inspiring the outraged protest of the Regno's Florentine merchants and the Florentine Signoria. Ultimately, both men regained their lands, and Angelo even succeeded his father as grand seneschal, but the reaction to Johanna's move against them reveals how thin was the veneer of her new reputation.[117] Giannozzo Sacchetti, brother of the more famous poet, Franco, and an associate of the magnates who formed the core of the Florentine Guelf party, attacked her in poetry:

> Johanna, little girl and no queen,
> not a woman, but an ignorant wench,
> ungrateful and fraudulent.

He also characterized her as "a house of lust" ("albergo di lossuria").[118] The old slurs remained, ready to emerge with the slightest provocation. Johanna might have reshaped her reputation, but it was fragile, and the old "harlot queen" still lurked beneath the surface.

---

117. Léonard, *Les Angevins de Naples*, 416.

118. Giannozzo Sacchetti, "V," in *Poeti minori del trecento*, ed. Natalino Sapegno (Milan: R. Ricciardi, 1952), 160.

❦ CHAPTER 5

The Schism of the Western Church and the Division of Johanna of Naples

> Reputation is no less indispensable than chastity. . . .
> A woman, in behaving well, performs but half her
> duty; as what is thought of her, is as important to
> her as what she really is. . . . Opinion is the grave of
> virtue among men; but its throne among women.
>
> Jean-Jacques Rousseau, *Émile*

> This regard for reputation, independent of its being
> one of the natural rewards of virtue, however, took its
> rise from a cause that I have already deplored as the
> grand source of female depravity, the impossibility of
> regaining respectability by a return to virtue, though
> men preserve theirs during an indulgence of vice. It
> was natural for women then to endeavor to preserve
> what once lost—was lost forever.
>
> Mary Wollstonecraft, *A Vindication of the Rights
> of Women*

On May 6, 1379, Catherine of Siena wrote to her friend Johanna of Naples. Whereas once their correspondence had centered on plans to promote the faith through crusade, Catherine wrote now with a wholly different purpose. "It is shameful to make yourself such a spectacle to others," she berated the queen, calling her to account for the drastic change her public persona underwent in late 1378, in the opening months of the Western Schism, after she abjured Pope Urban VI.[1] Johanna had become respected for her piety, wisdom, and loyalty to the papacy; suddenly, she was again notorious. Her transfer of obedience to Clement VII shattered her previous reputation, which, at least among Urbanists, was lost forever. She became, virtually overnight, a symbol of the division of the Church.

On October 31, 1378, Johanna became the first European monarch to recognize Clement VII as pope. It was a decision that, as one recent historical survey notes, proved "very unpopular in the Regno and poorly received

---

1. Catherine of Siena, Letter T348/G317, in *Letters*, 4:166–70, at 168.

in Provence."[2] The schism was nothing short of catastrophic for Johanna's realm and reputation. It bifurcated both, dividing them as it divided Western Christendom, leaving them splintered even after the reconciliation of the Church. Her lands were plunged into civil war by rival contenders for her throne, to be fitfully reunited for short periods before being divided forever. At the same time, Johanna's fateful choice transformed her in the eyes of her contemporaries, giving rise to vying Clementist and Urbanist versions of her. It also led directly to her deposition, imprisonment, and death.

Johanna played an integral part in what Renate Blumenfeld-Kosinski has called the *imaginaire* of the schism.[3] The trials of Naples and those of the Church mirrored one another, while Johanna herself was at the nexus of both interrelated calamities in the early years of the schism. For the Clementists, she was a martyr who adhered to religious principal despite horrible, unjust consequences. For the Urbanists, her support of Clement VII was indicative of destructive self-interest, motivated by and intimately associated with the iniquitous selfishness that had led to Andrew of Hungary's murder. The disastrous outcome of her decision, for herself and for her kingdom, was represented as the consequence of her foolhardiness and, ultimately, as divine retribution for the sins of her early reign. On the one hand, she was a tragic, selfless queen who placed her faith and Church ahead of her own well-being, while on the other, she was self-servingly and perversely stubborn, feigning piety even as she cut her subjects off from security and salvation. Commentators on both sides pondered her crucial first step—whose motivations were as obscure to contemporaries as they are to the modern historian—along the path that rent Western Christendom as they sought to explain the origins of the schism. The explanatory narratives that sprang from their contemplations of the schism, as of Johanna's career and legacy, gave birth to new images of the long-reigning queen that would determine how posterity remembered her. At the same time, her critical presence in the histories generated by both sides shaped how the conflict was described by those who attempted to make sense of it.

Johanna and the Origins of the Great Schism

From the very beginning of the schism, there was disagreement between Clementists and Urbanists as to what drove Johanna to recognize Clement

---

2. Martin Aurell, Jean-Paul Boyer, and Noël Coulet, *La Provence au Moyen Âge* (Aix-en-Provence: Publications de l'Université de Provence, 2005), 277.

3. Renate Blumenfeld-Kosinski, *Poets, Saints, and Visionaries of the Great Schism, 1378–1417* (University Park: Penn State Press, 2006).

VII as pope. From testimony gathered by both camps in the 1380s, two very different narratives emerge that impute different actions and motivations to Urban, to Johanna, and to those closest to the queen. Only a bare outline of events is possible without straying into these competing histories.

In 1378, Gregory XI died. His death was followed by a dramatic and controversial conclave that elected Bartolomeo Prignano (1318–89) pope. Prignano seemed the perfect choice: Neapolitan-born and of Pisan family, he had close ties to the mostly French papal Curia. He was an archbishop but not a cardinal—and, thus, a compromise candidate.[4] After an early career in Naples, he had entered the pontifical chancellery in Avignon, where his career flourished. He became the chaplain of the Limousin cardinal of Pampeluna (Pamplona), and was, according to Prignano himself, considered nearly French by the cardinals.[5] He had accompanied Gregory XI to Rome, where he was named archbishop of Bari in 1377.[6] He was a known quantity, a trusted colleague familiar to and with the Curia. Yet his election marked a shift away from the Limousin popes of the Avignon period and, apparently, a gesture of conciliation to the anxious (and reportedly murderous) mob that surrounded the conclave and demanded a Roman, or at least an Italian, pope.

Johanna was, according to numerous sources, overjoyed by Urban's election. Niccolò Moschini, the Dominican inquisitor in Naples at the time, later testified that news of Prignano's elevation was greeted in the city by revelry and bonfires.[7] Johanna, Moschini reported, refused to take part in the celebrations until she received official confirmation from the cardinals, but afterward, she made her joy known:

> She prepared a great celebration and commanded that another general celebration be made in the city. To me, however, she said, "Rejoice, because we now have a pope who will heed us, and we will make you a bishop." To which I responded, "My lady, you could even make me a cardinal."[8]

---

4. Salvatore Fodale, *La Politica Napoletana di Urbano VI* (Rome: Salvatore Sciascia, 1973), 8.

5. Walter Ullmann, *The Origins of the Great Schism: A Study in Fourteenth-Century Ecclesiastical History* (Hamden, CT: Archon Books, 1967), 12. Ullmann draws his account directly from Urban's *Factum Urbani*, drafted to refute the protestations of the ultramontane cardinals against his election. For the full text of the *Factum Urbani*, see Cesare Baronio et al., *Annales ecclesiastici, denuo et accurate excusi*, ed. August Theiner (Paris: Barri-Ducis, 1880), 26:348 and passim, and Noël Valois, *La France et le Grand Schisme d'Occident*, 4 vols. (Paris: A. Picard, 1896), 1:35–55.

6. Fodale, *La Politica Napoletana di Urbano VI*, 9.

7. Moschini's testimony is printed in Michael Seidlmayer, *Die Anfänge des grossen abendländischen Schismas: Studien zur Kirchenpolitik insbesondere der Spanischen Staaten und zu den geistigen Kämpfen der Zeit* (Münster: Aschendorff, 1940), 250. See also Fodale, *La Politica Napoletana di Urbano VI*, 7. Moschini was among the new cardinals created by Urban in 1378.

8. Seidlmayer, *Die Anfänge des grossen abendländischen Schismas*, 250.

Johanna's elation was to be expected. Urban VI's election promised a continuation of the partnership Johanna had enjoyed with Urban V and Gregory XI, both of whom had also had preexisting ties to Naples. There was every reason to believe that Johanna would remain the pope's staunch ally, as that the pope would emulate his predecessors in supporting her. Indeed, Urban himself, in an account of his election known as the *Factum Urbani*, recognized their connected interests, identifying himself as "by birth of the kingdom of Naples, which was now ruled by Queen Johanna, a princess very devout and loyal to the Church."[9]

At first, the relationship between Urban and Johanna fulfilled the expectations of both. Otto of Brunswick, Johanna's husband, and her chancellor, Niccolò Spinelli, traveled to Rome to congratulate and honor the new pontiff. In the summer of 1378, even after relations between Urban and the cardinals soured and the friendship between the courts of Rome and Naples was said to have cooled, Johanna supported Urban against Breton and Gascon mercenaries. In answer to the pope's call, she sent troops—including one hundred foot soldiers drawn, according to the *Chronicon Siculum*, from the queen's own guards—to his aid.[10] Johanna thus upheld her status as papal champion, even as Urban's position deteriorated.

Yet their relationship grew strained as Urban alienated not only the ultramontane cardinals but also those of Italian birth. Urban took one of the first steps toward schism on May 3, 1378, when he attacked the habits and lifestyles of the cardinals, including Giacamo Orsini, whom he called crazy, Pietro Corsini, whom he called a thief, and Robert of Geneva, whom he accused of debauchery, in a public consistory.[11] Urban's hostile treatment of the cardinals—whether motivated, as he maintained, by reforming zeal or by an altered or newly revealed evil character, as the Clementist cardinals

---

9. Ullmann, *The Origins of the Great Schism*, 13.

10. De Blasiis, *Chronicon Siculum*, 31; cf. Fodale, *La Politica Napoletana di Urbano VI*, 26 and n. 35; Ullmann, *The Origins of the Great Schism*, 50, 56. How many soldiers Johanna sent is disputed. Ullmann, following the testimony of the bishop of Cordova, argues that Johanna sent a token troop of two hundred "to keep up appearances" (ibid., 50). It is worth noting that the bishop offers the sending of these forces as evidence of Johanna's continued devotion, arguing that "dicta regina Neapolitana fuit spiritualis filia et devota dicti pape Urbani post separacionem et reprobacionem ipsius factam per cardinales usque in finem mensis augusti" (cf. Étienne Baluze, *Vitae paparum Avenionensium*, ed. G. Mollat [Paris: Letouzey et Ané, 1914–27], 2:647, and Seidlmayer, *Die Anfänge des grossen abendländischen Schismas*, 280). Fodale, on the other hand, cites the *Chronicon Siculum* and a letter by Marcilius de Inghen reporting that Johanna sent two thousand lances and one hundred foot soldiers to argue that Johanna remained staunchly loyal to Urban at this juncture (cf. Fodale, *La Politica Napoletana di Urbano VI*, 26).

11. Robert Ch. Logoz, *Clément VII (Robert de Genève): Sa chancellerie et le clergé romand au début du Grand Schisme (1378–1394)* (Lausanne: Payot, 1974), 62.

claimed—drove them from his side.[12] By Pentecost, only seven cardinals remained in Rome.[13] On July 20, they were summoned to join their colleagues in Anagni. On August 9, the cardinals declared Urban's election invalid (because coerced), the Holy See vacant, and Urban a usurper.

On August 27, the cardinals moved to Fondi, whose count, Onorato Caetani (ca. 1336–1400), was angry because Urban refused to repay a substantial loan made to Gregory XI.[14] Hosted by Caetani, the cardinals prepared to elect a new pope. They sent representatives and letters to those they hoped would support them, including Johanna, decrying Urban's defective character and election. Caetani sought an alliance with Naples at the same time, betrothing his daughter to Otto of Brunswick's brother, thus creating important political ties between the dissidents and the Neapolitan court.[15] Urban retaliated, excommunicating the cardinals who had abandoned him. On September 18, he created several new cardinals, most of whom were Italian and many of whom were Neapolitan, revealing his intention to foster a strong Urbanist base in Naples.[16] On September 20, the rebel cardinals elected Robert of Geneva, who took the name Clement VII, pope.[17]

Johanna's loyalty became an important prize, and the rival camps fought to win her allegiance. While the cardinals still deliberated, their residence in Fondi, within the Regno's borders, drew attention to Johanna from all quarters. Indeed, the cardinals took care to keep their movements within the Regno, where they could hope for Johanna's protection.[18] Urban appealed to her to serve as arbitrator in July, after the three remaining Italian cardinals—Orsini, Corsini, and Simone Borzano—deserted him.[19] Late in the summer, Emperor

---

12. Ibid., 63.

13. Ibid.; Ullmann, *The Origins of the Great Schism*, 50.

14. Logoz, *Clément VII*, 63; Ullmann, *The Origins of the Great Schism*, 50.

15. Fodale, *La Politica Napoletana di Urbano VI*, 38.

16. Ibid., 40; Arnold Esch, "Le Clan des familles napolitaines au sein du Sacré Collège d'Urbain VI et de ses successeurs et les Brancacci de Rome et d'Avignon," in Centre National de la Recherche Scientifique, *Genèse et Débuts du Grand Schisme d'Occident (Avignon, 25–28 septembre 1978)* (Paris: Centre National de la Recherche Scientifique, 1980), 494. Among the cardinals created by Urban in 1378, seven of twenty-five were Neapolitan. The trend continued: of six cardinals created in 1381, three were Neapolitan; of those created between 1382 and 1384, two of three were Neapolitan; in the final creation (1384) of Urban's pontificate, five of the nine new cardinals were Neapolitan (Esch, "Le Clan des familles napolitaines," 494).

17. Ullmann, *The Origins of the Great Schism*, 54–55.

18. This has been noted by Paolo Brezzi, "Il Regno di Napoli ed il grande Schisma d'Occidente (1378–1419)," in *Studi di storia cristiana ed ecclesiastica*, 2: *Medioevo* (Naples: Libraria Scientifica Editrice, 1966), 365.

19. Léonard, *Les Angevins de Naples*, 455.

Charles IV entreated her to use her influence to heal the breach between the cardinals and pope.[20] In early October, Catherine of Siena wrote to Johanna as well, attacking the cardinals as "incarnate devils" and begging her to "recognize [that] these men who have been set as pillars of holy Church have so abominably sown the poison of heresy that it is poisoning them as well as anyone who comes near them."[21]

The cardinals, for their part, were eager for Johanna's support and sent Cardinal Orsini and Niccolò Brancaccio, archbishop of Cosenza, to Naples at the end of July.[22] Johanna received them with honor and granted them an audience, during which they swore to the illegitimacy of Urban's election and consequent vacancy of the Holy See.[23] Brancaccio—created a cardinal by Clement VII in December of that year—later reported that rumors about Urban's invalid election worried Johanna, and that, after assuring her that they were true and her anxiety justified, Orsini attempted to convince her that he himself should become pope, hoping that her backing would ensure his election. According to Brancaccio, Johanna accepted Orsini's argument regarding Urban but suggested that Corsini, the so-called cardinal of Florence, would make a more suitable pontiff.[24]

It is impossible to know whether Johanna was truly convinced of Urban's illegitimacy as early as Brancaccio claims. Officially, at least, she remained neutral for nearly three months, recognizing Clement VII more than a month after his election, on October 31.[25] On November 22, she publicly declared her obedience to Clement, arresting Urban's emissaries and making a census payment of 64,000 florins to Clement. In both Naples and Provence, Clementist officials and clerics replaced Urbanist incumbents, precipitating lively resistance. Under Johanna's protection in Naples, the Franciscan general chapter declared its obedience to Clement.[26] The Angevin Piedmont and Montferrat, of which Otto of Brunswick was regent,

---

20. Valois, *La France et le Grand Schisme d'Occident,* 1:265, n. 6; cf. Ullmann, *The Origins of the Great Schism,* 62.

21. Letter T312/G315, in Catherine of Siena, *Letters,* 3:287–92, at 288.

22. Walter Ullmann attributed the cardinals' attentions to Johanna's kinship with Charles V, ignoring her central role in ecclesiastical politics and influence within Italy—surely the most important motivating factors (Ullmann, *The Origins of the Great Schism,* 88).

23. Ibid., 88–89.

24. Baluze, *Vitae paparum Avenionensium,* 2:620. Baluze reproduces Brancaccio's testimony in full. Cf. Ullmann, *The Origins of the Great Schism,* 88–89.

25. Léonard, *Les Angevins de Naples,* 454.

26. Valois, *La France et le Grand Schisme d'Occident,* 1:180.

became Clementist at the same time, as did the prefect of Rome and Gio-
rando Orsini, lord of Marino.[27]

Europe was rapidly divided between the rival popes. Charles V of France
and his brother, Louis of Anjou, emerged, with Johanna, as Clement's leading supporters. Many of Clement's key adherents were petty princes, such as
Leopold III, duke of Austria, and most, like Jean, duke of Berry, had ties to
the French court. Aragon and Castile and León ultimately chose the Avignon
obedience, as did Robert II of Scotland and Peter II of Lusignan, king of Cyprus.[28] Emperor Wenceslaus, who succeeded Charles IV at the end of 1378,
declared his allegiance to Urban and persuaded the Diet of Frankfurt to do the
same in February 1379.[29] Richard II of England, Louis of Hungary, and most
of the northern Italian communes did as well, cutting Johanna off from polities and rulers with whom she had long-standing, vital political connections.
Even Florence—where antipapal sentiment was rife and Urban viewed with
suspicion or outright dislike—ultimately submitted to the Roman obedience,
despite Johanna's appeals to honor their long alliance and recognize Clement.[30]

Beyond the realm of politics, the situation had become dire. Urban hired the
English mercenary captain John Hawkwood, who attacked Clement's Breton
mercenaries; papal politics erupted into full-scale warfare.[31] Clement, who initially held the upper hand, found his position in Italy deteriorating. Following
a disastrous defeat at Marino in May 1379, he retreated to Naples, where he
was welcomed by Johanna and given the run of the ancient fortress of Castel
dell'Ovo.[32] Many of Johanna's subjects, however, rioted when they learned of
Clement's presence in the city. According to multiple sources, public sentiment
turned—violently—against both Clement and Johanna. On May 13, Clement fled (in a ship Johanna provided) to Provence. He processed solemnly into
Avignon, where he would remain for the rest of his life, on June 20, 1379.[33]

Johanna was left to deal with her outraged subjects, who reportedly demanded her death or deposition. Probably in response, she declared her obedience to Urban VI on May 18, 1379, and, on June 3, sent representatives to Rome
to submit her abjuration of Clement.[34] Then news reached Naples that Otto

27. Léonard, Les Angevins de Naples, 458, Valois, La France et le Grand Schisme d'Occident, 1:160–61.
28. Logoz, Clément VII, 138.
29. Ullmann, The Origins of the Great Schism, 93.
30. Lewin, Negotiating Survival, 53–64. See esp. 53.
31. Ullmann, The Origins of the Great Schism, 95.
32. Ibid.; cf. Fodale, La Politica Napoletana di Urbano VI, 46.
33. Logoz, Clément VII, 131–32.
34. Valois, La France et le Grand Schisme d'Occident, 1:177.

of Brunswick was returning with his troops to the city. Johanna retransferred her obedience to Clement and carried out reprisals against Urban's supporters in the Regno.[35] From that time forward, Johanna was lost to the Urbanist cause.

Her second disavowal led Urban to excommunicate and depose Johanna. The Regno's proximity to Rome, the revenue it provided, and its role as a source of military support made having an ally at its helm of paramount importance. At first, Urban proceeded firmly but cautiously against Johanna, whom he hoped would reconsider. On November 29, 1379, he promulgated the bull *Nuper cum vinea*, excommunicating Spinelli—widely regarded as the instigator of Johanna's rebellious behavior—and Caetani. He continued to pursue more diplomatic channels with the queen herself.[36] At Urban's behest, Catherine of Siena appealed to Johanna to convert. For a time, there was discussion of sending Catherine and Katherine of Vadstena to Naples, but that plan never came to fruition. Finally, at the end of April 1380, Urban excommunicated Johanna. In a bull issued on May 11, he denounced her as schismatic, heretical, and blasphemous, labeled her a conspirator against the Church, and declared her guilty of lèse-majesté, deposing her, in his capacity as Naples's suzerain, as punishment for her heresy.[37]

Urban then moved to replace Johanna with her heir apparent, her cousin Louis of Durazzo's son, Charles. Charles, who had been living in Buda, was summoned to Rome. Urban's entreaties that he should take up Naples's crown were echoed by Bologna, Florence, and Siena, who hailed Charles as the clear leader of the Urbanist cause, and by Catherine of Siena, who had appealed to Louis of Hungary and Charles to intercede as early as the fall of 1379.[38] Johanna retaliated by adopting Louis of Anjou, Clement's most active

---

35. Ibid., 178; cf. Fodale, *La Politica Napoletana di Urbano VI*, 48 and n. 8. Both the *Chronicon Siculum* and *Diurnali del Duca di Monteleone* report military action against Urban's partisans, including an armed confrontation ("pulsata ad arma") in Naples's cathedral (De Blasiis, *Chronicon Siculum*, 47).

36. Fodale, *La Politica Napoletana di Urbano VI*, 49.

37. Naples, Biblioteca Nazionale, MS Brancaccio IV B 7, fols. 145v–146v. Cf. Fodale, *La Politica Napoletana di Urbano VI*, 50; Léonard, *Les Angevins de Naples*, 462. The bull of excommunication is published in Camera, *Elucubrazioni storico-diplomatiche su Giovanna I.a*, 287.

38. Léonard, *Les Angevins de Naples*, 460. Catherine wrote to Louis in October 1379 (Letter T357/G188) and to Charles later the same month (Letter T372/G189). While Catherine says nothing explicit about Charles assuming Naples's throne, her letter suggests that the plan was already being discussed by Urban's supporters. She asked Charles to learn from the examples of King David and Charles's own *beatus stirps*, Louis IX. Catherine praised these kingly exemplars: "They held their kingdoms in actuality, but not with inordinate attachment and desire. . . . They weren't like those who are reigning today, in whom there is so much selfish love for themselves that they would make a god of this tyrant, the world." This observation serves both as a model for Charles to follow and as an implied criticism of Johanna, whom Catherine chastised in her letters for "selfish love." See Catherine of Siena, *Letters*, 4:236–42, 301–6.

supporter, on June 29, 1380, naming him her successor in both Provence and the Regno.[39] Charles, answering Urban's call, began his military expedition into Italy on July 12, 1380, and was crowned Charles III of Naples in Rome on June 1, 1381.[40] On June 4, 1381, Johanna published the articles of adoption, which she had previously kept secret, and appealed to Louis of Anjou to protect her from Charles.[41] By letters patent, she proclaimed that Louis had been transformed into her son ("converte in filium nostrum") and was to enter into the governance of her territories and be obeyed by her subjects as her true and legitimate heir.[42]

Charles set out from Rome on June 8, determined to conquer his new kingdom. Otto of Brunswick, a seasoned campaigner, led Naples's defense, but his efforts were to no avail. The city of Naples fell on July 16, 1381. Charles then moved against Johanna's followers, hunting Otto and besieging Johanna herself in Castel Nuovo.[43] Johanna defended the castle through the summer, waiting for deliverance from Provence that never arrived. Louis of Anjou, much as he desired Naples, sought first to ensure his position in Provence. In mid-September, he was still haggling and, in places, at war with his reluctant new subjects, who finally swore to submit if he rescued their countess; Louis vowed to "go and do all in his power to deliver her by force from the hands of Charles."[44] It was too little too late. Charles captured Otto on August 25, and Johanna surrendered on September 2.[45]

News of Castel Nuovo's fall reached Provence on September 25. Spurred on by the impending loss of his new kingdom, Louis sprang into action. He appealed to his nephew, Charles VI of France, for assistance; Charles, apparently believing Johanna would make peace with Charles of Durazzo, declined.[46] Louis continued to press Clement VII for support while he sent representatives into Italy to assert his claim to the Regno. He was determined, according to his chancellor, Jean le Fèvre, to rely on chivalry both to rescue

39. Léonard, *Les Angevins de Naples*, 462; cf. Valois, *La France et le Grand Schisme d'Occident*, 1:189.

40. Léonard, *Les Angevins de Naples*, 462, 464.

41. One of the letters patent announcing the adoption is preserved in AMM, BB 28, fols. 131v–132r. Cf. Valois, *La France et le Grand Schisme d'Occident*, 2:9–10.

42. AMM, BB 28, fol. 131v.

43. Valois, *La France et le Grand Schisme d'Occident*, 2:10, 12–13; Fodale, *La Politica Napoletana di Urbano VI*, 64.

44. Jean le Fèvre, *Journal de Jean le Fèvre, évêque de Chartres, chancelier des rois de Sicile Louis I et Louis II d'Anjou*, ed. H. Moranvillé, 2 vols. (Paris: A. Picard, 1887), 1:11–12; cf. Aurell, Boyer, and Coulet, *La Provence au Moyen Âge*, 285–86.

45. Valois, *La France et le Grand Schisme d'Occident*, 2:10.

46. Ibid., 16; cf. Jean le Fèvre, *Journal*, 1:8–11.

the queen and to defend the Church.[47] On February 22, 1382, Clement VII entitled Louis duke of Calabria, strengthening his rhetorical claim to the Neapolitan throne. Writing to Marseille some months later, Louis stressed that his infeudation stemmed from necessity and was to Johanna's glory, a measure to secure her interests rather than his own.[48]

On March 3, Clement excommunicated Charles of Durazzo and his supporters. He cast the mission to rescue Johanna in a spiritual light, promising indulgences to those who accompanied Louis to Naples.[49] He announced that Louis would descend into Italy as the papal champion, charged to punish Charles and liberate Naples (and its queen), thus equating Louis's mission with that undertaken by Charles I—another duke of Anjou—when he seized the Regno from the Hohenstaufen for Clement IV.[50] Clement hosted a grand reception for Louis in Avignon in February. A contemporary observer described Louis's march through Provence, saying that Clement, "who was his intimate friend," welcomed him at a public audience. Louis was greeted by high-ranking ecclesiastics, then by each cardinal, and finally by Clement, who "rose from his throne . . . and took [Louis] lovingly in his arms to give him the kiss of peace."[51]

Aided by this papal endorsement, Louis levied a large army. His forces included many Provençal and French nobles, despite Charles VI's refusal to involve France militarily. The venture was, however, subsidized by a large French loan, pledged in mid-February by Charles "to rescue our most dear and most beloved cousin, the Queen of Sicily, who is at present in the hands of her enemies, the adversaries of Holy Church."[52] Johanna's liberty was thus equated by Clementists with that of the Church, and the mission to rescue her took on the trappings of a crusade. Louis took care to present it as

---

47. Jean le Fèvre, *Journal*, 1:11: "il entreprendra à faire son effort de delivrer la Roynne et promouvoir le faict de l'eglise par force de chevalerie."

48. Letter from Louis dated Carpentras, June 8, 1382. AMM, BB 28, fol. 136: "domino Clemente papa Septimo domino nostro tam dicte domine et matris nostre quam etiam nostro successorum nostrorum nomine de Regno Sicilie suscepimus pro evidenti utilitate et comadosa necessitate ac etiam ad gloriam maximam ipsius domine."

49. Valois, *La France et le Grand Schisme d'Occident*, 2:24.

50. Ibid., 19–20; cf. Jean le Fèvre, *Journal*, 1:45.

51. The description derives from a contemporary diary, a copy of which is contained in Avignon, Bibliothèque Ceccano, MS 2395, fol. 89r.

52. Valois, *La France et le Grand Schisme d'Occident*, 2:25, n. 1; cf. Léonard, *Les Angevins de Naples*, 466. Valois quotes an act of February 12, 1382, preserved in Paris, Bibliotheque nationale de France, MS fonds français 6537, n° 1, and cited by E. Jarry, *La vie politique de Louis de France, duc d'Orléans* (Paris: Alph. Picard, 1889), 19.

such, but he also publicized his fidelity to his new mother, announcing that he undertook the mission out of gratitude for the "very great love" she had shown him.[53] There was a great deal of public theater associated with the enterprise: Louis's pronouncements of filial affection were accompanied by public consistories denouncing Charles of Durazzo and detailing the charges against Urban, called simply "Barthelemi" in Provence.[54] When galleys in the port of Marseille raised Louis's battle standard, the city was reportedly filled with cries of "Long live Pope Clement! Long live Madame, Queen Johanna! Long live Monseignour the Duke of Calabria, her son!"—a testament to the degree to which Clement and Louis succeeded in associating Johanna's fate with that of the Church and perpetuating the legal fiction that Louis was her son.[55]

While Louis and Clement readied their crusade, matters in Naples progressed rapidly. Johanna was soon beyond the aid of those in whom she had placed her trust. When Louis's forces left Carpentras on June 13, 1382, Charles was already comfortably established in his new realm.[56] He had spent the months Louis devoted to raising an army subduing the Regno, seeking reprisals against Johanna's followers and the Clementist clergy, who were quickly replaced by Urbanists.[57] Urban swiftly reasserted his hegemony, which he clearly understood as both temporal and religious; he redistributed the goods confiscated from Clementist clerics, and he made generous payments to his supporters as well as to Charles's.[58] Charles's victory was marked by a second coronation in Naples on November 25, 1381, at which time his wife, Margaret, and their young son, Ladislaus, were also crowned. Ladislaus

---

53. Jean le Fèvre, *Journal*, 1:14.

54. Ibid., 45.

55. Ibid., 29; cf. Valois, *La France et le Grand Schisme d'Occident*, 2:23. By contrast, the *Chronique romane* of Montpellier reports that the rioters cried, "Viva madama la reyna e papa Urba de Roma, e mueyra lantipapa de Fundis e totz los Frances," casting their discontent in nationalistic terms, as opposition to French interference, rather than to Johanna herself, to whom the chronicler represents her subjects as loyal. See Ferdinand Pegat, Eugène Thomas, and Desmazes, eds., *La Chronique Romane*, in *Thalamus Parvus: Le Petit Thalamus de Montpellier*, ed. De Saint.-Paul et al. (Montpellier: Société Archéologique de Montpellier, 1836), 397.

56. Léonard, *Les Angevins de Naples*, 466; Valois, *La France et le Grand Schisme d'Occident*, 2:38.

57. Valois, *La France et le Grand Schisme d'Occident*, 2:11–14; Fodale, *La Politica Napoletana di Urbano VI*, 65, n. 24. Fodale and Valois both follow the *Chronicon Siculum*, which reports that the two Clementist cardinals captured with Johanna were publicly humiliated in the square outside the Church of Santa Chiara, where they were forced to renounce Clement and burn their hats and mantles. Lower prelates were defrocked as well, and their garments consigned to the same fire (De Blasiis, *Chronicon Siculum*, 40).

58. Fodale, *La Politica Napoletana di Urbano VI*, 66.

was entitled duke of Calabria, identifying him as his father's successor.[59] Charles's kingship was thus well asserted and his posterity assured. He enjoyed the support of most of Italy and the subsidy of Johanna's longtime ally, Florence, which hailed his victory as an act of God and celebrated Johanna's capture with a solemn mass.[60]

Charles boasted all the trappings of kingship, his position within the Regno threatened only by Johanna's presence and the possibility that her supporters might attempt to restore her throne. Matters soon took a decisive turn in Charles's favor. On or near July 27, 1382 (the date given by Charles in the circular announcing the news), Johanna died in prison, leaving Charles, a Neapolitan born and raised, the uncontested monarch within the Regno, challenged only by an outsider whose claim must have seemed dubious to many.[61] Because she died excommunicate—at least in Urbanist eyes—Johanna was denied both Christian funeral rites and burial among her forebears in the church of Santa Chiara; the location of her grave is disputed. Although Johanna's body was displayed publicly in Santa Chiara, the tomb that she had intended for herself near those she had commissioned for Robert and Sancia went instead to her sister, Mary—the mother of Charles's wife, Margaret—an act that constituted a form of *damnatio memoriae*.[62] Mary's reburial in Johanna's tomb symbolized the legitimacy of the new line of Anjou-Durazzo and quite literally removed Johanna from the ranks of Naples's monarchs and from honor in public memory.

The cause of Johanna's death was immediately debated. Charles reported that she died of natural causes, but both Clementist and Urbanist sources insist that he murdered her. Louis of Anjou's mission was now framed as vengeance. His forces reached Aquila in late September 1382; the war for Johanna's throne began in earnest in October.[63] Both sides characterized the

---

59. Ibid., 67. Fodale points out that Charles's decision to designate his son as his successor at this early date was in direct contravention of his agreement with Urban, an early indicator of the autonomy Charles would assert as Naples's king. Cf. De Blasiis, *Chronicon Siculum*, 42–44.

60. Valois, *La France et le Grand Schisme d'Occident*, 2:31.

61. Léonard, *Les Angevins de Naples*, 467.

62. On Johanna's burial, see Émile G. Léonard, "La captivité et la mort de Jeanne Iʳᵉ de Naples," *Mélanges d'archéologie et d'histoire* 41 (1924): 65–67. Cf. Léonard, *Les Angevins de Naples*, 468, and Gaglione, *Donne e potere a Napoli*, 52. There is some scholarly confusion, largely owing to the destruction during World War II of many of the Angevin tombs, as to whether Johanna's sepulcher went to her mother, Marie of Valois (as Léonard says), or to her sister (as Gaglione claims). On the royal tombs in Santa Chiara, see Bruzelius, *The Stones of Naples*, 150–51, and Caroline Bruzelius and William Tronzo, *Medieval Naples: An Architectural and Urban History, 400–1400* (New York: Italica Press, 2011), 102–4.

63. Léonard, *Les Angevins de Naples*, 472.

struggle as a crusade, the rival claimants supported by the rival popes, each insistent on his sacred position as the Regno's suzerain. The war raged intermittently for decades, interrupted by Louis's death from gangrenous angina in 1384 and Charles's assassination in Hungary—whose throne he seized upon Louis of Hungary's death—in 1386, only to be continued by their wives, Marie of Blois (1345–1404) and Margaret of Durazzo (1347–1412), during their sons' minorities, and then again by those sons, Louis II of Anjou (d. 1417) and Ladislaus of Anjou-Durazzo (d. 1414). With the exception of brief periods during which the French Angevins gained control of the Regno, Johanna's realm remained divided, Provence under the dominion of Louis of Anjou's descendants and Naples under the house of Anjou-Durazzo, which retained its hegemony until shortly before the Regno fell to Aragon in 1442.

The Dynastic Politics of the "French" Royal Houses

Dynastic competition that predated the schism drove much of what followed Johanna's transfer of obedience. Papal politics became interwoven with the dynastic politics of the three "French" monarchies—those of France, Naples, and Hungary—and the purportedly religiously motivated struggle over Naples was in fact as rooted in ongoing competition for Johanna's throne as in pious sentiments. In order to understand Johanna's actions—particularly given the tendency of her contemporaries and later historians to describe them as privileging the French over the Italian—it is necessary to understand preexisting debates about the succession to Johanna and how they became entangled with the schism.

In the 1370s, the question of who would succeed Johanna became increasingly fraught. By law, Johanna, a childless monarch, should be succeeded by Mary's eldest eligible child, with sons preferred before daughters. Because Mary had only daughters, the kingdom would pass from a woman to a woman. Two of Mary's daughters were ineligible: Johanna of Durazzo's illicit marriage disqualified her, while her younger sister, Agnes, had renounced her rights to the throne when she married. The third sister, Clementia, died in 1363, making Mary's youngest daughter, Margaret of Durazzo, Johanna's heir.

Louis of Hungary, also childless, had not given up his plans for a unified Angevin kingdom, nor was he content to allow Naples's crown to pass from Johanna to Margaret, preferring instead that his closest eligible male relative should inherit both Hungary and the Regno. That heir was Charles of Durazzo, who had been resident at the Hungarian court since the 1360s. In

1370, Louis entitled Charles prince of Sclavonia and Croatia, titles custom-arily reserved for the heir to the Hungarian throne, thereby signaling that he would succeed him.[64]

Louis's plans for Charles were ambitious. In January 1370, Louis and Johanna negotiated the marriage of Charles, for whom Johanna had briefly cared after his father's death, to Margaret of Durazzo, his first cousin. The union appeared likely to unite Hungary and Naples and ensure that Louis's heir sat on the Neapolitan throne.[65] A contemporary French genealogy of the Angevin house—prepared for the watchful Charles V, who observed his cousins' negotiations with interest—commented that the marriage placed Johanna at risk but served Louis's interests, as Charles was "of his lineage and to his liking, because he ha[d] no children."[66] Charles and Margaret returned to Buda after their marriage, removing both from Johanna's influence and placing them under Louis's sway.[67] At the same time, the potential Angevin empire expanded: Louis succeeded his maternal uncle, Casimir III (1310–70), as king of Poland in late 1370.[68] Charles and Margaret stood poised to rule a realm that stretched from Provence to Albania and included all of the Regno, Hungary, and Poland, promising a new age for the dynasty.

Then the Hungarian dynastic outlook changed drastically. In 1370, Louis's queen, Elizabeth of Bosnia (ca. 1339–87), gave birth to a daughter, Catherine, who was followed by two more daughters, Maria (b. 1371) and Jadwiga (b. 1373).[69] Charles's imperial prospects evaporated. Louis, who had opposed Johanna's and Margaret's successions partially on the grounds that women should not inherit when eligible male relatives existed, found himself the protector of three daughters for whom he wanted kingdoms and whose interests he placed before those of Charles. He determined to divide the crowns of Poland and Hungary, and he once again set his sights on Naples. He accordingly revived his claims to the Neapolitan throne and declared Johanna a usurper. His lawyers worked to demonstrate his superior claims compared to those of Mary's daughters, arguing that direct descent from

---

64. Ibid., 429–30.

65. Ibid., 430; Lecacheux, *Lettres secrètes et curiales du Pape Urbain V*, 539, no. 3120 (Reg. Vat. 250, fol. 107r); cf. Cerasoli, "Urbano V e Giovanna I di Napoli," 624, n. 144.

66. L. Ovàry, "Negoziati tra il Re d'Ungheria e il Re di Franchia per la successione de Giovanna I. d'Angiò," *ASPN* 2 (1877): 152.

67. Léonard, *Les Angevins de Naples*, 430, n. 3.

68. Ibid., 443.

69. Ibid., 444.

Charles II placed Louis "closer [to the throne] than the daughters of the sister of . . . Queen Johanna."[70]

Louis's interests coincided with those of the French court, which had long desired Provence and began to assert a claim to Naples as well. Ironically, the Valois monarchy, which owed its crown to the so-called Salic law's prohibition of female succession, based its claim on descent from Charles II's daughter, Margaret of Anjou (d. 1299).[71] Even within the Valois family, there was competition for Johanna's lands. In 1374 and 1375, Louis of Anjou, taking advantage of his residence in Avignon and his active role in the crusade against the Visconti, sought to parlay papal favor into territorial gains and add both Provence and Majorca to his conquests, even as Charles V sought to secure the county for his younger son.[72] Louis had, in fact, been making military incursions into Provence since the 1360s, prompting Johanna to urge her subjects to resist temptations from French agents, warning them that the duke—identified as her enemy—would be disappointed in his "iniquitous intention."[73]

Hoping to protect his sons' interests, Charles V formed an alliance in 1374 with Louis of Hungary that promised to fulfill both monarchs' dynastic ambitions. The alliance enjoyed papal support: Urban V approved a plan to wed Louis of Hungary's niece to Charles's youngest brother, while Gregory XI supported a plan to place a French prince on the Hungarian throne as the husband of one of Louis's daughters.[74] That same year, Louis and Charles began to discuss a marriage between Catherine of Hungary and Charles's son, Louis of Valois (b. 1372), with the Regno and Provence as Catherine's dowry (a stipulation that did not receive papal backing). That August, they signed a treaty that betrothed Catherine and Louis, with the expectation that they would one day rule Johanna's realm.[75]

Margaret of Durazzo remained an obstacle to these plans. In December 1375, the French king and Hungarian representatives drew up an accord concerning the "recuperation" (*recuperatione*) of the Neapolitan

---

70. Ovàry, "Negoziati tra il Re d'Ungheria e il Re di Franchia," 145–46: "dictus dominus rex Vngarie esset proximior quam filie sororis dicte domine regine Johanne."

71. Léonard, *Les Angevins de Naples*, 445.

72. Ibid. Margaret married Charles of Valois in 1290; their son became Philip VI, the first Valois king of France.

73. "dux ipse in sua iniqua intencionem falletis." Letter written by Johanna against Louis of Anjou, June 25, 1368, AMM, AA 140 1.

74. Léonard, *Les Angevins de Naples*, 446.

75. Jarry, *La vie politique de Louis de France*, 7–8.

throne.[76] Among other things, it stipulated that Margaret should, with her husband's approval, renounce her claims in favor of Louis of Hungary, "who ha[d] fostered them" ("qui eos nuttrivit") and would "splendidly" compensate them.[77] Should Louis's line fail, the kingdom would revert to any male heir of Margaret and Charles of Durazzo. In the absence of a male heir, the Church would appoint a suitable monarch.[78] Interestingly, the accord ignores the traditional Angevin provision for female succession, although presumably Louis's daughters would have been permitted to succeed him; the document states that at Johanna's death, Louis or his heir should succeed her "without impediment."[79]

In 1378, the dynastic map changed again. Catherine of Hungary died, as did the impending marital alliance between France and Hungary. Before the schism, Louis of Valois might have married another Hungarian princess, but religious politics intervened. For Naples, the most significant outcome of Catherine's death was that Louis of Hungary once again promoted Charles of Durazzo as heir to the Neapolitan throne, while continuing to favor Maria and Jadwiga as his heirs in Hungary and Poland. Charles, suddenly assured again of inheriting a kingdom, was determined to protect his interests. He and Louis of Hungary jointly championed the Roman pope with the understanding that their allegiance bought them Naples.[80]

The schism also opened a new opportunity to obtain Naples and Provence either for Louis of Anjou or for Charles V's heirs. Like Charles of Durazzo, Louis of Anjou acted quickly. Adherence to Clement VII furthered his ambitions. When the news of Clement's election reached him in Toulouse, before Charles V acknowledged that he was aware of the newly proclaimed pope, Louis commanded his subjects to abjure Urban, ordering *Te Deums* sung in the city's churches and a solemn mass in the cathedral to honor Clement VII.[81] From that time forward, he was Clement's foremost supporter, sending ambassadors into Italy ahead of his brother's and making overtures on Clement's behalf to others who might support him.[82] He remained firmly committed to Clement even as he faced opposition in France after he became regent for his nephew, Charles VI, in 1380. He took a firm

---

76. Ovàry, "Negoziati tra il Re d'Ungheria e il Re di Franchia," 126–31, at 127. Cf. E. Miskolczy, "Le pretese di Lodovico il Grande sul trono di Sicilia," *Samnium* 2 (1929): 50–82.

77. Ovàry, "Negoziati tra il Re d'Ungheria e il Re di Franchia," 128.

78. Ibid., 129–30.

79. Ibid., 130.

80. Léonard, *Les Angevins de Naples*, 459.

81. Valois, *La France et le Grand Schisme d'Occident*, 1:151–52.

82. Ibid., 154.

stand against the University of Paris, which advocated compromise, while Louis—who needed Clement to triumph—insisted that Urban's forced abdication was the only suitable end to the schism.[83]

Among those Louis approached as a potential ally was Johanna, who openly regarded him as her enemy. She had little reason to align herself with Louis, and her eventual adoption of him was in direct contravention of her Provençal subjects' wishes and interests. Yet his role as papal champion prompted Louis to court Johanna's favor and position himself—her former adversary—as her committed ally. He addressed complimentary letters to her, praising her for her "fruitful labors" on behalf of the Church and chastising Francesco del Balzo (then rebelling in Provence), against whom Louis offered both righteous indignation and military aid. He stressed their shared blood—repeatedly calling Johanna his "beloved kinswoman"—and interests.[84] He likewise made overtures to Otto of Brunswick.[85] Conveniently forgetting that he had himself recently menaced Johanna's territory, Louis styled himself the defender of her sovereign rights. The generosity of his gesture covered its pragmatism: Louis needed Johanna's friendship for himself and for Clement, to whom Johanna's loyalty was vital.

Louis's efforts were not without their price. Even before his adoption by Johanna, Louis's reward, should Clement triumph, was to be a kingdom. By a bull of April 17, 1379, Clement created the (purely hypothetical) Kingdom of Adria for Louis, cobbled together from Church lands then under Urban's control. If realized, Adria would have incorporated Ravenna, Ferrara, Bologna, the Romagna, the province of Massa Trabaria, the March of Ancona, Perugia, Todi, and the duchy of Spoleto.[86] It was in effect a second kingdom on the Neapolitan model; indeed, the bull that created Adria was copied directly from that which bestowed Sicily on Charles I. Clement thus created an imaginary papal island in Tuscany and the region around Rome, encompassed by loyal vassal kingdoms, Naples to the south and Adria to the north.[87]

In the struggle between Clement and Urban, Johanna found herself confronted not only by two rival popes but also by two papal champions. On the

---

83. R. N. Swanson, *Universities, Academics and the Great Schism* (Cambridge: Cambridge University Press, 1979), 67.

84. Bibl. Barberini, MS XXX 174, fol. 8r, cited in Valois, *La France et le Grand Schisme d'Occident*, 1:156, n. 1, n. 2 and 181, n. 1.

85. Bibl. Barberini, MS XXX174, fol. 10v, cited in Valois, *La France et le Grand Schisme d'Occident*, 1:182, n. 1.

86. Valois, *La France et le Grand Schisme d'Occident*, 1:167.

87. Ibid., 168

one hand, she faced French interests that jeopardized Provence and threatened to materially alter the balance of power in Italy, while on the other, she faced a joint Italian and Hungarian threat to her crown and kingdom. On the face of things, Johanna had little reason to throw her lot in with Clement and Louis. She and Robert of Geneva shared a long-standing animosity dating back to the struggle over Johanna of Durazzo's marriage (see chapter 3). There was little love lost between them, as Brancaccio noted afterward.[88] Furthermore, at least according to Brancaccio, Johanna had wished to see Pietro Corsini, rather than Robert, pope: it had been two Italian prelates who approached her regarding Urban's illegitimacy, and she had, apparently, hoped to see a third wear the papal tiara. There was, thus, nothing to suggest that she would favor an ultramontane pope or that she would be disposed to cooperate with Louis. Her vaunted French descent notwithstanding, her interests and allegiances were primarily Italian.

For reasons that remain uncertain—whether pragmatic, personal, or religious—Johanna awarded her obedience not to her former subject, Bartolomeo Prignano, but to her old enemy, Robert of Geneva. The die cast, Johanna was forced to make the best of the situation. Menaced by Charles of Durazzo, she had little choice but to select a new heir and trade her kingdom for protection from Charles. The most logical choice was Louis of Anjou. Louis and Clement faced a pressing need to protect Johanna—the Regno was of the utmost importance in the struggle for the papacy. Clement subsidized Johanna's defense, sending her 35,000 florins in the summer of 1379.[89] Louis did his part too, addressing her, as Noël Valois puts it, "numerous compliments from the month of July [1379], accompanying these with flattering praise for . . . her husband" while assuring her that his forces were formally engaged to aid her.[90] Most significantly, he offered material aid in exchange for her entire realm, including Provence, after her death. In return for the adoption he proposed, he promised armed galleys, liberal financial assistance and military aid, on-the-spot defense of Provence, freedom from his interference in government, and a guarantee to honor whatever provisions Johanna made for Otto after her death.[91]

---

88. Deposition of archbishop of Cosenza, Paris, Bibliothèque nationale de France, MS fonds latin 11745, fol. 43r: "Et scit bene quod domina regina non diligebat nimis istum dominum Clementum quando erat cardinalis. Ymo fuerat aliqua dissenssio inter predictam dominam et dominum cardinalem Bononiensem [i.e., Guy de Boulogne], avunculum istius" (cited in Valois, *La France et le Grand Schisme d'Occident*, 1:159, n. 5).

89. Valois, *La France et le Grand Schisme d'Occident*, 1:179 and n. 6.

90. Ibid., 181.

91. Ibid., 184 and n. 1. Valois cites Paris, Archives nationales, J 375, n°5; J 512, n° 31; J 848, n° 3.

Johanna acquiesced. She did so with the express approval of Clement VII, who had issued bulls on February 1, 1380, claiming that he had learned that Johanna wished to console herself for her childlessness by adopting Louis and stating that he would override Naples's laws of inheritance out of consideration for her.[92] The adoption—quickly ratified by Clement[93]—was framed exactly as such. Indeed, the French royal chronicle, the *Grandes Chroniques de France*, represents Louis as nobly disinterested, agreeing to the adoption only because of Johanna's need for an heir and to the invasion of Naples out of a desire to serve Clement.[94] Louis began self-consciously styling himself Johanna's loving son despite the fact that the two probably never met and their relationship was purely legal.

Thus, the allegiances between the popes and their champions formed along dynastic lines. Johanna's seeming preference for the "French" over the "Italian"—for Louis over Charles—was an artifact of dynastic politics that coalesced around her. Even before the schism, her cousins had schemed to place either a French prince or Charles of Durazzo on Johanna's throne, regardless of her preference. The schism accelerated the process by which the candidates were chosen and pitted Charles and Louis against one another, leaving Johanna caught between. Having chosen Clement, she had little choice but to also choose Louis. Her choice of pope, made early, before the splintering of Europe, had ramifications that she may not have foreseen, resulting in the division of her realm and in the parallel division of her public persona into French (or Clementist) and Italian (or Urbanist) figures.

The Clementist Johanna

According to Clementist commentators, Johanna's decision to transfer her obedience to Clement stemmed purely from religious conviction. This was the explanation Johanna herself offered. In a letter to Duke Stephen III of Bavaria (r. 1375–1413) dated June 5, 1380, written in response to Stephen's offer to help her reconcile with Urban, she explained that she had laid aside her personal inclinations to adhere to the counsel of theologians, prelates, and canonists that the true pope was Clement VII, the man elected "unanimously"

---

92. Valois, *La France et le Grand Schisme d'Occident*, 1:184. Valois cites Paris, Archives nationales, J 375, n° 4; J 512 n⁰ˢ 31, 31; J 848, n° 3.

93. Clement's confirmation of Louis's adoption is ADBR, B 150.

94. Paulin Paris, ed., *Les Grandes Chroniques de France, selon que elles sont conservées en l'Église de Saint-Denis en France* (Paris: Techener, 1838), 6:477.

by the cardinals.[95] Her argument is ecclesiological, locating ultimate authority in the cardinals and the body of the universal Church rather than in the person of the pope himself. Given the choice between Urban and the Church more broadly construed, her choice was clear. Her decision, as she presented it, had far less, therefore, to do with personal or political considerations than with commitment to the teachings of the Church and the guidance of those to whom she looked as its representatives. Her transfer of obedience was, from this perspective, an expression of her filial obedience to the Church—here identified as the universal Church, rather than the pope.[96]

Added to these considerations, however, was indignation with both Urban and Charles of Durazzo. In a letter to Rinaldo Orsini, count of Tagliacozzo, written in August 1380, after she learned that Charles was hiring Florentine bandits, Johanna avers that she is prepared to fight and has "long known of [Charles's] perverse disposition."[97] In her letter to Stephen, however, Johanna expresses astonishment and outrage with Charles, whom she describes as "ungrateful and unmindful of his faith and the kindnesses he received," recalling her care for him after his father's death. The letter speaks of her sense of betrayal and conviction in the moral rectitude of her stance; she insists upon her trust in "the goodness of God, and in the justice of our position and the loyalty of our kingdom."[98]

Johanna's argument echoes that of the Clementists in general. In a bull of October 1378 announcing his election, Clement likewise insists on the unanimous voice of the cardinals. He describes the riotous behavior of the Roman populace, which forced the cardinals to elect the "intruder," Urban.[99] Clement's election, on the other hand, was the result not of mob coercion but of sober consideration by the assembled cardinals, gathered together as one (in unum) to elect a pastor for the widowed Church.[100] It was the product of

95. Bologna, Biblioteca comunale dell'Archiginnasio, MS B 1145, fols. 19r–20v. Valois cites and provides a brief description of the letter. Cf. Valois, La France et le Grand Schisme d'Occident, 1:78, n. 2; 178, n. 3; 2:8, n. 2.

96. That Johanna was inclined to view the Church this way was suggested by the Dominican inquisitor Moschini in his 1380 deposition, when he stated that Johanna awaited confirmation from the cardinals before celebrating Urban's election.

97. The letter is Archivio Lante, B. 77, an edition of which is published in Pietro Egidi, "La scrittura segreta di Giovanna I di Napoli in una sua lettera dell'A. 1380," ASPN 31 (1906): 369, 377.

98. Bologna, Biblioteca comunale dell'Archiginnasio, MS B 1145, fol. 20v. Cf. Valois, La France et le Grand Schisme d'Occident, 2:8, n. 2.

99. AMM, AA 141 2.

100. Ibid.: "predicti fratres nostri congregati in unum ut viduate ecclesie de pastore ydoneo providerent."

consensus, arrived at not through fear but by reasoned, informed deliberation that gave Clement's election validity that Urban's lacked.

The central motif in the Clementist story of Johanna's conversion was her unflinching obedience to the Church. Peter, cardinal of Vernio, reported when deposed that Johanna was "assured by [Cardinal Orsini] that [Urban] was not pope and that the Holy See was vacant"—an assurance that she accepted.[101] Brancaccio later claimed that the embassy he and Orsini undertook to Naples was at Johanna's invitation. He testified that Johanna's anxiety about Urban's rumored illegitimacy prompted her to summon Orsini, "whom the lady queen trusted greatly," to ask him whether the rumors regarding Urban's election were true.[102]

> Then this lady queen . . . said to [Orsini] . . . that she should be told whether this archbishop of Bari were not the pope, and that she was asking him that he tell her the truth. And the cardinal declared under oath, laying his hand on his breast, that he truly was not pope. And the queen also received the cardinal's hand, and in her hand he declared to her and swore that what he said was true.[103]

Here again, ecclesiological argument predominates: Her conscience troubled, Johanna turned to the cardinals as the voice of authority. Brancaccio presents her concerns as the result of pious anxiety about the state of the Church, for which she felt responsibility. The double oath she required Orsini to swear underscores her concern with the truth, highlighting her desire to know and be guided by it.

The Clementist explanation for Johanna's conversion thus hinged on ecclesiological argument. According to Clementist accounts, Johanna's anger and sense of betrayal followed her decision to support Clement and stemmed not from the danger presented by Urban and Charles—whom she insisted she did not fear—but from her former ward's shameless ingratitude after her pious decision. Her transfer of obedience was an act of faith, rather than self-interest, while her campaign against Charles and Urban was a defense of her sovereign rights, as well as those of the Church, which their actions usurped.

---

101. Testimony of Peter, cardinal of Vernio, in Baluze, *Vitae paparum Avenionensium*, 2:619–20.

102. Testimony of Niccolò Brancaccio, in Baluze, *Vitae paparum Avenionensium*, 2:620: "domina regina confidebat valde de eo."

103. Ibid.: "Tunc ipsa domina regina . . . dixit predicto cardinali, . . . quod dicebatur sibi quod ille Barensis non erat papa, et quod rogabat eum quod ipse diceret sibi veritatem. Et ipse cardinalis firmavit sub juramento, ponendo manum ad pectus, quod vere non erat papa. Et regina ultra illud recepit manum cardinalis, et in sua manu firmavit sibi cardinalis et asseruit istud quod dicebat esse verum."

Johanna's Role in the Schism

The Clementist cardinals gathered testimony in Avignon in 1380 and 1386, seeking to understand the schism, including Johanna's behavior. Their explanations for Johanna's transfer of obedience stressed that she had no personal reason to reject Urban. Indeed, in a deposition of May 17, 1380, Brancaccio insisted that before the schism, Johanna "was a good friend of [Prignano's] and loved him greatly."[104] Brancaccio was with Urban when the newly elected pontiff received money and troops from Johanna; Urban's gratitude prompted him to say that "he had two masters, namely, his lady the queen and his lord the cardinal of Pampeluna."[105] Urban was supposedly so sure of Johanna's support that he sent John Lemosini, canon of Bazas, to Naples with the letters announcing his election, promising John that he would be amply rewarded by the delighted queen.[106]

Once pope, however, Urban reportedly revealed an evil character previously hidden. Among his sins was high-handed behavior toward monarchs, over whom he claimed extraordinary terrestrial jurisdiction. Brancaccio reported that Urban demanded that the French king and other sovereigns appear before him in Rome, asserting that he could rule their lands better than they.[107] In addition, Urban's former secretary and bodyguard, Stephen de Millarisis, testified that Urban had so little respect for kingship that he often sent forged letters—bearing skillful imitations of the seals of various kings—in praise of himself, appropriating the voices of Christendom's leaders to extol his virtues.[108] This attitude extended even to Johanna. Urban's promises to John Lemosini revealed that he believed he could dispose of the Regno's goods as he chose. Such reports suggest that he saw his jurisdiction over Naples as complete and Johanna merely as his vassal.

As the division within the Church deepened, so too did the gulf separating Johanna—identified with the true Church—from Urban. Stephen de Millarisis testified in 1386 that Urban's altered behavior drove him to Naples, where his true loyalties lay:

---

104. Baluze, *Vitae paparum Avenionensium*, 2:778.

105. Deposition of Cardinal Nicholas of Cosenza (Niccolò Brancaccio), in Seidlmayer, *Die Anfänge des grossen abendländischen Schismas*, 245–46.

106. Deposition of Johannes Lemosini, Summer 1386, in Seidlmayer, *Die Anfänge des grossen abendländischen Schismas*, 310–13.

107. Deposition of Cardinal Nicholas of Cosenza (Niccolò Brancaccio), in Seidlmayer, *Die Anfänge des grossen abendländischen Schismas*, 246: "Item dicebat publice: Pereant michi reges Francie et alii, quia melius regit ista quam aliquis ipsorum!"

108. Deposition of Stephen de Millarisis, in Seidlmayer, *Die Anfänge des grossen abendländischen Schismas*, 314.

And seeing this same Bartolomeo being imbued with every vice and stripped of all conscience and virtues, ever committing enormities and ever accumulating more wicked sins, I forsook him and went to my natural lady, Queen Johanna.[109]

The theme of seeking refuge with Johanna appears as well in the testimony of Peter Flandrin, cardinal deacon of Saint Eustace, who described the efforts of the cardinals to persuade Urban to agree to a general council. When Urban refused and no compromise could be reached, Peter says, the cardinals retreated "in total discord," many to sanctuary "within the dominion of the most serene queen of Sicily."[110] Opposition between Johanna and Urban thus came to represent the struggle within the Church. Johanna was a safe haven, her pious obedience to the Church and uncompromising fidelity providing stark contrast to Urban's "enormities" and finally necessitating the break between them.

The greatest proof of Johanna's obedience was, of course, her captivity and death. While she was still imprisoned, Clement evoked the fight for her liberty to rally support. He held her up as a beacon of faith and constancy, contrasting her virtue to Charles's and Urban's wickedness. In a bull granting indulgences to the Church of St. Victor, Clement praised the people of Marseille for their loyalty:

> They devote their constant, unshaken fidelity to our most dear daughter in Christ, the illustrious queen of Sicily, their temporal mistress. They have stood firm up to now and persist in efforts for the liberation of this queen, who unhappily is held captive under the tyrannous savagery of perfidious schismatics, which we have recalled, groaning, with bitterness of heart.[111]

Johanna was thus a figurehead for the Clementist cause. The loyalty she inspired in her devoted subjects could be equated with loyalty to the Church, while Charles personified the "perfidious schismatics" who exercised tyranny not only over the Church's faithful, beleaguered daughter, but also over the Church itself.

---

109. Testimony of Stephen de Millarisis, in Seidlmayer, *Die Anfänge des grossen abendländischen Schismas*, 314.

110. Baluze, *Vitae paparum Avenionensium*, 2:633. Cf. Franz Plazidus Bliemetzrieder, *Literarische Polemik zu beginn des grossen abendländischen Schismas* (Vienna: F. Tempsky, 1910), 88; Ullmann, *The Origins of the Great Schism*, 59.

111. AMM, AA 5, fols. 2v–3r, at fol. 2v.

Once dead, Johanna became a Clementist martyr. There was, in Clementist accounts, little doubt that she had been murdered. Official proclamation of her death and her funeral were delayed until 1384, largely to ensure that sentiment in Provence remained favorable to Louis of Anjou (who failed to keep his promise to rescue her).[112] When, however, Clement did publicly announce her death, he ordered a mass—preached by Brancaccio—in honor of the dead queen, "murdered by Charles of Durazzo."[113] Cities across Provence held their own funerals that December; a diarist in Arles described the service in the Church of St. Trophime, where there was "a beautiful sermon and a solemn mass" attended by the city's population, its people dressed in black and carrying candles.[114]

Clement returned to Johanna's death in a 1385 bull addressed to Marseille's vicar and syndic. His description of her murder set the tone for future Clementist treatments of it: He stated that Johanna had been "inhumanly killed" by the "wicked" Charles, whom he abused as a "faithless traitor" and labeled "a second Nero" and "most evil matricide . . . to be abhorred by all men."[115] Nero's barbarity would have been well known to Clement's intended audience.[116] *The Golden Legend*'s life of St. Peter records the rumor that Nero's mother, Agrippina, died as the result of her son's unnatural desire to see the interior of her uterus.[117] Clement's bull compares Charles's treatment of Johanna—called his mother, in a deliberate overstatement—with Nero's depraved assault on the womb that bore him, as, by association, with his persecution of Christians and Christ's first vicar, St. Peter. Charles's crime was thus double: Clement's equation of Charles to Nero was a reminder

---

112. The official records for the funeral date from 1384, as do most chronicle reports of Johanna's death. The *Chronique romane* of Montpellier says that the news of Johanna's death reached Provence in 1383, the earliest date recorded for the announcement, although the chronicler appears to have been writing from memory (Pegat, Thomas, and Desmazes, "La Chronique Romane," 408). It is unclear when people in Provence actually learned of Johanna's death, although the municipal council in Marseille believed her to be alive as late as January 27, 1383 (council deliberations, AMM, BB 29, fol. 245). Cf. Léonard, "La captivité et la mort de Jeanne Iʳᵉ de Naples," 63, n. 1.

113. Jean le Fèvre, *Journal*, 105; cf. Baluze, *Vitae paparum Avenionensium*, 2:779.

114. Paris, Bibliothèque nationale de France, MS fonds français 4317, fol. 9r–v.

115. Bull of June 16, 1385, asking the people of Marseille to remain loyal to Louis of Anjou's son, Louis II, during his minority, AMM, AA 65 6.

116. Agrippina's murder was notorious among medieval audiences familiar with *The Golden Legend*, as with descriptions of Nero in works like Boccaccio's *De casibus virorum illustrium* (book VII) and *De mulieribus claris* (chapter XCII), although Boccaccio characterizes the murder as a politically expedient measure that freed Nero from Agrippina's influence.

117. See "Saint Peter, Apostle," in Jacobus de Voragine, *The Golden Legend—Readings on the Saints*, trans. William Granger Ryan (Princeton: Princeton University Press, 1993), 1:340–50, at 347.

that the emperor had attacked not only his own flesh and blood but also the Church, in the person of the first pope.

Johanna far more greatly resembles a martyred saint in the pope's description of her, however, than she does Agrippina. Employing hagiographic language, Clement insists that Johanna should be remembered not only for the "detestable way" in which she had been murdered, but also—and especially—for

> her ineffable ways, which made her among all illustrious women of the ages like a rose, surrounded by thorns, yet emitting fragrance; she spread her inimitable odors of sweetness over us and the Roman Church, just as over you and all her other subjects.[118]

Like an uncorrupted saint, Johanna spread sweet fragrance over the faithful. And, like the early martyrs, she suffered persecution, not only by Charles *qua* Nero but also by the "remarks and whispers of detractors, who freely pursue lies and flee from the truth, in order to sow scandal."[119] She was a martyr to the schism and the slander of her opponents, and Clement insists that despite her tribulations, she remained a paragon among women. The bull was meant to demonize Charles—whose evil is compounded by the saintly virtue Clement ascribes to Johanna—and inspire outrage against him, but it also re-created Johanna as a symbol of the Clementist cause. To that end, Clement describes her not as a sovereign queen valiantly struggling against heretics but as a passive victim, characterized not by valor but by sweetness and significant for her endurance of suffering rather than for the strength of her resistance. She embodied the *paciencia* of the late medieval saint, purified and feminized by having her power and influence stripped from her.

That Johanna had been cruelly murdered became a commonplace in Provençal and French histories of the period. In Provence in particular—where strife between Urbanist and Clementist forces continued until 1387—Johanna was an important symbol. Her murder validated not only the new Angevins' campaign against their adversaries but also the Clementist struggle. Her adoptive family took up the story of her murder and wielded it as a rhetorical weapon in their efforts to assert their legitimacy in Provence and their right to the Regno. They, too, described Johanna's death as matricide. Angevin propaganda transformed Charles into a "treacherous, impious . . . most ungrateful traitor, a notorious violator of fidelity and faith," characterized

---

118. AMM, AA 65 6.
119. Ibid.

by "cruel impiety" compounded by "horrible ingratitude and abominable cruelty," whose perfidy was such that it could never be forgiven, nor could peace ever be made with him.[120] Louis and his family thus linked Johanna's murder to Charles's transgression against the Church. This allowed Clement and Louis to represent their fight as one against active, palpable evil, re-creating Johanna as a murdered innocent whose demise exposed their opponents' wickedness. They used her death to frame their fight as a battle between good and evil in terms to which Johanna's subjects would respond, tied to and yet outside of the realm of ecclesiology. The assassination of an innocent woman, not to mention a reigning queen, provided an ideological construct around which to base their attacks on their enemies.

Johanna in Clementist Chronicles

It fell to chroniclers to record and interpret the schism's beginning for posterity. The descriptions of Johanna and stories of her death propagated by Clement and his supporters coalesced in the *Chroniques* of Jean Froissart (1337–1410). In earlier annals of the period penned by authors with Clementist sympathies, Johanna is an important, if somewhat vague, figure. In the *Grandes Chroniques de France*, she is the first person, after the cardinals, to recognize Clement as pope.[121] The portion of the chronicle dedicated to Charles V's reign closes with Louis of Anjou's adoption and mission to rescue Johanna, her fate unknown.[122] Likewise, in the *Chronique romane* of Montpellier, Johanna appears as a supporter of Clement VII, on whose behalf Louis, having become "her first-born son" agrees to reclaim the Regno from Charles of Durazzo and "that Bartolomeo . . . calling himself pope."[123]

Froissart, whose chronicle provides a syncretic transregional historical narrative of the period, built on the foundation laid by Clement and Louis and by other chroniclers, transforming Johanna into a tragic heroine. He embroidered her story with magic and intrigue and portrayed her as the embodiment of chivalrous queenship, the equal of any noble, doomed damsel conjured by writers of Arthurian romance. Unlike the authors of the *Grandes Chroniques* or *Chronique romane*, he told Johanna's story as a coherent tale, centered on the events leading to her death and Louis's efforts to recapture Naples.

---

120. Letter of Marie of Blois against Charles of Durazzo, 1385, AMM, AA 141 5.
121. Paris, *Grandes Chroniques*, 6:446.
122. Ibid., 477.
123. Pegat, Thomas, and Desmazes, "La Chronique Romane," 404.

Johanna's role in Froissart's chronicle differs from that she plays elsewhere. He represents Charles V and his brothers as the first to recognize Clement and places Johanna on a list of other supporters behind the king of Spain, the count of Savoy, and the ruler of Milan.[124] Louis of Anjou is Froissart's hero, and Johanna's story adds depth and color to his. Froissart endows Louis with clairvoyant insight that might have averted the schism altogether, had Gregory XI heeded his warning that, in going to Rome, he went "into a country and among people by whom [he was] little loved," abandoning France, "the fountain of faith and the land where the Church has the greatest voice and more excellence than anywhere in the world."[125] Froissart's Louis even predicts the unrest that led to Urban's election:

> If you die there—which is very likely, as your physicians tell me—the Romans, who are terrible and traitors, will be the lords and masters of all the cardinals, and they will make a pope to their liking by force.[126]

He thus emerges as an ideal prince, one whose excellence derives from his French blood and is expressed in his sage counsel and concern for the welfare of the Church.

Johanna's story begins in earnest soon after. Finding herself without an heir and menaced by Hungary, Johanna bestows all of her lands on Clement to give to "a high prince . . . of the kingdom of France, who had the strength necessary against those who wished her death, who descended from the kingdom of Hungary."[127] The struggle for her kingdom is thus a national one: French blood is correlated with righteousness and is prerequisite for inheritance in Naples. Humbling herself before Clement, Johanna confides all of her secrets to him, including recounting the final words said to her by her father, whom Froissart calls King Louis of Sicily:

> My beautiful daughter, you are the heir to many riches and great lands, and I believe that many great lords will seek to have you for a wife for the magnificent heritage and goods that you hold. Take care to marry a lord great enough to have the power to hold you and your heritage in peace. And if it should be that God wills that you should have no heir

124. Jean Froissart, *Les Chroniques de Sire Jean Froissart, qui traitent des merveilleuses emprises, nobles aventures et faits d'armes advenus en son temps en France, Angleterre, Bretaigne, Bourgogne, Escosse, Espaigne, Portingal et ès autres parties*, ed. J. A. C. Buchon (Paris: Desrez, 1837), 2:60.

125. Ibid., 21.

126. Ibid.

127. Ibid., 61.

of your body, place all of your holdings in the hand of whomever is then pope; because King Robert, my father, on his deathbed so charged me as well—so I charge you, my beautiful daughter, and so discharge my oath.[128]

Froissart thus establishes Johanna's adoption of Louis as part of her queenly duty, the fulfillment of an oath and in keeping with royal law. He eschews the fiction of maternal and filial affection insisted on by Louis and Clement. Louis is not Johanna's choice, nor the pragmatic solution to the situation in which she found herself, but Clement's selection in Johanna's time of need—the choice of wisdom and right, conditioned by Louis's French blood.

Johanna goes on to give Clement a full rendition of her life—one that differs from her true history in interesting particulars, many of which are likely by design. In Froissart's tale, Johanna succeeds not her grandfather but her father, with little question that she is his legitimate successor. After his death, "with the consent of the nobles of Sicily and of Naples," she married Andrew of Hungary. The union produced no heirs, "because he died young in Aix-en-Provence." Her second husband was Charles, prince of Taranto, with whom she had a daughter before Louis of Hungary—angered by his brother's death—went to war against Charles, whom he captured and imprisoned in Hungary, where he died. Her third marriage, to James of Majorca, was also arranged by agreement with the nobles of her kingdom. It too ended unhappily, when, despite her entreaties and offers to maintain him "in such a state as he wished," James insisted on reconquering his kingdom.[129] Johanna begged him to seek Charles V's help, but James did not heed her and died. At the same time, Johanna appealed to Charles to send "a noble man of his blood" to Naples to marry her daughter so that her lands would not be left without an heir.[130] Charles complied, sending his cousin, Robert of Artois.

Widowed yet again, Johanna married Otto of Brunswick, drawing the ire of Charles of Durazzo, who anticipated that Johanna would wish Otto to rule after her death. Charles attacked, trapping and besieging Johanna and Otto

in the Castel dell'Ovo by enchantment, so that it seemed to us in the castle that the sea was so high that it must cover us. We were in

---

128. Ibid., 62.
129. Ibid.
130. Ibid., 63.

that hour so consternated and so frightened that we four gave our-
selves over to my lord Charles . . . to save our lives. He held us in
prison—myself and my husband, my daughter and her husband—and
it so happened that my daughter and her husband died. Afterward, by
treaty, we were delivered, while all of Apulia and Calabria remained
in his control; and he intends to succeed to Naples, to Sicily, and to
Provence and seeks alliances everywhere. And he strives to the right
of the Church as though I were dead. . . . Which is why, Holy Father,
I wish to acquit myself before God and before you, as before the souls
of my predecessors.[131]

Johanna then renews her appeal to Clement to accept her lands and give
them to a worthy prince.

Froissart deemphasizes Johanna's power and political importance while
simultaneously softening and feminizing her. Some of his errors are surely
the product of faulty information—such as his misnaming of Louis of
Taranto—but others appear calculated to frame his tale as a celebration of
French blood, and particularly of Louis of Anjou. His Johanna is not a sovereign eager to protect her position—she recognizes her limitations, abdicates,
and steps aside to allow Clement and Louis to care for her kingdom (as her
husbands had earlier done). Froissart also removes the stigma of childlessness
from his heroine. Whereas Johanna's three children died young, Froissart
gives her a daughter who lived to adulthood and would have succeeded
her, but for Charles's cruelty. This is not pure invention—Johanna of Durazzo married Robert of Artois in 1376, and they remained loyal to Johanna
during the schism. Both died in the Castel dell'Ovo—although in 1387,
considerably after the elder Johanna. Froissart, looking back at events from
the distance of some years, re-created the historical Johanna of Durazzo as
Johanna's daughter to suit the exigencies of his narrative.

Froissart's liberties with history make Johanna a maternal figure, presenting her adoption of Louis as necessary because of recent bereavement, rather
than as consolation for childlessness. The death of her daughter in prison
lends Johanna an air of tragedy. Indeed, Froissart's Charles is doubly monstrous, having not only deposed Johanna but also killed the legitimate heir
to her throne. His power in Naples comes through the abuse and deaths
of helpless women. Furthermore, portraying Johanna of Durazzo as Johanna's daughter allows Froissart to emphasize Naples's reverence for and
dependence on French blood, which, in Froissart's history, is endowed with

131. Ibid.

a natural, recognized superiority. Froissart accordingly obscures the political expedients that drove Johanna to adopt Louis, whom, significantly, he presents as completely divorced from the proceedings. His Louis is no opportunist. He lacks cupidity or self-interest and is prompted to reconquer Naples only from a heroic desire to assist a vulnerable, disenfranchised woman.

In the interest of making Johanna femininely weak and innocent, Froissart glosses over or ignores portions of her biography that would have been well known. By insisting that she inherited her kingdom from her father, he removes any implication that Johanna might hold a dubious claim to the throne—thus obscuring any rights that either Louis of Hungary or Charles of Durazzo might assert. Similarly, no mention is made of Andrew of Hungary's murder, although the chronicle mentions Louis of Hungary's invasion, establishing precedent for the Hungarian menace to Naples. Johanna's rumored role in Andrew's death—like her rumored adulteries—is omitted. Froissart also locates Andrew's death in Aix-en-Provence, which enhances Johanna's ties to Provence.

Significantly, Froissart depicts the first Neapolitan-Hungarian war as waged between Johanna's husband and Louis of Hungary, removing Johanna from the conflict entirely. Read against the deathbed counsel of her father that she should marry a man strong enough to hold her and her kingdom, it appears that Froissart was determined to represent Johanna as sovereign in blood but not in power, allowing her husbands—two of whom, we are told, were chosen by her nobles—to rule in her stead. His Johanna is no virago and no she-wolf. Her life is filled with tragedy—war, widowhood, bereavement—encountered in the course of following her father's final directives, to which she continues to adhere in offering her kingdom to Clement.

Like other Clementists, Froissart stresses Johanna's obedience to and reverence for the Church, and he presents the Neapolitan monarchy as absolutely dependent upon the pope. He represents both Johanna and Louis as loyal papal servants. Their shared French blood binds them together, and Froissart draws attention to it, having Clement swear to Johanna to find her "an heir of your blood, noble, powerful, and strong enough to resist all who want to harm him."[132] Louis, the embodiment of chivalry, is the perfect choice, and he promptly promises to aid her:

> The duke of Anjou, who always sought high lordships and high honors, took the gifts to himself most magnificently and accepted them for himself and for his heirs. And he told the pope that he would go

---

132. Ibid.

in strength from that place as soon as possible, in order to combat all nuisances to the Queen of Naples.[133]

A man of his word, Louis travels to Naples, where Johanna has died and Charles claims to be king. Louis, however, adds a wrinkle to his plans, for—Froissart says—Johanna's subjects wanted no one but him to rule them.[134] While in Naples, Louis has ample opportunity to demonstrate his virtue. Tempted by the enchanter who helped Charles—who relies on sorcery rather than knightly skill—he is offered the opportunity to triumph by magic, if only he and his men will not make the sign of the cross, which would break the enchantment. A true Christian knight, Louis trusts in his abilities and his faith. The enchanter—whom Louis blames for the deaths of Johanna and her family—is beheaded, and Louis continues on his quest.[135] Froissart leaves little doubt that he would have triumphed, had he not died soon afterward.[136]

The schism, as Froissart represents it, pitted righteous, noble Frenchmen against irreligious foreign enemies. One such foreigner, Charles of Durazzo, exemplifies the craven evil of the Urbanists, willing to consort with the devil—for in buying the magician's help he must have promised not to pray or make the sign of the cross—to defeat their opponents. If Louis is the chivalrous hero of Froissart's tale, Johanna appears to advantage as well. Her past whitewashed, she is re-created as a devout queen who loses everything in the fulfillment of her duties. Froissart says nothing of how she died—to do so would emphasize that Louis failed to protect her—but he presents her as the innocent victim of malevolent forces.

By the time Froissart wrote his chronicle, Johanna had become a Clementist heroine. Her virtue was necessary to Clementist commentators, whose version of history hinged on her righteousness. Froissart's Johanna could not have existed without the narrative seeds sown by figures like Brancaccio, Stephen de Millarisis, and Clement and Louis themselves. Their celebrations of her piety, obedience, selflessness, and newly found maternal sentiment formed the basis of Froissart's romantic reimagining of Johanna, allowing him to transform the Clementist martyr into a tragic chivalric queen.

---

133. Ibid., 64.
134. Ibid., 184–85.
135. Ibid., 186.
136. Louis's death is discussed by Froissart in *Chroniques*, 302–3.

The Urbanist Johanna

The Urbanist cardinals, like their Clementist counterparts, collected depositions in the early years of the schism. Their tales of the schism's inception reveal a preoccupation with explaining Johanna's decision that went beyond that discernible in Clementist accounts. The question of why she would abandon Urban, her natural ally, for men who had formerly been her enemies was troubling and perplexing. Johanna's defection had profound ramifications for the Roman pope's security, finances, and prestige, and many Urbanist commentators described it as a definitive moment. Her behavior was all the more problematic in that it pitted her against former allies, forcing a reevaluation of her by those who had long been her supporters.

Two lines of argument emerge in early considerations of Johanna's decision. Some observers presented her actions as the result of a colossal, but perhaps not altogether unwarranted, misunderstanding, most likely instigated by Niccolò Spinelli and Otto of Brunswick. Indeed, many Urbanist commentators acknowledged that Urban behaved badly toward Johanna, but they faulted her defection, which they described as fueled by self-interest, nonetheless. Others, including Catherine of Siena, argued that she was motivated by jealousy of her power, which caused her to reveal her true character when presented with a pope who took his suzerainty over Naples seriously. In her cowardice and selfishness, she allowed herself to be seduced by the antipope. Even if her initial renunciation of Urban derived from misunderstanding, her persistence in it was perversely, foolishly stubborn, bespeaking a defective character and lack of concern for her people's welfare.

Almost all Urbanist considerations of Johanna tie her betrayal of the Roman pope to her sex. For some, her recognition of Clement was indicative of feminine fickleness; for others, it was a sign of Johanna's weak resolve, easily broken when manipulated by men cleverer than herself, and her inferior intellectual capacity, which made her easily duped. Like all women, she was apparently "susceptible to unsavory influences" and easily bent to others' wills.[137] Still others described her actions as exemplary of a typically feminine irrationality. Such arguments ultimately fell back on the well-worn tropes of medieval antifeminism, which described women as inferior due to the natural "weakness of their reason."[138] Implicitly, they also hearkened back

---

137. Dyan Elliott, "From Sexual Fantasy to Demonic Defloration: The Libidinous Female in the Later Middle Ages," in Elliott, *Fallen Bodies: Pollution, Sexuality, and Demonology in the Middle Ages* (Philadelphia: University of Pennsylvania Press, 1999), 43.

138. Cadden, *Meanings of Sex Difference in the Middle Ages*, 140.

to old insinuations about Johanna's lustfulness, for medical discourse identified women's sexuality as "an expression of irrationality and lack of control which suggested a dimension of female weakness."[139] These themes appear, often intertwined, in the arguments of Urbanists who pondered Johanna's decision and its effects.

For the Urbanist cardinals, as for their Clementist counterparts, Johanna's initial loyalty to Urban was vital to explaining what had happened. Urban himself, describing her preschism behavior, called her "Queen Johanna, then most devoted."[140] Menendus, bishop of Cordova, testified in the spring of 1381 that he knew that Johanna was "a spiritual daughter and devoted to Urban" even after the cardinals renounced him, and that she remained so at least until late August 1378.[141] The pope's confessor, Thomas Gundisalvus, who contemptuously called Johanna "that woman who was then queen" when he testified in 1379, acknowledged that she initially demonstrated herself "a great friend" to Urban and sent representatives to congratulate him upon his election.[142] Didacus Martini of Orduña, canon of Toledo, testified that he had seen Hugh of San Severino and Spinelli arrive in Rome to pay their respects to Urban on Johanna's behalf,[143] while Peter Roderici, canon of Cordova, testified that he had seen Otto of Brunswick come to Rome, where he was received with honor.[144]

The most straightforward Urbanist explanation for Johanna's behavior was that she balked at Urban's active overlordship, which threatened her hegemony in Naples.[145] Many of the cardinals reported that Johanna turned on

---

139. Ibid., 151.

140. Baronio et al., *Annales ecclesiastici*, 26:333 (letter of Urban to Juan of Castile): "Joanna tunc regina devotissima."

141. Deposition of Friar Menendus, bishop of Cordova, in Seidlmayer, *Die Anfänge des grossen abendländischen Schismas*, 280. Cf. Baluze, *Vitae paparum Avenionensium*, 2:647.

142. Deposition of Friar Gundisalvus, in Seidlmayer, *Die Anfänge des grossen abendländischen Schismas*, 296; Baluze, *Vitae paparum Avenionensium*, 2:620.

143. Deposition of Didacus Martini, in Baluze, *Vitae paparum Avenionensium*, 2:647.

144. Deposition of Peter Roderici, ibid., 2:645.

145. This is the position argued by Salvatore Fodale (see Fodale, *La Politica Napoletana di Urbano VI*, 18). There are several problems with his theory, not the least of which is his dependence on Urbanist accounts. As others have noted, Fodale's determination to present Urban's attitude vis-à-vis Naples as entirely rational and in keeping with an extremely literal interpretation of papal suzerainty leads him to emphasize evidence supporting his argument while discarding as erroneous or biased evidence that doesn't. See, for instance, William Perry's critique of Fodale: "Review: *La Politica napoletana di Urbano VI*," *Speculum* 51 (October 1976): 740–41. Among other things, Fodale far overstates the degree of papal interference during Johanna's reign, representing her as without political power or influence.

Urban after he expressed a desire to reform the Regno's government, whose problems he was said to attribute to long rule by a woman. Some witnesses stipulated that Urban spoke frankly and impoliticly about the matter. Indeed, they identified Urban's lack of tact as the source of much of his opponents' disillusionment with him. In Johanna's case, Urban's behavior, according to some, was decidedly bad. Didacus Martini, for instance, claimed that Urban's reception of the Neapolitan delegation was far from civil:

> And when they made their reverence to him on the queen's behalf . . . the newly elected pontiff told them he wished to correct and emend the queen, and that the Regno had been poorly led and governed for a long time by a woman, and that he wanted to give it to a man to lead and govern . . . and that he whom he wanted to appoint was Charles of [Durazzo], and he wanted the queen to enter the religious order of her choice.[146]

His harsh comments prompted Johanna's representatives to protest that "the queen had ruled and yet ruled the kingdom well, and that she was married, and thus could not enter an order, and that everyone in the Regno was content with her."[147]

Others insisted that such reports were vicious rumors. Peter Roderici testified that "it had been suggested to [Johanna]—but contrary to the truth—that the first-elected pope intended to deprive her of her kingdom."[148] Both Menendus and Angelus, the Urbanist minister general of the Franciscan order, echoed this statement in 1384, Menendus saying that Johanna had been told that Urban planned to confine her to a convent and Angelus that she had heard false rumors about Urban's desire to depose her.[149] Whether or not the story that Urban planned to replace Johanna with a man and cloister her is true, it had the ring of plausibility, particularly in that it recalled criticisms of Johanna early in her reign. It was believable that such a thing might happen, and that she would hear the report, credit it, and react strongly, even rashly.

All of the witnesses agreed that Johanna's defection was due to the interference of some outside person. Angelus identified Cardinal Orsini as the culprit, citing his trip to Naples as the cause of Johanna's transformation into

---

146. Deposition of Didacus Martini, in Baluze, *Vitae paparum Avenionensium*, 646.

147. Ibid.

148. Deposition of Peter Roderici, ibid., 646.

149. Depositions of Brother Menendus and Brother Angelus, ibid., 647, 620.

Urban's "persecutor" (*persecutrix*).[150] Others were less willing to see her actions as the result of religious conviction. Menendus alleged that Johanna had been convinced of Urban's hostility by "certain false bulls" fabricated by a group of conspirators—including the Clementist Franciscan minister general, Brancaccio, and Spinelli.[151] Bartolomeo Mezzavacca, bishop of Rieti, one of the cardinals created by Urban in 1378, also stated that Johanna was tricked by forgeries into believing that Urban planned her forced claustration. He insisted that Spinelli had forged a letter in Urban's name to Louis of Hungary that maligned Johanna in "shameful" (*opprobriosa*) terms and spoke of her deposition—a story the inquisitor Moschini confirmed.[152] Thus, the rumors to which the Urbanist cardinals attributed Johanna's transformation were carefully designed—whether by Spinelli and his coconspirators or in the minds of the cardinals themselves—to strike fear into Johanna.

At the heart of the matter was an understanding of Johanna's vulnerability as a woman. The rumors the cardinals testified to built on precedent, but they went further, suggesting that Johanna—explicitly because of her sex—was unfit to rule. They also drew on Johanna's long-standing rivalry with Louis of Hungary. In essence, the cardinals suggested that Urban had or was thought to have sided with Louis—something no other pope had done—and accepted not only his claims to the Regno (perhaps including his charge that Johanna was a viricide) but also his stance against female succession. Finally, the explanation that Johanna feared claustration spoke to her perceived desire for autonomy. Even if Urban never suggested enclosing Johanna in a convent, the cardinals' testimony provides evidence that such expedients were discussed and that Johanna's sex continued to trouble even those who had seemed to support her.

The cardinals agreed that Johanna was vulnerable to manipulation. Otto and Spinelli were most often identified as the architects of her defection. Roderici said that he had heard Johanna wished Urban to crown Otto as her coruler—something at variance both with Johanna's style of rule and her best interests, not to mention in violation of their marriage agreement. Roderici claimed that Urban refused, angering Johanna.[153] His tale was to some extent corroborated by the theologian Alvarus Martini, who claimed that Johanna not only wished Otto to rule alongside her but also to rule

---

150. Ibid., 620.

151. Ibid., 647.

152. Deposition of Cardinal Moschini, Rome, Summer 1380, in Seidlmayer, *Die Anfänge des grossen abendländischen Schismas*, 251, 253.

153. Baluze, *Vitae paparum Avenionensium*, 2:645.

after her death—something to which Urban could not agree.[154] Such stories provide a rationale for why Otto might have turned against the pope, as well as an explanation for how Urban might have first offended Johanna. Their suggestion, however, that the question of Otto's power lay at the root of the break between Johanna and Urban is significant. The possibility that Johanna might be controlled by an influential man had been omnipresent in critiques of her reign. Otto was yet another such man, and Johanna—Roderici and Martini suggested—was victim yet again to a woman's weakness. At best, her rejection of Urban after he refused to crown Otto was an expression of childish petulance, but at worst, it was evidence that Johanna, dominated by womanly passions, allowed her husband's ambitions to drive her not merely to act against the Regno's interests but also into heresy and schism.

According to Didacus Martini, it was not Otto but Spinelli whose clash with Urban led to Johanna's defection. Spinelli's meddling and excessive influence are common themes in the Roman depositions, and the question of why he should have worked against Urban was important. Martini theorized that Urban had wounded Spinelli's overweening pride. Spinelli had been a frequent and favored guest of former popes. Martini reported that he had been invited by Urban to a feast, where he sat in his usual seat of honor. Urban, however, objected when he saw "some prelates seated after Niccolò, because he did not want him to be above prelates." Angry, Urban "ordered him to arise from that place." Spinelli protested that he had only accepted the seat assigned to him—that customarily accorded him, "both as the queen's chancellor and as the Seneschal of Provence." He left in high dudgeon, telling the pope that "he would go to his own home and sit wherever he liked."[155] Johanna was so dismayed by the lack of respect shown to Spinelli and the abuse heaped on her by Urban that she allied herself with the dissident cardinals.

The implicit assumption common to such accounts was that one pitfall of entrusting a kingdom to a woman was the threat that she would fall prey to the men upon whom she must rely, who could steer her by appealing to her baser instincts—especially vanity and anger. The Urbanist cardinals thus overwhelmingly attributed Johanna's decision not to religious conviction but to easily manipulated irrational fear and jealousy of her power. Her passions were too easily aroused, and this made her weak. Her natural feminine defects—foolishness, rage, jealousy, irrationality—made her both a failed queen and an unwitting agent of schism.

---

154. Deposition of Alvarus Martini, ibid., 646.
155. Ibid.

Saintly Animosities

The cardinals were not the only Urbanist commentators to consider Johanna's behavior and role in the schism. Among these others were Johanna's erstwhile friends, Birgitta of Sweden's followers and Catherine of Siena. The Birgittine response was subtle, but it was effective and lasting: Around 1380, Prior Peter of Alvastra added Birgitta's harsh visions for Johanna to book VII of the *Revelations* (*Rev.* VII.11:23), incorporating the saint's invective into both the Birgittine canon and the ongoing discussion of Johanna (see chapter 4). Birgitta's visions sexualized Johanna and recalled characterizations of her after Andrew of Hungary's death. They could be—and surely were—read as evidence that Birgitta had foreseen the schism: She warned Johanna, whom she saw besmeared in semen and compared to a blood-drinking lioness, that she was dangerous, and that if "she succeed[ed] in her will, many [would] be in tribulation."[156] Thus, private visions intended to inspire Johanna's personal reform became proof of Birgitta's prophetic insight and Johanna's integral part in the miseries that accompanied the schism.

Alfonso of Jaén and Katherine of Vadstena remained largely silent regarding Johanna's betrayal. It is perhaps significant that, although he wrote two treatises on the schism, Alfonso did not mention Johanna. Perhaps he hoped not to taint her support for Birgitta's canonization. Urban sought without success to enlist Katherine's aid. For a time, he contemplated sending her with Catherine of Siena to Naples, hopeful that they could sway Johanna.[157] Raymond of Capua later reported that Katherine refused to go—whether from fear or from anger is unclear—but Katherine permanently disassociated herself from Johanna. Catherine of Siena, however, was eager to undertake the journey. She wrote to Johanna that she "would much rather tell [her] the truth in person than in writing," believing that her presence would have more effect.[158] In the end, the men who advised the two women decided that the journey was too dangerous, particularly as Johanna (Raymond noted, subscribing to the idea that she was easily influenced) "egged on by the followers of Satan—and there were plenty of them around her!—could easily have ordered unprincipled men to do them some injury."[159]

---

156. Ibid.; *Rev.* VII.11.28, VII.11:30 in Birgitta of Sweden, *Revelaciones Lib. VII*, 143.
157. Raymond of Capua, *The Life of St. Catherine of Siena*, 306. Cf. Beattie, "Catherine of Siena and the Papacy," 90.
158. Letter T317/G316 (early December 1378), in Catherine of Siena, *Letters*, 4:5–11.
159. Raymond of Capua, *The Life of St. Catherine of Siena*, 306.

Catherine, too, attributed Johanna's behavior to the influence of unscrupulous men and, ultimately, to demonic or satanic interference. She was present in Rome as the cardinals discussed Johanna, and she was clearly part of a larger conversation in ecclesiastical circles about the queen, her decision, and its consequences. Far more than the cardinals did, however, Catherine cast the struggle within the Church (as within Johanna's conscience) in eschatological terms as a battle between the true Church and Antichrist. She wrote numerous letters to Johanna in the opening months of the schism, alternately pleading with and chiding her. Before she was even aware of Johanna's recognition of Clement, Catherine wrote to warn her that those who renounced Urban took on "the work of devils."[160] During the period when she knew the dissident cardinals were wooing Johanna, trying to turn "an obedient and respectful daughter . . . away from [her] father," Catherine warned her against them, calling them "incarnate devils bereft of the light of truth and covered with the falsehood of self-centeredness."[161]

Raymond called Catherine a "martyr of patience," but Catherine longed for true martyrdom.[162] She urged martyrdom on Johanna, begging her to "prefer death to working against the Church."[163] She was sorely disappointed when Johanna refused. In Catherine's view, Johanna should have sacrificed herself to Urban's whim, accepting humiliation, correction, and even deposition if he so required. Catherine argued that she gave in to "a disordered fear, a fear of losing [her] temporal position, which is as fickle and as passing as the wind," preferring the fleeting pleasures of power in this life to a martyr's crown in the next.[164] She took Johanna to task as a "blind fool" for not understanding that she doomed herself and her subjects to damnation.[165] Indeed, she argued that Johanna, when she could have become a martyr, selfishly chose instead to persecute the Church, her actions constituting far more than rebellion against Urban: "You have persecuted not Pope Urban VI but the truth and our faith—the faith I expected you, my mother and my daughter, with the help of divine grace, to spread among the unbelievers as you wrote me you would."[166] Although Catherine had once seen Johanna

---

160. Letter T312/G315 (October 7, 1378), in Catherine of Siena, *Letters*, 3:287–92, at 288.

161. Ibid., 288–89. On Catherine's letters to Johanna about the schism, see Blumenfeld-Kosinski, *Poets, Saints, and Visionaries of the Great Schism*, 51–52.

162. Kieckhefer, *Unquiet Souls*, 67–68.

163. Letter T312/G315 (October 7, 1378), in Catherine of Siena, *Letters*, 3:290.

164. Letter T317/G316, in Catherine of Siena, *Letters*, 4:5–11, at 10.

165. Ibid., 6.

166. Letter T348/G317 (May 6, 1379), in Catherine of Siena, *Letters*, 4:166–70, at 168.

as a fellow crusader, she now saw her as an enemy of Christianity. Indeed, Johanna was wholly transformed in Catherine's eyes:

> I address you with [no] respect, because I see the great change in your person. You who were a lady have become a servant and slave of that which has no being. You have subjected yourself to falsehood and to the devil, who is the father of lies.[167]

Her actions led Catherine to question whether Johanna had ever been what she seemed: "You seem not to have known God's truth . . . for if you had known it you would sooner die than mortally offend God."[168]

Catherine described Johanna as "ruled by passion, as one who is weak and overpowered by that passion." Following her passions, the queen went horribly astray, forsaking the true pope for "the antipope, who is really Antichrist, a member of the devil."[169] This was a sign of the inadequacy of Johanna's rational faculties. Catherine bemoaned the fact that Johanna was "so ignorant or so cut off from the true light that [she didn't] know about the villainous lives of these men who had led [her] into such heresy."[170] The truth was so plain that the only possible explanations for Johanna's behavior were stupidity and weakness (failings intimately associated, for Catherine, with femininity)—flaws that led her, like Eve, not to recognize evil when it was in front of her.

Like the cardinals, Catherine believed Johanna vulnerable to pernicious counsel. She charged that "a cursed talebearer incited [her] to hatred and contempt and fear" that deprived her of reason:

> you yourself have relinquished your claim to the very thing you feared losing, and so have been robbed of light and knowledge. And because of your obstinacy in this evil you don't know the truth or see the judgment that is about to come upon you.[171]

Catherine's understanding of what led to Johanna's betrayal thus tallies with explanations put forward by the cardinals: Spinelli (the "cursed talebearer"), for his own selfish reasons, caused Johanna to fear that she would be deposed, and in her fear, she turned away from logic, truth, and the Church. More overtly than the cardinals, however, Catherine pointed out the flawed

---

167. Letter T317/G316, in Catherine of Siena, *Letters*, 4:6.
168. Ibid., 7.
169. Ibid.
170. Ibid., 8.
171. Ibid., 9.

thinking behind Johanna's decision: She failed to see either Spinelli's ulterior motives or the consequences of foreswearing Urban, which included losing her throne. Yet, as time dragged on and Johanna refused to repent, Catherine came to believe that hers was "no offense committed in ignorance or lack of knowledge"—that she had come to see the error of her ways but was kept (irrational creature that she was) from amending them, because "the sword of [her] perverse selfish will" robbed her "of knowledge and willpower."[172]

Catherine quickly came to advocate Johanna's ouster. She told her that she should lose her goods and title because she had "forfeited them—and justly."[173] She was briefly swayed by Johanna's seeming return to the Urbanist fold. She rejoiced in 1379 that "the heart of Pharaoh is broken—I mean the heart of the queen," likening herself to Moses and Johanna to Pharaoh, who too ignored abundant evidence of God's will and might.[174] When Johanna's repentance proved fleeting, Catherine despaired of her, telling her that her sin in turning away the second time was "more serious and more displeasing to God and to other people than [her] earlier sin" and reproaching her for having lied to Catherine herself in a letter.[175] To Raymond, who planned a mission to Hungary, Catherine lamented of Naples, "There is so much evil there that God must apply his own remedy."[176] Part of that remedy was Johanna's removal from power, and Catherine wrote to hasten Louis of Hungary's intervention, demanding, "Will you tolerate Antichrist (a member of the devil) and a woman to subject our whole faith to ruination and darkness and confusion?" She thus equated Johanna's sex with her betrayal, presenting her as an agent of evil whose actions left "the whole world . . . divided . . . and racing toward hell."[177]

Catherine made explicit the gendered critiques left implicit in the cardinals' testimony. Throughout her letters, Catherine (appropriating a hagiographic commonplace) equates virility with courage and right action. It was something to which she aspired and to which she encouraged both Johanna and her male correspondents. Catherine implored Johanna to fight the Clementists manfully, saying that her opposition would demonstrate "that you are no longer weak and effeminate but have become courageous

---

172. Letter T348/G317, in Catherine of Siena, *Letters*, 4:168.

173. Ibid.

174. Letter T353/G337, to a group of Neapolitan women (May 18, 1379), in Catherine of Siena, *Letters*, 4:196–201, at 201.

175. Letter T362/G318 (early August 1379), in Catherine of Siena, *Letters*, 4:222–27, at 225.

176. Letter T344/G101 (late August 1379), in Catherine of Siena, *Letters*, 4:228–35, at 231.

177. Letter T357/G188 (late August 1379), in Catherine of Siena, *Letters*, 4:236–42, at 240.

and strong."[178] In so doing, she echoed the wisdom of hagiographers and of natural philosophers like Albert the Great who, a century earlier, had argued, "there is no woman who would not naturally want to shed the definition of femininity and put on masculinity."[179] Johanna's abjuration of Urban was the opposite of virile, as Catherine defined it. She perversely proved herself the extreme expression of womanhood by rejecting the obviously better state. The saint denigrated her to Louis of Hungary as "this poor little woman, the queen," contrasting Johanna's base femininity with the glorious virility she urged Louis to demonstrate on behalf of the Church.[180]

In giving in to her passions, Johanna succumbed to her femininity and would, if she could, drag others into sin and degradation:

> You have been and still are encouraging the people and all your subjects to be more against than with you, because they've found little truth in you personally, not a courageous and manly heart but effeminate weakness with no firmness or stability—like a woman who whirls about like a leaf in the wind. . . . Now I see you turned around like an unstable woman. . . . Oh miserable passion! You want to give them the sickness you yourself have![181]

Catherine thus directly links Johanna's actions to her sex and gender. While her subjects needed and looked for a man—defined either spiritually or biologically—they were left with a mere woman, one who did not deserve their fidelity. Catherine saw Johanna's lack of regard for them as unnatural and cruel, and she angrily chastised her for losing sight of their interests when she had "guided them for so long with such diligence and in such peace."[182] Recalling Johanna's former glory, Catherine asked rhetorically, "And where is the truth we are accustomed to finding in the queen's mouth, the truth which normally is and should be good news (*evangelio*)?"[183] Like the "courageous and manly heart" Catherine now despaired of finding in Johanna, it was gone; gospel truth had been replaced with heresy.

---

178. Letter T312, in Catherine of Siena, *Letters*, 3:290. Noffke notes that Catherine literally says that Johanna will have "lost the condition of a woman and have become a courageous man" (290, n. 14).

179. Albertus Magnus, *Quaestiones de animalibus*, book X, q. 4., quoted in Cadden, *Meanings of Sex Difference in the Middle Ages*, 160.

180. Letter T357/G188 (late August 1379), in Catherine of Siena, *Letters*, 4:236–42, at 240.

181. Letter T353/G337 (after May 18, 1379), in Catherine of Siena, *Letters*, 4:196–201, at 201.

182. Letter T362/G318, in Catherine of Siena, *Letters*, 4:224.

183. Ibid., 226.

Johanna in Urbanist Chronicles

Chroniclers completed the task of codifying Johanna's place in the Urbanist cultural imaginary. Like Catherine, they often characterized her as irrational and easily manipulated and placed an emphasis on defects explicitly defined as feminine that led Johanna to make a foolish, selfish decision—one with far-reaching implications that generated widespread suffering. They portrayed her defection as key to understanding the schism, although the degree to which they held her culpable for the disasters that followed varies. As narratives of a pan-European crisis, chronicle accounts also examine the aftermath of Johanna's decision, offering interpretations of her character and legacy that act as referenda on her reign as a whole, even as they weigh her actions against those of her opponents. Their accounts offer ruminations on female rule, and many present moral portraits of Johanna as a queen and woman that recall those penned in the aftermath of Andrew of Hungary's death. In the process, they resurrected the she-wolf. Indeed, Andrew's death became a touchstone in Urbanist histories of the schism, an act of brutality that foreshadowed and was echoed by Johanna's betrayal of Urban.

Not all chroniclers with Urbanist sympathies unequivocally condemned Johanna. This was particularly true of Italians, who offered more nuanced readings of Johanna than did chroniclers further afield, their schism stories informed by Johanna's history as a major force in Italian politics, as by their own proximity to the struggle over the Regno. An anonymous Florentine chronicler, for instance, describes the ambivalence with which Johanna's defeat was greeted in his city, saying that some people advocated celebration while others did not.[184] Her abandonment of Urban constituted a betrayal of her former allies, but many perceived the complexities of her situation.

Like Coluccio Salutati, many Italian commentators viewed Johanna's defeat as just but were hesitant to describe her as evil. Salutati reminded Charles of Durazzo, even in congratulating him on his victory, that Johanna had demonstrated "virtue of leadership, mercy, justice, and benevolence," and that he would "discover no woman among the feminine sex" comparable to his vanquished foe. Yet, Salutati suggests, Johanna's feminine "mildness of character" proved unequal to the task of holding "the king's throne"—a seat rightly pertaining to a man.[185] Her sex rendered her an exemplar of feminine

---

184. *Cronaca prima di Anonimo* (1378–87) conosciuta sotto il nome di *Cronaca dello Squittinatore*, in Gino Scaramella, ed., *Il Tumulto dei Ciommpi—Cronache e Memorie*, vol. 13, pt. 3 of *RIS*, new ed. (Bologna: Nicola Zanichelli, 1934), 96: "Recesene festa di questo, chi sì, chi no."

185. Salutati, *Epistolario*, 2:24–25.

virtue rather than of effective sovereignty; Charles was the true king, the man finally able to stabilize the Regno.

Ambivalent Italian chroniclers, like Salutati, ascribed what they presented as Johanna's eventual failure to the shortcomings of her sex. Some represented her femininity as an insurmountable obstacle to peace and stability; others faulted Johanna for her choice of obedience but presented sympathetic portraits of her, not least because they objected to Charles of Durazzo or even to Urban himself. Indeed, for many chroniclers, Johanna figured most prominently to illustrate Charles's perfidy, her role in the schism all but ignored. Charles, who broke with Urban not long after gaining Naples and went on to betray Louis of Hungary by seizing the Hungarian throne, figures in many Urbanist accounts as an unsuitable replacement for Johanna and an even more unsuitable champion of the Church. He went so far as to openly wage war on the Roman pope, besieging him in Nocera (where Urban reportedly imprisoned and tortured cardinals who disagreed with him)—an act of betrayal that many chroniclers treated as equivalent to or greater than Johanna's own.[186] Johanna's death at his hands was proof positive of his treacherous nature in many Urbanist accounts, and she became, if not a martyr, at least a victim of his unscrupulous grasping for power.

The Italian chronicler most kindly disposed toward Johanna was the Venetian chancellor Raphaynus de Caresinis (d. 1390). Although Venice adhered to Rome, the republic had a long history of enmity with Louis of Hungary—who disputed its claims to Dalmatia—and Charles of Durazzo.[187] Antipathy for Charles colors Raphaynus's treatment of Johanna, whom he describes as having "peacefully and most wisely" ruled the Regno. Charles's triumph is marked by ignominy, marred because he "wickedly killed the captive queen in Castel dell'Ovo." His wickedness obscures Johanna's guilt; her death and defeat are no credit to Charles, the magnitude of whose crimes are emphasized by the absence of any suggestion that Johanna deserved punishment. Her death, the sole action in which she is involved, demonstrates Charles's sin and corruption. So too does Charles's own murder in Hungary,

---

186. For a concise description of the struggle between Charles and Urban, see Ullmann, *The Origins of the Great Schism*, 164–68, and De Blasiis, *Chronicon Siculum* (on which most modern authors draw), 50 and passim.

187. On the Hungarian action against Venice and its impact on the timing of Charles's conquest, see Egidi, "La scrittura segreta di Giovanna I di Napoli," 376. Cf. G. Wenzel, *Magyar Diplomacziai emlékek az Anjou-Korbol*, in *Monumenta Hungariae Historica*, vol. 3 (Budapest: A. M. Tud. Akadémia, 1876), 187, n. 143.

which echoes and requites his betrayal of Johanna.[188] In the same vein, the early fifteenth-century *Diurnali del Duca di Monteleone* describes Johanna as a loving aunt who treated Charles and her nieces as though they were her own children.[189] Her actions in the chronicle have evil consequences but are not born from evil motives. The chronicler describes the furor in Naples over her choice of obedience, saying that the Neapolitans rose up against Clement, the "Carnival Pope," but he also recounts a skirmish between one of Urban's supporters and a "gentleman" who took umbrage at hearing the queen slandered.[190] He thus acknowledges that the struggle had two sides and that Johanna commanded the loyalty of noble men. His Johanna is maternal and kindly, the victim of her own poor choices and others' betrayal but ultimately a figure in whom the chronicler finds much to admire. The continuator of the Sienese chronicle attributed to Paolo di Tommaso Montauri, who began his addenda in 1381, provides a similarly sympathetic assessment of Johanna, whose captivity and death form the fulcrum around which the war between her two would-be heirs—the chronicler's main concern—revolves.[191] The schism is the backdrop to their struggle, and the chronicler, despite his commune's loyalty to Rome, expresses strong disapproval of Urban and Charles of Durazzo. His condemnation of them softens his stance on Johanna. Her role in the schism is reduced while her death is foregrounded—her guilt is not at issue, while Charles's evil is.

Thus, sympathetic treatments of Johanna are as much condemnations of her opponents as vindications of her. She was important primarily for what she demonstrated about the men who struggled against her. She was accordingly reduced to an innocuous, feminized figure—a wise and peaceful queen, a loving aunt, a surrogate mother—to highlight their guilt. By and large, however, Johanna's culpability is a given in Urbanist chronicles. At the very least, chroniclers portrayed her abandonment of Urban as partially responsible for the schism and as just cause for her

---

188. Raphaynus de Caresinis, *Cronica* [aa. 1343–1388], ed. Ester Pastorello, vol. 12, pt. 2 of *RIS*, new ed. (Bologna: Nicola Zanichelli, 1923), 66.

189. Michele Manfredi, ed., *I Diurnali del Duca di Monteleone*, vol. 25, pt. 5 of *RIS*, new ed. (Bologna: Nicola Zanichelli, 1958), 16, 18. The *Diurnali* are a collection of miscellanea relating Naples's history. The text becomes detailed with Johanna's reign, and this account appears to date to ca. 1400 or shortly after.

190. Ibid., 22–23. The *Chronicon Siculum* recounts the story too, providing a similarly complicated view of the uprisings in Naples that makes clear that not all of Johanna's subjects opposed her. Cf. De Blasiis, *Chronicon Siculum*, 36.

191. *Cronaca Senese conosciuta sotto il nome di Paolo di Tommaso Montauri (continuazione—Anni 1381–1431)*, in Lisini and Iacometti, *Cronache Senesi*, 687–845, at 695.

deposition.[192] A Bolognese chronicle describes the rage that gripped Naples during Clement's visit, leading the populace to rise up with cries of "Death to the Antipope and the queen!" and proclaim that they no longer recognized Johanna's sovereignty if she did not recognize Urban's.[193] The *Chronicon Siculum* likewise reports that Johanna's people shouted, "Death to Pope Clement with the cardinals, and also the queen, if she wants to defend him, and long live Pope Urban!"[194] The Sienese chronicle written by Donato di Neri and his son, Neri, also charges that Johanna's transfer of obedience occasioned scandal and unrest, precipitating her fall from power and eventual strangulation.[195] Such reports suggest that her subjects recognized Urban's lordship, even if Johanna did not, making her deposition justified.

Most often, Urbanist chronicles depict Johanna's transfer of obedience as the catalyst for a series of progressively worse disasters. Foremost among these was the German bishop Dietrich of Niem (or Nieheim), who had been a scribe and abbreviator in Urban's chancery and who finished his *De scismate libri tres*—whose single surviving manuscript has become one of the most important sources on the schism—around 1410.[196] Dietrich attributed Johanna's betrayal to fury with Urban—whose defects Dietrich was perfectly willing to acknowledge—after he publicly slighted Otto of Brunswick.[197] Although Dietrich acknowledges Urban's rudeness, he does not excuse Johanna, nor does he depict Otto as anything more than the unwitting instigator of Johanna's anger.[198] Johanna's abandonment of Urban

---

192. This was true of Urbanist chronicles from across Europe. Thomas Walsingham, writing sometime before 1400, only fleetingly mentions Johanna, saying that the French pope—no longer "clement" (*clemens*) but now "demented" (*demens*)—took refuge under Johanna's protection until his "schismatics" could spirit him away to Avignon. Walsingham offers no consideration of her motives; she is merely one of many heretics who wickedly support the deranged antipope and enable his success. See Thomas Walsingham, *The St. Albans Chronicle*, vol. 1: *1376–1394: The "Chronica Maiora" of Thomas Walshingam*, ed. John Taylor, Wendy R. Childs, and Leslie Watkiss, trans. Leslie Watkiss (Oxford: Oxford University Press, 2003), 274.

193. *Cronaca A*, in Sorbelli, *Corpus Chronicorum Bononiensium*, 359.

194. De Blasiis, *Chronicon Siculum*, 36. The anonymous author of the *Chronicon Siculum* was not an Urbanist—he called Urban "Bartholomeus Prignanus intrusus qui intitulabatur papa Urbanus" (88). Yet, as a Neapolitan, he offered complicated and nuanced readings of the situation that were not sympathetic to Johanna and were often in line with the interpretations offered by Urbanist chroniclers.

195. *Cronaca Senese di Donato di Neri e di suo figlio Neri [1352–1381]*, in Lisini and Iacometti, *Cronache Senesi*, 565–685, at 673.

196. Dietrich von Niem, *De scismate libri tres*, ed. George Erler (Leipzig: Veit, 1890), iii.

197. Ibid., 19.

198. Ibid., 34.

stems from wounded pride, which makes her so irrational that she refuses to listen to her husband's better, sounder judgment (so that she fails as a wife, as well as a queen).

Dietrich criticizes everyone involved in the transfer of power in Naples. His Charles of Durazzo is grasping and greedy, his Margaret of Durazzo duplicitous, and his Urban unscrupulous. Johanna and Otto are little more than bystanders, the victims of conspiracies and interests that shunted them aside and destroyed their family. Among the opportunists who threaten Johanna, Charles is by far the worst, and Dietrich saw little to celebrate in his victory. Indeed, it merely recalled Naples's violent past. In a savage repetition of history, an Angevin prince again shed noble German blood on Italian soil, when Otto's brother was executed on the spot where Charles I had executed Conradin of Hohenstaufen.[199] Evil fortune thus came again to Naples with this new Charles. His ascension to the throne is part and parcel of the cyclical tragedy Naples was doomed to suffer; indeed, Johanna herself is part of that destiny, both as the instigator of the latest cycle of violence and as its victim. Charles holds her captive in Abruzzo, where he orders her murder: "Soon after, it is said, the queen was praying in the castle's chapel; while genuflecting before the altar, she was strangled at Charles's command by four Hungarian courtiers."[200] Johanna dies at prayer, misguided but not faithless, overpowered by enemies against whom she cannot defend herself.

While Dietrich's Johanna is more tragic antiheroine than villainess, her wounded pride leads to catastrophe, and all that follows her transfer of obedience is punishment for her transgression. Her murder is an act of retributive justice, not just for her abandonment of Urban but also, implicitly, for Andrew of Hungary's murder—a thematic element that became integral to contemporary accounts. Her strangulation mirrors Andrew's; by attributing it to Louis of Hungary's agents, Dietrich implies that this, finally, is Louis's revenge. At the same time, Johanna's betrayal of Urban—an act of womanly vanity—is the catalyst for the degradation suffered by herself, her family, and, most importantly, her kingdom.

Dietrich's tale of Angevin tragedy functions as a warning against powerful women. All of his Angevin women—key players in the Neapolitan drama—share the vice of avarice. Johanna of Durazzo, we are told, suffered greatly, living in wretched captivity "like she was a poor servant."[201] Her fate

199. Ibid., 45–46.
200. Ibid., 48.
201. Ibid., 49.

was punishment for greed: Dietrich claims that she refused to help fund the struggle against Charles but quickly found money to bribe him after her capture (which Charles took without freeing her), allowing Dietrich to remind his reader that "there is no avarice greater than the avarice of women, as experience teaches." The elder Johanna's pride and love of power lead to her downfall, as Johanna of Durazzo's greed does to her captivity. Margaret of Durazzo completes the trinity of avaricious women: Dietrich describes her living sumptuously, aware of her sister's plight but doing nothing, until finally "the duchess died after long incarceration in squalor."[202] Rumination on feminine vice anchors his entire narrative, and Dietrich condemns feminine power for the iniquity it occasions, leading to suffering far beyond the silly women who abuse it.

Dietrich's account is in many senses emblematic of Urbanist histories of the period, particularly those that consider the schism's impact on Europe as a whole. The English author of the monastic *Westminster Chronicle*, probably writing in the later 1380s,[203] offers a similarly gendered account of Johanna in which her behavior is tantamount to adultery. He describes her early fondness for Urban, which Clement subverted in what amounts to an act of seduction:[204]

> Robert of Geneva, the usurper of the Roman papacy . . . made secret approaches to the queen, and when his intermediaries had done their work was welcomed by her in friendly fashion, eventually enticing her over to his side, so that she rejected Pope Urban and without hesitation or reserve accepted the Genevan as the true pope. . . . How easily women's minds can be altered! And no wonder, when their fickleness is an excuse for them.[205]

An adulteress to the faith, Johanna easily succumbs, turning away from the true pope whom she had earlier seemed to love. The chronicler thus describes Johanna's decision as the result of inborn moral frailty and feminine changeability that rendered her easily seduced.

The Westphalian historian and monastic reformer Gobelinus Person also describes the schism as a catastrophe, seeing its wider implications for the

---

202. Ibid., 50.

203. On the dating of the *Westminster Chronicle*, see L. C. Hector and Barbara F. Harvey, eds. and trans., *The Westminster Chronicle, 1381–1394*, Oxford Medieval Texts (Oxford: Oxford University Press, 1982), xiii, xxiii–xxx.

204. Ibid., 106, 108.

205. Ibid., 108 (trans. 109).

whole of Christian society, and he too links Johanna's betrayal of Urban to her sex. Naples was surely in Gobelinus's thoughts when he lamented that the schism brought with it "homicide, conflagrations, war, destruction—not just of lands but also of kingdoms." He attributes Clement VII's success partially to Johanna's support, thereby implicating her in the schism and the suffering it caused. Gobelinus claims that Johanna renounced Urban when he refused to crown Otto, citing the danger Johanna's childlessness after multiple marriages represented for the Regno's future.[206] In calling attention to Johanna's many marriages and lack of children, Gobelinus invoked her reputation for libidinousness: Medieval medical wisdom linked lust and childlessness, positing that women with active sex lives were "less likely to conceive" than those who were more abstemious.[207]

Gobelinus's Johanna displays the full spectrum of female vice, not merely lust. He attributes her renunciation of Urban to rage at having her will thwarted:

> And then certain crafty informers ran between the pope and the queen, so that each became angry with the other. Just as there is no head more evil than that of the snake, so is no wrath greater than the wrath of a woman (Eccl. 25:22–25:23). This queen . . . affirmed the antipope Robert to be the true vicar of Christ with obstinate fury of purpose, so that her husband could take up the kingdom's crown through him.[208]

She is thus endowed with irrational feminine temper, perversely set on achieving her desire. Gobelinus's Johanna may act in Otto's interests, but her fury is a force unto itself—it drives her actions and dominates her will with terrible repercussions.

Gobelinus explicitly links the schism to Andrew's death. He prefaces his story of the schism with that of Andrew's murder, reporting, "common repute taught that the queen was an accomplice" in this "wickedness."[209] He frames Charles's attack on Naples as an act of vengeance performed for Louis of Hungary, who "panted fervently for the queen's extermination,"

206. Gobelinus Person, *Cosmidromius Gobelini Person, und als Anhang desselben Verfassers, Processus translacionis et reformacionis monasterii Budecensis*, ed. Max Jensen, Veröffentlichungen der Historischen Kommission der Provinz Westfalen (Münster: Aschendorff, 1900), 84.

207. Cadden, *Meanings of Sex Difference in the Middle Ages*, 144.

208. Person, *Cosmidromius*, 87–88.

209. Ibid., 88: "rex Andreas frater eiusdem regis, primus ipsius regine Iohanne maritus, in Aversana civitate noctu in palacio strangulatus et de fenestra proiectus mortuus est, de mane repertus in orto, cuius sceleris ipsam reginam communis fama consciam predicabat."

tying her betrayal of Urban to her betrayal of Andrew and associating her death (and Naples's suffering) with both.[210] Charles is the instrument of Louis's revenge: Gobelinus describes him hurling body parts from catapults, pelting Naples with "hands, feet, or heads and other members" cut from his captives, which made the city's defenders vomit and fear suffocation.[211] Finally, Johanna, "nearly out of her mind for sorrow," surrenders, hoping to save those who remain alive.[212] Charles, however, feels no compassion, and Louis's vengeance is soon complete: "In revenge for King Andrew's death, it is said that he secretly had the queen's throat slit."[213]

Gobelinus thus reduces Johanna's reign to the linked crimes of Andrew of Hungary's murder and her renunciation of Urban VI. Both illustrate Johanna's iniquity and both stem from blind feminine rage and moral turpitude. Gobelinus denies Johanna any rational faculty. Her piety, sham or genuine, is never mentioned, and he never acknowledges even the pretense of reason behind Johanna's transfer of obedience. Like the Johanna of the *Chronicon Estense*, Gobelinus's Johanna is a caricature of femininity whose defects promote only violence and chaos, and her rule encompasses little beyond acts of overt evil for which she is fittingly recompensed.

Gobelinus was not alone in seeing a direct link between Andrew's murder and the schism. The Bolognese chronicler Matteo de' Griffoni (1351–1426), for instance, identifies Johanna as Andrew's murderer as he provides background to the schism.[214] Baldassare Bonaiuti (d. 1385), who wrote his *Cronaca Fiorentina* between 1378 and 1385, also provides Andrew's death as background.[215] He depicts Johanna's break with Urban as the result of the pope's desire to depose her, reporting that Urban proclaimed that "she was Johanna, a woman and no queen, and that the kingdom was not hers but the king of Hungary's."[216]

---

210. Ibid.

211. Ibid., 89–90.

212. Ibid., 90.

213. Ibid., 91.

214. Mattheo de' Griffoni, *Memoriale Historicum de rebus Bononiensium* [AA. 4448 a.C.–1472 d. C.], ed. Lodovico Frati and Albano Sorbelli, vol. 18, pt. 2 of *RIS*, new ed. (Città di Castello: S. Lapi, 1902), 56: "Mortuus est rex Andreas, frater regis Ungarie, seditione reginae Johannae ejus uxoris, que suspendi fect ipsum per gulam cum uno panno syrici." In dealing with the schism, however, Matteo focuses on Johanna primarily as the source of the struggle between Charles and Louis. He is more concerned with their war and its ramifications—particularly the devastation caused by their armies—than with Johanna as a historical figure.

215. Baldassare Bonaiuti [Marchionne di Coppo Stefani], *Cronaca Fiorentina*, ed. Niccolò Rodolico, in *Cronache Toscane*, vol. 30 of *RIS*, new ed. (Città di Castello: S. Lapi, 1903), xxiii; 224–25: "Dissesi la regina Giovanna, sua moglie, acconsentì al delitto detto."

216. Ibid., 312.

Johanna's sex and her status as a viricide underpin his narrative, these twin defects necessitating her removal from power. Indeed, Bonaiuti lays out the dynastic entanglements of Hungary and Naples as context and portrays Charles, as do Dietrich and Gobelinus, as the agent of Louis of Hungary's revenge.[217] Johanna's denial of Urban is brought within the scope of Louis's vendetta, and her status as a schismatic is intimately associated with her identity as a viricide. In both cases, she has sinned against the natural order, denying and subverting the authority of the man who should exercise power over her. The central issue is her evil feminine nature, and the final solution to the problem she poses is her death. The natural balance is restored when she is replaced by Charles of Durazzo, a male descended—Bonaiuti reminds us—from Charles I and untainted by the deficiencies that necessitated Johanna's removal from power.

As Thelma Fenster and Daniel Lord Smail have noted, a person often had "more than one *fama*, because different groups might have constructed facts or memories in ways that suited their own political or social interests."[218] Characterizations of Johanna during the schism reflect competing political and social interests, just as they reflect the confusion of the schism itself. Her disparate personae reflect *fama* as a "process," something "carried on through conversations . . . [in a way that] constructed, deconstructed, and reconstructed the things remembered."[219] In depositions, chronicle accounts, and correspondence describing the schism, we catch snippets of those conversations, and tracking them allows us to watch arguments, about both Johanna and the schism, develop and evolve.

In the case of the schism, a crisis that affected all of Western Christian society, throwing people's religious beliefs and affiliations as well their day-to-day lives into turmoil, the conversations that deconstructed and reconstructed Johanna's *fama* were part of a process of making sense of calamity. As Gobelinus Person reminds us, the schism was not merely an ideological struggle, nor was it limited to the men who strove for ecclesiastical primacy; it shook people's moral and religious foundations and inflicted "homicide, conflagrations, war, [and] destruction" on them, particularly in Johanna's lands.[220] Preoccupation with Johanna reveals that she was bound up in her contemporaries' understanding of the schism. She formed a crucial part of its *imaginaire*, variously interpreted in light of "the ideas, conceptions, and even prejudices" that

---

217. Ibid., 312–13.
218. Fenster and Smail, "Introduction," 6.
219. Ibid.
220. Person, *Cosmidromius*, 284.

underpin Blumenfeld-Kosinki's definition of *imaginaire*.[221] As such, defining and understanding Johanna was central to how both Clementist and Urbanist observers explained and codified the schism.

As Chris Wickham points out, "if you want to know about the boundaries of the everyday morality of, the sense of belonging to, a social group, then listening to how it gossips, if it will let you, is one crucial mechanism, maybe even the best one." He continues:

> What people gossip about, what stories they tell, will also tell you how their group socially constructs the world outside as meaningful, and about how it understands the processes of practical behaviour . . . which structure the way everyone deals strategically with that world. Gossip indeed focuses on these strategies: "don't you know why she really did that? it was because . . ."; or, "he ought to have known that so-and-so would react that way."[222]

Discussions of Johanna during the schism constitute precisely this kind of gossip, beginning in the explanations of churchmen, reflected in Catherine of Siena's knowledge of talk in Rome, disseminated among her *familia* through her letters, and finally transmitted in the stories heard, shaped, and retold by chroniclers. Gossip or "talk" (to use Fenster and Smail's term) about Johanna reveals the narrative strategies people used to make sense of the schism, to explain her role in it, and finally to understand her. Johanna as a real person was not at issue, whereas Johanna as a type was: What sort of woman would act as she did? Why did she take the steps that she did, and what were their consequences? Why did her actions have the results that they did? What sort of men succeeded her, and how did she reflect on them and they on her? In answering these questions, commentators crafted new *famae* for Johanna to suit their various agendas and fit their imagined histories.

On both sides, representations of Johanna were reductionist, designed to position her with reference to the struggle within the Church. And, on both sides, her previous reputation(s) and career were downplayed or ignored. She was recrafted to suit rival agendas and rival narratives. As a result, she was feminized in ways that heroized her—as in her representation as a Clementist martyr—or demonized her, as in her representation as the partner of Antichrist. The sovereign persona she had helped to shape disappeared, her history and legacy repurposed by adherents of the rival obediences who

---

221. Blumenfeld-Kosinki, *Poets, Saints, and Visionaries of the Great Schism*, 13.
222. Wickham, "Gossip and Resistance among the Medieval Peasantry," 12.

incorporated her into historical narratives that justified their positions and explained the predicament in which they found themselves.

Compared to Clementist depictions of Johanna—largely the product of official propaganda—the Urbanist Johanna was a quite complicated figure. The Clementist Johanna was a reduced version of the queen, her history whitewashed, her persona feminized and very nearly sanctified. The Urbanist Johanna, on the other hand, was the product of disparate voices with differing agendas trying to understand her role in a catastrophe that altered the politico-religious map of Europe, especially Italy. Once a trusted ally, she became a persecutor of the faith; once a pious daughter of the Church, she became a sexualized, irrational harridan; once a wise, serene queen, she became a tyrant who sacrificed her people's welfare to her own whim.

The closest thing that survives to an official Urbanist description of Johanna is that put forth in the bull that excommunicated her as a heretic, schismatic, and blasphemer. This description, it seems, did not satisfy Urbanist commentators, who expanded on it. At one extreme was Catherine of Siena's image of Johanna as the collaborator of devils, a weak woman who clung to earthly glory rather than accept a martyr's crown. At the other was the image propagated by Charles of Durazzo's opponents who, disillusioned with him, portrayed Johanna as a betrayed maternal figure to highlight Charles's inadequacies. (Louis of Anjou's supporters did precisely the same thing, with commentators on both sides appropriating Johanna as a means to characterize the man with whom they were truly concerned.) In the middle was the image of Johanna as a lifelong sinner whose evil had finally caught up to her, a woman deeply flawed ruling a kingdom not rightfully hers whose comeuppance was inevitable, ultimately realized by the vengeful hand of Louis of Hungary, working through Charles of Durazzo.

At the same time, such narratives scapegoated Johanna, associating the evils of the schism with the evil inherent in her character, ultimately blaming the calamities to which her lands were subject on her flawed femaleness. Such depictions telescoped her reign, seeking the roots of her collaboration with the dissident cardinals in the wicked character revealed by Andrew's death and identifying her as first and always a usurper and viricide. Commentators drew on what Edward Muir calls "the terminology of revenge" to describe the outcome of Johanna's decision, crafting historical narratives that read her fate as part of a vendetta story and giving her life and the disaster of the schism a coherent, comprehensible framework.[223] They collapsed her

223. Muir, *Mad Blood Stirring*, xxi, xxv.

reign onto itself, ignoring its successes to focus on the two great scandals that bookended it. The ultimate explanation for Johanna's behavior, in such a view, was her inherently wicked nature, whose mischief was facilitated by the iniquity that she was allowed to reign and redressed only when Charles deposed her and restored right order to the Regno.

Behind all of these portraits are reductionist treatments of femininity. Johanna had managed, between Louis of Taranto's death and the schism, to reinvent herself, but that revised image could not stand up to the exigencies of explaining her role in the schism. As in the period after Andrew of Hungary's death, commentators fell back on stereotypes of femininity. If she was able, during a period of relative calm, to rise above her *mala fama* and participate in shaping her own reputation, in extremis others shaped it for her, seeking explanations for her behavior in the glories or flaws of her sex. For Clementists, she was most useful as a self-sacrificing victim, the embodiment of feminine patience, humility, and obedience. Her nobility of character was amplified by making her, on the one hand, the betrayed mother of Charles of Durazzo and, on the other, the loving mother of Louis of Anjou, whose military campaign was sanitized and justified by representing him as a vengeful son. For Urbanists, she was a caricature of femininity, very nearly a personified version of feminine vanity, unreason, and rage. She embodied what her detractors saw as the weaknesses of her sex, and her destructive influence on their world was explained in light of these weaknesses, either because she was a tool manipulated by unscrupulous men or because she was driven by a woman's irrational passions, which led to destruction and suffering for those under her power.

Epilogue

The authors of a recent survey of Provençal history preface their chapter on Johanna of Naples's reign, entitled "Épilogue Tragique," with the observation,

> The time of "Good Queen Johanna" has become proverbial in Provence. There could hardly be a reputation less deserved, given that the region entered into one of the grimmest periods of its history at the end of the 1340s. The queen's golden legend is without basis.[1]

Their puzzlement is warranted, for if Provence enjoyed considerable autonomy during Johanna's reign, it was also beset with disasters ranging from plague to the depredations of mercenaries to civil war. It appears improbable that the period should be described as a golden age or that Johanna herself should be remembered fondly. Nonetheless, Johanna has been viewed in Provence as a heroic figure of romance, identified by Frédéric Mistral as the region's Mary, Queen of Scots.[2]

Perhaps because she has been conflated in historical memory with René of Anjou's wife, Jeanne de Laval (1433–98)—the county's other

---

1. Aurell, Boyer, and Coulet, *La Provence au Moyen Âge*, 275.

2. Frédéric Mistral, *La Reino Jano: tragedi prouvencalo*, ed. and trans. Émile G. Léonard (Toulon: L'Astrado, 1974). Cf. Michel, *La reine Jeanne de Naples et de Provence*, and Paladilhe, *La Reine Jeanne*.

Reine Jeanne—Provençal literature associates Johanna with poetry and the arts and credits her with passionate concern for her subjects' welfare. The sixteenth-century Périgordian historian Pierre de Bourdeille, lord of Brantôme, incorporated her into his *Les vies des dames galantes*, where he describes her romantic escapades and charges her with murdering both Andrew of Hungary and James of Majorca but also describes her as "the most beautiful queen and the greatest princess and woman in the world at that time."[3] The eighteenth-century historian François Bouche offers this flattering portrait in his *Essai sur l'histoire de Provence*:

> Queen Johanna was a woman endowed with all the agreeable traits possible in her sex: beautiful, spiritual, and sweet; a queen easy to approach, wanting to know the unhappy in order to soothe them; affable with the least of her subjects; an enemy of oppression, above all else protecting those of the third estate from the usurpations of the nobility; appearing often in public in order to spread her blessing; respecting private property and communal privileges.[4]

Such biographical accounts depict Johanna as intimately involved in her subjects' lives and actively protective of the Provençal communes—arguments common in histories of Provence up to the twentieth century. Even a set of spurious Avignon prostitution statutes attributed to Johanna reflects widespread belief in her anxiety for her people's welfare. As a prank, eighteenth-century forgers inexpertly inserted the false statutes—which purport to date to Johanna's residence in Provence in 1347–48—into a fourteenth-century manuscript. The text claims that the statutes were drafted because "this good queen" feared that the supposedly common Muslim practice of sodomy would spread to her subjects if brothels were not available.[5] Although the statutes owe a great deal to Johanna's sexualized reputation, they also draw on her vaunted concern for her subjects' moral and physical well-being. Indeed,

---

3. Pierre de Bourdeille, *Oeuvres du Seigneur de Brantôme*, 2:426. Brantôme explicitly states his preference for Froissart's literary portrait to that put forward by the Neapolitan Pandolfo Collenuccio, thereby preferring the "French" Johanna to the "Italian." I am indebted to William Monter and Robert E. Lerner for this reference.

4. François Bouche, *Essai sur l'histoire de Provence, suivi d'une des Provencaux célèbres* (Marseille: J. Mossy, père et fils, 1785), 1:384–85.

5. The text in question is Avignon, Bibliothèque Ceccano, MS 2834, fol. 64. Copies exist in a number of early modern miscellanies: see Avignon, Bibliothèque Ceccano, MS 1615, fols. 425r–427r; MS 2394, fol. 53; MS 2465–66, fol. 19*bis*; and MS 2430, fol. 41. On the forgery, see Pierre Pansier, "Histoire des prétendus statuts de la reine Jeanne et de la réglementation de la prostitution à Avignon au Moyen-Age," *Janus* 7 (1902), reprinted as an extract.

one nineteenth-century doctor read them as evidence of Johanna's efforts to protect her subjects not only from sin but also from syphilis.[6]

The romanticized Provençal portrait of Johanna must derive in part from her self-conscious relationship with Marseille—which asserted itself her most loyal city—as well as from the fact that her reign is remembered as the last period of independence before France swallowed Provence. For authors like Mistral who strove to reinvigorate the Provençal language and protect the region's distinctive culture, her reign represented a lost era when the true Provençal spirit thrived. Yet while these factors clearly helped shape Johanna's legacy in the county, her romantic legend also demonstrates the effectiveness of the propaganda campaign begun by Clement VII and aggressively pursued by Louis of Anjou's heirs. Marie of Blois and her son, Louis II, successfully crafted a new persona for Johanna, one discernible even through eighteenth- and nineteenth-century accretions. Without their deliberate refashioning of her, Johanna might have been remembered very differently.

Naples's She-Wolf

Johanna's enduring popular image in Italy differs starkly from that in Provence. The image of Johanna as a she-wolf triumphed in Italy, thanks largely to the efforts of fifteenth-century historians like Pandolfo Collenuccio of Pesaro (d. 1504), who retold the story of Andrew of Hungary's murder, explicitly tying Johanna's disordered lust to the crime.[7] A twentieth-century Neapolitan biographer, alluding to this legacy, wonders rhetorically, "Was she really the shameless nymphomaniac who has been handed down to us, or rather an unfortunate woman who sought in vain all her life for a true love?"[8] This question reflects the fact that in Neapolitan popular history, Johanna's insatiable sexual appetite is her defining trait, and she is most known for Andrew's murder and her rumored love affairs. A current tourism website for the Amalfi coast advertises visits to the Bagno della Regina Giovanna like this: "In one of the clefts of the cliffs there is a natural warm pool that is completely surrounded by rocks. Queen Giovanna of Naples is said to have spent many an hour there with her lovers."[9]

---

6. Hippolyte Mireur, *La syphilis et la prostitution dans leurs rapports avec l'hygiène, la morale et la loi* (Paris: Masson, 1875), 437.

7. Collenuccio, *Compendio delle historie del Regno di Napoli*, 143.

8. Vittorio Gleijeses, *La Storia di Napoli dalle origini ai nostri giorni* (Naples: Società Editrice Napoletana, 1974), 362.

9. "Vacations at the Amalfi Coast," http://www.vacation-amalfi.com/excursions/Sorrento.html.

As in Provence, Johanna's reputation doubtless owes something to her conflation with another queen by the same name, in this case her great-niece, Johanna II—the daughter of Charles III and Margaret of Durazzo—who also died childless and was known for rumored sexual voraciousness. Yet much of what is said about the first Johanna can easily be linked to her reputation during and immediately after her life, although certain charges, such as Suzanne Noffke's assertion that she suffered from an unrequited infatuation with Charles III of Durazzo, are difficult to trace back in time.[10] Some effort was made in Naples to recuperate Johanna's reputation. At its center was Tristan Caracciolo (ca. 1437–ca. 1528), who wrote an exculpatory biography of Johanna, the *Vita Joannae Primae Neapolis Reginae*.[11] His *vita* asserts at the outset that its aim is to defend Johanna against many false claims.[12] He presents her as well educated and refined and as a worthy successor to Robert. Much of Caracciolo's biography, which borders on hagiography, focuses on the aftermath of Andrew's death; he says little about the murder itself, although he does characterize Andrew as barbaric and uncouth, decidedly undeserving of Johanna.[13] He thus glosses over the greatest scandal of Johanna's reign, focusing instead on the suffering it brought her, and provides an elegiac portrait of the queen that represents her as the embodiment of Renaissance ideals of culture and refinement.

Caracciolo's voice was, however, drowned out by others far more critical of Johanna. The history of Florence by the great Florentine humanist Leonardo Bruni (ca. 1369–1444), for instance, focuses on Johanna's presumed guilt for Andrew's murder (framed as a play for power) and her resulting infamy.[14] He apportions her a share of the blame for the schism, and he frames her defeat by Charles of Durazzo in part as revenge by Louis of Hungary, thereby adhering closely to the narrative established by Urbanist chroniclers during the schism.[15] Johanna was, in his estimation, truly wicked, guilty of heresy and a schismatic, and he presents her as rightly having forfeited her kingdom as a result.[16]

---

10. Catherine of Siena, *Letters*, 4:301.

11. Tristano Caracciolo, *Opusculi Storici editi e inediti*, ed. Giuseppe Paladino, vol. 22, pt. 1 of *RIS* (Bologna: Nicola Zanichelli, 1934).

12. Ibid., 15: "sinistra et aeque falsa de ea recepta opinion."

13. Ibid., 9: "Andreas vero barbaricos mores feritatemque pannonicam penitus imbiberat."

14. Leonardo Bruni Aretino, *Historiarum Florentini populi, Libri XII, e Rerum suo tempore gestarum commentarius*, ed. Emilio Santini and Carmine di Pierro, vol. 19, pt. 3 of *RIS* (Città di Castello: S. Lapi, 1926), 173: "Consciam fuisse reginam tam atrocis facinoris creditum est; et auxit infamiam alter subinde coniunx ab illa susceptus."

15. Ibid., 226.

16. Ibid., 228.

The Carraran chronicler Andrea Gatari revisited the same narrative. Continuing the chronicle begun by his father in the fourteenth century and taken up by his brother in the fifteenth, he added his own meditations on the schism around 1450. His account of events in Naples is confused and riddled with errors, but it adheres to characterizations of Johanna that developed during the schism. For instance, he says that Andrew of Hungary traveled to Naples with his brother, the duke of Durazzo, to marry Johanna. She is said to have enjoyed an adulterous liaison with the duke and to have plotted Andrew's murder with him and other men—adhering to tradition in linking her murderous tendencies with her lustfulness.[17] Gatari—like other fifteenth-century historians—alleges that she also beheaded James of Majorca for committing adultery, thus branding her a hypocrite as well as a viricide.[18] Her eventual downfall is well deserved, the result of a life of crime, and is linked to Louis of Hungary's long-standing vendetta. Gatari even pens a speech for Charles III in which he calls the Neapolitans to be loyal to him because he has liberated them "from the iniquity of the present queen."[19] Johanna's evil, libidinous nature is the yoke from which Charles delivers Naples, and her fate is justified because of her sexually charged crimes. Likewise, Niccolò Acciaiuoli's fifteenth-century biographer, Matteo Palmieri, told stories not merely of Johanna's wickedness but also of her alleged adulteries. He repeated the old charges that Robert had designated not Johanna but Andrew his heir, characterizing her reign as illegitimate and alleging that her throne was secured through murder.[20] He thus adds to her reputation for infidelity and viricide, amassing evidence from her various marriages to portray her as insatiably debauched.

Collenuccio gathered these threads together in his *Compendio delle historie del Regno di Napoli*, propagating an image of Johanna indebted to Giovanni Villani and the *Chronicon Estense*. She is, like Boccaccio's she-wolf, a sexual being. Collenuccio, too, links her murderous instincts with her lust: He charges that Johanna murdered Andrew in part because "Andrew, who was still very young, was not well enough versed in venereal acts" to satisfy her "unbridled appetite." According to Collenuccio, even in his day ("ancora al di d'hoggi"), a century after Johanna's death, people in Naples told the

---

17. Galeazzo Gatari and Bartolomeo Gatari, *Cronaca Carrarese confrontata con la redazione di Andrea Gatari* [AA. 1318–1407], ed. Antonio Medin and Guido Tolomei, 3 vols., vol. 17, pt. 1 of *RIS*, new ed. (Città di Castello: S. Lapi, 1909), vol. 2, appendix, XLI.

18. Ibid., XLII.

19. Ibid., XLV: "liberata che sia la patria vostra dall'iniquità della presente regina."

20. Palmieri, *Vita Nicolai Acciaioli*, 8–9.

story of Andrew's murder and described the queen fashioning a cord out of gold with which to strangle her young, innocent husband.[21] He conjures an enduring portrait of Johanna as the subject of gossip, a lustful monstrosity whose crimes continued to fascinate the people of Naples. The process begun during the schism of tying Johanna's betrayal of Urban to her murder of Andrew was complete, and Johanna as the She-Wolf of Naples was codified as a character in the region's history.

Johanna's Provençal Persona and the New Angevin Quest for Legitimacy

Johanna's Italian reputation was, by and large, the result of the accretion and mutation of gossip that, as Collenuccio testifies, continued long after her death. Nothing like an official Neapolitan portrait emerged after she died. Charles of Durazzo, suspected of having smothered or garroted Johanna, could hardly refer to her to legitimize his position. Even Charles's supporters described her death with distaste; the sense that he had betrayed a woman who was nearly a mother to him arose quickly and spread widely. Silence was the best policy. Instead, Johanna's legend grew and evolved in chronicles and the popular imagination, remaining firmly tied to contemporary accounts of her life even as new facets—such as the story of James of Majorca's beheading—were added to it.

In Provence, the situation was quite different. Louis of Anjou was an outsider who represented long-standing, acquisitive French interests. Provençal autonomy depended on the remote Neapolitan crown, which accorded the communes privileges and levied taxes but otherwise left them unmolested. The sudden appearance of a resident royal family changed Provençal life and politics substantially; the new dynasty needed to campaign actively to gain acceptance and assert its legitimacy. Accordingly, the representatives of the second Angevin line deliberately strove to tie themselves to Johanna, re-creating her as a loving maternal figure and attacking Charles III of Durazzo as a matricide. They refashioned her, discarding her history of childlessness and of war with Louis of Anjou, ignoring the scandals that had plagued her reign to present her as their innocent, murdered mother and themselves as her vindicators. In so doing, they asserted a right to Provence that derived from her will, as from their relationship to her, embroidering the legal fiction that Louis had been transformed into Johanna's firstborn son.

---

21. Collenuccio, *Compendio delle historie del Regno di Napoli*, 143.

Louis's succession proved divisive in Provence. The Estates General convened in April 1382 to discuss Johanna's provisions for her throne. The nobles and prelates declared themselves for Louis; some communes, including Marseille and Apt, did the same, while others, including the capital, Aix, rebelled.[22] Louis left the county in disarray when he departed for Naples. The opposition movement, known as the Union of Aix, grew in strength and numbers, appointing its own governor to replace the Angevin seneschal and sending ambassadors to Naples to treat with Charles of Durazzo. When the news of Johanna's death reached Provence, the Union decreed Charles her legitimate successor; by January 1383, Nice was flying Charles's standard, and a new Provençal government had formed to rival that established by Louis. Active hostilities between the rival factions began in February, when papal forces entered the county, which descended into civil war.[23]

Louis's death in Bari on September 21, 1384, escalated tensions in Provence. The threat that France would absorb the county loomed; Charles VI and Jean, duke of Berry, courted the dissidents while offering to help Louis's widow, Marie of Blois, conquer Naples. Marie, however, a shrewd and able regent, was determined to protect her son's rights in the county as well as in Italy. She reacted strongly and swiftly, moving into Provence and taking aggressive action against the rebels. She also hastened to have her son swear fealty to Clement VII for Johanna's lands, establishing him as the late queen's heir and securing Clement's support.[24] A second meeting of the Estates assured Marie of the high nobility and won several new communes for Louis II, while it also negotiated a twenty months' truce between Marie and the Union of Aix, which had no wish to see the county under French dominion.[25]

Marie turned to Johanna for aid, wielding her public image to legitimate Louis II's claims. She built on the foundation laid by Clement VII and her husband during Johanna's captivity, branding Charles a usurper and matricide and calling on Johanna's memory to inspire her subjects' devotion. Indeed, the bull of 1385 by which Clement all but sanctified Johanna (see chapter 5) formed part of this effort. Issued in Avignon on June 16, 1385, it called upon the people of Marseille to remain loyal to Louis II during Marie's regency.[26] Clement's attack on Charles as a second Nero and praise

---

22. Aurell, Boyer, and Coulet, *La Provence au Moyen Âge*, 285.
23. Ibid., 286.
24. Ibid.; Léonard, *Les Angevins de Naples*, 474.
25. Aurell, Boyer, and Coulet, *La Provence au Moyen Âge*, 287.
26. AMM, AA 65 6.

for Johanna's saintly attributes set the tone for letters patent sent to the city by Marie two months later.

Marie sought not only to assert Johanna's virtue but also to associate Louis I with it, insisting that he had died while pursuing justice, filled with ardor for the faith and zeal for charity.[27] He died, Marie reminded Marseille, in the service of Johanna, as of the Church, making him, too, a martyr. His object was to vanquish the "notorious" Charles of Durazzo, whom Marie excoriates as the "most ungrateful violator of faith and fidelity."[28] She compounds Charles's iniquity by representing him as the murderer of "the most serene lady Johanna of illustrious memory, queen of Jerusalem and Sicily and our natural mother (*matrem nostram naturalem*), as well as the liege lady of the aforesaid Charles."[29] Marie explicitly calls Johanna her "natural" mother, using the Latin word (*naturalis*) that designated a blood rather than an adoptive relationship. Indeed, she stresses her filial bond to Johanna and the late queen's glory far more than she praises or laments Louis I, depicting herself as personally injured by Charles's crime. Johanna was the adoptive mother of Marie's husband, and the two women certainly never met, but Marie evoked an intimate kinship with the slain queen, a sacred bond severed by Charles.

Not only had Charles committed the unforgivable sin of murdering Marie's mother, he had also at the same time murdered his own "most mild and most pure mother."[30] Building on the saintly reputation for which Clement VII had laid the foundation, Marie went so far as to implicitly equate Johanna with the Virgin Mary, Christ's most pure mother (*mater purissima*). Charles's crime, according to Marie, went beyond matricide: He murdered Johanna faithlessly (*infideliter*), impiously (*impie*), and ungratefully (*ingratissime*). The murder was thus not only a crime against Johanna's human flesh but also against God and the Church, and Marie represents Johanna as a martyred saint, the holy mother she is sworn to avenge.

Marie offers her own grief to contrast Charles's faithlessness: "The iniquitous deed having been accomplished, having been dressed in mourning clothes, with beaten breast, disarrayed hair, torn face, and mourning eyes, with horrible cries and indescribable wailing, demanding a suitable vengeance," she set herself to seek justice.[31] Johanna's newly established purity

---

27. AMM, AA 141 5: "Serenissimi domino consortis noster, cui deus partat ardore fidei et caritatis zelo virilius prosequamur."

28. Ibid.: "ingratissimum fidelitatis et fidei violatorem notorium Carolum de duracio."

29. Ibid.

30. Ibid.: "clementissimam et p[u]rissimam matrem suam."

31. Ibid.

and her association with the Church lent Marie's mission of vengeance, like that of Louis I, a religious dimension. Marie amplified this by depicting herself as a bereaved child sworn to avenge her blameless mother, ennobling herself through her loving distress.

At the heart of Marie's diatribe is an argument regarding Charles's fitness to rule. She says that she has searched chronicles and the works of ancient authors, but neither in antiquity nor in modern times "is there to be discovered such cruel impiety, such horrible ingratitude, and such abominable cruelty gathered together in one man."[32] Charles's faults are a detriment to the realm, because this "notorious violator of fidelity, along with his confederates in wickedness" is collecting "ingratitude, treachery, and impiety" in the Regno.[33] Above all else, he is a traitor to his own blood ("fraterni sanguinis violata"), something demonstrated not merely in his murder of his "natural lady and most pure mother" but also by the fact that he "held her captive in hard and inhumane prison in his Castel dell'Ovo."[34] Charles's iniquity contrasts starkly with Marie's grief and regard for Johanna. He is inhuman, a trait that led him to commit a cowardly murder: "Charles, hearing of the advent of our consort, the duke, of happy and honored memory, cruelly and inhumanly suffocated the lady queen, his most pure mother, between two pillows, which thing it is most bitter to recall."[35] Marie's sorrow and outrage argue for her greater legitimacy, while her loyalty and that of her family demonstrate their superior claims to Johanna's kingdom. They, and not Charles, are her true heirs.

Marie's letter evokes a dramatic conflict between herself, the avenger of her murdered mother, and Charles, her unnatural brother. The dispute revolves around the figure of Johanna as a saintly mother, the focus of Marie's grief and source of her rage. Marie returns repeatedly to the image of Johanna as "most pure mother," representing her as chaste and innocent to highlight Charles's iniquity. At the same time, she erases Johanna's sexualized reputation, restoring her virginity even as she asserts a new maternal identity for her. In life, Johanna had been childless, and the traumas visited on her lands after her death sprang in part from her lack of an heir. Marie remade her into a mother of many children, both virtuous and evil, cut down

---

32. Ibid.

33. Ibid.: "fidelitatis notorius violator cum sue nequicie complicibus quos ingratitudo prodicio et impietas sibi congragavit in unum Regnum Amasit."

34. Ibid.

35. Ibid.: "autem Carolus ipse felicem clare memorie duci dominum consortis noster ad Regium sesiit adventum ipsam dominam Reginam p[u]rissimam matrem suam inter duo matracia quo amarissime Refferimus crudeliter et inhumaniter suffocare fecit."

by her faithless son while her other children, Louis I, Louis II, and Marie herself, sought justice on her behalf. If in Italy, Johanna was immortalized as a she-wolf, her detractors calling up Andrew's ghost and describing her adulteries in order to defame her, in Provence, Marie cleansed her image, describing her as the pinnacle of feminine virtue, pure and untouched but still the mother of many loving "natural" children. If she does not go so far as to claim that she and her son were conceived immaculately, there is an implicit suggestion that their transformation into the children of a pure mother—a filial relationship lacking the sin inherent in conception—has a holy dimension. Indeed, by extension, Marie suggests that Louis of Anjou's transformative adoption—overseen by the pope, his holy father—was miraculous, making him the supernaturally conceived son of a pure and sinless mother, born anew as the son of the pope and the pure, saintly queen. His flesh was, Marie suggests, transubstantiated, making him truly Johanna's natural son and affirming Clement's role as God's representative on earth.

Marie re-created Johanna to validate herself, promoting herself and her son as Johanna's champions. In so doing, she called upon the loyalty of Johanna's subjects, reminding them of what they had lost and representing herself—Johanna's natural daughter—as Provence's rightful protector. Purified, Johanna became a symbol for the new dynasty. She was also a symbol of continuity, and Marie asks her subjects to recognize this, demonstrating her devotion to Johanna to tie them to her.

During the truce negotiated with the Union of Aix, Marie pressed her advantage. Arles reunited with the crown in November 1385, Brignoles in May 1386, and Sisteron in June 1386, isolating the Union. Although Margaret of Durazzo attempted to keep Charles's death in February 1386 a secret, the news made its way to Provence, leading more communes to negotiate with Marie in the spring of 1386. Marie continued her diplomatic efforts into the autumn of 1387, achieving a peace accord with most of the communes in June of that year.[36] Aix finally capitulated on September 17. Pockets of resistance remained: Nice continued to hold out, and the remaining Carlist communities fell under the control of Savoy in 1388.[37] Despite her losses, however, Marie had won back most of the county, establishing a base of power for Louis II. She was free to turn her attention to Naples, which became her primary concern from early 1388.

Marie's rhetorical need for Johanna did not end with her victory in Provence. Indeed, she and Louis II continued to evoke Johanna, insisting

---

36. Aurell, Boyer, and Coulet, *La Provence au Moyen Âge*, 287–88.
37. Ibid., 288.

on their rights as her appointed successors. They consistently stressed their kinship to her, and she remained the dynasty's loving mother, its fictional progenitor. In the chapters of peace agreed upon between Marie and the city of Aix, for instance, Marie called Johanna's shade as a witness, referring to her as "the lady our mother, whose spirit Paradise possesses."[38] Similarly, in a 1399 letter, she commended a Guichard of Villanova for his loyalty against "that most criminal traitor, Charles of Durazzo, invader and occupier of our kingdom of Sicily," the "reckless matricide of our lady mother."[39] The same marks of respect and love were extended to Johanna in the official correspondence of Louis II, who referred in an act of 1400 to his desire to "cultivate afresh the memory of the most reverend lady Queen Johanna."[40]

The new image of Johanna disseminated by Marie and Clement VII took root in Provence, reflected in communal rhetoric during the civil war. A notarial formulary containing a lamentation for Johanna's death bears witness to their campaign's success, as to characterizations of Johanna and of her death current in Provence at the time. Drawn from a formulary belonging to the notarial family of Borrilly, it is one of a collection of diverse types of documents copied for future reference.[41] Maurice Raimbault, who first described it, classifies the text as a model of satire or diatribe originally composed during the civil war by an Angevin partisan loyal to Johanna's memory and most likely a resident of Marseille.[42] The anonymous author was clearly familiar with descriptions of Johanna by Clement and Marie, and he likens Johanna to such biblical exemplars as the queen of Sheba, Judith, and Esther, although she surpassed even these women.[43] He goes on to enumerate her virtues, saying that she was

> fervent in goodwill, steadfast in her promises, predisposed to compassion, stern in oversight, and . . . upright in judgment, modest in speech, diligent in command, wise in counsel, gracious in her responses and equally circumspect; presenting herself to companions of lesser rank,

---

38. ADBR, B 1403, fol. 65r.

39. ABDR, B 8, fol. 52r: "nephandissimo proditori charolo de duracio Regni nostri Sicilie Invasori et occupatori ac serenissime domine Regine Johanne dei gratia Jerusalem et Sicilie . . . domine matris nostre temerario matricida."

40. Ibid., fol. 54v: "Recolende memorie reverendissime domine Johanne Regine."

41. Maurice Raimbault, *Un Pamphlet contemporain sur la mort de la Reine Jeanne*, Ext. des Comptes rendus et Mémoires du Congrès de Marseille 1928 (p. 58) (Marseille: Institut Historique de Provence, 1931), 1. The manuscript is Aix-en-Provence, Bibliothèque Arbaud, MS Raimbault D 25, fol. 156.

42. Raimbault, *Un Pamphlet contemporain sur la mort de la Reine Jeanne*, 2.

43. Ibid., 5: "Non regina Sabe, non Judic, non Ester fureunt sibi similes in virtutibus neque pares cum inclita ipsa domina fuerit ad mores composite."

[she was] stern toward arrogance, kindly toward humility, merciful toward the penitent and inflexible toward the obstinate, neither had anyone been so greatly endowed among her subjects nor among her natural kin (*suis naturalibus*) so greatly loved.[44]

His praise thus prefigures that offered by later historians like Bouche, whose elegiac description of Johanna descends from such closely contemporary characterizations.

Given its relationship to other pro-Angevin rhetoric of the time, the lamentation is closer to diatribe than to satire. Its praise of Johanna is perhaps extreme, but it was likely not meant as mockery. Indeed, the author's description of Johanna is probably drawn in part from Giovanni Boccaccio's *De mulieribus claris*. He adapts the arguments current in royal and papal discussions of Johanna, amplifying and expanding on them. He also adds rhetorical flourish that pushes his praise even further than Clement and Marie dared.

It is clear that Marie's re-creation of Johanna lies behind the unknown author's elegy. He begins by calling on God, begging the Almighty to "teach me your outraged anger that there had been so many sons and so many princes of our Lady Queen" through whose machinations "her kingdom and her legitimate adopted successor" are left to bemoan Johanna's "premature, miserable, and severe death."[45] The depiction of the childless queen as the mother of too many sons reflects Marie's comparison of herself as Johanna's natural daughter to Charles, the unnatural matricide. Charles is on this author's mind as well, and he draws on the Clementist portrait of Charles as treacherous to kin and ungrateful for Johanna's care, calling him a "destroyer of the womb" (surely recalling Clement's comparison of him to Nero) and a matricide. Charles is "ungrateful for the benefits he received," scornful of the ties that should have bound him to Johanna as "a son and nephew" after she had "delicately nurtured him in his boyhood." His betrayal martyred Johanna, the author argues—making explicit what Clement and Marie have implied—her patience in the face of death winning her the martyr's palm (*palmam martirii*).[46] The lamentation thus completes the process begun by Clement and Marie, unequivocally declaring Johanna a martyr and making the sainthood with which they had flirted literal. Its portrait of Johanna, if embroidered for

---

44. Ibid.

45. Ibid., 4: "aprehendit me indignicio ire sue ut que fueram tanti filii tantique principis domine nostre Regine per eam in Regem et successorem suum legitimum adoptati solatio destitute, premature, miserabilis, cevera [*sic*] et lugenda mors prefacte domine nostre regine."

46. Ibid., 5: "matri uteri corrosor et . . . matricida."; "benificiorum receptorum ingrates . . . a dicta domina nostra et sua, sic in sua puericia delicate nutritus."

rhetoric's sake, represents an extreme point in the Provençal reinvention of Johanna. She is a mother, a saint, a martyr, and an exemplar of queenly virtue. During the civil war that followed her death, she became a loyalist symbol, a veritable patron saint for the faithful communes. In death, she rose again to become enshrined in the county's "golden legend" as the perfect queen.

The Johanna immortalized in Provence was, thus, the product of Angevin propaganda. Marie of Blois and Louis II of Anjou, building on a foundation laid by Louis I and Clement VII, refashioned Johanna as the founder of their new dynasty. They deliberately obscured their distant kinship to her, Marie and Louis I both depicting themselves as her loyal children. In her efforts to secure Provence for her son, Marie elaborated on this kinship, obscuring what was merely a legal relationship beneath her self-identification as Johanna's "natural" daughter. In so doing, she played on the representation of Charles of Durazzo as a matricide: His behavior was unnatural, making him an unnatural son, while her devotion transformed her into a natural daughter. The word "natural" was thus polysemous, employed to mean both that Marie was Johanna's biological daughter and that her behavior was appropriate while Charles's was inhuman, unnatural. She deployed the emotional language of kinship to depict herself as a fitting successor to the murdered queen, whose virtue she enhanced and whose history she ignored. Charles, through his faithlessness, had forfeited any rights he might have had to Johanna's throne, while Marie—the representative of Johanna's designated heir and her faithful daughter—earned the right to it through her love and outraged grief. At the same time, she asserted her right to be Provence's regent, representing the relationship between her family and Johanna as transcending legal nicety, binding them together in a spiritual kinship that obliterated any doubt as to the second Angevin line's legitimacy.

The image of Johanna as violated mother and progenitor of the new dynasty endured, finding its way, alongside Froissart's depiction of the tragic queen, into Provençal legend. Good Queen Jeanne lived on to rival the She-Wolf. The author of the lamentation on Johanna's death enshrined her as the county's own martyred saint, a paragon of virtue and the embodiment of just queenship. Both are caricatures of femininity, the one approaching virginal saintliness, the other embodying female lasciviousness in its most dangerous, most violent form. The negative characterizations of Johanna revived and amplified during the schism evolved in Italy, working their way into Neapolitan history. In Provence, Marie of Blois recuperated Johanna, giving rise to a tender maternal image that eventually surpassed historical memory of the trials of Johanna's reign so that all that remained was a legendary golden-age queen of unmatched piety and virtue.

Conclusion

The evolution of Johanna of Naples's reputation reflects shifting, inconsistent responses to female sovereignty. Reactions to Johanna's reign were inseparable from her sex, and descriptions of it were always gendered. Her contemporaries typed her and she typed herself according to accepted gender norms, describing her as a good or bad woman according to culturally constructed definitions of femininity. Those wishing to defame and delegitimize her described her as a she-wolf, viricide, and harlot, faulting her for inconstancy and irrationality. Those who upheld her sovereignty or—in the case of the second Angevin line—drew on her image to legitimate themselves cast her as a model of positive feminine virtues, such as maternal affection, piety, filial obedience, and patient endurance. She herself took part in this process, manipulating her *fama* and crafting a modified form of Angevin sovereignty that stressed her allegiance to the papacy and patronage of religious projects, thereby neutralizing her reputation for unbridled, dangerous sexuality.

Johanna's evolving reputation highlights how *fama* worked in late medieval Europe. Johanna's *fama* was largely determined by her femininity: an active, powerful woman was always sexualized, and queens in particular were commonly portrayed as sexually licentious. Johanna and her apologists could—and did—cloak her sex in the positive attributes of femininity, but they could not escape gendered assumptions about women in power.

During times of crisis, accepted negative stereotypes of femininity shaped contemporary responses, so that political scandal inevitably became sexual scandal, and criticism of Johanna as a ruler shaded into attacks on her as a woman. Thus, the making of Johanna's reputation was the product of constant struggle between competing forces—Johanna's public performance of queenship, her cultural commissions, the descriptions of her supporters and opponents, and the perpetual mutation of gossip and rumor—some of which Johanna could direct and some of which were outside her control.

A close inspection of Johanna's constantly shifting *fama* reveals that her reign was not perceived during her lifetime as the unmitigated disaster it has often been described as, nor was she herself a marginal figure. She looms large in her time's cultural imaginary, the preoccupation with her reign and personality revealing her importance during her life. If her reign began and ended in disaster, Andrew of Hungary's death and the schism were separated by a long period during which Johanna, rather than being perceived as an ineffectual and libidinous queen with little real power, instead became an illustrious ruler in the true Angevin vein and the embodiment of feminine virtue. Her career and reputation traced a parabolic path. At its height, Johanna's *fama* reveals that the idea of regnant queenship was viable when her sexuality was bounded and contained by rhetorical subservience to the papacy and active displays of piety, while at the depths that defined either extreme of her reign, her sovereignty was described as invalid because of the natural defects of her sex.

In times of crisis, Johanna's detractors consistently fell back on well-worn tropes of medieval antifeminist argument. Their criticisms were hackneyed, but they were intended to defame her in comprehensible terms during moments of perceived failure. Her discursive infamy argued against her right and fitness to rule, demonstrating the illegitimacy of her succession and the pitfalls inherent in allowing women to exercise sovereign authority. Her critics' characterizations of her were most negative when she was seen as most independent and unbridled and when her actions had the greatest impact on European society. During the worst moments of crisis—the aftermath of Andrew of Hungary's murder and the early years of the schism—Johanna's rule was described as a carnivalesque inversion of natural order. According to the anonymous *Diurnali del Duca di Monteleone*, Johanna's subjects rose up against *lo Papa delo Carnevale* when Clement VII traveled to Naples. Johanna could herself be seen as part of the inverted order of carnival, the queen and her antipope forming the reversed reflection of right order, represented by Charles III of Durazzo and Urban VI. The same inversion is visible in earlier accounts of her reign, particularly in analyses of her relationship to Andrew of Hungary, whose sovereignty in marriage and in the Regno she was argued to have usurped. Female sovereignty, at critical moments in Johanna's career, was argued to constitute an inversion, a violation of the laws of nature that placed husbands above wives and kings above queens.

Yet attitudes toward sovereign queenship, as toward Johanna, were not so simple. Disordered femininity and irrationality could explain her failures, but belief in natural female inferiority did not bar Johanna from the throne, despite antifeminist rhetoric and political theories drawn on by commentators who argued that sovereignty was reserved to men. Early in her reign, especially after Andrew's death, Johanna was portrayed as monstrously female to demonstrate the illegitimacy of her rule as well as to explain Andrew's murder. The years that followed, however, yielded new descriptions of Johanna that reveal ambiguities in the concept of regnant queenship, as in the very idea of sovereignty. Indeed, it was the papacy—the most male-dominated institution in Western Christendom—that supported her rule until 1378. Sovereignty might be gendered male, but Johanna's apologists ascribed feminine attributes to it, and Johanna herself ably shaped her performances of queenship to reflect ideals of both femininity and monarchy. Her success reveals both her considerable personal presence and her skill at self-presentation. Her supporters offered her feminine virtues as proof of her effective, beneficent rule, femininity's positive attributes serving to legitimate her position as much as its negative characterizations served to invalidate it. Boccaccio described her as "soft-spoken, . . . affable, compassionate, gentle, and kind," asking rhetorically, "What greater qualities would one seek in the wisest King?"[1] Femininity could be a disqualification for sovereignty, but it could also be associated with its successful exercise.

The question of Johanna's legitimacy as a regnant queen was complicated, and the same commentators—for instance, Boccaccio and Petrarch—sometimes argued both sides of the issue. Contemporary natural philosophical and literary discourse posited that women should not rule over men and that they in fact lacked the capacity to do so. At the same time, the hereditary principle of rulership favored succession in the direct line, and Johanna was (arguably) the legitimate heir to the Neapolitan throne according to that principle. Whether depicting her as its continuator or its destroyer, stories about Johanna's rule consistently return to the necessity of preserving the dynasty. Recognizing the crucial importance of lineage, she strove to associate herself with her ancestors, relying on their memory to legitimate her position. She celebrated her kinship with *beata stirps* like Louis of France and

---

1. Giovanni Boccaccio, *De mulieribus claris*, CVI, in Brown, trans., *Famous Women*, 232.

Louis of Toulouse, as to Robert and Sancia, whose piety she stressed both in describing and in emulating them.

Louis of Taranto's reign brought the matter of blood to the forefront, and those who had been eager to see a strong man at the Regno's helm were ultimately glad to see sovereignty vested once again in Robert of Anjou's heir, even if that heir were a woman. Louis might exercise sovereignty, but Johanna embodied it. As such, her contemporaries recognized that sovereignty (at least in Naples) could be legitimately transmitted to and through women. Indeed, Johanna's successors in Provence insisted that it could in their portrayal of themselves as her natural children, seeking to obscure their intrusion into the dynasty, while her Italian detractors during the schism argued that she had sought to disrupt dynastic succession by having her nondynastic husband succeed ahead of Charles III. Charles's usurpation was justified as a means to protect the Angevin bloodline—indeed, he effectively erased Johanna from it after her death—and Johanna's deposition was presented as necessary due to her violation of dynastic principle.

Another contentious issue was whether Johanna, despite being the legitimate sovereign through descent from Robert, could legitimately exercise the sovereignty she embodied. Discussions of Johanna worked on two levels, demonstrating that queens, like kings, had two bodies. On the one hand, she was the inheritor of Angevin sovereignty; on the other, she was a woman and a wife, and she needed the appearance of a traditional marriage that subjected her to a husband in order to construct and maintain her *fama* for virtue. It was unacceptable for her to rule over her husband, but it was equally unacceptable for her husband to usurp her sovereignty (at least if he exercised it poorly). Her four marriages tested the ambiguities and contradictions inherent in the notion of the king-consort, and she struggled to find a balance that protected her power without drawing criticism for usurping her husband's authority.

The period between Louis of Taranto's death and the beginning of the schism saw the elaboration of a form of sovereign queenship that Johanna's contemporaries were largely willing to accept. She was perhaps most successful at navigating the perceived problems of unbounded femininity during this period. Marriage and active piety helped counteract her reputation for uncontrolled sexuality, while her patronage of chaste, holy women associated her with their reputations for sanctity. She marshaled contemporary depictions of virtuous femininity to redefine herself, appropriating them for her image while representing herself as a papal champion in a way that combined traditional aspects of queenship with those of Angevin kingship. At the same time, she adopted a humble stance with regard both to her papal suzerains and to her saintly friends, demonstrating a feminine meekness that softened her assertions of sovereignty. Her reputation for piety and as a member of the papal league testifies to the success not only of Johanna's efforts to reshape her *fama* but also of the idea of female rulership, which her contemporaries tolerated and even celebrated. Indeed, by the 1380s, regnant queens ruled kingdoms throughout Europe.

This is not to say that the idea of female sovereignty as Johanna articulated it and her contemporaries described it was an unqualified triumph. It had limitations, and Johanna, in tailoring her performances of queenship and shaping her *fama*, clearly recognized them. Perhaps she was even a victim of her own success; the relationship she forged with the papacy proved her undoing when the schism began and she asserted her right to take a leading role in the struggle that followed. Her actions were proscribed within the discourse on femininity, and her transgressions of gender norms could be pushed only so far. Her legacy, in both Provence and Italy, reflects the conditions of her time. She was redefined according to gendered tropes that suited the needs of those describing her, and her reputation became reduced and flattened when she could no longer act on it. Her self-definition and her successes largely vanished in historical memory, while the stereotypically feminine images disseminated by her critics and posthumous apologists remain.

 Bibliography

Archival Sources

Archives départementales des Bouches-du-Rhône, B 3, B 5, B 8, B 150, B 165, B 168,
B 176, B 181, B 205, B 269, B 483, B 539, B 550, B 559 2, B 559 3, B 1403.
Archives municipales de Marseille, AA 5, AA 64 1, AA 64 2, AA 64 3, AA 65 6, AA
76 1, AA 140 1, AA 141 2, AA 141 5, BB 20, BB 21, BB 28, BB 29.
Archivio di Stato di Firenze, Capitoli, t. XVI.
Bullaire d'Avignon, Archives de Vaucluse, AA 5.

Manuscript Sources

Aix-en-Provence, Bibliothèque Arbaud, MS Raimbault D 25.
Aix-en-Provence, Bibliothèque Méjanes, MS 771 [1064].
Avignon, Bibliothèque Ceccano, MS 1615, MS 1706, MS 2394, MS 2395, MS 2430,
MS 2465–66, MS 2834.
Bologna, Biblioteca communale dell'Archiginnasio, MS B 1145.
Leuven, Maurits Sabbe Bibliotheek, MS 1.
London, British Library, MS Cotton Claudius B. I.
Naples, Biblioteca Nazionale, MS Brancaccio IV B 7.
New York, Pierpont Morgan Library, MS M. 498.
Palermo, Biblioteca Centrale della Regione Siciliana, MS IV.G.2.
Paris, Bibliothèque nationale de France, MS fonds français 756–57, MS fonds français
4274, MS fonds français 4317, MS fonds français 6537, n° 1, MS fonds français
30025, MS fonds latin 11745.
Tours, Bibliothèque municipale, MS 520.
Uppsala, Universitätsbibliothek, MS C 15.
Vienna, Österreichische Nationalbibliothek, Cod. 1921.
Warsaw, Biblioteka Narodowa, MS 3310.
Zwettl, Zisterzienserstift, Cod. 169 8, Cod. 169 20.

Printed Primary Sources

Agnes of Harcourt. *The Writings of Agnes of Harcourt: The "Life of Isabelle of France"
and the "Letter on Louis IX and Longchamp."* Edited and translated by Sean L.
Field. Notre Dame: University of Notre Dame Press, 2003.
Albertus de Bezanis. *Cronica pontificum et imperatorum.* Edited by Oswald Holder-Egger.
Monumenta Germaniae Historica, Scriptores rerum Germanicarum in usum
scholarum separatim editi 3. Hannover: Hahn, 1908.

Andreas Capellanus. *Andreas Capellanus on Love.* Edited by P. G. Walsh. London: Duckworth, 1982.

Aquinas, Thomas. *Summa Theologiae.* Edited by Pietro Caramello. 3 vols. Turin: Marietti, 1952–76.

Aretino, Leonardo Bruni. *Historiarum Florentini populi, Libri XII, e Rerum suo tempore gestarum commentarius.* Edited by Emilio Santini and Carmine di Pierro. Vol. 19, pt. 3 of *Rerum Italicarum Scriptores.* Città di Castello: S. Lapi, 1926.

Arienzo, Luisa d', ed. *Carte reali diplomatiche di Pietro IV il ceremonioso, re d'Aragona, riguardanti l'Italia.* Padua: Casa Editrice Dott. Antonio Milani, 1970.

Ayala, Pero Lopez de. *Crónica del Rey Don Pedro y del Rey Don Enrique, su hermano, hijos del rey don Alfonso Onceno.* Edited by Germán Orduna. Buenos Aires: Incipit-Ediciones Criticas, 1994.

Baluze, Étienne. *Vitae paparum Avenionensium.* Edited by G. Mollat. 2 vols. Paris: Letouzey et Ané, 1914–27.

Barbi, Silvio Adrasto, ed. *Storie Pistoresi* [1300–1348]. Vol. 11, pt. 5 of *Rerum Italicarum Scriptores: Raccolta degli Storici Italiani dal cinquecento al millecinquecento,* edited by L. A. Muratori, new ed. Città di Castello: S. Lapi, 1907.

Baronio, Cesare, et al. *Annales ecclesiastici, denuo et Accurate excusi.* Edited by August Theiner. Paris: Barri-Ducis, 1880.

Battagli da Rimini, Marco. *Marcha di Marco Battagli da Rimini* [AA. 1212–1354]. Vol. 16, pt. 3 of *Rerum Italicarum Scriptores,* edited by Aldo Francesco Massèra, new ed. Città di Castello: S. Lapi, 1912.

Begani, Orsini, ed. *Breve Chronicon Monasterii mantuani sancti Andree ord. Bened. di Antonio Nerli* (AA. 800–1431). Vol. 24, pt. 13 of *Rerum Italicarum Scriptores,* edited by Ludovico Muratori, new ed. Città di Castello: S. Lapi, 1910.

Bertoni, Guilio, and Emilio Paolo Vicini, eds. *Chronicon Estense, cum additamentis usque ad annum 1478.* Vol. 15, pt. 3 of *Rerum Italicarum Scriptores: Raccolta degli Storici Italiani del cinquecento al millecinquecento,* edited by L. A. Muratori, new ed. Città di Castello: S. Lapi, 1908.

Birgersson, Ulf. *Vite Katerine.* Edited by Tryggve Lundén. Uppsala: Almqvist & Wiksell, 1981.

Birgitta of Sweden. *The Liber Celestis of St. Bridget of Sweden: The Middle English Version in the British Library MS Claudius B I, together with a Life of the Saint from the Same Manuscript.* Edited by Roger Ellis. 2 vols. Early English Text Society 291. Oxford: Oxford University Press, 1987.

——. *Sancta Birgitta—Revelaciones, Book I, with Magister Mathias' Prologue.* Edited by Carl-Gustaf Undhagen. Samlingar utgivna av Svenska Fornskriftsällskapet, Series 2: Latinska Skrifter 7.1. Uppsala: Almqvist & Wiksell, 1978.

——. *Sancta Birgitta Revelaciones, Book IV.* Edited by Hans Aili. Samlingar utgivna av Svenska Fornskriftsällskapet, Series 2: Latinska Skrifter 7.4. Stockholm: Almqvist & Wiksell, 1992.

——. *Sancta Birgitta Revelaciones Lib. VII.* Edited by Birger Bergh. Samlingar utgivna av Svenska Fornskriftsällskapet, Series 2: Latinska Skrifter 7.7. Uppsala: Almqvist & Wiksell, 1967.

Blamires, Alcuin, ed. *Woman Defamed and Woman Defended: An Anthology of Medieval Texts.* Oxford: Oxford University Press, 1992.

Boccaccio, Giovanni. *Amorosa Visione*. Edited by Vittore Branca. Vol. 3 of *Tutte le Opere di Giovanni Boccaccio*, edited by Vittore Branca. Milan: Arnoldo Mondadori, 1974.

———. *The Corbaccio, or the Labyrinth of Love*. Edited and translated by Anthony K. Cassell. Binghamton: State University of New York Press, 1993.

———. *De casibus virorum illustrium*. Edited by Pier Giorgio Ricci and Vittorio Zaccaria. Vol. 9 of *Tutte le opere di Giovanni Bocaccio*. Milan: Arnoldo Mondadori Editore, 1983.

———. *Famous Women*. Edited and translated by Virginia Brown. The I Tatti Renaissance Library. Cambridge, MA: Harvard University Press, 2001.

———. *Eclogues*. Translated and edited by Janet Levarie Smarr. New York: Garland, 1987.

———. *Epistole e Lettere*. Edited by Ginetta Auzas. Vol. 5 of *Tutte le Opere di Giovanni Boccaccio*, edited by Vittore Branca. Milan: Arnoldo Mondadori, 1992.

Bonaiuti, Baldassare [Marchionne di Coppo Stefani]. *Cronaca Fiorentina*. Edited by Niccolò Rodolico. In *Cronache Toscane*, vol. 30 of *Rerum Italicarum Scriptores*, new ed. Città di Castello: S. Lapi, 1903.

Bresc, Henri, ed. *La Correspondence de Pierre Ameilh, Archêveque de Naples puis d'Embrun (1363–1369)*. Sources d'Histoire Médiévale 6. Paris: Centre nationale de la recherche scientifique, 1972.

Caracciolo, Tristano. *Opusculi Storici editi e inediti*. Edited by Giuseppe Paladino. Vol. 22, pt. 1 of *Rerum Italicarum Scriptores*. Bologna: Nicola Zanichelli, 1934.

Catherine of Siena. *The Letters of Catherine of Siena*. Edited and translated by Suzanne Noffke. 4 vols. Tempe: Arizona Center for Medieval and Renaissance Studies, 2000–8.

Cerasoli, F., ed. "Clemente VI e Giovanna I di Napoli—Documenti inediti dell'Archivio Vaticano, 1343–1352." *Archivio storico per le province napoletane* 21 (1896): 3–41, 227–64, 427–75, 667–707.

———, ed. "Gregorio XI e Giovanna I, regina di Napoli." *Archivio storico per le province napoletane* 23 (1898): 471–501, 671–701.

———, ed. "Gregorio XI e Giovanna I di Napoli." *Archivio storico per le province napoletane* 24 (1899): 3–24, 307–28, 403–27.

———, ed. "Gregorio XI e Giovanna I di Napoli—Documenti inediti dell'Archivio Vaticano, 1370–1378." *Archivio storico per le province napoletane* 25 (1900): 3–26.

———, ed. "Innocenzo VI e Giovanna I di Napoli: Documenti inediti dell'Archivio Vaticano." *Archivio storico per le province napoletane* 22 (1897), 183–203, 351–70, 507–28.

———, ed.. "Urbano V e Giovanna I di Napoli—Documenti inediti dell'Archivio Vaticano, 1362–1370." *Archivio storico per le province napoletane* 20 (1895): 72–94, 171–205, 359–94, 598–645.

Chaucer, Geoffrey. *The House of Fame*. In Geoffrey Chaucer, *Dream Visions and Other Poems*, edited by Kathryn L. Lynch, 39–92. New York: W. W. Norton, 2007.

———. "The Legend of Good Women." In *The Complete Works of Geoffrey Chaucer*, edited by Walter William Skeat, 6:349–95. Oxford: Oxford University Press, 1903.

Christine de Pizan. *The Book of the City of Ladies*. Translated by Earl Jeffrey Richards. New York: Persea Books, 1982.

———. *Le Livre de la Mutacion de Fortune.* Edited by Suzanne Solente. 4 vols. Paris: Picard, 1959–66.

———. *Le Livre des Trois Vertus: édition critique.* Edited by C. C. Willard and Eric Hicks. Bibliothèque du XVe siècle 50. Paris: H. Champion, 1989.

———. *The Treasure of the City of Ladies, or the Book of the Three Virtues.* Translated by Sarah Lawson. London: Penguin, 1985.

Clausdotter, Margareta. *Chronicon de genere et nepotibus S. Birgittae, auctore Margareta Clausdotter, abbatissa Vadstenensi.* In *Scriptores Rerum Svecicarum Medii Aevi,* edited by Claudius Annerstedt, 3.2:207–16. Graz: Akad. Dr.-u. Verlag-Anst, 1966.

Cola di Rienzo. *Epistolario di Cola di Rienzo.* Edited by Annibale Gabrielli. Fonti per la storia d'Italia 6. Rome: Forzani, 1890.

Collenuccio, Pandolfo. *Compendio delle historie del Regno di Napoli, composto da messer Pandolfo Collenutio iurisconsulto in Pesaro.* Vinegia: Michele Tramezino, 1548.

Collijn, Isak, ed. *Acta et Processus Canonizacionis Beate Birgitte.* 2 vols. Samlingar utgivna av Svenska Fornskriftsällskapet. Series 2: Latinska Skrifter. Uppsala: Almqvist and Wiksells, 1924–31.

Dati, Gregorio. *L'Istoria di Firenze dal 1380 al 1405.* Edited by L. Pratesi. Norcia: Tonti Cesare, 1902.

De Blasiis, Joseph, ed. *Chronicon Siculum incerti auctoris ab anno 340 ad annum 1396, in forma diario ex inedito Codice Ottoboniano Vaticano.* Società Napoletana di Storia Patria. Monumenti Storici—Serie Prima: Cronache. Naples: Francisco Giannini & Fil., 1887.

Déprez, Eugène, ed. *Clement VI (1342–1352): Lettres closes, patentes et curiales publiées ou analysées d'après les registres du Vatican.* Paris: E. de-Boccard, 1958.

Déprez, E., J. Glénisson, and G. Mollat, eds. *Clement VI (1342–1352): Lettres se rapportant à la France, publiées ou analysées d'après les registres du Vatican.* Paris: A. Fontemoing, 1925.

Dietrich von Niem. *De scismate libri tres.* Edited by George Erler. Leipzig: Veit, 1890.

Domenico da Gravina. *Chronicon de Rebus in Apulia Gestis [AA. 1333–1350].* Edited by L. A. Muratori. Vol. 12, pt. 3 of *Rerum Italicarum Scriptores: Raccolta degli Storici Italiani dal cinquecento al millecinquecento,* new ed. Edited by Albano Sorbelli. Città di Castello: S. Lapi, 1903.

Egidi, Pietro. "La scrittura segreta di Giovanna I di Napoli in una sua lettera dell'A. 1380." *Archivio storico per le province napoletane* 31 (1906): 360–84.

Eiximenis, Francesc. *Lo Libre de les Dones.* Edited by Frank Naccarato. Barcelona: Curial, 1981.

Fejér, Georgii, ed. *Codex diplomaticus Hungariae ecclesiasticus ac civilis,* vol. 9, pt. 7. Buda: Typis typogr. Regiae Universitatis Ungaricae, 1829.

Filangieri, Riccardo, et al. *I registri della concellaria angioina.* Naples: Accademic Pontaniana, 1950–2006.

Froissart, Jean. *Les Chroniques de Sire Jean Froissart, qui traitent des merveilleuses emprises, nobles aventures et faits d'armes advenus en son temps en France, Angleterre, Bretaigne, Bourgogne, Escosse, Espaigne, Portingal et ès autres parties,* v. 2. Edited by J. A. C. Buchon. Paris: Desrez, 1837.

Fumi, Luigi, ed. *Ephemerides Urbevetanae, dal Cod. Vaticano Urbinate 1745.* Vol. 15, pt. 5 of *Rerum Italicarum Scriptores,* edited by Ludovico Muratori, new ed. Città di Castello: S. Lapi, 1903.

Gatari, Galeazzo, and Bartolomeo Gatari. *Cronaca Carrarese confrontata con la redazione di Andrea Gatari* [AA. 1318–1407]. Edited by Antonio Medin and Guido Tolomei. 3 vols. Vol. 17, pt. 1 of *Rerum Italicarum Scriptores*, new ed. Città di Castello: S. Lapi, 1909.

Gejrot, Claes, ed. *Vadstenadiariet*. Stockholm: Kungliga Samfundet för utgivande av handskrifter rörande Skandinaviens historia, 1996.

Geoffrey of Monmouth. *The History of the Kings of Britain*. Translated by Lewis Thorpe. London: Penguin Books, 1966.

Giovanni da Bazzano. *Chronicon Mutinense* [AA. 1188–1363]. Edited by Tommaso Casini. Vol. 15, pt. 4 of *Rerum Italicarum Scriptores: Racolta degli Storici Italiani del cinquecento al millecinquecento*, edited by L. A. Muratori, new ed. Bologna: N. Zanichelli, 1917–19.

Gratian. *Decretum Magistri Gratiani*. Edited by A. Friedberg. In *Corpus Iuris Canonici*, vol. 1, pt. 2. Leipzig: Unveränd. Nachdr., 1879–81; repr. Graz: Akademische Druck-u. Verlagsanstalt, 1959.

Green, Monica, ed. *The Trotula: An English Translation of the Medieval Compendium of Women's Medicine*. Philadelphia: University of Pennsylvania Press, 2002.

Hector, L. C., and Barbara F. Harvey, eds. and trans. *The Westminster Chronicle, 1381–1394*. Oxford Medieval Texts. Oxford: Oxford University Press, 1982.

Hegel, Karl, ed. *Chronicon Moguntinum*. Monumenta Germaniae Historica, Scriptores rerum Germanicarum in usum scholarum separatim editi 20. Hannover: Hahn, 1885.

Heyligen, Louis. "Breve Chronicon Clerici Anonymi." In *Receuil des Chroniques de Flandre*, edited by J. J. de Smet, vol. 3. Brussels: Commission Royale d'Histoire, 1856.

Isidore of Seville. *Etymologiarum sive originum libri XX*. Edited by W. M. Lindsay. Oxford: Oxford University Press, 1911.

Isoldi, Francesco, ed. *La Mesticanza di Paolo di Lello Petrone (XVIII Agosto MCCCCXXIV – VI Marzo MCCCXLVII)*. Vol. 24, pt. 2 of *Rerum Italicarum Scriptores*, edited by Ludovico Muratori, new ed. Città di Castello: S. Lapi, 1910.

Jacobus de Voragine. *The Golden Legend—Readings on the Saints*. Vol. 1. Translated by William Granger Ryan. Princeton: Princeton University Press, 1993.

Jean le Fèvre. *Journal de Jean le Fèvre, évêque de Chartres, chancelier des rois de Sicile Louis I et Louis II d'Anjou*. Edited by H. Moranvillé. 2 vols. Paris: A. Picard, 1887.

John of Rupescissa. *Liber ostensor quod adesse festinant tempora*. Edited by André Vauchez, Clémence Thévenaz, and Christine Morerod-Fattebert. Rome: École française de Rome, 2005.

——. *Liber secretorum eventuum: Edition critique, traduction et introduction historique*. Edited by Robert E. Lerner and Christine Morerod-Fattebert. Fribourg: Éditions Universitaires, 1994.

John of Winterthur. *Die Chronik Johanns von Winterthur*. Edited by Friedrich Baethgen. Monumenta Germaniae Historica, Scriptores rerum germanicarum, new series, 3. Munich: Monumenta Germaniae Historica, 1982.

Juvenal. *Satires*. Edited by Susanna Morton Braund. New York: Cambridge University Press, 1996.

Kaup, Matthias, and Robert E. Lerner, eds. "Gentile of Foligno Interprets the Prophecy 'Woe to the World,' with an Edition and English Translation." *Traditio* 56 (2001): 149–211.

Kelly, Samantha, ed. *The "Cronaca di Partenope": An Introduction to and Critical Edition of the First Vernacular History of Naples (c. 1350)*. Leiden: Brill, 2011.

Kezel, Albert Ryle, ed. and trans. *Birgitta of Sweden: Life and Selected Revelations*. Classics of Western Spirituality. Mahwah, NJ: Paulist Press, 1990.

Lecacheux, Paul, ed. *Lettres secrètes et curiales du Pape Urbain V (1362–1370) se rapportant à la France, publiées ou analysées d'après les registres du Vatican*. Paris: Fontemoing, 1902.

Lisini, Alessandro, and Fabio Iacometti, eds. *Cronache Senesi*. Vol. 15, pt. 6 of *Rerum Italicarum Scriptores*. Bologna: Nicola Zanichelli, 1931.

Ljubic, Sime. *Commissiones et relationes venetae*, vol. 2. Monumenta Spectantia Historiam Slavorum Meridionalium. Zagreb: Sumptibus Academiae Scientiarum et Artium, 1876.

Lope de Vega. *La reina Juana de Nápoles: Obras de Lope de Vega*. Edited by Marcelino Menéndez [y] Pelayo. Biblioteca de Autores Españoles 15. Madrid: Real Academia Española, 1966.

Manfredi, Michele, ed. *I Diurnali del Duca di Monteleone*. Vol. 25, pt. 5 of *Rerum Italicarum Scriptores*, new ed. Bologna: Nicola Zanichelli, 1958.

Mathias of Neuenburg. *Die Chronik des Mathias von Neuenburg*. Edited by Adolf Hofmeister. Monumenta Germaniae Historica, Scriptores rerum Germanicarum, new series, 4. Berlin: Weidmann, 1955.

Mattheo de' Griffoni. *Memoriale Historicum de rebus Bononiensium* [AA. 4448 a.C.– 1472 d. C.]. Edited by Lodovico Frati and Albano Sorbelli. Vol. 18, pt. 2 of *Rerum Italicarum Scriptores*, new ed. Città di Castello: S. Lapi, 1902.

Mistral, Frederic. *La Reino Jano: tragedi prouvencalo*. Edited and translated by Émile G. Léonard. Toulon: L'Astrado, 1974.

Mollat, G., ed. *Lettres secrètes et curiales du pape Grégoire XI (1370–1378), intéressant les pays autres que la France, publiées ou analysées d'après les registres du Vatican*. Paris: E. de Boccard, 1962.

Musto, Ronald G., ed. and trans. *Medieval Naples: A Documentary History, 400–1400*. New York: Italica Press, 2013.

Ovàry, L. "Negoziati tra il Re d'Ungheria e il Re di Franchia per la successione de Giovanna I. d'Angiò." *Archivio storico per le province napoletane* 2 (1877): 101–57.

Ovid. *Ars Amatoria*. In *Ovid's Erotic Poems*, translated by Len Krisak. Philadelphia: University of Pennsylvania Press, 2014, 113–90.

Palmieri, Matteo. *Vita Nicolai Acciaioli*. Edited by Gino Scaramella. Vol. 13, pt. 2 of *Rerum Italicarum Scriptores*, new ed. Bologna: Nicola Zanichelli, 1934.

Papon, M. *Histoire générale de Provence*. Vol. 3. Paris: Impr. de P.-D. Pierres chez Moutard, 1784.

Paris, Paulin, ed. *Les Grandes Chroniques de France, selon que elles sont conservées en l'Église de Saint-Denis en France*, vol. 6. Paris: Techener, 1838.

Pegat, Ferdinand, Eugène Thomas, and Desmazes, eds. *La Chronique Romane*. In *Thalamus Parvus: Le Petit Thalamus de Montpellier*, edited by De St.-Paul et al., 313–475. Montpellier: Société Archéologique de Montpellier, 1836.

Pere III of Catalonia [Pedro IV of Aragon]. *Chronicle*. Translated by Mary Hillgarth. Edited by J. N. Hillgarth. 2 vols. Toronto: Pontifical Institute of Mediaeval Studies, 1980.

Person, Gobelinus. *Cosmidromius Gobelini Person, und als Anhang desselben Verfassers, Processus translacionis et reformacionis monasterii Budecensis*. Edited by Max Jensen.

Veröffentlichungen der Historischen Kommission der Provinz Westfalen. Münster: Aschendorff, 1900.

Petrarch, Francesco. *Epistolae de Rebus Familiaribus et Variae*, vol. 1. Edited by Joseph Fracassetti. Florence: F. Le Monnier, 1859.

——. *Le Familiari*. Critical edition. Edited by Vittorio Rossi. Florence: G. C. Sansoni, 1968.

——. *Rerum familiarium libri, I–VIII*. Translated by Aldo S. Bernardo. Albany: State University of New York Press, 1975.

——. *Rerum familiarium libri, IX–XXIV*. 2 vols. Translated by Aldo S. Bernardo. Baltimore: Johns Hopkins University Press, 1982–1985.

Pierre de Bourdeille. *Oeuvres du Seigneur de Brantome*. Vol. 2: *Contenant des dames illustres Françoises et étrangeres*. London: Aux dépens du Libraire, 1779.

Pliny the Elder. *C. Plini Secundi Naturalis historiae libri XXXVII*. 6 vols. Edited by Ludwig Ianus and Charles Mayhoff. Stuttgart: Teubner, 1967–70.

Pseudo-Albertus Magnus. *Women's Secrets: A Translation of Pseudo-Albertus Magnus' "De Secretis Mulierum," with Commentaries*. Edited and translated by Helen Rodnite Lemay. Albany: State University of New York Press, 1992.

Radice, Betty, trans. *The Letters of Abelard and Heloise*. Revised ed. London: Penguin Books, 2003.

Raimbault, Maurice. *Un Pamphlet contemporain sur la mort de la Reine Jeanne*. Ext. des Comptes rendus et Mémoires du Congrès de Marseille 1928 (p. 58). Marseille: Institut Historique de Provence, 1931.

Raphaynus de Caresinis. *Cronica* [AA. 1343–1388]. Edited by Ester Pastorello. Vol. 12, pt. 2 of *Rerum Italicarum Scriptores*, new ed. Bologna: Nicola Zanichelli, 1923.

Raymond of Capua. *The Life of St. Catherine of Siena*. Translated by George Lamb. London: Harvill Press, 1960.

Rosell, Cayetano, ed. *Cronicas de los Reyes de Castilla, desde Don Alfonso el Sabio hasta los Catolicos Don Fernando y Doña Isabel*. Biblioteca de Autores Españoles, desde la Formacion del Lenguaje Nuestros Dias 66. Madrid: Ediciones Atlas, 1953.

Rousseau, Jean-Jacques. *Emilius and Sophia: or, a New System of Education*. Translated by W. Kenrick. London: T. Becket and P. A. de Hondt, 1767.

Sacchetti, Giannozzo. "V." In *Poeti minori del trecento*, edited by Natalino Sapegno, 160–63. Milan: R. Ricciardi, 1952.

Sacchi, Bartolomeo. *Platynae Istorici—Liber de vita Christi ac omnium pontificum* [AA. 1–1474]. Edited by Giacinto Gadia. Vol. 3, pt. 1 of *Rerum Italicarum Scriptores*, new ed. Città di Castello: S. Lapi, 1913.

Salutati, Coluccio. *Epistolario di Coluccio Salutati*. Edited by Francesco Novati. 4 vols. Rome: Forzani E. C. Tipografi del Senato, 1891–1911.

Scaramella, Gino, ed. *Il Tumulto dei Ciompi—Cronache e Memorie*. Vol. 13, pt. 3 of *Rerum Italicarum Scriptores*, new ed. Bologna: Nicola Zanichelli, 1934.

Sorbelli, Albano, ed. *Corpus Chronicorum Bononiensium*. Vol. 18, pt. 1 of *Rerum Italicarum Scriptores*, new ed. Bologna: Nicola Zanichelli, 1939.

Theiner, August, ed. *Vetera monumenta historica Hungariam sacram illustrantia maximam partem nondum edita ex tabulariis Vaticanis deprompta collecta ac serie chronologica disposita*. Vol. 1: *ab Honorio III. usque ad Clementem VI*. Rome: Typis Vaticanis, 1859.

Undhagen, Carl-Gustaf. "Une source du prologue (Chap. 1) aux Révélations de Sainte Brigitte par le cardinal Jean de Turrecremata." *Eranos* 58 (1960): 214–26.

de Viel-Castel, Horace, ed. *Status de l'Ordre du Saint-Esprit au Droit Desir ou du Noeud, institue a Naples en 1352 par Louis d'Anjou, premier du nom, roi de Jérusalem, de Naples et de Sicile—Manuscrit du XIVME siècle, conservé au Louvre dans le Musée des Souverains Français. Avec une notice sur la peinture des Miniatues et la description du manuscrit par M. le Comte Horace de Viel-Castel, conservateur du musée des souverains français au Musée Impérial du Louvre.* Paris: Engelmann and Graf, 1853.

Villani, Giovanni. *Nuova Cronica.* Edited by Giuseppe Porta. 3 vols. Parma: Ugo Guanda, 1991.

Villani, Matteo. *Cronica, con la continuazione di Filippo Villani.* Edited by Giuseppe Porta. 2 vols. Parma: Ugo Guanda, 1995.

Walsingham, Thomas. *The St. Albans Chronicle.* Vol. 1: *1376–1394: The "Chronica Maiora" of Thomas Walshingam.* Edited by John Taylor, Wendy R. Childs, and Leslie Watkiss. Translated by Leslie Watkiss. Oxford: Oxford University Press, 2003.

Wenzel, G. *Magyar Diplomacziai emlékek az Anjou-Korbol.* Vol. 3 of *Monumenta Hungariae Historica.* Budapest: A. M. Tud. Akadémia, 1876.

Wollstonecraft, Mary. *A Vindication of the Rights of Woman: With Strictures on Political and Moral Subjects.* In D. L. Macdonald and Kathleen Scherf, eds. *The Vindications: The Rights of Men, The Rights of Woman.* Peterborough, ON: Broadview Press, 1997.

Secondary Sources

Abulafia, David. *Frederick II: A Medieval Emperor.* Oxford: Oxford University Press, 1988.

——. "The Italian South." In *The New Cambridge Medieval History*, edited by Rosamond McKitterick, Timothy Reuter, David Abulafia, Michael Jones, and C. T. Allmand, 6:488–514. Cambridge: Cambridge University Press, 1995.

——. *A Mediterranean Emporium: The Catalan Kingdom of Majorca.* Cambridge: Cambridge University Press, 2002.

——. "Southern Italy and the Florentine Economy, 1265–1370." *Economic History Review* 34 (August 1981): 377–88.

——. *The Two Italies: Economic Relations between the Norman Kingdom of Sicily and the Northern Communes.* Cambridge: Cambridge University Press, 1977.

Aili, Hans, and Jan Svanberg. *Imagines Sanctae Birgittae: The Earliest Illuminated Manuscripts and Panel Paintings Related to the Revelations of St. Birgitta of Sweden.* 2 vols. Stockholm: Royal Academy of Letters, History and Antiquity, 2003.

Akehurst, F. R. P. "Good Name, Reputation, and Notoriety in French Customary Law." In Fenster and Smail, *Fama*, 75–94.

Ascoli, Albert Russell. *Dante and the Making of a Modern Author.* Cambridge: Cambridge University Press, 2008.

Aurell, Martin, Jean-Paul Boyer, and Noël Coulet. *La Provence au Moyen Âge.* Aix-en-Provence: Publications de l'Université de Provence, 2005.

Baddeley, Welbore St. Clair. *Queen Joanna I of Naples, Sicily, and Jerusalem, Countess of Provence, Forcalquier and Piedmont: An Essay on Her Times.* London: W. Heinemann, 1893.

——. *Robert the Wise and His Heirs, 1278–1352.* London: W. Heinemann, 1897.

Baratier, Édouard. *Histoire de la Provence.* Toulouse: E. Privat, 1969.

Barbero, Alessandro. "La Propaganda di Roberto d'Angiò, Re di Napoli." In Cammarosano, *Le forme della propaganda politica nel due e nel trecento,* 111–31.

Barraclough, Geoffrey. *The Medieval Papacy.* Norwich: Harcourt, Brace & World, 1968.

Beattie, Blake. "Catherine of Siena and the Papacy." In *A Companion to Catherine of Siena,* edited by Carolyn Muessig, George Ferzoco, and Beverly Mayne Kienzle, 73–98. Leiden: Brill, 2012.

Bechtold, Joan. "St. Birgitta: The Disjunction Between Women and Ecclesiastical Male Power." In *Equally in Gods Image: Women in the Middle Ages,* edited by Julia Bolton Holloway, Joan Bechtold, and Constance S. Wright, 88–102. New York: Peter Lang, 1990.

Benton, John F. "Consciousness of Self and Perceptions of Individuality." In *Renaissance and Renewal in the Twelfth Century,* edited by Robert L. Benson and Giles Constable, 263–95. Cambridge, MA: Harvard University Press, 1982.

Bestor, Jane Fair. "Bastardy and Legitimacy in the Formation of a Regional State in Italy: The Estense Succession." *Comparative Studies in Society and History* 38 (July 1996): 549–85.

Bianchini, Janna. *The Queen's Hand: Power and Authority in the Reign of Berenguela of Castile.* Philadelphia: University of Pennsylvania Press, 2012.

Bignami-Odier, Jeanne. "Jean de Roquetaillade (de Rupescissa): Théologien, polémiste, alchimiste." *Histoire littéraire de la France* 41 (1981): 75–209.

Birg, Birger. *Heliga Birgitta: Åttabarnsmor och profet.* Lund: Historiska Media, 2002.

Bliemetzrieder, Franz Plazidus. *Literarische Polemik zu beginn des grossen abendländischen Schismas.* Vienna: F. Tempsky, 1910.

Blumenfeld-Kosinski, Renate. *Poets, Saints, and Visionaries of the Great Schism, 1378–1417.* University Park: Penn State Press, 2006.

Bologna, Ferdinando. *I pittori alla corte angioina di Napoli, 1266–1414, e un riesame dell'arte nell'età fridericiana.* Edited by Giuliano Briganti. Saggi e studi di storia dell'arte 2. Rome: Ugo Bozzi, 1969.

Bonnot, Isabelle, ed. *Marseille et ses Rois de Naples: La diagonale angevine 1265–1382.* Marseille: Edisud, 1988.

Bornstein, Daniel. "Women and Religion in Late Medieval Italy: History and Historiography." In Bornstein and Rusconi, *Women and Religion in Medieval and Renaissance Italy,* trans. Schneider, 1–27.

Bornstein, Daniel, and Roberto Rusconi, eds. *Women and Religion in Medieval and Renaissance Italy.* Translated by Margery J. Schneider. Chicago: University of Chicago Press, 1996.

Boscolo, Alberto. *Saggi di storia Mediterranea tra il XIV e il VI secolo.* Fonti e Studi del Corpus Membranarum Italicarum, Prima Serie: Studi e Ricerche 19. Rome: Il Centro di Ricerca, 1981.

Bouche, François. *Essai sur l'histoire de Provence, suivi d'une des Provencaux célèbres.* Marseille: J. Mossy, père et fils, 1785.

Boulton, D'Arcy Jonathan Dacre. *The Knights of the Crown: The Monarchical Orders of Knighthood in Later Medieval Europe, 1325–1520.* Bury St. Edmunds: St. Martin's Press, 1987.

Bowman, Jeffrey. "Infamy and Proof in Medieval Spain." In Fenster and Smail, *Fama,* 95–117.

Boyer, Jean-Paul. "La 'Foi Monarchique': Royaume de Sicile et Provence (MI-XIII ͤ–MI-XIV ͤ siècle)." In Cammarosano, ed. *Le forme della propaganda politica nel due e nel trecento*, 85–110.

Branca, Vittore. *Boccaccio: The Man and His Works*. Translated by Richard Monges. New York: New York University Press, 1976.

Bräm, Andreas. *Neapolitanische Bilderbibeln des Trecento: Anjou-Buchmalerei von Robert dem Weisen bis zu Johanna I*. 2 vols. Wiesbaden: Reichert, 2007.

Brezzi, Paolo. "Il Regno di Napoli ed il grande Schisma d'Occidente (1378–1419)." In *Studi di storia cristiana ed ecclesiastica*, 2: *Medioevo*, 359–75. Naples: Libraria Scientifica Editrice, 1966.

Brundage, James A. *Law, Sex, and Christian Society in Medieval Europe*. Chicago: University of Chicago Press, 1987.

———. "Sex and Canon Law." In Bullough and Brundage, *Handbook of Medieval Sexuality*, 33–50.

———. "Widows and Remarriage: Moral Conflicts and Their Resolution in Classical Canon Law." In *Wife and Widow in Medieval England*, edited by Sue Sheridan Walker, 17–32. Ann Arbor: University of Michigan Press, 1993.

Bruzelius, Caroline. "Queen Sancia of Mallorca and the Church of Sta. Chiara Naples." *Memoirs of the American Academy in Rome* 40 (1995): 69–100.

———. *The Stones of Naples: Church Building in Angevin Italy, 1266–1343*. New Haven: Yale University Press, 2004.

Bruzelius, Caroline, and William Tronzo. *Medieval Naples: An Architectural and Urban History, 400–1400*. New York: Italica Press, 2011.

Bullough, Vern L. "Cross Dressing and Gender Role Change in the Middle Ages." In Bullough and Brundage, *Handbook of Medieval Sexuality*, 223–42.

Bullough, Vern L., and James A. Brundage, eds. *Handbook of Medieval Sexuality*. New York: Routledge, 2000.

Bynum, Caroline Walker. "'. . . And Woman His Humanity': Female Imagery in the Religious Writing of the Later Middle Ages." In *Fragmentation and Redemption: Essays on Gender and the Human Body in Medieval Religion*, 151–79. New York: Zone Books, 1992.

———. "Did the Twelfth Century Discover the Individual?" *Journal of Ecclesiastical History* 31 (1980): 1–17.

Cadden, Joan. *Meanings of Sex Difference in the Middle Ages: Medicine, Science, and Culture*. Cambridge: Cambridge University Press, 1995.

Caferro, William. "Slaying the Hydra-Headed Beast: Italy and the Companies of Adventure in the Fourteenth Century." In *Crusaders, Condottieri, and Cannon: Medieval Warfare in Societies around the Mediterranean*, edited by L. J. Andrew Villalon and Donald J. Kagay, 285–304. Leiden: Brill, 2002.

Calabrese, Michael A. "Feminism and the Packaging of Boccaccio's Fiammetta." *Italica* 74 (Spring 1997): 20–42.

Camera, Matteo. *Elucubrazioni storico-diplomatiche su Giovanna I.a, regina di Napoli, e Carlo III di Durazzo*. Salerno: Tipografia Nazionale, 1889.

Cammarosano, Paolo, ed. *Le forme della propaganda politica nel due e nel trecento*. Rome: École Française de Rome, 1994.

Casteen, Elizabeth. "Sex and Politics in Naples: The Regnant Queenship of Johanna I." *Journal of the Historical Society* 11 (June 2011): 183–210.

Cheyette, Fredric L. *Ermengard of Narbonne and the World of the Troubadours.* Ithaca: Cornell University Press, 2001.

Chibnall, Marjorie. *The Empress Matilda: Queen Consort, Queen Mother, and Lady of the English.* Oxford: Wiley-Blackwell, 1991.

Chojnacki, Stanley. "Patrician Women in Early Renaissance Venice." *Studies in the Renaissance* 21 (1974): 176–203.

Classen, Albrecht, and Marilyn Sandidge, eds. *Friendship in the Middle Ages and Early Modern Age: Explorations of a Fundamental Ethical Discourse.* Berlin: De Gruyter, 2011.

Collins, Amanda. *Greater than Emperor: Cola di Rienzo (ca. 1313–54) and the World of Fourteenth-Century Rome.* Ann Arbor: University of Michigan Press, 2002.

Coulter, Cornelia C. "Boccaccio and the Cassinese Manuscripts of the Laurentian Library." *Classical Philology* 43 (October 1948): 217–30.

Crane, Susan. *The Performance of Self: Ritual, Clothing, and Identity during the Hundred Years War.* Philadelphia: University of Pennsylvania Press, 2002.

Dean, Trevor. "Marriage and Mutilation: Vendetta in Late Medieval Italy." *Past and Present* 157 (November 1997): 3–36.

——. "The Sovereign as Pirate: Charles II of Anjou and the Marriage of His Daughter, 1304." *English Historical Review* 11 (April 1996): 350–56.

Deane, Jennifer Kolpacoff. "Archiepiscopal Inquisitions in the Middle Rhine: Urban Anticlericalism and Waldensianism in Late Fourteenth-Century Mainz." *Catholic Historical Review* 92 (2006): 197–224.

Denifle, Henri. *La Guerre de cent ans et la désolation des églises, monastères et hôpitaux en France.* Vol. 2. Paris: A. Picard et Fils, 1899.

DuBois, Thomas Andrew, ed. *Sanctity in the North: Saints, Lives, and Cults in Medieval Scandinavia.* Toronto: University of Toronto Press, 2008.

Duggan, Anne J. "Introduction." In Duggan, *Queens and Queenship in Medieval Europe*, xv–xxii.

——, ed. *Queens and Queenship in Medieval Europe.* Bury St. Edmunds: Boydell Press, 1997.

Dunbabin, Jean. *Charles I of Anjou: Power, Kingship and State-Making in Thirteenth-Century Europe.* London: Longman, 1998.

——. *The French in the Kingdom of Sicily, 1266–1305.* Cambridge: Cambridge University Press, 2011.

Dupuy, Mark. "The Unwilling Prophet and the New Maccabees: John de Roquetaillade and the Valois in the Fourteenth Century." *Florilegium* 17 (2000): 229–50.

Duran, Michelle M. "The Politics of Art: Imaging Sovereignty in the Anjou Bible." In Watteeuw and Van der Stock, *The Anjou Bible*, 73–94.

Earenfight, Theresa. *The King's Other Body: Maria of Castile and the Crown of Aragon.* Philadelphia: University of Pennsylvania Press, 2009.

——, ed. *Queenship and Political Power in Medieval and Early Modern Spain.* Aldershot: Ashgate, 2005.

——. *Queenship in Medieval Europe.* London: Palgrave Macmillan, 2013.

Ehrle, Franz. "Zur Geschichte des papstlichen Hofceremoniells in 14 Jahrhundert." *Archiv für Literatur und Kirchengeschichte des Mittelalters* 5 (1889): 565–602.

Elliott, Dyan. *Fallen Bodies: Pollution, Sexuality, and Demonology in the Middle Ages.* Philadelphia: University of Pennsylvania Press, 1999.

———. "From Sexual Fantasy to Demonic Defloration: The Libidinous Female in the Later Middle Ages." In *Fallen Bodies: Pollution, Sexuality, and Demonology in the Middle Ages*, 35–60. Philadelphia: University of Pennsylvania Press, 1999.

———. *Proving Woman: Female Spirituality and Inquisitional Culture in the Later Middle Ages.* Princeton: Princeton University Press, 2004.

———. *Spiritual Marriage: Sexual Abstinence in Medieval Wedlock.* Princeton: Princeton University Press, 1993.

Elliott, Janis, and Cordelia Warr, eds. *The Church of Santa Maria Donna Regina: Art, Iconography and Patronage in Fourteenth Century Naples.* Farnham: Ashgate, 2004.

Erler, Mary C., and Maryanne Kowaleski, eds. *Gendering the Master Narrative: Women and Power in the Middle Ages.* Ithaca: Cornell University Press, 2003.

———. "Introduction: A New Economy of Power Relations: Female Agency in the Middle Ages." In Erler and Kowaleski, *Gendering the Master Narrative*, 1–16.

Esch, Arnold. "Le Clan des familles napolitaines au sien du Sacré Collège d'Urbain VI et de ses successeurs et les Brancacci de Rome et d'Avignon." In Centre National de la Recherche Scientifique, *Genèse et Débuts du Grand Schisme d'Occident (Avignon, 25–28 septembre 1978)*, 493–506. Paris: Centre National de la Recherche Scientifique, 1980.

Falconieri, Tommaso di Carpegna. *The Man Who Believed He Was King of France: A True Medieval Tale.* Translated by William McCuaig. Chicago: University of Chicago Press, 2008.

Fedele, Pietro. "L'amore di Giovanna di Durazzo per Aimone III di Ginevre." In *Miscellanea di Studi Storici in Onore di Antonio Manno*, 2:635–53. Turin: Officina Poligrafica Editrice Subalpina, 1912.

Fenster, Thelma, and Daniel Lord Smail, eds. *Fama: The Politics of Talk and Reputation in Medieval Europe.* Ithaca: Cornell University Press, 2003.

———. "Introduction." In Fenster and Smail, *Fama*, 2–11.

de Feo, Italo. *Giovanna d'Angiò, regina di Napoli.* Naples: F. Fiorentino, 1968.

Ferrando, J. Ernest Martínez. *La Tràgica Història dels Reis de Mallorca.* Barcelona: Ed. Aedos, 1960.

Field, Sean. *Isabelle of France: Capetian Sanctity and Franciscan Identity in the Thirteenth Century.* Notre Dame: University of Notre Dame Press, 2006.

Fine, John V. A. *The Late Medieval Balkans: A Critical Survey from the Late Twelfth Century to the Ottoman Conquest.* Ann Arbor: University of Michigan Press, 1994.

Fleck, Cathleen A. *The Clement Bible at the Medieval Courts of Naples and Avignon: A Story of Papal Power, Royal Prestige, and Patronage.* Farnham: Ashgate, 2010.

Fleischman, Suzanne. "On the Representation of History and Fiction in the Middle Ages." *History and Theory* 22 (October 1983): 278–310.

Fodale, Salvatore. *Comes et Legatus Siciliae: Sul privilegio di Urbano II e la pretesa Apostolica Legazia dei Normanni di Sicilia.* Palermo: U. Manfredi, 1970.

———. *La Politica Napoletana di Urbano VI.* Rome: Salvatore Sciascia, 1973.

Fradenburg, Louise O. "The Love of Thy Neighbor." In Lochrie, McCracken, and Schultz, *Constructing Medieval Sexuality*, 135–57.

Fraher, Richard M. "Conviction According to Conscience: The Medieval Jurists' Debate Concerning Judicial Discretion and the Law of Proof." *Law and History Review* 7 (Spring 1989): 23–88.

Franklin, Margaret Ann. *Boccaccio's Heroines: Power and Virtue in Renaissance Society.* Aldershot: Ashgate, 2006.

Frede, Carlo de. "Da Carlo I d'Angiò a Giovanna I, 1263–1382." In *Storia di Napoli,* vol. 3: *Da Carlo I d'Angiò a Giovanna I, 1263–1382,* edited by E. Pontieri, 1–333. Naples: Edizioni Scientifiche Italiane, 1969.

Friedman, Joan Isobel. "MS Cotton Claudius B.I.: A Middle English Edition of St Bridget of Sweden's *Liber Celestis.*" In *Prophets Abroad: The Reception of Continental Holy Women in Late-Medieval England,* edited by Rosalynn Voaden, 91–113. Cambridge: D. S. Brewer, 1996.

Froio, Felice. *Giovanna I d'Angiò.* Milan: Mursia, 1992.

Frugoni, Chiara. "Female Mystics, Visions, and Iconography." In Bornstein and Rusconi, *Women and Religion in Medieval and Renaissance Italy,* trans. Schneider, 130–64.

Gaglione, Mario. *Donne e potere a Napoli: Le sovrane angioine; Consorti, vicarie e regnanti (1266–1442).* Catanzaro: Rubbettino Editore, 2009.

Gaposchkin, Cecilia. *The Making of Saint Louis: Kingship, Sanctity, and Crusade in the Later Middle Ages.* Ithaca: Cornell University Press, 2009.

Giesey, Ralph E. *Le rôle méconnu de la Loi Salique: La succession royale, XIVᵉ–XVIᵉ siècles.* Translated by Franz Regnot. Paris: Les Belles Lettres, 2007.

Gilli, Patrick. "L'intégration manquée des Angevins en Italie: Le témoignage des historiens." In Istituto Storico Italiano per il Medio Evo, *L'État Angevin: Pouvoir, culture et société entre XIIIᵉ et XIVᵉ siècle. Actes du colloque international organizé par l'American Academy in Rome, l'École française de Rome, l'Istituto storico italiano per il Medio Evo, l'U.M.R. Telemme et l'Université de Provence, l'Università degli studi di Napoli "Federico II" (Rome-Naples, 7–11 novembre 1995),* 11–33. Rome: Istituto Storico Italiano per il Medio Evo, 1998.

Gleijeses, Vittorio. *La Storia di Napoli dalle origini ai nostri giorni.* Naples: Società Editrice Napoletana, 1974.

Gleijeses, Vittorio, and Lidia Gleijeses. *La Regina Giovanna d'Angiò.* Naples: T. Marotta, 1990.

Gluckman, Max. "Papers in Honor of Melville J. Herskovits: Gossip and Scandal." *Current Anthropology* 4 (June 1963): 307–16.

Goldstone, Nancy. *The Lady Queen: The Notorious Reign of Joanna I, Queen of Naples, Jerusalem, and Sicily.* London: Walker and Company, 2009.

Green, Louis. *Chronicle into History: An Essay on the Interpretation of History in Florentine Fourteenth-Century Chronicles.* Cambridge: Cambridge University Press, 1972.

———. "Historical Interpretation in Fourteenth-Century Italian Chronicles." *Journal of the History of Ideas* 28 (April 1967): 161–78.

Greenblatt, Stephen. *Renaissance Self-Fashioning: From More to Shakespeare.* Chicago: University of Chicago Press, 1980.

Grierson, Philip, and Lucia Travaini. *Medieval European Coinage: With a Catalogue of the Coins in the Fitzwilliam Museum, Cambridge.* Vol. 14: *Italy (III): (South Italy, Sicily, Sardinia).* Cambridge: Cambridge University Press, 1998.

Grudin, Michaela Paasche. "Making War on the Widow: Boccaccio's *Il Corbaccio* and Florentine Liberty." *Viator* 38 (2007): 127–57.

Guadette, Helen. *The Piety, Power, and Patronage of the Latin Kingdom of Jerusalem's Queen Melisende.* New York: City University of New York Press, 2005.

Hamburger, Jeffrey F. "Medieval Self-Fashioning: Authorship, Authority, and Autobiography in Suso's *Exemplar*." In *The Visual and the Visionary: Art and Female Spirituality in Late Medieval Germany*, 233–78. New York: Zone Books, 1998.

Harris, Marguerite Tjader, ed. *Birgitta of Sweden, Life and Selected Revelations*. Translated by Albert Ryle Kezel. New York: Paulist Press, 1990.

Haseldine, Julian, ed. *Friendship in Medieval Europe*. Stroud: Sutton, 1999.

Hazard, Harry W. *A History of the Crusades*. Vol. 3: *The Fourteenth and Fifteenth Centuries*. Edited by Kenneth Meyer Setton (general editor). Madison: University of Wisconsin Press, 1975.

Hillgarth, J. N. *The Spanish Kingdom, 1250–1516*. Vol. 1: *Precarious Balance*. Oxford: Oxford University Press, 1976.

Houben, Hubert. *Roger II of Sicily: A Ruler between East and West*. Translated by G. A. Loud and D. Milburn. Cambridge: Cambridge University Press, 2002.

Housley, Norman. *The Avignon Papacy and the Crusades, 1305–1378*. Oxford: Oxford University Press, 1986.

———. *The Italian Crusades: The Papal-Angevin Alliance and the Crusades against Christian Lay Power, 1254–1343*. Oxford: Oxford University Press, 1982.

Howell, Margaret. *Eleanor of Provence: Queenship in Thirteenth-Century England*. Oxford, Blackwell Publishers, 2001.

Huneycutt, Lois L. "Female Succession and the Language of Power in the Writings of Twelfth-Century Churchmen." In Parsons, *Medieval Queenship*, 189–201.

———. *Matilda of Scotland: A Study in Medieval Queenship*. Rochester, NY: Boydell Press, 2003.

Jaeger, C. Stephen. *Ennobling Love: In Search of a Lost Sensibility*. Philadelphia: University of Pennsylvania Press, 1999.

Jansen, Katherine Ludwig. *The Making of the Magdalen: Preaching and Popular Devotion in the Later Middle Ages*. Princeton: Princeton University Press, 2000.

Jarry, E. *La vie politique de Louis de France, duc d'Orléans*. Paris: Alph. Picard, 1889.

Jorday, Mark D. "Homosexuality, *Luxuria*, and Textual Abuse." In Lochrie, McCracken, and Schultz, *Constructing Medieval Sexuality*, 24–39.

Jørgensen, Johannes. *Saint Bridget of Sweden*. 2 vols. Translated by Ingeborg Lund. London: Longmans, Green, 1954.

Jussen, Bernhard. *Der Name der Witwe: Erkundungen zur Semantik der mittelalterlichen Bußkultur*. Göttingen: Vandenhoeck und Ruprecht Verlag, 2000.

Kantorowicz, Ernst. *The King's Two Bodies: A Study in Mediaeval Political Theology*. Princeton: Princeton University Press, 1997.

Karras, Ruth Mazo. *Common Women: Prostitution and Sexuality in Medieval England*. Oxford: Oxford University Press, 1998.

———. *From Boys to Men: Formations of Masculinity in Late Medieval Europe*. Philadelphia: University of Pennsylvania Press, 2003.

———. "Prostitution in Medieval Europe," In Bullough and Brundage, *Handbook of Medieval Sexuality*, 243–60.

———. *Sexuality in Medieval Europe: Doing unto Others*. New York: Routledge, 2005.

Keen, Maurice. *Chivalry*. New Haven: Yale University Press, 1984.

Kelly, Samantha. "Intercultural Identity and the Local Vernacular." *Medieval History Journal* 14, no. 2 (2011): 259–84.

———. *The New Solomon: Robert of Naples (1309–1343) and Fourteenth-Century Kingship.* Leiden: Brill, 2003.

Kieckhefer, Richard. *Unquiet Souls: Fourteenth-Century Saints and their Religious Milieu.* Chicago: University of Chicago Press, 1984.

Klaniczay, Gábor. *Holy Rulers and Blessed Princesses: Dynastic Cults in Medieval Central Europe.* Translated by Éva Pálmai. Cambridge: Cambridge University Press, 2002.

———. "La noblesse et le culte des saints dynastiques sous les rois angevins." In *La noblesse dans les terroires angevins à la fin du moyen âge,* edited by N. Coulet and J.-M. Matz, 511–26. Rome: École française de Rome, 2000.

———. *The Uses of Supernatural Power: The Transformation of Popular Religion in Medieval and Early Renaissance Europe.* Princeton: Princeton University Press, 1990.

Labande, L.-H. "Le cérémonial romain de Jacques Cajétan." *Bibliothèque de l'École des Chartes* 54 (1893): 45–74.

de Laincel, L. "Sault." *Revue de Marseille et de Provence* 5 (1869): 65–79.

Lambert, Sarah. "Queen or Consort: Rulership and Politics in the Latin East, 1118–1228." In Duggan, *Queens and Queenship in Medieval Europe,* 153–69.

Lansing, Carol. "Gender and Civic Authority: Sexual Control in a Medieval Italian Town." *Journal of Social History* 31 (Autumn 1997): 33–59.

Layher, William. *Queenship and Voice in Medieval Northern Europe.* New York: Palgrave Macmillan, 2010.

Laynesmith, J. L. *The Last Medieval Queens: English Queenship, 1445–1503.* Oxford: Oxford University Press, 2005.

Lea, H. C. *A History of the Inquisition in the Middle Ages.* 3 vols. New York: MacMillan, 1901.

Lee, Charmaine. "Boccaccio's Neapolitan Letter and Multilingualism in Angevin Naples." *Mediaevalia* 34 (2013): 7–21.

———. "Naples." In *Europe: A Literary History, 1348–1418,* edited by David Wallace. Oxford: Oxford University Press, forthcoming.

Lee, Patricia-Ann. "Reflections of Power: Margaret of Anjou and the Dark Side of Queenship." *Renaissance Quarterly* 39 (Summer 1986): 183–217.

Leff, Gordon. *Heresy in the Later Middle Ages: The Relation of Heterodoxy to Dissent, c. 1250–c. 1450.* Manchester: Manchester University Press, 1967.

Léonard, Émile G. "Un abrégé illustré de la Reine Jeanne dans un tableau des droits de Louis XII sur le Royaume de Naples." Ext. des Comptes rendus et Mémoires du Congrès de Marseille 1928 (p. 72). Marseille: L'Institut Historique de Provence, 1931.

———. *Les Angevins de Naples.* Paris: Presses Universitaires de France, 1954.

———. "La captivité et la mort de Jeanne Iʳᵉ de Naples." *Mélanges d'archéologie et d'histoire* 41 (1924): 42–77.

———. *Histoire de Jeanne Iʳᵉ, reine de Naples, comtesse de Provence (1343–1382).* 3 vols. Monaco: Imp. de Monaco, 1932–36.

Lerner, Robert E. *The Age of Adversity: The Fourteenth Century.* Ithaca: Cornell University Press, 1968.

Lewin, Alison Williams. *Negotiating Survival: Florence and the Great Schism, 1378–1417.* Madison, NJ: Fairleigh Dickinson University Press, 2003.

Lochrie, Karma, Peggy McCracken, and James A. Schultz, eds. *Constructing Medieval Sexuality*. Minneapolis: University of Minnesota Press, 1997.

Loconte, Aislinn. "Constructing Female Sanctity in Late Medieval Naples: The Funerary Monument of Queen Sancia of Majorca." In *Representing Medieval Genders and Sexualities in Europe: Construction, Transformation, and Subversion, 600–1530,* edited by Elizabeth L'Estrange and Alison More, 107–25. Farnham: Ashgate, 2011.

Loenertz, Raymond-J., O. P. "Hospitaliers et Navarrais en Grèce, 1376–1383: Regestes et documents." *Orientalia christiana periodica* 22 (1956): 319–60.

Logoz, Robert Ch. *Clément VII (Robert de Genève): Sa chancellerie et le clergé romand au début du Grand Schisme (1378–1394).* Lausanne: Payot, 1974.

Lowden, John. "The Anjou Bible in the Context of Illustrated Bibles." In Watteeuw and Van der Stock, *The Anjou Bible,* 1–25.

Luongo, F. Thomas. *The Saintly Politics of Catherine of Siena.* Ithaca: Cornell University Press, 2006.

Luttrell, Anthony. "The Principality of Achaea in 1377." *Byzantinische Zeitschrift* 57 (1964): 340–45.

Maclean, Ian. *The Renaissance Notion of Woman: A Study in the Fortunes of Scholasticism and Medieval Science in European Intellectual Life.* Cambridge: Cambridge University Press, 1980.

Mango, Antonino. *Relazioni tra Federico III di Sicilia e Giovanna I di Napoli: Documenti degli Archivi de Vaticano.* Documenti per servire alla storia di Sicilia, Series 1: Diplomatica 22. Palermo: Società Storia Patria Palermo, 1915.

Mann, Jill. *Feminizing Chaucer.* Cambridge: Boydell & Brewer, 2002.

Marrocco, Dante. *Gli Arcani Historici di Nicolò di Alife.* Naples: Arti Grafiche "Ariello," 1965.

Martin, Therese. *Queen as King: Politics and Architectural Propaganda in Twelfth-Century Spain.* Leiden: Brill, 2006.

Martin-Chabot, Eugène. "Le Registre des lettres de Pierre Ameil, archevêque de Naples (1363–1365), puis de Embrun (1365–1379)." *Mélanges d'archéologie et d'histoire* 25 (1905): 279–92.

Maurer, Helen E. *Margaret of Anjou: Queenship and Power in Late Medieval England.* Woodbridge: Boydell Press, 2003.

Mazzoleni, Jole. "Les archives des Angevins de Naples." In Bonnot, *Marseille et ses Rois de Naples,* 25–29.

McCracken, Peggy. *The Romance of Adultery: Queenship and Sexual Transgression in Old French Literature.* Philadelphia: University of Pennsylvania Press, 1998.

McNamara, Jo Ann. "Women and Power through the Family Revisited." In Erler and Kowaleski, *Gendering the Master Narrative,* 7–30.

Michel, Louise. *La reine Jeanne de Naples et de Provence: Histoire et légendes.* Grasse: TAC Motifs, 1995.

Migliorino, Francesco. *Fama e Infamia: Problemi della società medievale nel pensiero giuridico nei secoli XII e XIII.* Catania: Editrice Giannotta, 1985.

Mireur, Hippolyte. *La syphilis et la prostitution dans leurs rapports avec l'hygiène, la morale et la loi.* Paris: Masson, 1875.

Miskolczy, E. "Le pretese di Lodovico il Grande sul trono di Sicilia." *Samnium* 2 (1929): 50–82.

Mollat, Guillaume. *Les papes d'Avignon (1305–1378)*. 10th ed. Paris: Letouzey et Ané, 1964.

Monter, E. William. "Gendered Sovereignty: Numismatics and Female Monarchs in Europe, 1300–1800." *Journal of Interdisciplinary History* 41, no. 4 (Spring 2011): 533–64.

———. *The Rise of Female Kings in Europe, 1300–1800*. New Haven: Yale University Press, 2012.

Monti, Gennaro Maria. *Dal Duecento al Settecento: Studi Storico-Giuridici*. Biblioteca di coltura meridionale 1. Naples: I.T.E.A. Editrice, 1925.

Morris, Bridget. *St. Birgitta of Sweden*. Woodbridge: Boydell Press, 1999.

Muir, Edward. *Mad Blood Stirring: Vendetta in Renaissance Italy*. Reader's edition. Baltimore: Johns Hopkins University Press, 1998.

Murray, Jacqueline. "Hiding Behind the Universal Man: Male Sexuality in the Middle Ages." In Bullough and Brundage, *Handbook of Medieval Sexuality*, 123–52.

Musto, Ronald G. *Apocalypse in Rome: Cola di Rienzo and the Politics of the New Age*. Berkeley: University of California Press, 2003.

———. "Franciscan Joachimism at the Court of Naples, 1309–1345: A New Appraisal." *Archivum Franciscanum Historicum* 90 (1997): 419–86.

———. "Queen Sancia of Naples (1286–1345) and the Spiritual Franciscans." In *Women of the Medieval World: Essays in Honor of John H. Mundy*, edited by Julius Kirschner and Suzanne F. Wemple, 179–214. Oxford: Blackwell, 1985.

———. "Review: Lieve Watteeuw and Jan Van der Stock, eds., *The Anjou Bible: A Royal Manuscript Revealed* and Cathleen A. Fleck, *The Clement Bible at the Medieval Courts of Naples and Avignon: A Story of Papal Power, Royal Prestige, and Patronage*." *Renaissance Quarterly* 64 (Summer 2011): 587–90.

Newman, Barbara. *From Virile Woman to WomanChrist: Studies in Medieval Religion and Literature*. Philadelphia: University of Pennsylvania Press, 1995.

Noland, Kathleen, ed. *Capetian Women*. New York: Palgrave Macmillan, 2003.

Nordenfalk, Carl. "Saint Bridget of Sweden as Represented in Illuminated Manuscripts." In *De Artibus Opuscula XL: Essays in Honor of Erwin Panofsky*, edited by Millard Meiss, 1:371–93. New York: New York University Press, 1961.

Norwich, John Julius. *The Normans in the South, 1016–1130*. London: Longmans, 1967.

Nyberg, Tore. "The Canonization Process of St. Birgitta of Sweden." In *Procès de canonisation au Moyen Âge / Medieval Canonization Processes*, edited by Gábor Klaniczay, 67–85. Rome: École française de Rome, 2004.

Österberg, Eva. *Friendship and Love, Ethics and Politics: Studies in Mediaeval and Early Modern History*. Budapest: Central European University Press, 2010.

Paladilhe, Dominique. *La Reine Jeanne, Comtesse de Provence*. Paris: Perrin, 1997.

Pansier, Pierre. "Histoire des prétendus statuts de la reine Jeanne et de la réglementation de la prostitution à Avignon au Moyen-Age." *Janus* 7 (1902), reprinted as an extract.

Parsons, John Carmi. "Introduction: Family, Sex, and Power: The Rhythms of Medieval Queenship." In Parsons, *Medieval Queenship*, 1–11.

———, ed. *Medieval Queenship*. New York: Palgrave Macmillan, 1998.

Perry, William. "Review: *La Politica napoletana di Urbano VI*." *Speculum* 51 (October 1976): 740–41.

Peters, Edward. "*Vox populi, vox Dei.*" In *Law in Medieval Life and Thought*, edited by Edward B. King and Susan J. Ridyard, 91–120. Sewanee, TN: University of the South Press, 1990.

——. "Wounded Names: The Medieval Doctrine of Infamy." In *Law in Medieval Life and Thought*, edited by Edward B. King and Susan J. Ridyard, 43–90. Sewanee, TN: University of the South Press, 1990.

Phillips, Susan E. *Transforming Talk: The Problem with Gossip in Late Medieval England.* University Park: Pennsylvania State University Press, 2007.

Pollastri, Sylvie. "La Noblesse napolitaine sous la dynastie angevine: L'aristocratie des comtes (1265–1435)." PhD dissertation. Université Paris X-Nanterre, 1994.

Pournot, Joëlle. "Monnaies en Provence et dans le royaume de Naples (1246–1382)." In Bonnot, *Marseille et ses Rois de Naples*, 51–60.

Pratt, Karen. "The Image of the Queen in Old French Literature." In Duggan, *Queens and Queenship in Medieval Europe*, 235–62.

Pryds, Darleen. *The King Embodies the Word: Robert d'Anjou and the Politics of Preaching.* Leiden: Brill, 2000.

Runciman, Steven. *The Sicilian Vespers: A History of the Mediterranean World in the Later Thirteenth Century.* Cambridge: Cambridge University Press, 1958.

Rychterová, Pavlína. *Die Offenbarungen der Heiligen Birgitta von Schweden: Eine Untersuchung zur alttschechischen Übersetzung des Thomas von Štítné (um 1330–um 1409).* Cologne: Böhlau Verlag, 2004.

Sabatini, Francesco. *Italia Linguistica delle Origini: Saggi editi dal 1856 al 1996.* 2 vols. Lecce: Argo, 1996.

Sahlin, Claire L. *Birgitta of Sweden and the Voice of Prophecy.* Woodbridge: Boydell Press, 2001.

Salisbury, Joyce E. "Gendered Sexuality." In Bullough and Brundage, *Handbook of Medieval Sexuality*, 81–102.

Seidlmayer, Michael. *Die Anfänge des grossen abendländischen Schismas: Studien zur Kirchenpolitik insbesondere der Spanischen Staaten und zu den geistigen Kämpfen der Zeit.* Münster: Aschendorff, 1940.

Setton, Kenneth M. "Archbishop Pierre d'Ameil in Naples and the Affair of Aimon III of Geneva (1363–1364)." *Speculum* 28 (October 1953): 643–91.

Shadis, Miriam. *Berenguela of Castile (1180–1246) and Her Family: Political Women in the High Middle Ages.* New York: Palgrave MacMillan, 2009.

Silleras-Fernandez, Nuria. *Power, Piety, and Patronage in Late-Medieval Queenship: Maria de Luna.* New York: Palgrave MacMillan, 2008.

Smail, Daniel Lord. "Hatred as a Social Institution in Late-Medieval Society." *Speculum* 76 (January 2001): 90–126.

Soldevila, Ferran. *Història de Catalunya.* 3rd ed. Barcelona: Editorial Alpha, 1972.

Spiegel, Gabrielle M. "History, Historicism, and the Social Logic of the Text in the Middle Ages." *Speculum* 65 (January 1990): 59–86.

Stafford, Pauline. "The Portrayal of Royal Women in England, Mid-Tenth to Mid-Twelfth Centuries." In Parsons, *Medieval Queenship*, 143–67.

Steinberg, Justin. "Dante and the Laws of Infamy." *PMLA* 126 (October 2011): 1118–26.

Stern, Laura Ikins. "Public Fame in the Fifteenth Century." *American Journal of Legal History* 44 (April 2000): 198–222.

Stern-Gillet, Suzanne, and Gary M. Gurtier, eds. *Ancient and Medieval Concepts of Friendship*. Albany: SUNY Press, 2014.

St. John, Lisa Benz. *Three Medieval Queens: Queenship and the Crown in Fourteenth-Century England*. New York: Palgrave Macmillan, 2012.

Strohm, Paul. *Hochon's Arrow: The Social Imagination of Fourteenth-Century Texts*. Princeton: Princeton University Press, 1992.

Sumption, Jonathan. *The Hundred Years War: Trial by Fire*. Vol. 2. Philadelphia: University of Pennsylvania Press, 2001.

Swanson, R. N. *Universities, Academics and the Great Schism*. Cambridge: Cambridge University Press, 1979.

Théry, Julien. "*Fama*: L'opinion publique comme preuve judiciare. Aperçu sur la révolution médiévale de l'inquisitoire (XIIe–XIVe siècle)." In *La preuve en justice de l'Antiquité à nos jours*, edited by Bruno Lemesle, 119–47. Rennes: Presses Universitaires de Rennes, 2003.

Thibault, Paul R. *Pope Gregory XI: The Failure of Tradition*. Lanham, MD: University Press of America, 1986.

Tocco, Francesco Paolo. *Niccolò Acciaiuoli: Vita e politica in Italia alla metà del XIV secolo*. Istituto Storico Italiano per il Medio Evo, Nuovi Studi Storici 52. Rome: Nella sede dell'Istituto Palazzo Borromini, 2001.

Topping, Peter. "The Morea: 1311–1364." In *A History of the Crusades*, general editor Kenneth Meyer Setton, vol. 3: *The Fourteenth and Fifteenth Centuries*, edited by Harry W. Hazard, 104–40. Madison: University of Wisconsin Press, 1975.

——. "The Morea: 1364–1460." In *A History of the Crusades*, general editor Kenneth Meyer Setton, vol. 3: *The Fourteenth and Fifteenth Centuries*, edited by Harry W. Hazard, 141–66. Madison: University of Wisconsin Press, 1975.

Torelli, Pietro. "Antonio Nerli e Bonamente Aliprandi cronisti mantovani." *Archivio storico Lombardo*, 4th series, 15, no. 38 (1911), 209–30.

Trexler, Richard C. *The Spiritual Power: Republican Florence under Interdict*. Studies in Medieval and Reformation Thought 9. Leiden: E. J. Brill, 1974.

Tuchman, Barbara. *A Distant Mirror: The Calamitous Fourteenth Century*. New York: Random House, 1978.

Ullmann, Walter. "The Development of the Medieval Idea of Sovereignty." *English Historical Review* 64 (January 1949): 1–33.

——. *The Origins of the Great Schism: A Study in Fourteenth-Century Ecclesiastical History*. Hamden, CT: Archon Books, 1967.

Vallerani, Massimo. *Medieval Public Justice*. Translated by Sarah Rubin Blanshei. Washington, DC: Catholic University of America Press, 2012.

——. "Modelli di Verità: Le prove nei processi inquisitori." In *L'Enquête au Moyen Âge*, edited by Claude Gauvard, 123–42. Rome: L'École française de Rome, 2008.

Valois, Noël. *La France et le Grand Schisme d'Occident*. 4 vols. Paris: A. Picard, 1896.

Vauchez, André. "'*Beata Stirps*': Sainteté et lignage en Occident aux XIIIe et XIVe siècles." In *Saints, Prophètes et Visionnaires: Le pouvoir surnaturel au Moyen Âge*, 67–78. Paris: Albin Michel, 1999.

——. *Sainthood in the Later Middle Ages*. Translated by Jean Birrell. Cambridge: Cambridge University Press, 2005.

Vitolo, Paola. *La Chiesa della Regina: L'Incoronata di Napoli, Giovanna I d'Angiò, e Roberto d'Oderisio*. Rome: Viella, 2008.

Vones, Ludwig. *Urban V. (1362–1370): Kirchenreform zwischen Kardinalkollegium, Kurie und Klientel*. Päpste und Papsttum 28. Stuttgart: Anton Hiersemann, 1998.

Warr, Cordelia, and Janis Elliott, eds. *Art and Architecture in Naples, 1266–1713: New Approaches*. Oxford: Wiley-Blackwell, 2010.

Watteeuw, Lieve, and Jan Van der Stock, eds. *The Anjou Bible, Naples 1340: A Royal Manuscript Revealed*. Paris: Peeters, 2010.

Weimer, Christopher B. "The Politics of Husband-Murder: Gender, Supplementarity and Sacrifice in Lope de Vega's 'La reina Juana de Nápoles.'" *Hispanic Review* 69 (Winter 2001): 32–52.

Wickham, Chris. "*Fama* and the Law in Twelfth-Century Tuscany." In Fenster and Smail, *Fama*, 15–26.

——. "Gossip and Resistance among the Medieval Peasantry." *Past and Present* 160 (August 1998): 3–24.

Wilkins, Ernest H. *Petrarch's Correspondence*. Padua: Antenore, 1960.

——. "Petrarch's *Exul ab Italia*." *Speculum* 38 (July 1963): 453–60.

——. *Studies in the Life and Works of Petrarch*. Cambridge, MA: Mediaeval Academy of America, 1955.

Witt, Ronald G. *Hercules at the Crossroads: The Life, Works, and Thought of Coluccio Salutati*. Durham, NC: Duke University Press, 1983.

Wolf, Armin. "Reigning Queens in Medieval Europe: When, Where, and Why." In Parsons, *Medieval Queenship*, 169–88.

Woodacre, Elena. *The Queens Regnant of Navarre: Succession, Politics, and Partnership, 1274–1512*. New York: Palgrave Macmillan, 2013.

——, ed. *Queenship in the Mediterranean: Negotiating the Role of the Queen in the Medieval and Early-Modern Eras*. New York: Palgrave Macmillan, 2013.

Zaccaria, Vittorio. "Le due redazioni del '*De casibus*.'" *Studi sul Boccaccio* 10 (1977–78): 1–26.

——. "Le fasi redazionali de '*De mulieribus claris*.'" *Studi sul Boccaccio* 1 (1963): 253–332.

Zacour, Norman P. *Talleyrand: The Cardinal of Périgord (1301–1364)*. Transactions of the American Philosophical Society. Philadelphia: American Philosophical Society, 1960.

Zarri, Gabriella. "Living Saints: A Typology of Female Sanctity in the Early Sixteenth Century." In Bornstein and Rusconi, *Women and Religion in Medieval and Renaissance Italy*, trans. Schneider, 219–303.

INDEX